D0072866

Building Leaders For Church Education

Building Leaders For Church Education

by
KENNETH O. GANGEL

MOODY PRESS
CHICAGO

To my family—Betty, Jeff, and Julie—
at once my greatest responsibility
and greatest joy

This book, with certain revisions, is a combination of *Leadership for Church Education* and *Competent to Lead.*

The use of selected references from various other versions of the Bible in this publication does not necessarily imply publisher endorsement of the versions in their entirety.

Library of Congress Cataloging in Publication Data

Gangel, Kenneth O.
Building leaders for church education.

Includes bibliographical references and index.
1. Christian education. I. Title.
BV1475.2.G29 268 81-16766
ISBN 0-8024-1592-X AACR2

Printed in the United States of America

Contents

Part V
ADMINISTRATIVE PERSONNEL IN THE CHURCH

Part VI
THE LEADER WORKING WITH PEOPLE

Part VII
THE LEADER TRAINING OTHER LEADERS

Diagrams

Foreword

In *Building Leaders for Church Education,* Kenneth Gangel has drawn together basic ideas from the standard works on Christian education, ventilated this imposing structure with adequate "for instances," and then added some inspiring and challenging innovative suggestions of his own.

For persons already engaged in Christian education, Gangel provides the answers to the twin questions, What ought to be done? and, How do I get people to work? Not content with being merely theoretical, the author includes at every possible point some helpful "how to do it" advice.

For students, or for pastors and other Christian workers who recognize the growing importance of Christian education in the local church, this book will be a gold mine of insights and new ideas.

Written not out of the ivory tower but from considerable personal experience and bedrock research, *Building Leaders for Church Education* may well become an outstanding source of facts and motivation for years to come.

Robert A. Cook
President
The King's College

Preface

The field of Christian education is moving rapidly. Each passing year witnesses worthy additions to a growing body of literature in the field. I have been involved directly in Christian education for twenty-three years as a college and seminary teacher, pastor, and consultant in many churches in the area of educational programming. Two problems have presented themselves over and over again during ministry in more than a thousand churches during the past two decades. This book is an attempt to speak to those problems.

The first problem concerns a *lack of genuine Bible knowledge* on the part of adults in evangelical churches in America. Several reasons could be offered in explanation of this lack, but certainly a primary one is the inadequacy of the program of education in local churches. The pulpit is essential, but it is simply not enough. Yet it is forced too often by a lack of satisfactory organization in the instructional program to carry all the weight of Christian nurture in the local church. The first part of the book, therefore, is an attempt to come to grips with the development and organization of a properly functioning ministry of Christian education in the local church.

A second problem focuses on the *lack of leadership* in local churches. Leadership is used here in the broadest sense of pastors, directors of Christian education, Sunday school teachers, youth sponsors, and other workers. When the original text of this book was prepared in 1968, no evangelical author had produced a work that dealt adequately with the technical aspects of leadership. Since that time several helpful works by Ed Dayton, Ted Engstrom, and Lyle Schaller have become available along with my own *Competent To Lead,* which is now being blended into this volume.

This new volume is designed to build upon the 1981 Moody Press release *Introduction to Biblical Christian Education,* edited by Werner Graendorf. Many of the chapter subjects dealt with in that volume have been deliberately avoided here, and the reader is asked to study the two books as complementary. Some of the same crucial areas, such as the chapters on "Professional Church Leadership in Christian Education," "The Organizational Structure," and "The Pastor and Christian Education," are dealt with here, it is hoped with a different point of view, because of their strategic significance in the organization of the educational program. The focus of the entire volume is the local church rather than the broader field of Christian education.

I am indebted to many for the material that appears in this book. My philosophy of Christian education has been profoundly influenced by the writings of Dr. Frank E. Gaebelein. Insights into the field of Christian education have been provided by a number of teachers in four different graduate schools, including Dr. C. Adrian Heaton, Dr. Milford Henkel, Dr. Mark Fakkema, Sr., Dr. Donald Deffner and Dr. Harold C. Mason. Colleagues in the field have read manuscripts of the various chapters and have provided helpful comments and criticisms, which have been incorporated into the present structure of the volume. Secretaries have labored long over manuscripts. The greatest debt is to the Head of the church, Jesus Christ, God's Son, not only for the eternal salvation but for the privilege of a call to give a lifetime of service in Christian education.

Miami, Florida
1981

Introduction

The introductory sentences in Weldon Crossland's book *Better Leaders for Your Church* assert: "Four indispensables are to be found in every successful church. They are program, organization, morale, and leadership; but the greatest of these is leadership."[1] Vernon Jacobs agrees when he says, "There is hardly a congregation to be found in which there is not a scarcity of leaders."[2] In his chapter on "The Christian Teacher" in *Introduction to Biblical Christian Education,* Gilbert Peterson states, "In church education, the training situation is usually critical. . . . In a survey taken by this author of over one thousand churches across the United States, 15 percent indicated no leadership training programs whatever, and another 33 percent reported only a yearly meeting of some type."[3]

A cross-section of personal observation is of sufficient magnitude to convince one that the problem to which these writers speak is not limited to one or two churches, nor to a certain geographical area of the United States. Indeed, it is a problem that has existed from the days of Christ. We read in the New Testament that He said to His disciples, "The harvest is plentiful, but the workers are few. Therefore beseech the Lord of the harvest, to send out workers into His harvest" (Matt. 9:37-38).

Definition of Leadership

Pastors have worried and churches have prayed about the question of personnel to equip the church for its many tasks in carrying out the work of Christ's kingdom here on earth. Most Christian leaders verbalize concerning this problem and possible solutions to it, but relatively few have been able to alleviate satisfactorily the shortage of laborers for the harvest.

Our framework is defined as the context of the educational program of the local church. Since the local church is at the foundation of all Christian service, if the problem of lack of leadership can be solved at this level, all other Christian organizations directly and organically connected with it will reap the benefits in improved leadership in their ranks, both quantitatively and qualitatively.

Various authors offer many different definitions to the word "leadership." Ordway Tead says that "leadership is the activity of influencing people to cooperate toward some goal which they come to find is desirable."[4] Ross and Hendry accept no such simple definition. They prefer rather to think of leadership as partaking of elements from three different conceptions of leadership theory: leadership as a trait within the individual leader; leadership as a function of the group; or leadership as a function of the situation. After discussing each of these, the authors conclude that "each of the three theories of leadership discussed briefly above has a good deal to support it. Yet none of them, taken separately, provides an adequate theory of leadership."[5]

Other secular definitions of leadership emphasize such things as the *central person* who is able to polarize the behavior of the group around him; the *functional person* who is able to lead the group toward apparent goals; the *sociometric choice* of a given group; the *person who most forcibly influences a given group* to his way of thinking; and the *person who most thoroughly demonstrates leadership behavior.*

In considering a definition of leadership in the light of Christian theology and the work of the church, definitions like the one developed by Crossland are prevalent.

> Leadership, then, in the local church is the noble art of cooperatively planning and unitedly achieving the goals God has set for mankind in the life and teachings of Jesus Christ. In the life of the church leadership is far more than methods of machinery or techniques or holding an office. In essence, a leader is a Christ-like personality, whose wisdom, self-sacrifice and labor cooperate with others in finding and doing the will of God.[6]

Some writers prefer not to write a definition but merely to compile some aspects which are a part of the leadership "role." Bell describes leadership as relative to such elements as personality, symbolism, position and title.[7]

One of the parts of a questionnaire used some years ago was a question which asked pastors "to write a brief definition of 'leadership' without consulting books or other persons." Some of the responses were as follows:

> One with proper training in certain fields, who knows the problems—and has ability to meet the problems—one who has ability to lead others.
>
> Leadership is to know what needs to be done, know how to do it, and then to get others to follow.

> Leadership is taking the responsibility in a group activity and leading others in the doing of that activity.
>
> The ability needed to direct a group or person toward a set goal.
>
> Leadership is the art of carrying out on your own an assignment involving other people—the capacity to improvise when needed and to command when necessary.

In almost every one of the definitions written by the pastors surveyed, three elements came to the fore: leadership is an *ability;* leadership involves *working with other people;* and leadership involves *progressing toward some kind of a goal.* If these three items were embodied in a definition acceptable for the scope of this book, it might look something like this: *Leadership is the exercise by a member of a group of certain qualities, character and ability which at any given time will result in his changing group behavior in the direction of mutually acceptable goals.* This definition views only the broad application of the term and makes no attempt at this point to define *Christian* leadership.

Reviewing the Need

One of the major elements of research for the first release of *Leadership for Church Education* was a national survey on church leadership needs conducted in 1965. No similar research instrument has been employed for this revision, but a subject of analysis of evangelicalism as we enter the decade of the 1980s indicates that the leadership crisis in local churches continues. That is not to suggest that nothing has been done. Seminaries, for example, have become much more active in the development of courses geared to preparing pastors and other church leaders for managerial and administrative tasks. As indicated in the preface, the literature is significantly expanded from ten years ago. Local churches are attempting to meet the problem through short-term seminars, denominational conferences, and discipleship programs. But as the society becomes more complex and knowledge continues to spread across the culture, demands for intelligent and alert leadership in the church increase, and we simply have not been keeping up with the need. The problem continues to be a genuine one, and again it is the intent of this book to make some contribution toward solving it.

FOR FURTHER READING

Adams, A. M. *Effective Leadership for Today's Church.* Philadelphia: Westminster, 1978.

Dayton, Edward R., and Engstrom, Ted W. *Strategy for Leadership*. Old Tappan, N.J.: Revell, 1975.

Eims, Leroy. *Be the Leader You Were Meant To Be*. Wheaton, Ill: Victor, 1975.

Engstrom, Ted W. *The Making of a Christian Leader*. Grand Rapids: Zondervan, 1976.

Gangel, Kenneth O. *Competent To Lead*. Chicago: Moody, 1974.

Hocking, David L. *Be a Leader People Follow*. Glendale, Calif.: Regal, 1979.

NOTES

1. Weldon Frank Crossland, *Better Leaders for Your Church* (Nashville: Abingdon, 1955), p. 9.
2. J. Vernon Jacobs, *Ten Steps to Leadership* (Cincinnati: Standard, 1961), p. 5.
3. Gilbert A. Peterson, "The Christian Teacher," in Werner C. Graendorf, *Introduction to Biblical Christian Education* (Chicago: Moody, 1981), p. 84.
4. Ordway Tead, *The Art of Leadership* (New York: McGraw-Hill, 1963), p. 20.
5. Charles E. Hendry and Murray G. Ross, *New Understandings of Leadership* (New York: Association, 1957), p. 31.
6. Crossland, p. 12.
7. A. Donald Bell, *How To Get Along with People in the Church* (Grand Rapids: Zondervan, 1960), pp. 29-42.

PART I

Foundations of Church Education

1

The Nature of the Church

THE ABSENCE OF CAPABLE LAY LEADERSHIP throughout evangelical Christianity today—the ignorance of the Bible and doctrine on the part of a great portion of the laity—the lack of a genuine commitment to the Lord by many Christians—these and other problems pinpoint the failure of many churches to provide a superior quality, life-transforming church program.

The great majority of Christians get their only contact with Christian education through the local church. Such a responsibility necessitates a program of education on the local church level that is superior rather than inferior, progressive rather than regressive and flexible rather than rigid.

If we are to have better church leadership, a better informed laity and a deeper dedication to Christ, Christian education in the local church needs to be based squarely on biblical concepts. This means, for one thing, having a biblical perspective on, and understanding of, the nature of the church. In much of Christianity today the heart of the problem seems to be that we have forgotten what it means to "be the church."

The process of Christian education must properly proceed from theology to philosophy to practical implementation in the form of curriculum and methodology. It is imperative, therefore, that a book which deals with the totality of the educational program of the church begin with a theological examination of the church itself.

Much of the confusion that we are facing today in the educational program of the church has stemmed from the lack of a clear-cut philosophy of education, carrying with it the weight of specific objectives which have their epistemological and axiological foundation laid firmly in the Word of God. It is essential that the church's educational program should be pedagogically respectable. It is even more essential, however, that it be thoroughly biblical.

CONTEMPORARY CONFUSION REGARDING THE NATURE OF THE CHURCH

SECULAR ANALYSIS

In the 1950s and 1960s abundant literature provided a sociological analysis of the church's problems from such noted educators as Gibson Winter, Martin Marty and R. J. Havighurst. The religious book market has been flooded with volumes analyzing the church as though it were the local supermarket or a branch of a major industry. From such examination the church can well learn some of the organizational defects into which it has fallen through the years. It has had ample opportunity to study its irrelevance, tradition-bound immobility, and inability to meet the needs of modern society. Much of the criticism has been good and much of it has been helpful. Nevertheless there is one basic erroneous note that flows through most of the literature dissecting the church in recent decades. It has viewed the church largely as an *organization* and failed to realize that it is also an *organism*.

THE DISTORTED IMAGE OF FICTION

Another problem that the church faces today is the image that it has inherited in contemporary fiction and the cinema. The image of Jonathan Edwards thundering the truth of God to a people who trembled before His sovereignty has now given way to a distorted picture of Elmer Gantry ranting his way up and down the land, grasping for personal profit in religious merchandise. After identifying modern man as confused, complacent, chaotic, rebellious and desperately in need of help, the writers of twentieth-century fiction have been able to construct nothing better than a "picaresque saint." The voices of Kafka and Camus have been heard more clearly on college campuses than the voice of God. The educated American has nearly lost sight of what the New Testament church was all about.

EXTERNAL RENEWAL

There are those within the church, of course, who call loudly for renewal. Existential religious education, following in the footsteps of its parent existential theology, offers to drape the old form of evangelical jargon with a new dress more adapted to the modern society. Sara Little talks about getting back to the Bible in Christian education, but the Bible to which she would go is not the Bible of Wesley, Luther, Calvin and Augustine.[1]

Findley Edge, Professor of Religious Education at Southern

Baptist Seminary, spoke to the combined commissions of the National Sunday School Association in September 1966. He pointed out that the renewal movement emphasizes the external man to the exclusion of a sound theology which deals accurately with man's inner problems. Edge called for a combination of evangelism and social involvement to lift the church from its doldrums of confusion.

THE GOSPEL OF A CAUSE

Still another voice clamoring to be heard in the darkness is what may be called "The Gospel of a Cause." Strangely enough, prophets of this position can be found in the ranks of both theological extremes. Their paths are different and their traveling gear diverse, but they end up at the same crossroads—the banner of a *cause*. Some tell us the church must become more involved in civil rights, using the influence of pastor and parish to push for open housing, school integration, job opportunities and a dozen other aspects of that pressing social problem.

Others would press the church into the battle for world peace. Only in such a noble and worldwide cause for the benefit of the human race, they threaten, can the church redeem itself from its years of apathy and injustice. Still others tell us that the church must be in the foreground fighting communism. Since the church is basically theistic and communism is categorically atheistic, the logical conclusion for this group must be an active anticommunist crusade.

The difficulty of all the above causes (and dozens more like them) is that they have often failed to distinguish between the supernatural work of regeneration and its accompanying results in individual behavior and in society. The fact of the matter is that satisfactory civil rights on earth are not to be equated with heavenly citizenship; world peace (even should it be attained) is a shoddy substitute for the eternal peace of God in the human heart; and American democracy is not biblical Christianity. The problem of the gospel of a cause, therefore, is that it has offered itself as a substitute for the gospel of the cross!

POLARIZATION OF A PHILOSOPHY OF MINISTRY

There have been a number of beliefs and behaviors that have divided evangelicals through the twentieth century—levels and extent of separation; arguments over prophecy; disputes related to systems of Bible interpretation; and more recently, positions on the doctrine of inerrancy. Increasingly obvious as a divisive force is the attitude toward how the church should minister and what forms that ministry should take. Part of the issue, for example, is size. One wing of conservative Christianity focuses on what we have come to call the "super church" with its vast busing program, strong evangelistic emphasis, and constant concerns with attendance. The opposite extreme stresses the importance of small groups, discipleship training, and a heavy emphasis on "sharing." Obviously, there are local churches representing almost every point on a continuum line between those extremes, and there are people who feel comfortable in many and varied ministerial styles.

Because the Scripture is hardly dogmatic on philosophy of ministry, it becomes a matter of personal taste coupled with the leading of the Holy Spirit as individuals and families feel drawn to a particular kind of church.

One of the positive by-products of the debate over philosophy of ministry has been a renewed study of the nature of the church. Another by-product has been an awareness by many of the wide gap we had placed between ourselves and the church of the New Testament by overemphasizing *organization* almost to the exclusion of *organism*. The renewal movement advanced significantly by Ray Stedman (*Body Life*) and Gene Getz (*Sharpening the Focus of the Church*) has helped immeasurably in directing our attention again to the basic biblical components of the New Testament church.

THE MEANING OF THE WORD "CHURCH"

THE ENGLISH WORDS

The English word *church* is one of the most abused and misused words in the twentieth-century vocabulary. Unfortunately, like Caesar, it suffers more at the hands of its friends than at the hands of its enemies. There are four common uses which many Christians make of the word *church*, certainly with no deliberate attempt to wrench the word from its proper biblical context.

Building. Many people refer to the building in which the congregation assembles as the "church." A man may say to his wife, "I am going down to the church to pick up my hat which I left there after the morning service," fully knowing that no other individual will be in the building at the time he arrives.

Denominations. It is quite common to speak of a collection of churches which have assembled themselves together in some kind of organization or association as "the Baptist church," "the Methodist church," or "the Presbyterian church."

Universal church. The universal church is a reference to all members of the Body of Christ in all places and all ages. Some theologians have referred to this as the "church invisible," but in actuality the church has never been invisible.

Local church. The local church is a given geographical representation of the universal church. It is this usage of the word which is most in focus throughout the pages of this book.

Of the four common usages of the word *church* mentioned above, only two are biblical. The first two have grown up in the jargon of the ecclesiastical years. It is not necessarily a great error to use the word *church* in this way unless, by so doing, one forgets that in the emphasis of the New Testament, the church is always *people.* The last two usages, universal and local, are the only scriptural usages of the concept of church.

THE GREEK WORD

The Greek word used to designate either universal church or local church in the New Testament is the word *ecclesia.* To the Greeks the word indicated an assembly of free citizens; however, to the Jews it would have more theocratic connotations. In the New Testament the word has three basic uses:

1. *A political assembly of free citizens.* The word *ecclesia* appears in this context in Acts 19:32, 39, 41. The English word used in the authorized translation is the word *assembly,* which is quite proper in describing the situation. God had worked various miracles through Paul at Ephesus, and Demetrius, representative of the silversmiths, was afraid that their patron deity was in jeopardy because of the increasing number of people who were turning to the gospel of Christ. In the confusion that followed, mob violence was averted by the speech of the town clerk. It is interesting to note that when the mob was in complete chaos as well as when it was formally dismissed by the town clerk, it is referred to as an *ecclesia.*

2. *Jewish assembly of the Old Testament.* In the sermon just before his martyrdom, Stephen speaks of Moses and "the church in the wilderness" (Acts 7:38). The word *ecclesia* in this context obviously cannot be a reference to the New Testament church but speaks in a general way of the congregation or the gathering of the people in the wilderness under the leadership of Moses.

3. *The Christian church.* Almost all the New Testament pas-

sages (excluding the two mentioned above) deal with the Christian church in either its universal or local form. Because of the extreme importance of this concept, one cannot properly perceive of the doctrine of the church without a thorough understanding of these two uses of the word *ecclesia*. The universal church contains only true believers, whereas the local church may include professing Christians who have not had an experience of regeneration.

THE UNIVERSAL CHURCH

In the Old Testament the church was presented in typological form. Sample types might include Ruth, the Gentile bride; and Israel, God's remnant in the world.

In the gospels God's revelation of the church proceeds to a prophetic form as the Lord Jesus Christ Himself pronounces, "Upon this rock I will build My church" (Matt. 16:18). The book of Acts describes the history of the church in its early days, and the spread of the gospel through the church, beginning at Jerusalem and today around the world, is in literal fulfillment of Acts 1:8.

It is not until one reads the epistles, however, that he is confronted with any kind of formalized church doctrine, since in God's sovereign plan such information was largely confined to the writings of the apostle Paul. The crown of church doctrine is the epistle to the church at Ephesus; and its most glittering jewel is chapter 4, particularly verses 11-16, a passage which comes into focus frequently throughout the pages of this book.

The universal church includes all Christians (1 Cor. 1:1-2), only Christians (Eph. 5:23-27), and is represented by those brought together through the Holy Spirit. The teaching on spiritual gifts in 1 Corinthians 12 is clear evidence of the nature of the church as an organism. The universal church is, in the language of the apostle Paul, "the body of Christ."

THE LOCAL CHURCH

God's pattern has always been that the universal church be manifest in the local church (Rom. 16:16), and Acts 2:41-47 represents the local church at Jerusalem carrying out the purposes and program of the universal church. There is no evidence in the Word of God that Christ ever abandoned the program and format of the local church as the basic foundation stone for all forms of service and mission in the world.

Membership. Membership in the local church seems to have been taken for granted by New Testament believers. Various passages seem to indicate that specific rolls were kept, but there is very little clearcut teaching on the nature of membership rules (Acts 1:15; 2:41; 6:2-5; 1 Cor. 5:13; 1 Tim. 5:9).

Organization. Like the matter of membership, church organization is not specifically outlined in the New Testament. It is somewhat assumed by Christ in Matthew 18 when He talks about establishing the facts of a dispute through collective hearing by the church. As apostolic authority passed off the scene, collective organization seems to have taken its place. In Acts 8, for example, Peter remonstrates with Simon the sorcerer on the basis of unilateral authority. Just a few years later the apostle Paul writes to the church at Corinth that they have the collective responsibility to judge wicked persons in their midst (1 Cor. 5:13).

In a sense the indigenous principle of missions is a more refined development of this earliest principle of organization. Another characteristic of organization in the early church is that it arose largely in response to the needs and problems which the church encountered. The selection of the deacons in Acts 6 is probably the most obvious example of this.

Government. An important part of organization in the local church is its government. Although there is a difference of opinion among evangelicals regarding the significance of such words as *episkopos* (bishop or overseer) and *presbuteros* (elder), there are several biblical principles of church government which are enunciated in the New Testament.

CHURCH GOVERNMENT SHOULD BE BIBLICAL IN CONSTITUTION

Young Timothy is a valid representative of early church leadership, and to him the apostle Paul writes that leaders in a church are to be in constant conformity to "sound words, those of our Lord Jesus Christ, and with the doctrine conforming to godliness" (1 Tim. 6:3). Of course some would immediately point out that the reference here to "words" is to the words of the living Son of God and not to the words written in the Bible. Nevertheless, our understanding of the words of Christ is exclusively dependent upon God's inspired record of those words. One of the great errors of liberal theology down through the years has been a fabricated separation of the written Word from the incarnate Word.

CHURCH GOVERNMENT SHOULD BE PARTICIPATORY IN FORM

The existence of numerous evangelical denominations with varying attitudes regarding church government is demonstration enough that the Scriptures are not explicit on the issue. Some interpret the New Testament to teach congregational government, others favor a presbyterian form, and still others the more hierarchical episcopalian structure. Quite obviously, each group will defend its preference from Scripture and history. The only point I wish to make here, therefore, is the renewed emphasis on the church as people. Evidence throughout the book of Acts strongly suggests that whatever emphasis may have been placed on the role of elders, the New Testament church leaders never forgot the participatory role of people in the operation of the church. That was an omission brought about by later corruption of medieval forms.

CHURCH GOVERNMENT SHOULD BE REPRESENTATIVE IN FUNCTION

How easy it would have been in Acts 6 for the apostles to select those seven men whom they desired to serve in the "daily ministration" (KJV). Nevertheless, they carefully restrained themselves and asked the entire group to make the selection. The statement of verse 5 is quite clear: "The whole multitude . . . chose" (KJV).

CHURCH GOVERNMENT SHOULD BE SPIRITUAL IN FUNCTION

The biblical, democratic, and spiritual aspects of church administration find their clearest practical application in the selection of the first missionaries. It is obvious in Acts 13 that the process of selecting and sending those missionaries was dependent solely upon the sovereignty of the Holy Spirit through prayer. The Holy Spirit selected the missionaries, and the Holy Spirit sent them to a particular place. The local church was an intermediary agency, a physical representation of the hand of God in His world.

THE PURPOSE OF THE CHURCH

Without a clear-cut set of objectives, any organization suffers. The church has been less than outstanding in its clarification of a raison d'etre in the twentieth century. Edward L. Hayes warned us over fifteen years ago that

> evangelical Christian education is proceeding into the late sum-

> mer of the twentieth century without clearly defined statements of purpose. Local church educational endeavors, at best, tend to revolve around a simplistic set of objectives which utterly fail to denote theological intent and educational methodology. Devoid of comprehensive statements of educational objectives, evangelical church education is in danger of being driven further and further into frantic activism.[2]

Not all church leaders have been silent, however, and at least one leading educator has specified in print an attempt to answer the question, What is the church for?

> The answer is no mystery. Scripture makes it plain that the church is to be a worshipping body, committed to "show forth the praises of him who has called (it) out of darkness into his marvelous light"; that it is to proclaim the saving gospel of Jesus Christ to all the world; and that it is to obey all the teachings of Jesus Christ, its great head and Lord.[3]

For thirty years Dr. Frank E. Gaebelein has given careful thought to the issues of Christian education and philosophy. Unfortunately, however, no one individual can speak for all local churches, as each body of believers must reassess the purposes of its own existence and clarify its relationship to the universal church. The New Testament seems to set forth four basic objectives for the church, though church educators may verbalize them differently.

THE CHURCH STRUCTURES A CLIMATE FOR WORSHIP

A host of passages invite our attention on the subject of the church promoting worship. It may be beneficial, however, to confine the biblical support for the church's purpose to the epistle of Ephesians. In chapter 1 Paul immediately declares that the purpose of God's predestination and adoption is that His people might be "to the praise of the glory of His grace." Lest his readers miss the emphasis, the apostle repeats the worship theme in verses 12 and 14. The great benediction of chapter 3 also focuses on the concept of worship as Paul writes, "To Him be the glory in the church and in Christ Jesus to all generations forever and ever. Amen" (Eph. 3:21).

To say that one of the purposes of the church is worship is not to say that the church fully accomplishes this objective by providing opportunities for the individual Christian to pray, sing, hear Scripture, read publicly or engage in any other kind of physical or verbal activity. As a matter of fact, worship is not primarily activity but rather an *attitude* of heart and mind which comprehends God for what He is and rejoices in the realization.

THE CHURCH PROVIDES THE SETTING FOR FELLOWSHIP

A little phrase in Ephesians 3:18 is often overlooked. It is "with all the saints," words which speak volumes regarding the nature of the church. Monasticism has never been God's way, and biblical separation today should be interpreted neither as some kind of isolation from others nor insulation from the very world that needs the witness of the church. The apostle John writes of fellowship in his first epistle: "What we have seen and heard we proclaim to you also, that you also may have fellowship with us; and indeed our fellowship is with the Father, and with His Son Jesus Christ" (1 John 1:3). In other words, horizontal fellowship between God's people is dependent upon vertical fellowship between the individual Christian and his Lord. One of the purposes of the church is that the world may see Christians living together in a harmonious love relationship which is demonstrative of the Christ whom they serve (John 13:35).

THE CHURCH DEVELOPS A FORTRESS FOR EVANGELISM

Biblically, evangelism is the clear proclamation of the gospel of Jesus Christ which leaves the results entirely up to the sovereignty of the Holy Spirit. Unfortunately, too many churches have viewed evangelism as the only task of the church and have subordinated all other purposes to it. Such churches fill their rolls with baby Christians who, instead of growing week by week on the milk, bread, and meat of the Word, are subjected to a constant barrage of the elementary principles of the gospel.

Such excesses, however, should not cloud the fact that evangelism *is* a legitimate task of the church. There may, indeed, be those who have the special gift of evangelism, but their ministry does not excuse the responsibility of *every* Christian to communicate the gospel. Paul is representative of the church in Ephesians 3:8 when he says of himself, "This grace was given, to preach to the Gentiles the unfathomable riches of Christ." In Acts 8:4 when the apostles were held at Jerusalem for some reason during a mass persecution, Luke records that the church "went about preaching the word."

Some would prefer to describe this concept of the church's purpose as "service" since it is a more inclusive word. There are varied kinds of service which God's people render through the church, and not all of them have to do directly with evangelism. In this respect, perhaps we can say that the church *has a mission* in the world and that the church indeed *is mission* in the world.

THE CHURCH MAINTAINS A MINISTRY OF EDUCATION

Again it is quite possible to choose a different word and offer basically the same meaning. It is proper to say that the church has a responsibility for instruction or edification. In the final analysis the Great Commission is a teaching commission (Matt. 28:19-20; Acts 2:42). Murch has warned us to "teach or perish."

It is to this facet of the church's responsibility that this entire book is dedicated. Nevertheless, it is not possible to move on to the matters of organization and administration before coming once again to that golden deposit of truth, Ephesians 4:11-16, which speaks so clearly regarding the church's educational task. Note carefully the *New International Version* translation of the passage:

> It was he who gave some to be apostles, some to be prophets, some to be evangelists, and some to be pastors and teachers, to prepare God's people for works of service, so that the body of Christ may be built up until we all reach unity in the faith and in the knowledge of the Son of God and become mature, attaining to the whole measure of the fullness of Christ.
>
> Then we will no longer be infants, tossed back and forth by the waves, and blown here and there by every wind of teaching and by the cunning and craftiness of men in their deceitful scheming. Instead, speaking the truth in love, we will in all things grow up into him who is the Head, that is, Christ. From him the whole body, joined and held together by every supporting ligament, grows and builds itself up in love, as each part does its work.

In this passage there are several facts which form a biblical basis for the church's educational program:

1. The church's educational ministry is carried on by those who are first gifted by the Holy Spirit to lead and then given to the church for that purpose (v. 11).

2. The purpose of the church's educational ministry is to make God's people mature so that they can minister. Maturation is an edification, or a "building up," process (v. 12).

3. If the church's educational ministry is properly carried on, the end result will be maturity in individual believers and a harmonious relationship between the believers collectively. The

process of growing into this maturity and harmony is the process of becoming more like Jesus Christ (v. 13).

4. The church's educational ministry is highly theological, producing discerning students of truth who are able—because of their understanding of truth—to detect and avoid error (v. 14).

5. A properly functioning church educational ministry will effectively combine truth and love, and not sacrifice either one on the altar of the other. A mature Christian (v. 15) will be like his Lord, "full of grace and truth" (John 1:14).

6. A properly functioning church educational program does not consist only of a few teachers and many learners but will actually be carried on for mutual edification as God's people help each other to grow in spirituality (v. 16).

To state it simply and yet biblically, *the overwhelming and all-encompassing objective of the church is total Christian maturity for all of its members.* Total Christian maturity includes an individual and collective life of biblical worship, biblical fellowship, and biblical evangelism, all of which are stimulated by and produced through properly functioning programs of biblical church education.

FOR FURTHER READING

Dobbins, Gaines S. *A Ministering Church.* Nashville: Broadman, 1960.
Edge, Findley B. *The Greening of the Church.* Waco, Tex.: Word, 1971.
MacArthur, John, Jr. *The Church, the Body of Christ.* Grand Rapids: Zondervan, 1973.
Saucy, Robert L. *The Church in God's Program.* Chicago: Moody, 1972.
Snyder, Howard A. *The Community of the King.* Downers Grove, Ill.: Inter-Varsity, 1977.
Stedman, Ray C. *Body Life.* Glendale, Calif.: Regal, 1972. (Revised and expanded, 1977.)
Zuck, Roy B. *Spiritual Power in Your Teaching.* Chicago: Moody, n.d.

NOTES

1. Sara Little, *The Role of the Bible in Contemporary Christian Education* (Richmond: Knox, 1961).
2. Edward L. Hayes, "Reconstruction in Christian Education—A Problem of Purpose," *Action* (September 1966), p. 11.
3. Frank E. Gaebelein, *A Varied Harvest* (Grand Rapids: Eerdmans, 1967), p. 160.

2

Toward A Biblical Philosophy of Church Education

ONLY WHEN ONE has properly understood the nature of the church and what the New Testament says about it, can he go on to formulate a satisfactory philosophy of church education. One's philosophy of education develops out of one's theology and is inseparably linked with it. Many problems now existing in church educational programs in evangelical circles are due to a lack of a clear-cut understanding of what we are really attempting to do in church education and how we must go about doing it.

To the extent that church education attempts to communicate a certain body of content to its constituency and to bring them to a higher level of maturity as a result of that communication, it is not unlike education in general. Many of the same apects of educational philosophy, therefore, which would be discussed in terms of a school situation are also relevant for a consideration of church education. The following paragraphs constitute a brief analysis of ten factors which must be reviewed in any analysis of educational philosophy. Each is present to a greater or lesser extent in church education, and each must be viewed from a genuinely biblical and evangelical point of view.

METAPHYSICS FOR CHURCH EDUCATION MUST BE GOD-CENTERED

Metaphysics has to do with the question of ultimate reality. It is the basic and pivotal postulate upon which any philosophy revolves, because it traces and identifies reality at its source. The claim of Christian philosophy is that this ultimate reality resides in the eternal God Himself (Gen. 1:1; John 1:1).

Even the casual reader will note that the Bible makes no attempt to prove the existence of God. It is the unprovable and assumed presupposition of all educational endeavors undertaken by those who rest their faith in the personal God of the universe. Church education which is genuinely Christian begins, proceeds, and ends with the concept of a triune God.

The Christian educator does not hesitate to welcome open investigation of the reality of his faith. The absence of detailed argument and defense of a scriptural metaphysic is patterned after the way biblical theology itself treats the issue.

THE EPISTEMOLOGY FOR CHURCH EDUCATION MUST BE REVELATION-CENTERED

It follows logically that after one has reached a conclusion concerning what is real, the next consuming philosophical passion would be to determine what is true. Epistemology deals with the essence of knowledge and how one knows what is true. Truth is neither manufactured by man nor discovered on a psychedelic trip within himself. The means of knowing truth for church education is God's revelation, both natural and special.

Natural revelation deals with the physical wonders of the universe which in their beauty and awesome intricacy speak of their divine Creator. How thrilling it must be to the scientist to uncover more and more of God's secrets in nature, particularly if he realizes that God has allowed him to discover something which He Himself has known all along.

Despite its weighty testimony, natural revelation is insufficient in itself. Gaebelein has said, "The world of nature bears overwhelming evidence to God and His greatness and essential being. But of the knowledge which is eternal life it does not directly state."[1]

Thus the Bible is the heart and core of Christian epistemology. For the Christian, an education (within or without the church) which disregards the Bible, is—in its very nature—inferior. To undertake learning while ignoring the source of all truth is foolishness at best and blasphemy at worst.

THE ANTHROPOLOGY OF CHURCH EDUCATION MUST BE IMAGE-CENTERED

Every educator must formulate a philosophy with respect to the nature of man, since his anthropological conclusions will affect his teaching process. If man is regarded as an essentially good being, as many educators in history have argued, the approach to teaching him will be considerably different than if one accepts the biblical position of depravity in human nature. The "image approach" to Christian anthropology is based on three biblical truths:

1. Man was created in the image of God (Gen. 1:26).

2. When sin entered the race through Adam, the image of God in man was marred (Rom. 5:19).

3. God has provided a means, Christ's death on the cross, through which man can be restored to salvation and fellowship with God (1 Cor. 15:22).

Since the aim of church education is to nurture those who are in Christ, it obviously follows that drawing men to the Savior must precede the nurturing process. The regenerate person receives a new nature, but the Adamic nature is not obliterated. In dealing with it, church education continually relies upon the Word of God as the sanctifying agent which carries on a cleansing process in the life of the Christian.

In Christian anthropology, both student and teacher understand that the grace of God must be operative not only in initial salvation but in the continuing process of edification and nurture which comprises church education. All church leaders must continually recognize that God's grace is crucial if the individual is to do anything worthy of God's blessing.

The Axiology of Church Education Must Be Eternity-centered

There are a number of choruses used in evangelical churches to minister to children and youth which carry very little theological value and, at times, even influence negatively. A worthy example of an effective chorus, however, is one entitled "With Eternity's Values in View." The words actually illustrate the axiological thrust of evangelical church education.

> With eternity's values in view, Lord,
> With eternity's values in view.
> May I do each day's work for Jesus,
> With eternity's values in view.

The current existential craze has created a spirit of what Bishop Whittmore calls "presentism." Because of his metaphysical position, the axiology of the secularist demands that his education be for the benefit of the present. For the Christian, on the other hand, the question of values occupies a much more broad and important position in his educational philosophy. Indeed, the entire structure is built on the premise that the purpose of education is to nurture individuals toward Christian maturity. All of life is really a preparation for eternal life. Paul writes to Titus,

> For the grace of God has appeared, bringing salvation to all men, instructing us to deny ungodliness and worldly desires and to live

> sensibly, righteously and godly in the present age, looking for the blessed hope and the appearing of the glory of our great God and Savior, Christ Jesus. [Titus 2:11-13]

In the midst of a materialistic society, the church must attempt to inculcate a value system that takes its roots from complete commitment to citizenship in heaven rather than a cabin at the lake. It must teach these values in its classrooms, preach them from its pulpits, and enable its parents to communicate them in day-by-day family living. The diametrical opposition of the world's value system to that of the Christian is demonstrated in numerous places in Scripture but never more clearly than when James writes that "friendship with the world is hostility toward God" (James 4:4). Similar passages are found in Colossians 3, 1 John 2, Philippians 3, and Matthew 6.

How can a Christian philosophy of church education avoid the pitfalls of relative values and situational ethics? Only by stressing the omniscience of God, His knowledge of all things, and their value in view of eternity (Rom. 8:23). Many Christian values may seem pointless in this society, but the Word of God reminds its readers that no man lives to himself and no man dies to himself. The values of the cross and the eternal city are not relative values. They rest in Him who transcends time and bids all men, like Paul, to count all things but loss in order to gain the excellency which is Christ.

The Objective of Church Education Must Be Christ-centered

No apology is necessary for the emphasis which is placed on clarity of objectives throughout this volume. Nothing can render an educational system in church or school less communicative and relevant to students than oblique aims which may or may not exist even in the minds of the educational leadership. As in all education, the objectives of church education are both general and specific. A general objective is to bring all men to maturity in Jesus Christ.

Comenius saw this task as threefold. First, man must know all things, including himself; second, he must be master of all things, including himself; and third, he must direct all things, including himself, to God. In order to attain these objectives the work of Christian education is to develop the pupil in knowledge and understanding, in moral insight and action, and in reference to God and in true spiritual living.[2]

The objective of church education is said to be Christ-centered because Christian maturity must always be based upon biblical truth and principles which, when related to life, cause regenerated personalities to become more like the Savior in the process of Christian nurture. The pastor and Christian education director can provide careful guidance for maturing Christians in channeling their sanctified efforts and energy effectively into society. But the genuine *desire* to have an impact on society with the gospel will utimately result only from Christian maturity itself.

The education of people in the evangelical church of today should be of such a nature that it results in the student's ability to evaluate all that he encounters in the light of God's Word and from what might be called "divine viewpoint." The education which is centered in Christ and in God's Word is the only kind that God will honor and approve (2 Tim. 2:15). Anything less than this is man-centered even though it may take place within the context of a church building. The statement of objective of church education is rather uncomplicated. The fulfillment of the objective, however, demands the best of sanctified ability that God has placed within the educational leadership.

The Curriculum of Church Education Must Be Bible-centered

Curriculum is a broad word which encompasses much more than the Sunday school quarterly or printed training-hour programs. These things are but a part of the curriculum and serve it well only when they reflect a clear and unadulterated biblical approach to the problems of human lives. Of course, the Scriptures must never be taught on the narrow, stuffy level of mere knowledge. They must be related to life through learning experiences and realistic application of truth. When this is done, Gaebelein reminds us that "no other book can compare in educating power with the Bible." He goes on to say:

> Let no Christian educator ever apologize to the sophisticated of the educational world for giving to the Bible the highest place. To take as the center of the curriculum the one book among all the other great books to which alone the superlative "greatest" can without challenge be uniquely applied—this is neither narrow nor naive. Rather it is simply good judgment to center on the best rather than on the second best.[3]

By now the philosophical house being constructed in this chapter begins to take on form. If God is ultimate reality, if truth is inseparably related to His revelation, and if the objective of church education is to make people like Jesus Christ, then the centrality of the Bible in the church's curriculum is a foregone conclusion.

The subtle approaches of existential religious education during the past three decades have undermined the role of the Bible in the church of today. The Kierkegaardian seed produced the neoorthodox plant which now gives forth an existential rose. But such a rose by any other name is still heresy, and any attempt to delete the Bible from the church's educational program or to compromise its message in any way can only result in victory for Satan and a surrendering of the objectives by default.

The Methodology of Church Education Must Be Interaction-centered

The methodology in any effective educational situation must result in satisfactory communication of the truth under consideration. A Christian teacher should always remember, however, that whereas the message is authoritative truth, the method does not have to be totalitarian and dictatorial. The content transmission of the traditional Herbartian church educational program did not result in producing generations of committed Christians whose lives were saturated with and surrendered to God's truth.

Without giving in to the premise of Dewey and his disciples, evangelical educators in the church can recognize the validity of some of their methodological conclusions. Dewey's talk about activity, interest, discussion and friendliness in the learning situation was not theological heresy but educational sense. The importance of interaction in a learning experience is biblically portrayed many times by the Lord Himself as He engaged Nicodemus, the woman of Samaria, and many others in dialogue about truth. The Sunday school teacher who involves his students in the lesson is not following John Dewey; he is following rather the example of Jesus Christ. In another publication the author has attempted to describe how it is possible to adopt Dewey's methodological conclusions without accepting his philosophical premises. Some of the values thus derived would include:

1. An emphasis on relevance.
2. A practical and expansive view of curriculum.
3. Pupil activity and participation in the learning process.
4. Problem-solving techniques.
5. Interest and dialogue in the learning process.
6. An attempt at emphasis on democracy in education.

7. Concern for the child as an individual.
8. An emphasis on creativity.[4]

The real dynamic of Christian methodology is the Holy Spirit. In the context of Christian education, He is operative in every learning situation. It is His particular ministry to guide the learner into all truth (John 16:12-15). Lois LeBar writes concerning the Holy Spirit in the teaching-learning situation:

> The infinite resources of heaven are at our disposal, waiting for us to be ready to receive fulness of life and power to teach. Think of the loss if we fail our generation, fail to transmit the gospel in its full force, fail to demonstrate the superiority of Christian teaching over secular teaching.[5]

The Discipline of Church Education Must Be Love-centered

Discipline is not to be equated with punishment. The term means rather a narrowing of the path thereby causing people to walk in the right way. Just as the Holy Spirit is dynamic in methodology, the dynamic of love pervades discipline in Christian education. The teacher in the church has the capacity through Christ to control the classroom situation in an atmosphere of love. This love, particularly when it is represented on a mutual level, is a distinctive feature of Christian education. Within the context of the Christian classroom, *agape* begets *agape*.

At times punishment will become a necessity when discipline fails. The Word patiently explains, "For those whom the Lord loves He disciplines, and He scourges every son whom He receives" (Heb.12:6). Such punishment can sometimes be the turning point in the education of a believer. The reproof in Hebrews 5:11 speaks out against the apathy of the writer's audience, a condition which forces him to dwell on primary principles of Christian doctrine instead of going on to the deeper truths and teachings so needful for the people to whom he writes. It is this situation in which many believers find themselves in the church today. It is a stagnation which may require occasional stern reaction to alleviate.

The Teacher for Church Education Must Be Spirit-centered

In the book of 1 Corinthians, Paul exhorts his readers to be followers of him even as he is of Christ. Such a responsibility requires that the teacher for church education be cleansed of sin and filled with God's Holy Spirit. Gaebelein lays down six qualifications for a Spirit-filled teacher:

> 1. Because the teacher is the communicator of truth, he must be openly and boldly a Christian. Christian education demands Christian teachers; anything less will not result in Christian education.
>
> 2. Every teacher must know the Bible. Because the Word of God is relevant to all subjects, this principle must apply to the teachers of these subjects as well as to those teachers of Bible subjects.
>
> 3. The Christian teacher must be committed in every aspect of his life and work, in all his being to the truth, including ordinary honesty.
>
> 4. The teacher must seek excellence. This is a seeking after intellectual excellence to the glory of God, and a Christian teacher should be content with nothing less than superiority in this area. The teacher should strive to meet the requirements of a demanding world, avoiding the sin of mediocrity.
>
> 5. The Christian teacher must truly love his students, seeking their highest good even when at times the way may be hard. Not only should he love his students, he should genuinely like and understand them. A God-given "like" is an essential in effective teaching.
>
> 6. Finally, the Christian teacher should exercise complete submission to the one great teacher. "This is my beloved Son: hear him" (Luke 9:35). Every teacher must listen to the Lord for his lessons and never should he think that he does not need to be taught of Him.[6]

Certainly on the human level no factor is as important to the educational process as the teacher. The discernment of Scripture is the potential of every Christian, but the ability to transmit to others the truth and principles of God's Word is a gift—the gift of teaching (Rom. 12:6-7; Eph. 4:11; 2 Tim. 2:2).

In the world today, the emphasis of teacher training is on the production of men and women well versed in liberal arts, demonstrating expertise in some academic discipline, and capable of raising questions and even doubts about the world in which they live. In contrast, the Christian teacher takes as his responsibility the instructing of students in an authoritative message based on the Word of God, and doing so within the enabling power of the Holy Spirit. Zuck well writes:

> First, the *aim* of Christian education necessitates born-again teachers. The transformation of lives, the growth of Christian personalities, the nurturing of pupils toward conformity to the will of God, demand that the teacher be one who possesses high spiritual objectives.
>
> Second, the *nature* of Christian teaching demands regenerate

instructors. Christian teaching is a divine calling, not simply a secular vocation. It is a ministry *divinely* ordained of God for the purpose of using *divinely* appointed persons to communicate truths of a *divinely* inspired Book, in order to help pupils lead *divine* lives.

Since the entire process is a divine one, only those who are divinely regenerated by God's Spirit qualify to engage in this ministry. An unsaved man, though religious, does not know God and therefore is incapable of communicating the truth and will of God to others.

Third, the *influence* of teachers' lives demands that teachers know Christ in salvation. The life, words, actions, attitudes, convictions, and objectives of the teacher all influence his pupils to one degree or another. A teacher who does not know Christ as Saviour is unable to influence his pupils with the realities of his own Christian life, because he has none. God's plan is to teach through regenerated personalities whom He indwells.[7]

THE EVALUATION OF CHURCH EDUCATION IS GROWTH-CENTERED

Since the objective of church education is maturity in Christ, the yardstick by which learning is measured relates to growth in that maturity. The evidence of growth, of course, is life change. Peter admonishes his readers to "grow in the grace and knowledge of our Lord and Savior Jesus Christ" (2 Peter 3:18). We may well apply evaluative questions to an observation of the growth pattern:

1. Does the pupil know truth?
2. Does the pupil understand truth?
3. Does the pupil practice truth?
4. Does the pupil perceive truth in himself?
5. Does the pupil differentiate truth in life?
6. Does the pupil relate truth to others?

Of course, "growth" in Christian maturity demands more than intellectual expansion. If this latter is the end result of all the church's educative efforts, it is contributing to society's pattern of creating "men without chests" as C. S. Lewis describes them.[8] Effective church education should teach the soul to love God and man while it encourages the spirit to grow close to the very heart of El Shaddai where it is nourished and tended by Him.

Actions and reactions are the fruit of philosophy. Because one acts in accordance with what he believes, it is only logical that he consider the basis for his beliefs, determining what is necessary to propagate those beliefs and eliminating those weights that only encourage complexity. Byrne sets down five values for thinking through a genuinely Christian philosophy of education:

1. A Christian philosophy co-ordinates the various spheres of life as a whole.
2. A Christian philosophy relates knowledge systematically.
3. A Christian philosophy examines the presuppositions, methods, and basic concepts of each discipline and groups of disciplines.
4. A Christian philosophy strives for coherence, the formulation of a world view.
5. A Christian philosophy consults data from total experience.[9]

Church education is God using His called leaders to put His children through a process which is known in theological terms as sanctification and in psychological jargon as maturation. The ten principles described and discussed in this chapter must be welded together into the essential nature of Christian education, which is the total integration of truth. Such a "wholistic" attitude toward education is made necessary by the assumption that there is only one truth, one way to know it, and one reason for knowing it. It is hoped that as the reader makes his way through the methodological sections of this book he will come again and again to these first two chapters which attempt to describe the reason for it all.

FOR FURTHER READING

Eavey, C. B. *History of Christian Education*. Chicago: Moody, 1964.
Gaebelein, Frank E. *The Pattern of God's Truth*. Chicago: Moody, 1968.
Holmes, Arthur F. *All Truth Is God's Truth*. Grand Rapids: William B. Eerdmans, 1977.
Richards, Lawrence O. *A Theology of Christian Education*. Grand Rapids: Zondervan, 1975.
Rood, Wayne R. *Understanding Christian Education*. Nashville: Abingdon, 1970.
Taylor, Marvin J., ed. *Foundations for Christian Education in an Era of Change*. Nashville: Abingdon, 1976.

NOTES

1. Frank E. Gaebelein, *Christian Education in a Democracy* (New York: Oxford, 1951) p. 37.
2. C. B. Eavey, *History of Christian Education* (Chicago: Moody, 1964), p. 174.
3. Frank E. Gaebelein, *A Varied Harvest* (Grand Rapids: Eerdmans, 1967), p. 41.
4. Kenneth O. Gangel, "John Dewey: An Evangelical Evaluation," *Bibliotheca Sacra* 493 (January-March 1967): 29.
5. Lois E. LeBar, *Education That Is Christian* (Westwood, N.J.: Revell, 1958), p. 244.
6. Frank E. Gaebelein, "Towards a Christian Philosophy of Education," *Grace Journal* 3 (Fall 1962): 28-32.
7. Roy B. Zuck, *The Holy Spirit in Your Teaching* (Wheaton, Ill.: Scripture Press, 1963), p. 9. (Reprinted by Moody Press, Chicago, as *Spiritual Power in Your Teaching*.)
8. C. S. Lewis, *The Abolition of Man* (New York: Macmillan, 1947), chap. 1.
9. H. W. Byrne, *A Christian Approach to Education* (Grand Rapids: Zondervan, 1961), p. 75.

3

The Balanced Church Program of Christian Education

In an era of anti-institutionalism, even the term *program* has fallen into disrepute. Phrases like "program seems more important than people," and "our church is overprogrammed" are representative of the criticism many churches have experienced throughout the 1970s. What happened, of course, is that the fragmented embryonic ministries of post-World War II church education took on rather fixed institutional forms during the 1960s. Having lost a good bit of their flexibility, they at times became masters rather than servants, and in such a situation we do well to criticize the obsolescence of forms that have outlived their function.

But most churches are still quite traditional in their educational ministries, and most traditional churches still think in terms of programs. Our concern in this chapter is to recognize an overall balance in church education that does not allow a single large ministry, such as Sunday school, to dominate the nurturing role of the church while other equally important educational ministries suffer from inadequate attention.

A balanced church program of Christian education is characterized by a number of factors. It is probably composed of a number of agencies or ministries which are educational in nature. It is kept running smoothly through a process of organization which maintains some principles of unification and correlation (discussed in chapter 16). One major characteristic should precede all others. It is by virtue of both its position and importance the most primary characteristic of any educational program, whether church or school, sacred or secular. Simply stated it is this: the educational program of the church must be solidly founded upon biblical objectives which clearly define what that educational program is trying to do.

Even though this is not a book on learning psychology, a brief review of the educational cycle may prove helpful here. Figure 1 is not the only form of the educational cycle, but it does conform generally to what most Christian educators see as the process of education as it develops either in a single class or in a total program.*

Notice that we begin with biblical objectives which are formulated from even more basic biblical imperatives.† It should become immediately clear once again why chapter 2, dealing with philosophy, is so important in a book on organization and programming. The educational program is built upon the educational philosophy. For the Christian, the educational philosophy is built upon a biblical theology. God has spoken and therefore the church acts upon that revelation.

A casual glance at the diagram will immediately demonstrate that from biblical objectives we develop local objectives; in other words, we apply the general goal put forth to all Christians in terms of our immediate environment and the needs of our people. In a sense, all educational objectives are built upon

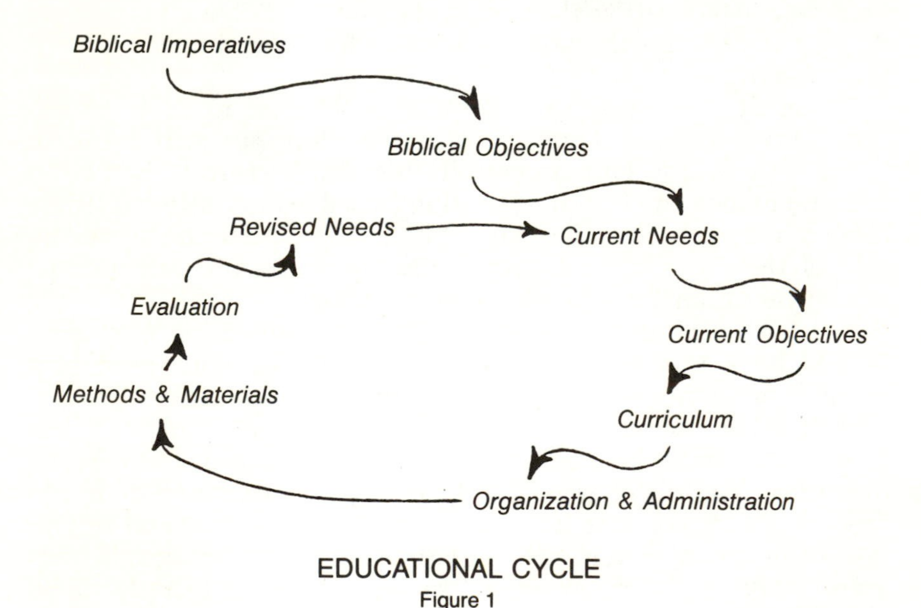

EDUCATIONAL CYCLE
Figure 1

*Diagram by Dr. Lois LeBar with revisions by Dr. Gene Getz and the present author.

†For example, a biblical imperative is clearly found in Matt. 28:18-20. The objectives which evangelicals derive from this imperative are world evangelization and congregational nurture.

needs, though the needs might not be realized by those for whom the educational program is being constructed.

Moreover, it becomes evident from the diagram that methodology, curriculum, administration—aspects which seem so strategically important in the educational process—only fall into place after objectives have been clearly defined. Each serves the purposes of those which precede it and, in turn, is only as strong as the biblical soundness of its predecessors. Methodology is extremely important in teaching; but if the curriculum is unsound, no amount of superb methodology can redeem the educational program.

The great irony of the total field of religious education today is that sometimes those who have the least to communicate are the most concerned with the process of communication. Liberal churches which have rejected the authority of God's Word often make very clear-cut efforts to improve educational programs which now are engaged in the business of propagating the ideas of man.

The process of evaluation is at the end of each round of the cycle. Evaluation pertains to all of the steps in the educational cycle, and every facet of the program must come under careful scrutiny. Observe that evaluation is inseparably related to the objectives, for in a sense it merely answers the question, Are we effectively accomplishing what we set out to do? All of the other steps in the process are tools which enable us to accomplish what we set out to achieve according to our stated objectives.

It is important to notice that the arrow of the educational cycle does not move up to include an evaluation of the biblical imperatives and objectives upon which the total program is based. It returns immediately to a reconsideration of objectives and perhaps a reformulation of them. The point is that God's Word is absolute and never changes. Therefore, if the imperatives and the objectives were genuinely biblical in the first place, there is no need for evaluation. Any change at this point would be a weakening rather than a strengthening of the educational program. This is a practical demonstration of the necessity of the principle of absolute truth.

There has been confusion in some of the literature on Christian education about the use of the terms "objectives," "goals," "purposes" and "aims." I see no value to be gained by attempting a technical differentiation between these terms, so I use them synonymously throughout the book. It is possible, therefore, to adopt Eavey's definition of aim and apply it to any of the above words. The definition states that "an aim is attention brought to focus to make possible expenditure of energy for achieving a predetermined purpose."[1]

Rather than attempt some kind of paper-thin distinction between these words, it would seem more practical to adopt the approach of Findley Edge when he simply defines the different types of objectives by the use of adjectives. There are, for example, "yearly aims," "quarterly aims" and "weekly aims." This is a classification of educational objectives by time.[2] Objectives may also be classified by types of learning and experiences, and the classic list in this category is offered by a secular educator Benjamin Bloom. He defines six levels of learning experiences and urges that teachers develop educational objectives in conjunction with these areas: knowledge, comprehension, application, analysis, synthesis and evaluation.[3]

Several lists of objectives have been written and are available for study in many of the books listed at the end of this chapter. For the sake of completeness, another list is offered here. The Christian education program of the local church should seek to lead a person to:

1. a biblical understanding of the triune God and a personal relationship with Him through Jesus Christ His Son
2. a biblical relationship with other Christians in a vital participation with them in the universal church
3. a biblically constant and thorough program of Christian nurture which has emphasis on doctrine, development of personal Christian convictions, and a scriptural conduct of oneself in family and larger social groups
4. a biblical recommitment of oneself to Christ in discipleship
5. a biblical and enthusiastic participation in the witness of the gospel to the whole world

These five areas can be viewed as one unified general objective. If we have a genuinely biblical concept of what the church is, then we must conclude that what it does is to make people more like its Head, Jesus Christ. *Therefore, the generalized objective of Christian education in the local church is to produce total Christian maturity in the lives of people.* It is to this end that its educational program is dedicated and toward which all of its agencies focus. Perhaps the following diagram using the words "aim," "aspects" and "agencies" can help to illustrate the rela-

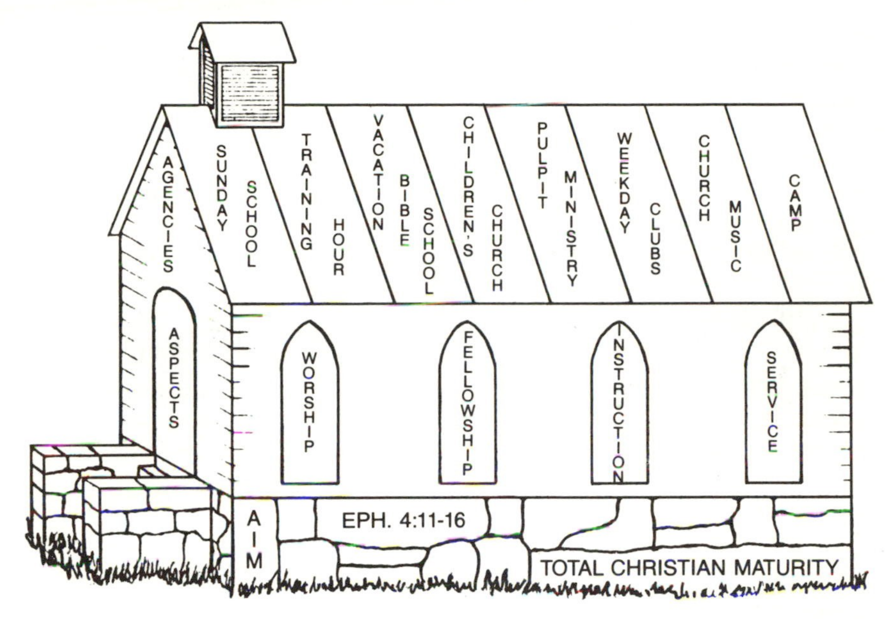

EDUCATIONAL AIM—ASPECTS—AGENCIES
Figure 2

tionship between objectives and programming in local church Christian education.

Notice that the "aspects" in the diagram are merely one-word designations of the objectives stated earlier. They are purpose turned into function. Through these channels we hope to bring people to total Christian maturity. The picture represents the total church program of Christian education. The point is that the foundation of the building is always laid before the roof is put on. How foolish it would be to attempt to nail the boards and shingles on the roof in the first step of the building process. Yet this is precisely what many churches attempt to do when they begin with the question, What educational agencies should we have at this church? First the foundation must be laid, and then we may construct the building. When we have carefully and prayerfully examined general and specific needs and written objectives to meet them, when we have set long-range plans and determined the route that must be followed to achieve them, then we are prepared to talk intelligently about the various agencies or ministries of the total church program.

FOR FURTHER READING

Bloom, Benjamin. *Taxonomy of Educational Objectives.* New York: McKay, 1969.

Bushnell, Horace. *Christian Nurture.* Reprint. Grand Rapids: Baker, 1979.

Church Educational Ministries. Wheaton, Ill. Evangelical Teacher Training Assn., 1980.

Dobbins, Gaines S. *A Ministering Church.* Nashville: Broadman, 1960.

Graendorf, Werner C., ed. *Introduction to Biblical Christian Education.* Chicago: Moody, 1981.

LeBar, Lois E. *Focus on People in Church Education.* Old Tappan, N.J.: Revell, 1968.

MacNair, Donald J. *The Birth, Care and Feeding of a Local Church.* Grand Rapids: Baker, 1976.

NOTES

1. C. B. Eavey, "Aims and Objectives of Christian Education," in *An Introduction to Evangelical Christian Education*, ed. J. Edward Hakes (Chicago: Moody, 1964), p. 55.
2. Findley B. Edge. *Teaching for Results* (Nashville: Broadman, 1956), chap. 6.
3. Benjamin Bloom, *Taxonomy of Educational Objectives.*

4

Unity and Community in the Body

WHAT IS THE GREATEST PROBLEM the church faces today? Is it the threat to orthodox theology by a militant liberalism? Certainly that threat is always there, but evangelical churches seem to be much more troubled, in these declining years of the twentieth century, by the immature behavior of Christians *within* their ranks than they are by the heresy from *without*. The issues of eccelesiology were the battleground of the 1970s, and it is imperative that a book attempting to describe the biblical way that God's people work together in church ministries should emphasize the issues of unity and community within the body of Christ.

The theological concept of the universal church is a reference to the spiritual unity of all of the redeemed in all ages and places. It includes believers who are Jews or Gentiles, in heaven or on earth, and stretches historically from the origin of the church at Pentecost to the final day when we shall be in heaven with the Lord. The objective of that unity, as Paul clearly declares in Ephesians 1, is a common redemption through the atonement of Calvary and a collective demonstration of the grace and glory of Jesus Christ.

UNDERSTANDING THE CHURCH

The eternal and invisible unity of the universal church is made contemporary and visible in the form of local churches. It is precisely this concept which in recent years has created so much confusion and controversy with respect to definition and description. Yet local churches have always been God's way of demonstrating the work of the universal church and, as one studies the New Testament, there seems to be at least a minimum boundary of inclusion which can be recognized by way of description of a local church. Writing out of the context of congregational polity, I would like to suggest that the local church is *a body of confessed believers joining together for worship, fellow-*

ship, instruction, and evangelism; led in their efforts by biblical officers (pastors and deacons); sovereign in polity; and including, as a part of its life and ministry, observance of the ordinances, discipline, and mutual edification.

My former colleague Dr. Robert Culver enumerates six characteristics of a local church: spiritual vitality, doctrinal instruction, fellowship, observance of the Lord's Supper, prayer, and Christian testimony.[1] The popular, contemporary apologist, Francis Schaeffer, indicates eight ingredients which must be a part of "the polity of the church as a church":

1. Local congregations made up of Christians
2. Special meetings on the first day of the week
3. Church officers (elders) who have responsibility for the local churches
4. Deacons responsible for the community of the church in the area of material things
5. A serious view of discipline
6. Specific qualifications for elders and deacons
7. A place for form on a wider basis than the local church
8. The observance of two sacraments, baptism and the Lord's Supper.[2]

Many additional pages could be filled with a statement of various views as well as a biblical exposition of the nature of the universal church and the local church, but that is not the primary purpose of this volume. What is of concern is that the reader recognize the *validity and essentiality of the local church as a visible, contemporaneous demonstration of the universal church and the primary importance that unity and community be demonstrated in its interpersonal relations.*

A theological concept that is closely aligned here is the matter of the priesthood of believers. Actually, there are only five passages, in two books of the New Testament, which refer directly to the priesthood of believers—few enough that they can be reproduced here (from the *New International Version*):

> You also, like living stones, are being built into a spiritual house to be a holy priesthood, offering spiritual sacrifices acceptable to God through Jesus Christ. [1 Peter 2:5]
>
> But you are a chosen people, a royal priesthood, a holy nation, a people belonging to God, that you may declare the praises of him who called you out of darkness into his wonderful light. [1 Peter 2:9]
>
> To him who loves us and has freed us from our sins by his blood,

> and has made us to be a kingdom and priests to serve his God and Father—to him be glory and power for ever and ever! Amen. [Rev. 1:5*b*-6]
>
> You are worthy to take the scroll and to open its seals, because you were slain, and with your blood you purchased men for God from every tribe and language and people and nation. You have made them to be a kingdom and priests to serve our God, and they will reign on the earth. [Rev. 5:9-10]
>
> Blessed and holy are those who have part in the first resurrection. The second death has no power over them, but they will be priests of God and of Christ and will reign with him for a thousand years. [Rev. 20:6]

One writer draws from these Scriptures five principles which speak to the issue of the relationship of believers in community as they seek to worship and serve God together:

1. The priesthood of the believer must be held in healthy tension with other basic concepts; it is not an absolute.
2. The believer can delegate some of the authority of his life and ministry to other believers.
3. The priesthood of the believers is conditioned by the gifts and roles in the life of the fellowship.
4. The priesthood of the believer implies shared responsibility and ministry as well as shared authority.
5. The priesthood of the believer is the basis for decision making in the church.[3]

Such a commitment to shared responsibility and authority is based on a proper understanding of what it means to be the church, and leads, I would think, to the kind of participatory democracy described in the first two chapters of this book. It emphasizes again that we are indeed "laborers together," not only with God, but also with each other, in carrying out the tasks of the church and establishing its witness in the world in any given era of its history.

Paul's Concept of the Body

There is, perhaps, no visual idea of the church receiving more attention today than the image of the body described by Paul in the twelfth chapter of 1 Corinthians. On every hand, we hear about "body life" and "body truth" and the exercise of spiritual gifts within the body. This is surely a healthy emphasis. It will help us to look again at the primitive notions (primitive in the sense of being authentic) which the early church had of itself and at the cardinal principles which governed its life and ministry in the first century.

The first Corinthian epistle was probably written from Ephesus, about A.D. 57. Corinth was a metropolis of the Roman province of Achaia, and a great commercial center of the Mediterranean world. Paul had visited the city twice and found it living up to its reputation as a center of sin and depravity. Corinth presented an enormous challenge to the gospel. To expect the principles of Christian faith to operate at Jerusalem, where the members of the early church had been schooled for years in Old Testament truth, was one thing; to motivate that kind of behavior in pagan Corinth was quite another.

Deplorable factions had split the Corinthian church into hostile fragments. Some of the believers claimed to follow Paul, others Apollos, others Peter, and some claimed such a pharisaical piety that they wished to bypass all of the contemporary leaders and refer themselves directly back to Christ. Paul deals with a number of the problems resulting from the schism which was destroying the unity and community at Corinth, and in chapter twelve he comes to an explanation of the nature and use of spiritual gifts. Interestingly, however, the bulk of the chapter does not deal with the specification of the gifts but rather with the kind of people who will be ministering them. The words of the old hymn "Onward Christian Soldiers" well depict the intent of 1 Corinthians 12. They remind the church, "We are not divided; all one body we, One in hope and doctrine, One in charity."

Paul is well known for his use of common illustrations to explain difficult spiritual truths. First Corinthians 12 demonstrates in detail how the unity of man's *physical* body offers a model for the kind of unity that ought to be exemplified in Christ's *spiritual* body. In verse 13 the apostle points out that the purpose of the baptismal ministry of the Holy Spirit is to place persons into the universal body of Christ, the church. Most evangelical scholars agree that the treatment of *baptism* here is less likely a reference to the ritual act of water baptism than to the spiritual act of implantation into the body. It is always important to remember that symbolical acts exist only to emphasize spiritual reality.

What comes through, in the essence of this chapter, is the old philosophical principle, "The whole is greater than the sum of its parts." Diversity of the parts is an essential ingredient of the operating body, but unity and community of the members is what allows the body to function properly. Paul draws the argument to ridiculous extremes in order to make his point: "If the whole body were an eye, where would the hearing be? If the whole were hearing where would the sense of smell be?" (v. 17). What kind of a functioning organism would one's body be if it were composed of nothing but one giant eye? Or perhaps one giant ear and no nose? Apparently, leaders exercising autocratic control were already manifesting their power in the early church. People whose strong personalities overwhelm the body of Christ and dominate its life and ministry have plagued the church from the first century until now. Such overpowering control by one member shows an inaccurate concept of what the church is.

After he focuses our attention on the functions of the physical body, Paul nails down the argument which is really his intent in this section of the epistle: *God has a place for everyone in the church, and everyone's place is important.* Remember the context of the passage, the issue of spiritual gifts. Every Christian has a spiritual gift, and some may have more than one. And just as all of the members have spiritual gifts, all of the members have distinct functions. God has gifted people for carrying on the work of the church and then placed them in the body for a particular purpose of ministry. Not only that, but He has done it in His own divine sovereignty, just as He arranged the organs of the physical body to create the best possible working relationship! Only when all of the members of the physical body are doing their task does that body function properly. The same is true of the church.

Distortion of the concepts of unity and community comes when some fail to exercise their proper gifts and roles in the body, or when certain members of the body are considered to be weaker or stronger, more necessary or less necessary, than others. When there is mutual care in the body, discord can be eliminated, but a ruptured organ can destroy the proper functioning of the system. An oversized gland creates abnormality, and the entire organism (or organization) suffers desperately.

In verse 26, Paul points out that there is perhaps no time in which the unity of the body is more apparent than during a time of pain or suffering. A broken leg sends splinters of pain throughout the entire system. Even the common cold can produce, at the same time, a runny nose, red and tired eyes, an earache, an aching head, a sore throat, an upset stomach, and general discomfort throughout the entire body.

In the same way, all of the members of the body of Christ share the suffering and unhappiness of any one of the members. Since the body is a unity which shares community, when one of its members is feeling well or enjoying some particular benefits, the entire body rejoices. This is true physically of the human body and spiritually of the church. In another place Paul wrote, "Rejoice with those who rejoice, and weep with those who weep" (Rom. 12:15).

The crucial application comes in verse 27 of our chapter: "Now you are Christ's body, and individually members of it." Note the emphasis on the word *you*. Even this fractured Corinthian church, with all of its doctrinal confusion and personal bickering, was a demonstration in the world of the body of Christ! The "bookends" of this passage fit the classic Pauline logic: "For even as the body is one" (v. 12) and, "Now you are Christ's body" (v. 27). Alan Redpath suggests that the kind of unity which Paul insists on in this chapter "is only possible as we recognize that within the church we have fellowship in our diversity, as we learn to love and to care for our brethren who are different, always recognizing the utter futility of identity."[4]

Francis Schaeffer speaks often about community. He emphasizes that horizontal relationship can only follow vertical relationship, because a Christian community can only be made up of individual Christians.

> Therefore, as we meet in our groups, we know who we are. We are not like those who march in our streets and do not know who they are—who call for community but have no basis for community beyond biological continuity. Now we are ready to begin real personal living, to practice the orthodoxy of community corporately as a community. Real personal Christian living individually and corporately as a community that rests upon the individual's and the community's personal relationship with a personal God gives us the possibility of Christian community before the eye of an observing world.[5]

The Implementation of Unity and Community

It would be delightful to spend the rest of the chapter continuing the discussion of the biblical nature of the "communited" church. But this is a book about church education and leadership development. Up to this point, I have tried to lay a biblical foundation for the drawing of some implications as to the kind of human relationships we must maintain if we are to work together harmoniously and effectively in the church or in other Christian organizations. Now let me deal briefly with four concepts which help to form a pattern of ministry which is based, if not on specific verses of 1 Corinthians 12, at least upon the general New Testament concept of the church as a unified body. There are, of course, a multitude of other Scriptures which could be brought to bear upon the issues.

A PEOPLE-CENTERED MINISTRY

In one sense it is correct to say that the church is the most person-centered organization in the world (or at least should be). In quite another sense, the church must be God-centered before it can be person-centered. Finding the proper balance between these two very important ingredients of biblical life has proved too great a responsibility for some churches, and they have slipped from the path either to the left (an overemphasis on humanism to the neglect of sovereignty of God) or to the right (a position which uses a "burden for souls" as an excuse for a lack of consideration of people's needs).

The biblical pattern of Christian love always finds its outworking within the context of relationships with people. Yet it is precisely at this point that so many Christian leaders and workers go sour. Many of our problems testify not so much to our inability to perform effectively in public ministries, as to our inability to get along with people in private, interpersonal relations. The church is and always has been *people,* and service in it at any given time is a necessary relationship with those people. Adequate leadership requires awareness of and sensitivity to human need all around us as well as an appreciation of how we can meet that need through the supernatural dynamics of God's truth and God's Spirit.

Consider, for example, a pastor who finds his own self-satisfaction and fulfillment amidst the books in his study, where he spends all of his time. Although his theology may be orthodox and his sermons scholarly, the dimension of reality could be missing from his ministry. His lifeline to meaningful ministry is in constant contact with *people,* so that he can learn to relate God's truth to real problems in real lives.

Our Lord's ministry was always centered on people, and, without doubt, He was primarily interested in meeting their spiritual and eternal needs. But this priority focus did not keep Him from showing an interest in temporal and physical needs as well. If the various bodily parts are going to function properly together, it will be because we have been able to discover and implement a new-covenant view of interpersonal relations.

THE GIFT OF LEADING

In conjunction with the gift of administration *(kubernēsis)*, there is also a concept of leadership which appears in Romans 12:8, which uses the word *prohistēmi.** It literally means "put before" or "to go before." Orginally it had the connotation of presiding, conducting, directing, or governing. I had often asked myself whether *kubernēsis* and *prohistēmi* represent two different spiritual gifts or two dimensions of the same spiritual gift, namely, congregational leadership. As closely as these ideas are linked, it may be preferable to think of leadership as merely one of the functions of the administrator.

In spite of the leadership role's accompanying prestige and necessary publicity, *the New Testament concept of leadership is service.* Those who exercise the gift of leadership and administration—the professional church staff and those who occupy significant, nonprofessional offices—are examples to the body. Somehow, a balance between delegated authority and loving concern must be the primary goal for biblical administration.

D. Swan Haworth identifies three interesting concepts of staff relationships:

1. A loosely organized staff which may have several "soloists" but no director, no regular rehearsals, and consequently very little harmony; people on such a staff relate to each other only by necessity
2. An integrated staff held together by one commander
3. A colleague relationship in which "each staff member trusts the other, despite their difference. This colleague relationship requires each member of the team to be a responsible person."[6]

It is quite obvious that the relationships of the professional staff stand as a model for the entire church. Confusion and bickering at the top will not only destroy the working effectiveness of the management team, but will filter down into the ranks to distort interpersonal relationships between other workers all the way up and down the line.

*For other appearances of *prohistēmi see* 1 Thessalonians 5:12; 1 Timothy 3:4, 12; 5:17; Titus 3:8, 14.

THE REQUIREMENT OF A BIBLICAL LIFE-STYLE

The Christian leader's behavior toward other people is determined by what he is in himself. To put it another way, interpersonal relations on a horizontal plane are determined by interpersonal relations with God on a vertical plane. One of the reasons we get into so many human relations problems in the church is that we have somehow confused ourselves into thinking that what we *do* for God is more important than what we *are* before God. A distinctly Christian life-style, with respect to shared ministries in a communal setting, requires the grace of mutual acceptance, a willingness to enter into mutual burden-bearing, and a generous dose of active love.

Understanding one's fellow workers involves seeing and knowing them as persons rather than as "other employees." Paul Tournier points out two great fears which keep people from understanding each other: fear of being judged and fear of being advised.[7] Harsh criticism and flippant answers to troubling problems are two clubs which can bludgeon human relations to a bloody hulk. For example, some adults have no ministry with teenagers because they greet every attempt at communication with a handy, "Oh yes, I used to feel like that. You'll get over it."

The immorality of manipulation is not confined to Madison Avenue. If manipulation is an immoral technique, it is just as wrong for the church leader as it is for the advertising executive whose task it is to design television commercials geared to trick people into buying what they do not need.

In our pressure-cooker society, it is extremely difficult to grasp and practice the biblical concept of patience. We tend to be obsessive and compulsive about our behavior, and frequently "come on too strong" in relationships with other people. I like the way one writer puts it: "Impatience is a heresy of the soul and an apostasy of the disposition."[8]

Schaeffer calls unity in love "the mark of the Christian" (in the book by that title) and refers to that unity as "the final apologetic." He points out that the world cares nothing for doctrine, but has been given the authority to judge the effectiveness and authenticity of the church on the evidence of a loving life-style among the members in its community.

UNDERSTANDING INTERPERSONAL ENCOUNTER

In one sense, we can think of the whole social order as a communications framework. If unity and community are to be realized, the third concept of communication (a term obviously related to the first two) must be functioning properly. Communication can be verbal or nonverbal, and should not be confused with the information theory of hardware and software systems. Some sociologists (the symbolic interactionists) remind us that no one person can be held responsible for communication; it is always a mutual process. The word *mutuality* becomes very important in recognizing the interrelated nature of communication.

Another term frequently used in sociological literature is *simultaneity*. Communication is not like a Ping-Pong game, in which messages are batted back and forth. Rather, the ongoing relationship between people who are communicating is a simultaneous process. If we would effectively relate to other people, we must recognize that our verbalizations to them and their verbalizations to us are all received through an emotional and cultural grid. (See chapter 27.)

When a Sunday school superintendent, for example, speaks to one of his teachers, the meaning of his words is not so much inherent in what he says, as it is in the way that she interprets them by placing her own meanings upon them. These two people are simultaneously active in the communications process and are therefore mutually responsible for what happens in their personal interaction. Each is loading up little trucks (words) with cargo (ideas) and sending them on their way. At the same time, each is unloading the trucks sent to him by the other person.

The main assumption of sociology is that human beings develop their human abilities through social interaction, and the community of church, school, or other institution provides the context for an analysis of relationships. We might also add that it provides the context for positive functioning together of believers as the body of Christ, in keeping with the kind of patterns delineated in 1 Corninthians 12 and other passages of the New Testament. We are certainly not passive recipients of everything that sociology and psychology tell us about human relationships. But we must be astute discerners of truth and willing to apply it as it fits our understanding of the special revelation of the Word of God.

Perhaps this chapter should end where it began, with some treatment of the church. Surely, any recognition of styles of relationship must stand under a proper delineation of the Lordship of Christ. Walter Liefeld has written:

> A local church . . . functions as a body of disciples devoted to their Lord and transmitting His teaching. The church remembers the past, insofar as it reminds itself and the world of its origin in the death and resurrection of Christ. It faces the future as an eschatological community in which the characteristics of the kingdom and the presence of the king are realized in its daily life.[9]

FOR FURTHER READING

Getz, Gene. *Loving One Another.* Wheaton, Ill.: Victor, 1979.

Madsen, Paul O. *The Small Church–Valid, Vital Victorious.* Valley Forge, Pa.: Judson, 1975.

Stedman, Ray C. *Body Life.* Glendale, Calif.: Regal, 1971. (Revised and expanded, 1977.)

NOTES

1. Ecclesiology class notes. Deerfield, Ill.: Trinity Evangelical Divinity School, 1970.
2. Francis Schaeffer, *The Church at the End of the Twentieth Century* (Downers Grove, Ill.: Inter-Varsity, 1970), pp. 62-66.
3. Ernest White, "Applying the Priesthood of the Believer to the Life and Work of a Church," *Search 2*, no. 2 (Winter 1972): 13-18.
4. Alan Redpath, *The Royal Route to Heaven* (Westwood, N.J.: Revell, 1960), p. 152.
5. Schaeffer, p. 56.
6. D. Swan Haworth, *How Church Staff Members Relate* (Nashville: Southern Baptist Sunday School Board, 1969), p. 1.
7. Paul Tournier, *To Understand Each Other* (Richmond: John Knox, 1968), pp. 19-25.
8. Robert Lofton Hudson, *What Makes for Patience?* (Nashville: Southern Baptist Sunday School Board, 1970), p. 7.
9. Walter Liefeld, "The Church: What Did Jesus Intend?" Deerfield, Ill.: Trinity Evangelical Divinity School, 1970.

5

Music in the Educational Program of the Church

MUSIC HAS ALWAYS been closely associated with Christianity. The apostle Paul encouraged the believers at Colossae to "let the word of Christ richly dwell within you, with all wisdom teaching and admonishing one another with psalms and hymns and spiritual songs, singing with thankfulness in your hearts to God" (Col. 3:16). Although music has had this foremost place in the church from the very beginning, now—as never before—it is used on a grand scale around the world.

Even people who do not play an instrument and cannot sing, enjoy music presented by others. The effectiveness of music depends largely upon the manner and degree in which it is used. Christian music is distinctive and should never be allowed to be poured into the world's mold.

I am aware that not all Christian educators share my enthusiasm for a focus on church music as an integral part of the total church program. However, this is not a new emphasis, as Heim reminds us:

> From the beginning music had a place in the American Protestant educational program. The earliest attempt at a volume of hymns for children was that of Isaac Watts, whose Divine and Moral Songs for Children was issued in 1715. This, with Charles Wesley's Hymns for Children (1763), and the old Bay Psalm Book of 1640 provided the musical element in the curriculum until Union Hymns was published in 1835 by the American Sunday School Union. After that a number of such titles appeared. Then followed the revivalistic song period and after that the development of the denominational and interdenominational hymns most favored at present.[1]

Since Christian music is distinctly related to the church, it becomes the task of the church to educate its constituency. Children, youth and adults should all be confronted with the best of

Christian music and, if they possess talent, be trained to use it for the Lord in the realm of music. This is music education.

The organizational factors involved here should be obvious. If music is not related to the total church program, it becomes a peripheral ministry; and the unification and correlation discussed in other chapters suffer a defeat. One of the reasons why some pastors have found the church's music department somewhat difficult to handle is that they have not properly related it to the total program of nurture.

The factor of need is also important here. Many evangelical churches are poverty areas when it comes to a recognition and utilization of good church music. Some have not even stopped to consider the quality and function of music in their programs.

Purpose of Christian Music

MUSIC FOR WORSHIP

Worship is almost a lost art in many churches. It is the attitude of man which causes him to reach out to perceive the character and attributes of God in wonder, adoration and thanksgiving. In the church's time of worship, the person in the pew should respond to God's revelation of Himself. The music should make the worshiper think of God, think of self in relation to God, and think of others. This was the experience of Isaiah recorded in Isaiah 6. My friend Bob Messner identifies three ways in which music helps people to worship:

1. Music calms the nerves and prepares people for an attitude of worship. Examples of hymns which could be used in this way are "Fairest Lord Jesus," "For the Beauty of the Earth," and "O Day of Rest and Gladness."
2. Music gives us an opportunity to express our own feelings and attitudes. Examples of hymns which can be used as expression include "My Faith Looks up to Thee" and "Guide Me, O Thou Great Jehovah."
3. Music may help in the development of a right conception of God. Examples of hymns with strong theological content would be "Alas and Did My Saviour Bleed," "And Can It Be," and "Holy, Holy, Holy, Lord God Almighty."[2]

MUSIC AS PREPARATION

The sermon is the center of any church service in which it appears. One of the purposes of the music should be to lead up to the sermon. To accomplish this, the music will have to fit the theme of the message as well as the atmosphere of the service.

Music can cause the minds of the congregation to dwell on a certain subject in preparation for the sermon on that subject. The music director should also gear his remarks and hymn introductions to lead people's thinking in this manner.

MUSIC IN SPECIAL SERVICES

Of course, it is easy to see how music fits the "special day" services of the church. Christmas, Easter and Thanksgiving all have their characteristic music which reminds people of the significance of that day. There is also a distinct place for music in special weeks of services, such as revival and evangelistic meetings or a missionary conference. Because Moody realized this in his evangelistic ministry, Sankey played a great part in the effectiveness of that great preacher.

Numerous gospel songs carry a message of challenge to Christians, such as, "Is Your All on the Altar?"; others have a definite evangelistic appeal, as "Where Will You Spend Eternity?" Yet others have a missionary message. Hymns and gospel songs should be used carefully to fit the purpose of the special service.

MUSIC AS INTEREST

Some would consider attraction to church attendance an unworthy purpose for music and say that church music is not to entertain. Yet there are people who would not enter the church to hear a sermon but are attracted by a good musical program. If they attend to hear the music and are reached by the message, then music has served a worthy purpose of interest awakener.

MUSIC AS INVITATION

The invitation music is an important part of the service in most evangelical and evangelistic churches. The hymn should be selected with great care, and the music director should be as inconspicuous as possible during the invitation. It is desirable that the people be familiar with the hymn and that the hymn reflect the invitation which the preacher is making. The music director must be alert and flexible during the invitation to blend with the preacher's wishes regarding number of verses, speed of singing, selection of verses, and so forth. The spiritual music director always remembers that the words of the invitation hymn may be used of the Holy Spirit to speak to needy hearts.

If the purpose of Christian music can be summarized in one brief statement, it would be a simple five-word imperative: *Music must convey a message!* It is not incidental to the service to be used only as a time-filler. Nor is it to be chosen on the basis of melody, although the hymn tune is important. Music can be a vehicle to carry a message of comfort, challenge, or conviction, and the musician should pray that his music will accomplish its desired purpose.

> The purpose of all church music is to enrich and blend with the entire purpose of the service, which includes worship and praise, devotion and need, purpose and conviction. It is the medium through which the soul and spirit reach out to God. Without it the service would be incomplete. It unifies thought, and in those who are not Christians, it prepares the way for the entrance of the Holy Spirit.[3]

The Organization of Church Music

Since the music of the church is important, the responsibility for coordinating, directing and improving the musical program must be properly placed. It has already been shown that the church's music program is related to the work of the board of Christian education and has adequate representation on that board. The chairman of the church music council represents music on the board of Christian education. More specifically, the following officers are responsible for the function and development of music in the church:

PASTOR

The pastor is the shepherd of the flock and therefore has an ex officio voice in every department of the church, including the music. Utmost cooperation must exist between the music director and the pastor. There must be love and understanding between the two to guarantee an effective music program. The wise pastor will let his director have charge of the music of the church and not treat him as a figurehead through whom he controls everything. On the other hand, the wise music director is alert to the pastor's suggestions and interests.

MUSIC DIRECTOR

This office is filled in various churches by individuals ranging from the accomplished musician holding a doctor's degree in the field of church music to the high school youth just learning to lead singing. The music director should be an elected or appointed officer of the church charged with the responsibility of guiding and directing a comprehensive program of church music. He may be a full-time, well-trained director who gives all of his time to music (actually called the minister of music), a combination minister of music and youth or Christian education, or a qualified musician whose service is avocational. The first two would be salaried staff members of the church, whereas the latter would probably be a volunteer worker. Staff music directors should be called by the congregation, not "hired" by the trustees.

The National Association of Directors of Christian Education does not advocate a multiplicity of responsibilities for the director in the local church. Nevertheless, because of the financial status of some churches and/or the interests and abilities of some directors, it is not unusual to find a director of Christian education also having responsibility for church music. The negative factor here is overload of the director. The positive factors could lead to recognition of the proper place of music in the church, coordination of the total music program, the training of youth and children in music, and a lessening of conflicts on the church calendar.

What kind of a person ought the music director to be? Here are ten qualifications, the majority of which should be characteristic of the church director:

1. a devout Christian character with sincere convictions and interest in spiritual things
2. the ability to sing and/or to play a musical instrument
3. good musical knowledge with some training and/or experience in Christian music
4. an enthusiastic, likeable personality
5. qualities of leadership and the ability to take charge of a situation or group
6. an organizational mind which enables him to see things in proper pattern and perspective
7. a devotion to his task and a belief that music can be used of God
8. a cooperative attitude and willingness to listen to ideas of others
9. pleasing platform presence, including neatness of dress and person
10. a progressive spirit which can overcome difficulties, be patient with people, and avoid procrastination of duties.

A highly developed theological sophistication is important for an effective music ministry. Some seminary training is highly desirable, since an educational background that has focused exclusively in secular institutions will probably be deficient in a theology of hymnody.

THE CHURCH MUSIC COUNCIL

The personnel of this council may include the director of church music, directors of the various choirs, church choir president, church organist, church pianist, representation from the official board, and the pastor as an ex officio member. The membership of the committee is arbitrary, but one thing is essential—*the members should know music and be genuinely interested in it.* "The general function . . . of the music committee is to advise and assist the minister of music in developing and maintaining the church-wide music program."[4] The care of musical property, selection of personnel, setting of policies, and budget-handling would all come under this general delineation of duties.

ACCOMPANISTS

The music director is only as effective as his pianist and organist. The accompanists can help or hinder any kind of music in the church. The director should always remember that he is to lead and the accompanists are to follow, whether in congregational, choral or solo music.

There must be harmony in relationships between the director and pianist or organist lest the spiritual ministry of music be hindered. If the program of the church is extensive, the accompanists should be able to transpose, modulate, and improvise on short notice. Punctuality, faithfulness, and humility are all desirable qualities in an accompanist.

VARIOUS FUNCTIONS OF CHURCH WORSHIP

CONGREGATIONAL SINGING

An essential part of almost every church service is congregational singing, and due consideration ought to be given it. Congregational singing benefits the group in many ways:

1. It tunes hearts with God.
2. It offers participation in the service for all.
3. It gives opportunity to voice praise and testimony.
4. It unifies minds and crystallizes thought.
5. It is a witness to all who hear.

6. It conveys a message to those singing.

The congregation ought always to be reminded to think on the words they are singing. Proper planning and consideration should be given to the choice of hymns for congregational singing so that they fit the theme and purpose of the service. The following is a list of practical suggestions for leading congregational singing:

1. Use new hymns occasionally but do not use too many new hymns in any one service; and, if possible, have the church choir prepare the new hymns before asking the congregation to sing them in a service.
2. Use only theologically sound hymns. This requires that the music director look over the words of all of the verses before a hymn is selected.
3. Vary the selection of hymns so as not to "wear out" old favorites.
4. Provide an adequate supply of books and make sure that the books are kept in good repair.
5. Keep the instruments tuned. There are actually three levels of tuning to watch: an instrument must be in tune with proper pitch; it must be in tune with any other instrument that is being played with it; and it must be in tune with itself.
6. Use an occasional hymn-story to add flavor to a service. Do not wear out this procedure and do not be verbose in any given presentation.
7. Plan well ahead for any service. Advance planning includes the selection of songs, the order of their use, the verses which will be used, and any comments or introductory remarks which are necessary.
8. Fit the theme of every service. Try to make all music lead toward the message of the hour.
9. Announce songs properly.
    a. Announce the number of the song more than once.
    b. Say "hymn number," not "page number."
    c. Allow time for all persons to find the hymn before beginning the singing.
    d. Let the congregation find the page before announcing that you wish them to stand for the singing.
10. Be in charge with confidence at all times.

CHORAL MUSIC

Most churches employ the use of choral music on some level.

Many churches have only one choir, whereas others have a developed, graded choir program of six or more choirs.

> The presentation of choir music is a very definite art. Careful preparation under able leadership is essential,—leadership that is well aware of the purpose of church music and has the inner spiritual life to express truthfully the message of the song and inspire the others to do the same.[5]

In the standard graded choir program there are six basic choirs:

1. the beginner choir—ages four and five
2. the primary choir—ages six through eight
3. the junior choir—ages nine through twelve
4. the teen or youth choir—ages thirteen through sixteen
5. the young people's choir—ages seventeen through twenty-four
6. the adult choir—twenty-four and up

The adult choir is the main choir of the church, and the others perform the task of music education leading to a ministry at this level. There may also be a men's chorus, women's chorus, or other special groups.

The choir's presentations should be carefully selected and thoroughly rehearsed. Members should consider it a ministry to participate in any choir, especially the adult choir. Discipline should prevail at rehearsals, and definite work be accomplished. Attendance is a must and punctuality very important. *The personnel of the adult choir should be selected by the music director on an audition basis to keep the standards high.*

Periodically full concerts, such as a Christmas or Easter cantata, should be planned to generate interest in the choir as well as provide a ministry to others. Vieth well reminds us, "A choir experience is a part of one's experience of Christian nurture, but rarely is it so regarded."[6]

ENSEMBLES AND SOLOS

The music director should seek to develop from among the choirs (or from those with musical ability who for some reason cannot participate in a choir) smaller musical groups such as octets, sextets, quartets, trios and duets, as well as soloists. These groups add variety to the musical program and give further outlets for service to those with talent. The church with fewer choirs should especially be alert to utilize these smaller groups.

It is generally agreed that the more talented an individual is musically, the smaller the group in which he can participate. The finest singers should be used in trios and duets and as soloists. The music director ought to work with these groups and encourage them by using them as frequently as possible. He should always know what they plan to sing well in advance of the service.

INSTRUMENTAL MUSIC

Aside from the accompanist, the church may use instrumental music in the form of soloists, small groups, or even a band or orchestra. Such groups need defined limitations and careful guidance. A well-trained orchestra can be used to great advantage in the Sunday evening congregational song service or in other church activities. More common would be the use of smaller groups, such as a trumpet trio or string ensemble. Instrumentalists who have unusual ability and training and are capable of solo performance can also be utilized along with a choir for variety in presentation.

In all of the church's music, vocal or instrumental, the director should be alert to proper placement of microphones and technical equipment. This responsibility is infinitely greater when recording or broadcasting.

A music director must be able to distinguish carefully between the different types of church music available for use in the program. Though definitions differ with writers, a *hymn* is generally considered to contain a text which directs one's thought toward God; whereas a *gospel song* is an exhortation or testimony to other people. *Choruses* are abbreviated forms of gospel songs and have their place in the music program, provided they are both theologically accurate and musically appropriate.

Spirituals, whether historical or contemporary, generally express in simple words and music the feelings of people about their faith. *Anthems* such as "The Lord Is My Shepherd" can be generally defined as more classic pieces of music set to words from the Bible. There are other types of church music, but these five make up the greater portion of music used in the church.

CHURCH MUSIC EDUCATION

The use of music itself, if properly conducted, is a method of education. The use of graded choirs provides a means of training directly related to Christian ministry. In addition, the musically progressive church will have special classes for promising accompanists and song leaders. If the music director or some member of the congregation is qualified, there could be a periodic music school with the teaching of hymnology and church music appreciation.

Various church music workshops are conducted around the country, some on an annual basis. Periodic attendance at continuing education programs like this will enhance the quality of the music director's ministry.

Literature published by Accent, the Church Music Department of the Southern Baptist Convention, and other sources can keep the church musician aware of current trends. The Southern Baptist periodical, *The Church Musician,* is of inestimable value to the music director and his staff.

Private lessons in voice and instrument can be part of the church's program of music education if qualified teachers are available. It is unfortunate that many talented children and young people must receive all of their music training in a secular context. In many years of working with college students, I have observed young people who have come from very fine churches and Christian homes whose musical ability has been narrowly confined to studies in the secular classics. The arrangement of a simple offertory hymn becomes a major chore because of their lack of training in Christian music. It would appear that if this lack is to be remedied, the church will have to step into the gap and come to grips with the issues of church music education.

In a survey taken by one of my students, a question was asked relative to the "Christian education values of the church music program." The responses were interesting and encouraging, for they demonstrated some progress on the part of churches in their thinking about the responsibilities of music education. The following are some of the values indicated:

1. Basic doctrines are learned and retained through participation in the choral program.
2. Children, young people, and adults are gaining experience in service for Christ through music.
3. Character development is taking place as people display increased devotion, loyalty and discipline in their Christian lives.
4. Worship concepts and attitudes are being established.
5. There is an extended retention of spiritual truth as people communicate it to others through music.

6. People are taking their proper place in the total church program through participation in its music.
7. As the musical standards of the church have been lifted, the spiritual standards have been raised.

Perhaps this chapter, as out of place as it may seem to some in a book on organization and leadership, will awaken in its readers a concern for aggressive improvement in the musical programs of evangelical churches. Hopefully, some of the comments can serve as an evaluation standard for present programs. It is not necessary for a church to be deprived in this most glorious area of the praise of God. Too much talent now lies latent in churches which could be put to use in the service of Christ by proper organization and direction. As Smith has said, "Music? Yes, let us have as much of it as we can . . . in every walk of life. There is value beyond the measure of gold in music!"[7]

FOR FURTHER READING

Eisenberg, Helen and Larry. *How To Lead Group Singing*. New York: Association, 1955. (Reprinted 1978 by Greenwood).

Hustad, Donald P. *Jubilate!* Grand Rapids: Hope, 1981.

Lunde, Alfred E. *Christian Education Through Music*. Wheaton, Ill.: Evangelical Teacher Training Association, 1978.

Nelson, Elizabeth R. *Practical Church Music*, Kansas City: Beacon Herald, 1964.

Wohlgemuth, Paul W. *Rethinking Church Music*. Rev. ed. Grand Rapids: Hope, 1981.

NOTES

1. Ralph D. Heim, *Leading a Church School* (Philadelphia: Fortress, 1968), p. 11.
2. Robert C. Messner, "Music Education in the Church" (Master's thesis, Grace Theol. Sem., 1959), p. 99.
3. Florence Smith, *Protestant Church Music* (Butler, Ind.: Higley, 1949), p. 70.
4. Messner, p. 33.
5. Smith, p. 70.
6. Paul H. Vieth, *The Church and Christian Education* (St. Louis: Bethany, 1963), p. 127.
7. Smith, p. 158.

PART II

The Nature of Leadership in the Local Church

6

Toward a New Testament View of Leadership

AS AESOP TELLS THE STORY, the frogs down on the pond wanted a king. They bothered Jupiter so much with their requests that he finally tossed a log into the pond, and for a while the frogs were happy with the new leader.

Soon, however, they discovered that they could jump up and down on the leader, run all over him, and he offered no resistance nor even a response. Not only that, but he had no direction or purpose to his behavior but just floated back and forth on the pond, a practice which exasperated the frogs, who were really sincere about wanting "strong leadership."

So back to Jupiter they went. They complained about their log leader and appealed for much stronger administrative oversight. Jupiter was weary of the complaining frogs, so this time he gave them a stork, who stood tall above the members of the group and certainly had the appearance of a leader. The frogs were quite happy with the new situation. Their leader stalked around the pond making great noises and attracting great attention. Their joy turned to sorrow, however, and ultimately to panic, for in a very short time the stork began to eat his subordinates.[1]

One of the major problems in implementing Christian leadership in the church, or in any other kind of Christian community, is failure to recognize not only a pragmatic, but also a biblical leadership style. Frequently we find ourselves gravitating to extremes and behaving like logs or storks in our relationship to the people with whom God allows us to work. The log was a "free-rein" leader, letting the followers do whatever they wanted to. The stork was at the opposite end of the continuum in his absolute autocracy.

In a *Harvard Business Review* article entitled "How to Choose a Leadership Pattern," authors Tannenbaum and Schmidt discuss the same problem with respect to secular functions of management science.

> The problem of how the modern manager can be "democratic" in his relations with subordinates and at the same time maintain the necessary authority and control in the organization for which he is responsible has come in to focus increasingly in recent years.
>
> Earlier in the century this problem was not so acutely felt. The successful executive was generally pictured as possessing intelligence, imagination, initiative, the capacity to make rapid (and generally wise) decisions, and the ability to inspire subordinates. People tended to think of the world as being divided into "leaders" and "followers."[2]

What is most interesting is that the leadership style which has evolved from multimillion dollars of research on the part of industrial management science is not far removed from the leadership style which Scripture delineates from the start! It is a style which recognizes the inherent value of the individual and the worth of human relations not only as a means to an end but as an end in itself within the Christian community. In a very real sense, it is correct to say that the church should be the most person-centered organization in the world. Indeed, the church which has its vertical relationships in order (theocentricity) will generally follow with proper horizontal relationships (anthrocentricity). Sometimes we get so busy "saving souls" that we forget to do anything for *people.* The church does not have to overemphasize the social gospel to recognize that souls are rather ethereal and invisible, but one sees people every day.

What is a biblical view of leadership? Perhaps we can best arrive at that answer by first dealing with the negative side of the question.

What New Testament Leadership Is Not

There is a marvelous passage in Luke 22 which holds some enormously valuable principles for helping us analyze our Lord's view of leadership. The passage itself is contained in verses 24 through 27, but the context is of great importance also. The Lord has just ministered to the disciples in their final supper together in the upper room. Commentators differ about whether the foot washing had taken place before the conversation or whether the conversation actually precipitated the foot washing. One thing is clear: they had just finished the bread and the cup and had experienced among themselves a worship relationship of the highest order, with the incarnate God in their midst and with the Father in heaven. It is almost unbelievable that the scene recorded in these verses could have followed that experience.

NEW TESTAMENT LEADERSHIP IS NOT POLITICAL POWER-PLAY

Immediately after sharing the symbolic representation of our Lord's flesh and blood, the disciples fell into a dispute. The word is *philoneikia* and literally means "rivalry." What is even more interesting is that this word does not describe an accidental falling into argument on occasion, but rather the possession of a habitually contentious spirit. To put it another way, because of their fondness for strife, the disciples verbally attacked one another in an attempt to gain political prominence in what they expected would be an immediately forthcoming, earthly kingdom! Martin Buber once said that persons' inability to "carry on authentic dialog with one another is the most acute symptom of the pathology of our time."

Political power-play in the church is even more reprehensible than it is in the world. Yet it is striking that even before the first church was organized at Jerusalem; before a pastor ever candidated for appointment to a congregation; before an official board ever met to design a building program, the church knew how to fight! Toward the end of the first century, John bemoaned that in one local church there was a man named Diotrephes who liked "to have the preeminence among them," and the Diotrephesian tribe has multiplied in nineteen hundred years of history.

NEW TESTAMENT LEADERSHIP IS NOT AUTHORITARIAN ATTITUDE

Luke 22:25 records our Lord's reaction to the arguments of his disciples. He offers first a comparison and then a contrast. The comparison is that their behavior at that moment was like the behavior of the Hellenistic monarchs who ruled in Egypt and Syria. Their leadership style is described as "exercising lordship"—the word *kurieuo,* which appears frequently in the pages of the New Testament. At times it is used to describe the authority of God (Rom. 14:9). Paul uses it often to refer to a negative control, such as death's attempt to hold dominion over Christ (Rom. 6:9); the power of sin in the life of the believer (Rom. 6:14); and the hold of the law on men freed by the gospel (Rom. 7:1).

A similar word, *katakurieuo,* is used to describe Gentile rulers; the control of demons over men (Acts 19:16); and as a negative example in prescribing the behavior of elders with saints in the church (1 Pet. 5:3). The verb form is never used positively of Christian leadership. To put it very simply, *Christian leadership is not authoritarian control over the minds and behavior of other people.* Peter remembered the lesson of this night, for in writing his epistle he warned the elders not to lord it over God's heritage.

The first part of Luke 22:26 is a strong contrast construction: "But ye . . . not so." The kings of the Gentiles wished to be called benefactor for any little deed of kindness they might show to their subjects, although it was expected that they would practice autocracy and demagoguery. Whether that is right or wrong is not the issue. The point is that *Christian* leadership is *not* that kind of authoritarian control. As a matter of fact, in defiance of the culture of the time, our Lord says in this verse that the one who is greatest in the church is actually *as* the younger, and the boss is *as* the worker.

NEW TESTAMENT LEADERSHIP IS NOT CULTIC CONTROL

One of the beautiful words describing the work of the church is the word *diakanos.* It means "service" and is precisely what Christ did for his disciples in that upper room. The question of verse 27 seems to be rhetorical: Who is more important, the waiter or the dinner guest? Obvious answer: the dinner guest, of course! But wait a minute, who is the guest and who is the waiter at this Last Supper? Answer: "I am among you as he that serveth." Conclusion: *New Testament Leadership is not flashy public relations and platform personality, but humble service to the group.* The work of God is to be carried on by spiritual power not personal magnetism, as Paul clearly points out in 1 Corinthians 1:26-31. Some leaders may *serve* the Word and some leaders may *serve* tables but all leaders *serve* (Acts 6)!

THE POSITIVE PATTERN OF CHRIST

The positive pattern of Christ in developing leadership in his disciples is clearly enunciated in A. B. Bruce's helpful book, *The Training of the Twelve.*[3] He suggests that the total report of the gospels covers only thirty-three or thirty-four days of our Lord's three-and-one-half-year ministry, and John records only eighteen days. What did Christ do the rest of the time? The clear implication of the Scriptures is that He was training leaders. What kind of leaders? How did He deal with them? What were the important principles of His leadership-development program?

Although it is not the purpose of this book to deal with the total subject of leadership development, certain principles may be helpful in making a transition to a positive declaration of what New Testament leadership is.

1. The leadership of our Lord focused on individuals. His personal conversation with Peter, recorded in John 21, is a good example of the way He gave Himself to His men in an attempt to build His life and ministry into them.

2. The leadership of our Lord focused on the Scriptures. His treatment of God's absolute truth was not diluted by relativistic philosophy. It held the Old Testament in highest esteem. The rabbis had distorted God's revelation, and the Leader of leaders now came to say, "You have heard that it was said, . . . but I say to you" (Matt. 5:21-48).

3. The leadership of our Lord focused on Himself. Remember, in John 14:9, how he found it necessary to say to one of the disciples, "Philip have you been so long with Me and you still have not known the Father? Take a good look at Me because if you understand Me you understand the Father" (author's paraphrase).

4. The leadership of our Lord focused on purpose. Christ had clear-cut goals for His earthly ministry, and a limited time in which to achieve them. If you knew you had to leave your present ministry within three-and-one-half years and turn it over completely to subordinates you would be allowed to develop during that period of time, how would you go about doing it? You could do no better than follow the example of Jesus, and the result would probably be a great deal like the leadership that characterized the New Testament church.

What New Testament Leadership Is

There is a temptation, in dealing with this issue, to turn to the book of Acts because of its vivid description of early church life. Yet the book of Acts is a historical narrative, not a developed ecclesiology. We will be better helped by looking at the epistles of Paul, who apparently was commissioned by the Spirit of God to organize local churches and to describe God's plan and pattern for the functioning of those churches. Some verses in the second chapter of 1 Thessalonians will serve us well as a model.

NEW TESTAMENT CHURCH LEADERSHIP IS NURTURE

Nurture is a botanical term which describes the care and feeding of a young plant so that it grows properly to maturity. In verses 7 and 8, Paul uses some distinctive words to describe what nurture really is in the eyeball-to-eyeball relationships that accompany leadership responsibility.

He speaks of being "gentle," the word *herioi,* used often of a teacher who is patient in the process of nurturing seemingly incorrigible students. As if that emphasis were not enough, he refers to the gentleness of a nurse, which is an obvious reference to a nursing mother, not a hired babysitter. The word is used in the Old Testament to describe Jehovah's care of Israel, and in 2 Timothy 2:24 Paul used the word to describe "the servant of the Lord."

But there is more to this emphasis on nurture. A gentle, nursing mother "cherisheth her children." The word is *thalpē,* which literally means "to soften by heat" or "to keep warm." Deuteronomy 22:6, in the Septuagint, uses the word to describe a bird caring for its young by spreading its feathers over them in the nest. Such a nurse is "affectionately desirous" of the growing children (v. 8), a term that seems cumbersome but appears in KJV, ASV, and RSV texts. The implication is a yearning after for the good of the group, which ultimately results in, as this verse indicates, a sacrifice on the part of the leader.

Where is the manliness in all of this? Where is the image of the sharp voice barking orders and "running a tight ship"? Again, a pagan culture distorts our understanding of spiritual reality. We identify masculinity with toughness and ruggedness, but God identifies it with tenderness. We think of leadership as "handling" adults, but God thinks of it as nurturing children.

NEW TESTAMENT LEADERSHIP IS EXAMPLE

The hard work of Paul's leadership spills out in verse 9. Both day and night, with great effort, he worked among the believers. His own life and those of his colleagues were examples of holiness, justice, and blamelessness before God. Note that this was behavior *before the believers,* not an attempt at evangelism.

In chapter 2, verses 5 and 6, Paul assured the Thessalonians that their leaders were men, not some kind of superhuman, ecclesiastical giants who wanted to run the organization by sheer executive skill and personal power.

NEW TESTAMENT LEADERSHIP IS FATHERHOOD

What does a father do? According to Ephesians 6:4, he is responsible for the nurture of children. Consequently, the model of the family is used not only to describe procreation in terms of infant birth, but also to describe leadership functions in terms of the teaching role of a father in the home.

In 1 Thessalonians 2:11, the words rendered *exhorted* and *comforted* are the words *parakalountes* and *paramuthoumenoi*. These are commonly used together in Paul's writing. The former is often used of divine ministry, but the latter is always a human word. It is never used directly to mean God's comfort but is descriptive of the way He uses people to minister to other people in the community of faith.

A father also "charges" his children (v. 11). The word has the idea of admonishing or witnessing truth so that they will walk in patterns acceptable to God.

Paul's Example

Earlier, we noted the positive pattern of Christ in leadership training. A word or two about the example of the apostle Paul may also be worth mentioning. The development of the New Testament church was the multiplication of the lives of the few people described in Acts 1. Many of the church leaders were personally trained by the apostle Paul. He was, in effect, the "pilot project." Timothy, Silas, Titus, Epaphroditus, the Ephesian elders, and many others were spin-offs from his own life and ministry.

There is, in some local churches today, the great curse of a one-man ministry, which looks much like the worldly leadership condemned by our Lord in Luke 22. If we are to serve our own generation with power and effectiveness, we must stop pretending that being a Christian leader is like being a king of the Gentiles.

For Further Reading

Engstrom, Ted W. *The Making of a Christian Leader.* Grand Rapids: Zondervan, 1976.

Gangel, Kenneth O. *Lessons in Leadership from the Bible.* Winona Lake, Ind.: BMH Books, 1980.

———. *So You Want To Be a Leader!* Harrisburg, Pa.: Christian Publications, 1973.

Richards, Lawrence O., and Hoeldtke, Clyde. *A Theology of Leadership.* Grand Rapids: Zondervan, 1980.

NOTES

1 "The Frogs and Their King," in *Aesop's Fables*.
2. Robert Tannenbaum and Warren H. Schmidt, "How to Choose a Leadership Pattern," *Harvard Business Review* 36 (March-April 1958): 95.
3. A. B. Bruce, *The Training of the Twelve* (New York: Harper, 1886).

7

Leadership Characteristics and Qualities

THE CONTEMPORARY sociological context of leadership emphasizes the place of the leader as a member of the group. Dictatorial and unilateral approaches to decision-making are now considered outdated, and idiographic approaches are recognized as most valid. Studies of leadership also point to a wide variety of leadership "roles" and demonstrate how the training of leaders for a specific task is a complex process.

Nevertheless, it is impossible and even undesirable to put all of the focus of leadership only on the context of the group. The leader *himself* is important. What he is and how he handles his responsibilities is a significant factor in the achievement of the group. The church will largely be the result of the efforts of its pastor, and the Sunday school class will grow spiritually in measure to the spiritual maturity and communication ability of its teacher.

WHAT IS A LEADER?

A leader is often conceived of as a person possessing certain characteristic traits which mark him as one who can occupy a status position somewhat higher than his peers. Current research argues that the "trait approach" to leadership has been largely discredited. Nevertheless, it is fair to ask if there are characteristic elements which seem to be common to most leaders. A positive response seems warranted. What is not warranted, however, is the conclusion that the mere possession of traits can equip a man to perform effectively in some role of leadership, particularly if that role is within the context of service for Jesus Christ.

Actually the leader represents a consequence of the needs and goals of a group of people. For example, an astronomer may be absolutely brilliant in his laboratory and, because of his extreme competence, emerge through the general respect of his coworkers or the appointment of his superiors as a definite "leader" in his field. The same man might be on vacation in the mountains of Colorado or Wyoming when a forest fire breaks out. Knowing the man in the next cabin is an efficient astronomer is of little comfort to his neighbor. He looks to the forest ranger to take charge of this different kind of situation.

These two concepts have sometimes been differentiated by reference to "the mythical leader" and "the functional leader." The first views the leader as a symbol and seeks out someone who is tall, handsome, forceful, fluent of speech, and possesses the qualities of "a natural leader." The point is that "the natural leader" is a myth and does not really exist.

The functional leader is chosen because of his dynamic value to a given group at a given time. The concern here is whether or not this individual can produce results for the group better than anyone else who might be chosen.

Five Approaches to Defining Leadership

THE LEADER IS THE CENTRAL PERSON

Sometimes the person who is able to polarize the behavior of the group around him is considered its leader. There is no question that a leader tends to be a central person, but not all central people are leaders. The strong soprano in the choir may never be elected to any popular office, but the choir director knows that she is the section leader. Her absence at any rehearsal or performance hampers the output of the section because most of the other singers are depending upon the strength of her voice.

On the other hand, consider the obnoxious drunk on a crowded sidewalk. He attracts the attention of all passersby and is therefore a central person. The thought that he is a leader, however, is ludicrous.

THE LEADER CAN ACHIEVE GROUP GOALS

It is merely a restatement of the functional approach to defining leadership to say that the leader can achieve group goals. That person who leads the group toward its apparent goals is viewed as the leader of the group. Some questions, however, must be considered. Do groups always know their goals? Are the goals of groups always worthy? What about the leader who leads toward negative goals? An emphasis only on the achievement of group goals leads to a recognition of Adolf Hitler and all mob rulers within the definition of leadership. In a sense they are "leaders," but not in any way that can help us formulate a Christian philosophy of leadership.

THE LEADER IS "THE PEOPLE'S CHOICE"

Sociometric selection is important in leadership studies, and many people severely limit their recognition of leadership only to whether or not the group has elevated one of its number to such a position. Unfortunately, such a choice is too often a popularity contest. One of the reasons why Christian education specialists suggest that Sunday school teachers should be appointed by the board of Christian education rather than elected by the class relates specifically to the problems involved in sociometric choice. The board will be more objective and will choose a person because of his ability. Election may elevate a man just because the group happens to think that "he's a nice fellow."

THE LEADER IS ONE WHO CAN INFLUENCE A GROUP

A combination of the trait and situation approach to defining leadership is to say that a leader is one who can influence the group. It states simply that the person who most forcefully influences the group to his way of thinking is the accepted leader. To this extent Fidel Castro is without doubt a leader. Again, such a definition of leadership is incomplete and largely unacceptable for purposes of church education.

THE LEADER IS ONE WHO POSSESSES LEADERSHIP BEHAVIOR

In this view of the leader possessing leadership behavior, different kinds of behavior indicate leadership in different situations. A basketball player is chosen captain of the team because he is able to perform satisfactorily as the "floor general" in the games. An individual is elected as choir president not only because he has a good bass voice but because he observes consistency in attendance at rehearsals and views his responsibility in the choir as a definite claim upon his life which requires faithfulness and commitment.

LEADERSHIP CHARACTERISTICS

The analysis of leadership characteristics occupies a large portion of the pages in Ross and Hendry's *New Understanding of Leadership.* The authors list five primary and six secondary ingredients of leadership. The list is introduced with this poignant sentence: "While one's capacity for leadership can undoubtedly be improved, we cannot suggest that mechanical practice of some of the factors we will list will either produce capable leaders or increase honesty in human relations."[1] Having warned against a "trait approach" to leadership, the authors nevertheless define the primary factors as empathy, group membership, consideration, surgency (talkativeness, cheerfulness, geniality, enthusiasm, expressiveness, alertness, orginality), and emotional stability.

The list of secondary characteristics includes a desire for leadership, intelligence, competence, consistency, self-confidence, and ability to share leadership. All of these items, both primary and secondary, have reference to qualities of the leader. In an attempt to relate these to leadership behavior in response to a group, Ross and Hendry further delineate nine "function ingredients" of leadership which are significant enough to bear reproduction here.[2]

VISCIDITY

This is a reference to "togetherness" or how the leader can guide the group to discipline their feelings toward each other to the end of producing a spirit of unity and cooperation when the group is operating together.

HEDONIC TONE

Successful group work needs a happy group relationship. Group activity should be something that is satisfying to the participants.

SYNTALITY

Prediction of group performance is a task of the leader.

GOAL ACHIEVEMENT

Groups want leaders who can lead them to an announced goal. At times, of course, this can be a negative feature. Hitler first convinced the people of an entire nation that they were a superrace and then convinced them to follow him in achieving his goal through war.

INITIATIVE

The leader is one who starts new ideas and projects, planting concepts which will come to fruition later in suggestions made by group members.

GROUP AND GOAL ANALYSIS

Bloom's *Taxonomy of Educational Objectives in the Cognitive Domain* lists evaluation as the highest level of learning.[3] A genuine leader is a constant evaluator who keeps in proper perspective the ultimate and immediate goals of the group and the progress which it is making in moving toward those goals.

Few problems in the study of administration get as much attention as the problem of communication. The leader should have a concern for both vertical and horizontal communication; that is, for clarity of directive from above and breadth of discussion and interaction among the members of the group.

ESTABLISHING STRUCTURE

The emphasis here is on job analysis, general organization, and the laying down of a framework which can produce satisfactory action by the group.

IMPLEMENTING PHILOSOPHY

The ingredient of implementing philosophy has to do with the leader's ability to make plans work. Organizations dependent upon volunteer workers have unique problems in implementing philosophy. Engstrom and Dayton suggest that participation in the planning process is the key.

> What many organizations do not realize is that planning can be a very useful way of involving many people in considerable depth. The act of asking individuals or groups to consider alternate or optimum ways of reaching their goal, or the act of asking them to propose specific goals against the higher purpose of the organization, can be a trigger for a series of events. It cannot only give people a feeling of having participated in the organization, but it can stimulate a host of new ideas. This is just as true for the local church as it is for the Christian organization which uses no volunteers.[4]

Hendry and Ross end their book by reproducing a quote from Robert N. McMurry written in an article entitled "Manhunt for Top Executives." The article appeared in the *Harvard Business Review* in January and February 1954. McMurry indicates that there are certain skills that can be inculcated into leaders through formal instruction. He suggests six areas in which a leader may make progress through formal courses.

1. The ability to see problems in broad perspective and to make decisions on the basis of long-run rather than short-run goals.

2. The capacity to delegate *authority* as well as responsibility.

3. An open-minded receptivity to suggestions and criticisms from peers and subordinates as well as superiors.

4. A willingness to risk the loss of the approbation and support of others, if necessary, by thinking independently and taking a firm stand (as, when necessary, saying "no" to administer discipline).

5. A knack for discovering and utilizing previously undetected relationships among the things and conditions of his environment.

6. Competence in carrying on, integrating, and coordinating a number of highly varied interests and activities simultaneously.[5]

Are leaders born or made? The overwhelming argument of contemporary research is that leaders are basically made. Accordingly, the development of leadership characteristics has occupied a number of pages in this study. However, the recognition of innate ability and characteristics is an important aspect of understanding leadership.

General Qualities of Leadership

PERSONALITY IS CENTRAL

Personality is a difficult concept to explain; attempts at definition have filled many volumes of psychology down through the years. Perhaps a simple approach to understanding the term is to describe it as the sum total of observable reactions of an organism. Of course, everyone has personality. Difference is determined by varying concomitant factors.

When personality characteristics are measured, they are called "traits." Then they can be thought of in categories such as emotional stability, emotional maturity, emotional complexities, temperament, and similar concepts.

One of the most common categories of personality traits in relation to leadership is the discussion of introversion and extroversion. In recognizing these aspects of leadership it is quite safe to say that an extrovert generally makes a better leader than an introvert, but ambiversion is probably preferable to both. An outgoing leader helps the group to feel that he is doing more, is more interested in them, and is better able to control situations. One of the important qualities of effective Christian leadership is the ability to adapt one's personality structure to a certain situation. Successful pastors who move from one church situation to another have learned the secret of such flexibility.

SYMBOLISM IS IMPORTANT

Previous paragraphs have emphasized the fallacy of choosing leaders purely on the mythical "popular" basis. This does not, however, negate the value of some symbolism in connection with leadership recognition. Babe Ruth's leadership in the field of baseball was so overwhelming that his very name has become a symbol of great athletes and sportsmanship. Billy Sunday is the symbol of flamboyant preaching. Moody Bible Institute has become a symbol of quality institute training in Bible education and Christian service development. It has been called "The West Point of Christian Service," indicating the importance of symbolism in leadership.

It takes time to build a symbol because the reality which it represents must be demonstrated to the groups served by the leadership offered. The various publics of a college, for example, must be convinced that the educational program is of quality before they are willing to speak of the college in glowing terms. When that latter state has been achieved, the college has become a symbol in the mind of its people.

Many Christian leaders have also found through the years that being a symbol is a difficult and responsible job. If the image becomes tarnished, there is an obvious reflection not only upon the individual and the church but also upon the reality of Christ Himself. This is why Paul writes to the Corinthians, "Giving no cause for offense in anything, in order that the ministry be not discredited" (2 Cor. 6:3).

POSITION HAS SOME SIGNIFICANCE

The term *ex officio* means "by virtue of office" and indicates that leadership carries with it a recognition of status and esteem. A young pastor, for example, may be no better a preacher after he is ordained than before. But the fact of his ordination somehow communicates to his people a validity of his ministry that was not possessed before.

Dr. Robert Hutchins, the great former president of the University of Chicago, was once asked by a group to send a speaker to an event which the group was having. The writer indicated that the group wished to hear "nobody lower than a dean." Hutchins reportedly responded by saying that there is nobody lower than a dean. Position may not convey the same image to some people as it does to others, but it is nevertheless an important part of leadership.

TITLES HAVE A PART

Sometimes titles can be a hindrance. It is generally agreed that a layman can witness more effectively for Christ among other laymen than can his pastor. The very title of "Reverend Smith" carries with it the connotation that the individual is being paid to direct the conversation around to spiritual things. Generally speaking, however, titles define a job and they must be properly understood by the group in which they are used. Such terminology as "chairman," "pastor" and "director" connotes a responsibility or an authority which may facilitate the exercise and function of leadership.

The challenge of leadership (especially in Christian work where almost all workers are voluntary) is to achieve desired results while still retaining hedonic tone and initiative. The methodology involved will probably lead the conscientious leader to a rejection of both the autocratic and "free-reign" or libertarian approaches. He will probably opt for a democratic "guiding" type of leadership which is basically group-centered and relates the leadership role to both the needs and objectives of the group, and the demands of a given situation.

FOR FURTHER READING

Engstrom, Ted W., and Dayton, Edward R. *The Christian Executive.* Waco, Tex.: Word, 1979.

Graendorf, Werner C., ed. *Introduction to Biblical Christian Education.* Chicago: Moody, 1981.

Schaller, Lyle E., and Tidwell, Charles A. *Creative Church Administration.* Nashville: Abingdon, 1975.

NOTES

1. Charles E. Hendry and Murray G. Ross, *New Understandings of Leadership* (New York: Association, 1957), p. 43.
2. Ibid., pp. 64-85.
3. Benjamin S. Bloom, ed., *Taxonomy of Educational Objectives in the Cognitive Domain* (Ann Arbor, Mich.: Edwards, 1956).
4. Ted W. Engstrom and Edward R. Dayton, *The Christian Executive,* pp. 117-18.
5. Hendry and Ross, p. 147.

8

Leadership in Organism and Organization

The church is both organism and organization. It is organism in that it is the Body of Christ and partakes of the spiritual qualities of that mystical assembly. It is organization because it partakes of many of the same kinds of characteristics that mark other organizations: institutional goals, trained personnel, budgets and accounts, hierarchy of leadership, and basic organizational structures.

The major difference comes in the attitude of leadership. One must maintain one's attitude of serving in this unique organism-organization. This is contrasted with the secular response of the kings of the Gentiles discussed in chapter 6. There are many points of similarity between Christian leadership and secular leadership, but the differences are much more important. In this chapter we will look at four of those differences: the source of authority, the historical precedent of biblical examples, the uniqueness of spiritual dynamic in leadership, and an analysis of bureaucracy in biblical leadership.

The Source Of Authority

Even preceding the Christian era, the great philosophers of ancient Greece grappled with the question of authority. Both Plato in *The Republic* and Aristotle in *Politics* were very much concerned with the questions of leadership, even though their concern related largely to the questions of such leadership in relation to the kind of democracy in operation at that time.

When one analyzes Plato's brand of philosophy, for example, he finds that the Platonic concept views the leader as a man possessed of special knowledge. It is not, however, the knowledge of the cobbler, the pilot, or the shepherd, for these have to do with a particular art or craft. We may call upon the river pilot to sail us safely across the water because the pilot's skill and knowledge are precisely proportionate to this particular task. But it would be foolish to ask him to mend a pair of shoes, to train horses, to till the earth, or take care of sheep; and it would be even more foolish to ask his advice on how to conduct the policy of the state or to determine laws. In short, the Platonic source of authority is *the particular task or relationship one has to the total operation of the state.*

Throughout the history of the Roman Catholic Church it has been characteristic that leadership take its authority from *the church* as its source. The doctrine of apostolic succession is the epitome of this concept and it carries through the entire hierarchical system of church leadership. Men become leaders of other men because the church has appointed them to this office. The church appoints them to this office because it has resident within it the authority to make such appointments.

Another view of leadership, however, is at variance with the foregoing. It holds that the principle of *sola scriptura,* recaptured for the church at the time of the Reformation, must today be the governing source of authority for Christian leadership. To determine what Christian leadership is, how people can be prepared for it, and how one exercises it within the community of the redeemed, the investigator must go directly to the inscripturated Word and develop therefrom a biblical perspective. The underlying theological assumptions are the doctrines of plenary inspiration and special revelation. In *Basic Christian Doctrines* Addison Leitch clearly states the nature of this authority:

> This is the Bible record of God's mighty acts and his authoritative Word about the revelatory acts and about himself. This is the climax and fulfillment of God's word to us in the living Word, even Jesus Christ. Natural revelation gives us direction and confidence in our search for God; God's special revelation gives us final authority and assurance regarding his own nature and his will for man. As Calvin suggests, in the Bible we have the "divine spectacles" which bring the truths of natural theology into focus.[1]

We see from these words that Christian leadership must take its cue from the Bible. This is the only acceptable source of authority by which the definition and function of Christian leadership can be determined. However, true Christian leadership is more than just an adherence to a printed page. It is the embodiment in the individual of the Spirit and truth of God. As Caemmerer says,

> His plan is that the small boys and their grandfathers and the whole church of God be people in whom He, God, is Himself at work and alive. Learning words and definitions help in the process, but that is only a help. The Bible is a means toward that end, but always only a means. The great objective of Christian nurture is that people belong to God, that He and His Spirit and His Son are enthroned as rulers in their hearts, and that these people therefore carry out the purposes for which God has placed them in the world and recaptured them from sin and the devil to fulfill His purposes.[2]

The working out of the authority of God in life can be observed in the pages of Scripture both in precept and example.

Not all "Christian educators," however, accept so high a view of Scripture as the source of authority for Christian leadership. Some attempt to reverse the position stated above by making the quality of life a judging factor for truth rather than allowing the truth of God's revelation to shine upon the life of leadership. Jahsmann warns that

> the chief assumption of Sherrill, Miller, Munro, and their followers is that "the quality of life within a congregation is the most powerful mediator of God's grace," and that "we live ourselves into religious thinking far more than we think ourselves into religious living." This teaching is clearly debatable, for, as we hope to demonstrate, the one type of learning experience finds its meaning in the other.[3]

Jahsmann's complaint against the existential views of those writers he names is that they have made the experience of men the final judge in matters of truth and have therefore followed Dewey into the kingdom where human experience reigns. It should be noted that the view of Leitch and Caemmerer emphasizes human experience also, but as a *result* of the activity of God rather than a *producer* of that activity. Jahsmann clearly states that human experience is not the measuring rod of eternal truth.

> For example, let us look again at the statements quoted at the beginning of this chapter. He who maintains that "religion emerges from within the natural relationships of a child" and that "it is impossible to teach the Christian faith without the context of the Church" makes vertical relationships with God dependent on horizontal relationships with people instead of making interpersonal Christian faith and at-one-ness with God.[4]

BIBLICAL EXAMPLES: MOSES, JOSHUA, PAUL

MOSES

As the slave child who became prince and lawgiver, Moses possessed almost all of the natural and educable attributes desirable in effective leadership. He grew up in Pharaoh's court and was in the line of heirship to the Egyptian throne. The hand of God reached down, snatched him from the royalties of the palace, and thrust him by divine sovereignty into a position which he did not want. William Sanford LaSor pinpoints several leadership qualities of Moses, indicating such things as singleness of purpose, organizational ability, faith, obedience, and faithfulness in service. LaSor notes that leadership potential was demonstrated early in Moses in that

> he was able to gather around him the elders of the people of Israel, who by this time had been in Egypt many years. . . . Yet Moses was able to fire the imagination of these people and elders of Israel; he was able to convince them that God was bent upon their deliverance, and he made them follow him. That is leadership.[5]

JOSHUA

The characteristics of godly leadership resident in Joshua are indicated clearly in verses 1-8 of chapter 1 of the book that bears his name.

> Now it came about after the death of Moses the servant of the LORD that the LORD spoke to Joshua the son of Nun, Moses' servant, saying, "Moses My servant is dead; now therefore arise, cross this Jordan, you and all this people, to the land which I am giving to them, to the sons of Israel. Every place on which the sole of your foot treads, I have given it to you, just as I spoke to Moses. From the wilderness and this Lebanon, even as far as the great river, the river Euphrates, all the land of the Hittites, and as far as the Great Sea toward the setting of the sun, will be your territory. No man will be able to stand before you all the days of your life. Just as I have been with Moses, I will be with you; I will not fail you or forsake you. Be strong and courageous, for you shall give this people possession of the land which I swore to their fathers to give them. Only be strong and very courageous; be careful to do according to all the law which Moses My servant commanded you; do not turn from it to the right or to the left, so that you may have success wherever you go. This book of the law shall not depart from your mouth, but you shall meditate on it day and night, so that you may be careful to do according to all that is written in it;

for then you will make your way prosperous, and then you will have success" [Joshua 1:1-8].

A number of elements in the above verses deserve delineation. First of all, Joshua was *called* to the task that he faced; he was not seeking to advance himself in the ranks of Israel. He had been around for a long time and had held various subordinate positions of authority, but there is no indication whatsoever that he was pushing to become Moses' successor. As in all authentic cases of Christian leadership, God reached down and selected the man to fill the ministry which was necessary to advance His cause at that time.

A second important feature is that Joshua had *paid the price of preparation*. This man who heard the call of God had been "Moses' minister." Although there is no specific indication of what it meant to be Moses' minister in those days, undoubtedly such a role included a great element of subordination to the leadership of the man God had been using up to this point in history. And all of these days and months and years of toil and subordination had been preparing Joshua for the task of leadership which now lay before him. God prepared Moses alone in a remote area of the desert. He chose to prepare Joshua in a constant apprenticeship situation so that his command over the people of Israel in a very real sense would be an extension of Jehovah's work through Moses.

Absolute dependency upon the Lord is clear in these verses. From the beginning God allowed Joshua to harbor no thoughts of self-sufficiency. Frequently throughout these verses one reads about the sovereign manipulation of the situation in such phrases as "I do give to them," "that have I given unto you," "I will be with thee," "I will not fail thee." Christian leadership requires that the leader always recognize his place of subordination within the spiritual line-staff relationships of the kingdom of God.

Joshua's leadership also demonstrates a definite emphasis on *courage* (vv. 6, 7, 9). Why does God give this triple revelation of command to His newly appointed captain? It is because godly leadership then, as now, requires a continual courageous relationship based on the faithfulness of God and His Son, Jesus Christ.

One final note of emphasis is Joshua's relationship to the Word, that is, to special revelation as it had progressed to his time. Verse 8 clearly indicates that Joshua was to operate within the framework of the Mosaic law. His leadership, in other words, was governed by the *authority of revelation*. Joshua's orders came not from his own ability and creativity but from a higher source, the world plan of a living God.

PAUL

In an excellent article in *Christianity Today* entitled "The Marks of Leadership," James Taylor, a Scottish Baptist pastor, writes:

> We are looking for Christians who are developing the same traits of character that made the Apostle Paul such a dynamic leader in the early days of the Christian church. He was God's man for the church to lead her forward in outreach and understanding. What can he tell us, centuries later, of the essential characteristics of leadership?[6]

Taylor delineates several specific characteristics possessed by the apostle Paul which should be found in Christian leaders today. He speaks first of all of "tenacity of mind," and by this has reference to specific objectives and aims which governed the apostle's life. The faithful Christian leader moves toward these goals with resolution of mind and will. Such tenacity includes conception of purpose and concentration of achievement. Paul's course did not deviate from one side to the other. When he testified that Christ was the controlling force in all of his life, he meant that this had practical implications in all that he did. Neither personal limitations, physical weakness, nor the adversities of life deterred the apostle in continually pursuing his goal of being like his Master.

Taylor also finds "conviction of belief" an important mark of the apostolic leadership. Paul knew that his message was an offense to many and that the proclamation of it carried the very danger of the loss of his own life. Yet he would not compromise, nor would he shirk the responsibility of proclaiming the gospel.

Taylor points out that the apostle was characterized by "breadth and largeness of vision." Today Paul would be called creative and innovative in his concern for communicating the gospel to the world. He put no stock in the view of those who would contain truth within the narrow confines of Judaism and carry over Old Testament legalism into the new life of grace. His vision spanned the Mediterranean to take in Asia Minor, Rome and even Spain. What mattered that he was a small man with no financial backing; he was a representative of the sovereign God of the universe.

Taylor indicates two final character traits in the apostle Paul which point to distinctive Christian leadership: "He was a man of deep affection and he had a genius for friendship." His ability to relate to people, to draw them to himself and to his Lord, was a demonstration of the inner motivation so essential to the Christian leader.

These three examples from both Old and New Testament days appear here only in brief form. However, the lessons indicated above are indicative of the many more which can be learned by studying Christian leadership through the biographies of the men God used.

The Dynamic of Spiritual Leadership

The experiences of Joshua and Paul demonstrate some obvious spiritual characteristics or qualities of Christian leadership which take precedence over all the sociological aspects of the leader's role. In reality, Christian leadership ought to be characterized by all of the legitimate earmarks of effective secular leadership *plus* the factors which make it distinctively Christian.

The obvious spiritual elements include such matters as faith, reliance upon prayer, the reality of the Holy Spirit in the life of the leader, and the absolute authority of God's inerrant Word as the basis for leadership. There are, however, some less obvious factors which mark a given exercise of leadership as "spiritual," which is compared with leadership which is either "natural" or "carnal," that is, totally secular, or exercised in the flesh.

Acceptance of Responsibility

Accepting responsibility is a basic discipline of all leadership which takes on added dimensions when that responsibility is defined in terms of God's call upon a life. Every Christian worker should strive to earn a reputation for being a person who can be counted upon. Someone has suggested that the best ability is dependability.

As a man settles finally to one woman who becomes his wife, so the Christian leader settles to the ministry to which God has called him. Sometimes this decision may push other legitimate and desirable things out of one's life. Such are the demands of the discipline of leadership. During the days following the resurrection, the apostle Peter may have thought fishing a more attractive occupation than evangelism. Ultimately, however, he had to face the claims of discipleship upon his life as the Master said to him, "Follow me."

MEEKNESS AND HUMILITY

The more mature one becomes in the Christian life and service for his Lord, the more he realizes that when he has done the best job he can possibly do and exerted all efforts to the task, he remains—when compared with the absolute perfection of God—an unworthy and unprofitable servant. The Christian leader cannot indulge himself in self-pity or dislike for others. He must minimize personality conflicts and allow the Spirit of God to work out an attitude of meekness before the Lord.

The Christian leader patterns his life after the Word of God wherein he sees countless examples of this kind of attitude in leadership. Moses had disciplined himself for many years to patiently listen to the murmuring and complaining of the children of Israel. The Hebrew children in Babylon renounced all possible political advantages to say that they would not be defiled with the king's meat. Daniel laid power and prestige on the line in prayer despite his high governmental position. Paul's missionary endeavors frequently took him into hard places, caused him to renounce himself, to bring his body under subjection, resulting in a complete commitment to Jesus Christ and His will.

TEACHABLENESS

Someone has aptly remarked that the teacher who ceases to learn ceases to teach. The following selected verses from Psalm 25 pinpoint David's attitude toward his own leadership in the light of teachableness:

> Make me know Thy ways, O Lord; teach me Thy paths. Lead me in Thy truth and teach me, for Thou are the God of my salvation; for Thee I wait all the day.
>
> Good and upright is the Lord; therefore He instructs sinners in the way. He leads the humble in justice, and He teaches the humble His way.
>
> Who is the man who fears the Lord? He will instruct him in the way he should choose. His soul will abide in prosperity, and his descendants will inherit the land. [Psalm 25:4-5, 8-9, 12-13]

CARE FOR HIS FOLLOWERS

The Christian leader exercises in his dealings with his group an *agape* relationship which is not a passive feeling but an aggressive commitment to their welfare which is motivated by faith. Such concern is not deterred by the failure of people to do what the leader expects them to do. It can weather disappointments and disillusionments in the difficult process of leadership. It is a reflection of Moses' concern for the people of Israel but an even greater resemblance to the life and ministry of the Son of God.

Bureaucracy and Biblical Leadership

What does bureaucracy have to do with a Christian organization? First of all, it must be recognized that bureaucracy is not the horrible specter of demonic control it is often conceived to be. In a discussion, a pastor friend of mine indicated that the church was "becoming too bureaucratic," and that that was one of its major problems. I asked him if he had ever read anything which attempted to deal with bureaucracy in a theological context, and his response was that he had never read *anything* about bureaucracy at all. It is one of those convenient words that we have learned to use when we want to speak out against something that is too big for us to understand, much less to handle.

As a matter of fact, bureaucracy is necessary in a democratic society and in a democratic organization. It is not *bureaucracy* that gives us the trouble, but rather the misuse and abuse of bureaucracy to the point that it becomes a hindrance rather than a help in our organizations. Bureaucracy, like many other tools of accomplishment, makes the proverbial good servant but bad master.

Contrary to popular notions, bureaucracy can be very efficient and an almost necessary tool to productivity. Blau suggests that the term describes a "type of organization designed to accomplish large-scale administrative tasks by systematically coordinating the work of many individuals."[7]

So it is not bureaucracy that causes our problems. It is, rather, a misunderstanding of its inherent evils as well as its helpfulness which leads us astray. It occurred to me, then, that our study might best take the form of pitting bureaucracy against several concepts which are generally considered contrary to it, in order to see the tension created when bureaucratic concentration of power destroys democratic processes.

Bureaucracy Verses a "Professional" View of Work

The word *professional* appears in quotation marks, because it is a technical term when used in the jargon of management science. Studies by Corwin, in the *Educational Administration Quarterly*, indicate a distinction between the behavior of what Corwin calls "a bureaucratic person" and that of "a professional person." It is not exactly a contrasting relationship, but there are some differences between the outlooks toward the whole matter of the employee's relationship to his institution.

To be more bureaucratic does not necessarily mean to be less professional. The same person could be oriented toward both bureaucratic and professional goals, but the double orientation would necessitate a constant struggle to bring together two things which tend to polarize themselves. A "professional" person in administration tends to emphasize individuals, research, freedom of relationships, skill development through training (rather than practice), decentralization of decision making, and sanctions by a given leader, rather than the constant serving of organizational goals.

Corwin would argue that administrators in a college tend to be more bureaucratic (serve the organization), whereas faculty tend to be more professional (serve their academic disciplines). It should be easy for us to understand that a person serving his academic discipline can also serve the organization and, if he is a Christian, he should serve Christ above either.

On the other hand, it is interesting to notice how often a professional faculty member becomes a bureaucratic administrator when appointed to a post as dean or, in some large universities, department chairman. Then there is the professional pastor whose prior concerns have always been for the autonomy of the local congregation. Now, as a district superintendent, he seems always to serve the goals and interests of the denomination, sometimes, it may seem, even to the lessening of emphasis on individual congregations within his sphere of authority.

BUREAUCRACY VERSUS EFFECTIVENESS

All of the research done on the subject of bureaucracy tends to conclude that the purely bureaucratic administrative structure is, from a technical point of view, capable of attaining the highest degree of efficiency. Of course, efficiency is measured in terms of product output and the achievement of the goals of the organization.

It is at this point that the concepts of Peter Drucker help us. He candidly offers a marked distinction between *efficiency* and *effectiveness* by suggesting that the former is the ability to do things right, whereas the latter is the ability to do the right things. Drucker pinpoints what he calls five practices, or habits, of the effective executive:

1. Effective executives know where their times goes.
2. Effective executives focus on outward contribution.
3. Effective executives build on strengths.
4. Effective executives concentrate on the few major areas where superior performance will produce outstanding results.
5. Effective executives make effective decisions.[8]

It should not be difficult to note that bureaucracy tends to emphasize *efficiency,* because it focuses on doing things right (task specialization, standardization, etc.), but *effectiveness* is much more concerned with achievement than with process.

BUREAUCRACY VERSUS A DEMOCRATIC VIEW OF ORGANIZATION

There are profound implications in a comparison of bureaucracy with democracy in organizational structure, since bureaucracy is primarily concerned with the systemization of the process of how one's own work fits together with the work of others. Blau's first chapter in *Bureaucracy in Modern Society* identifies three types of association, all of which are to some degree descriptive of the church and every other kind of Christian organization.

1. *The association which exists to produce certain end products and which, therefore, must concern itself with efficiency (doing things right).* Think about your church for just a moment. People who come together in the association that we call *congregation* do not actually create products, but their service to those not in the organization (the witness to the pagan culture and the outreach of world mission) is equivalent to the marketing of an industrial concern. We might also argue that the matter of "doing the right things" is important to the Christian if there are, indeed, biblical absolutes which define the way in which at least some of the work should be done in any age and place.

2. *The association which is established for the purpose of finding intrinsic satisfaction in common activities.* Here efficiency is less relevant, since the members in association are finding the end result of their togetherness in their relationship to each other. This we would call *koinonia* and think of as both an end and a means to an end (cf. chapter 4). Note that bureaucracy is important here, as well, since bureaucracy has to do with the process of how one's work fits together with the work of others.

3. *The association which exists for the purpose of deciding upon common goals and courses of actions.* Surely this also describes the church. To the extent that it has a job to do and a right way to do it, the church must of necessity be a bureaucratic organization. To the extent that the kind of leadership defined for the church in the New Testament (see Chapter 6) is essentially democratic when based on the concept of the universal priesthood of believers, the church must resist bureaucratization.

BUREAUCRACY VERSUS A CHRISTIAN VIEW OF SOCIETY

In his famous book, *The Lonely Crowd,* David Riesman delineates three periods in the development of any culture: the high growth potential period, characterized by tradition-direction; the transitional growth period, characterized by inner-direction; and the incipient decline of population, characterized by other-direction. The essential point of the book is that American society in the last half of the twentieth century is living in the "other-directed" period. Therefore the responsibility of the culture is to preserve individualism in the face of mass standardization.

Riesman suggests, "In large and bureaucratized organizations people's attention is focused more on products (whether these are goods, decisions, reports, or discoveries makes little difference) and less on the human element."[9] In this particular section of the book, Riesman is talking about the economic and industrial orientation of an inner-directed society. His obvious point is the overemphasis on efficiency. However, in discussing the matter of what he calls "the parental role in the stage of other-direction," Riesman argues, with Blau, that overbureaucratizing stifles the individuality that people in the other-directed phase of society claim they want so desperately.

The implication for the administrator in the Christian organization is that he should focus on the real issue of drawing out the work of the individual in a genuine way rather than glossing over the whole situation with some thin veneer of plastic "human relationism."

When he pours Riesman's theories through the sieve of special revelation, the evangelical Christian leader finds himself committed to a direction of children in the home, parishioners in the church, and students in the school. This direction receives its impetus from a power outside and beyond the administrative leadership in each of those organizations, and not merely from some kind of psychological gyroscope which is set into operation by the mature members of society.

BUREAUCRACY VERSUS A BIBLICAL VIEW OF MAN

Let us stay with Riesman just a moment longer. One's philosophy of anything always grows out of his theology, even if he does not admit to having any theology. This is notably true in education, and quite obviously, therefore, in the ministry of many Christian organizations, including the church. If one considers the social system to be in constant flux (which it certainly is, in Western culture), one is tempted to buy the presupposition of most secular psychologists and sociologists that the nature of man is therefore constantly formed by the environmental factors in that flux.

But the "inner-direction" of which Riesman speaks is not generated from the turbulent waters of the social system itself. It arises, rather, from moving and controlling the hearts of Christians, both individually and collectively, so that their work, in the process of association, transcends the norms and standards of society rather than constantly being formed and controlled by them. Living according to absolutes in a relativistic cultural system is not easy, but it is definitely necessary for the church. It always has been, and always will be.

When translated from a set of principles to a more formal definition, Christian leadership may be considered the exercise by a Christian member of the group of certain qualities and abilities given by the Spirit of God and based in Christian character, which at any given time, acting upon the call of God and the authority of His Word, he will offer in loving service to the group for the sake of Christ, in order to facilitate the change of group behavior in the direction of Christlikeness and toward the achieving of the eternal goals of His church.

FOR FURTHER READING

Eims, Leroy, *Be the Leader You Were Meant To Be.* Wheaton, Ill.: Victor, 1975.

Engstrom, Ted. W., and Dayton, Edward R. *The Art of Management for Christian Leaders.* Waco, Tex.: Word, 1976.

———. *The Christian Executive.* Waco, Tex.: Word, 1979.

Gangel, Kenneth O. *Lessons in Leadership from the Bible.* Winona Lake, Ind.: BMH Books, 1980.

Sanders, J. Oswald. *Spiritual Leadership.* Rev. ed. Chicago: Moody, 1980.

NOTES

1. Carl F. H. Henry, *Basic Christian Doctrines* (New York: Holt, Rinehart & Winston, 1962), pp. 5-6.
2. Richard R. Caemmerer, *Feeding and Leading* (St. Louis: Concordia, 1962), p. 34.
3. Allan Hart Jahsmann, *What's Lutheran in Education* (St. Louis: Concordia, 1960), p. 80.
4. Ibid.
5. William Sanford LaSor, *Great Personalities of the Old Testament* (Westwood, N.J.: Revell, 1959), p. 62.
6. James Taylor, "The Marks of Leadership," *Christianity Today* 8 (3 January, 1964): 5.
7. Peter Blau, *Bureaucracy in Modern Society* (Chicago: U. of Chicago, 1956), p. 14.
8. Peter Drucker, *The Effective Executive* (New York: Harper & Row, 1967), pp. 23-24.
9. David Riesman, *The Lonely Crowd* (New Haven: Yale U., 1950), p. 112.

9

The Leader and His Church

In the last chapter we talked about David Riesman's book *The Lonely Crowd*. There we were concerned about the role of bureaucracy in Christian leadership and how it forces us to take a look at the motives we utilize in working with people in the church. We want to broaden that idea now by emphasizing again that the church must be viewed as both organism and organization. To view it only as organization is secularistic naturalism, a position which has no role in a biblical understanding of Christian leadership. On the other hand, viewing the church *only* as an organism can lead to an ethereal piety which fails to take into consideration modern research and management theory in the development of leadership for church education. In this chapter we are focusing on the leader relating to his church as organization.

Two significant factors must be analyzed in an evaluation of the validity of Riesman's conclusions for the church administrator. The first is the sociological issue which asks whether Riesman's three cycles of the conditions of society are any more valid than Toynbee's cyclical approach to history or for that matter, Alvin Toffler's three waves. Although examples from history are offered as documentation for the theory, sociologists have challenged it and the issue is far from closed.

One prime factor here is of consequence to the church. Whether or not a society moves from tradition-direction through inner-direction to other-direction as smoothly as Riesman seems to suggest, may be open to question. What is not open to question is that society definitely finds itself today in a time of mass influence in which individualism and nonconformity are rare exceptions rather than the general rule!

The second basic question facing us deals with the theological significance of Riesman's work. Like most sociologists before and since, he views the lives of people and their impact on society merely from a naturalistic framework. Perhaps, then, our first concern is the spirit of rebellion that strives against almost all authority and every institution in contemporary Western culture.[1]

Following Lines of Authority

The position of Christian leadership lies somewhere between libertarian individualism and William White's "organization man." Every pastor, Sunday school superintendent, or teacher learns to relate himself to the church as an organization without destroying his own initiative and creativity or sacrificing any convictions which have been built into his own heart by the teaching ministry of the Spirit of God. As in other organizations, such a relationship situation can only be sustained in the church through a *proper following of the lines of authority.*

To facilitate harmonious relationships in the organization, the leader must know the lines of authority. Serving Christ through the church is not activity in a vacuum. It is a constant relationship with other people. A study of adequately drawn organizational charts as described in Chapter 16 is important; but even beyond this, the leader must understand his own role and its commensurate responsibility.

Span of control is an important concept here since it defines the extent and limitations of the leader's supervision of other people in the program. Only hard feelings and disruption of the ministry can result when a leader who is not in line of authority over another worker assumes a supervisory capacity.

THE LEADER MUST ACCEPT HIS ROLE IN THE TOTAL SCHEME OF THE ORGANIZATION

Knowing one's place and accepting one's place are two totally different mental and emotional positions. In the secular business world, the "cutthroat" ascent of the ladder of executive success is a normal procedure. In the work of the church, however, attitudes are to be refined by a spiritual recognition of one's call to a given office, and placement there by the sovereign selection of God. The usher who is disgruntled because he is not a deacon, and the Sunday school teacher who sets fleshly sights on the position of departmental superintendent, are not satisfactorily accepting their roles within the New Testament framework of humility and grace in the service of Christ.

THE LEADER MUST EXERCISE INTEGRITY IN THE CARRYING OUT OF HIS ROLE

To recognize the lines of authority is one thing; to function properly within them is quite another. Every organization is made up of individual people. The leader's honesty, kindness, and consideration toward his fellow workers depict his level of concern for the church and its ministry. Peter delineates several virtues which mark the spiritually mature Christian leader, particularly in his relations with other people:

> Now for this very reason also, applying all diligence, in your faith supply moral excellence, and in your moral excellence, knowledge; and in your knowledge, self-control, and in your self-control, perseverance, and in your perseverance, godliness; and in your godliness, brotherly kindness, and in your brotherly kindness, Christian love. For if these qualities are yours and are increasing, they render you neither useless nor unfruitful in the true knowledge of our Lord Jesus Christ. [2 Pet. 1:5-8]

THE LEADER MUST KNOW THE PROPER USE OF REPORTS AND FORMS

When the worker is responsible to someone else for achievement of his duties, the reporting of this achievement should be both written and regular. Even in organizations which do not require such reporting, the competent leader will exercise his own initiative in reporting regularly to his superiors. The line of reporting in most churches may proceed something like this: teacher—departmental superintendent—agency head—board of Christian education—director of Christian education—pastor—official board—congregation.

THE LEADER MUST DEVELOP PROPER ATTITUDES TOWARD AUTHORITY IN THE ORGANIZATION

From the various psychological systems put forth by secular theorists in the twentieth century, none has seemed more adaptable to Christian theism than phenomenology, particularly as it is developed by Snygg and Combs. Simply stated, the theorists argue that an individual behaves largely in the way he views himself and within the framework of the role which he sees as proper.

An individual's "phenomenal field" represents those things which he knows about but does not apply to himself. The inner circle describes those things and feelings with which he personally identifies. Intangible evidences of behavior such as "self-confidence" or "inferiority complex" are behavioral repesentations of how the individual sees his role in relation to other people and the organization.

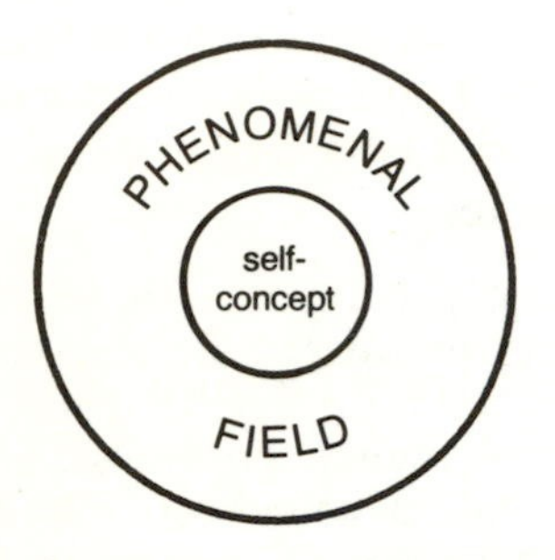

SELF-CONCEPT DIAGRAM
Figure 3

According to this theory, learning occurs in three basic ways:

1. By moving previously unknown information into the "phenomenal field" so that the individual becomes acquainted with it.

2. Through differentiation; in other words, a development of adequate perspective between factors which are already in the phenomenal field.

3. By changing one's self-concept to bring it more into conformity with reality—this is the best approach. The self-concept, according to which the individual behaves, is sometimes distorted. Therefore, the more the self-concept approximates reality, the more reasonable and mature one's behavior will become.

Dangers to a Healthy Self-Concept

The leader's reaction to authority will depend upon whether he sees that authority as a threat (the long arm of the organization seeking to beat him into submission) or a legitimate guideline under which he can function without fear. Within the context of the church, the leader ought not to be concerned about *self*-advancement. Rather, he should rejoice in the development of the organization since it represents an extension of the cause of Christ. Any of the following will be a detriment to leadership ministry in the church and, if carried to extreme, will actually lead to neurosis.

DEFENSIVENESS

Smooth running of any church can be disrupted by an individual who goes about his task with a chip on his shoulder. This is the fellow who is sure that everyone is out to get him. His perverted mind constantly conjures up images of plots against his social welfare. His self-concept begins to develop a persecution complex, and his ability to work with other people is seriously impaired, if not entirely dissipated.

INSECURITY

The word *insecurity* describes the individual who is afraid of his leadership situation and the result it may bring. He fears that his level of competence may not be equal to the task, and that perhaps people will not like it if he makes this decision or that one. What he really fears, of course, is himself. His self-concept has convinced him that his involvement in a given situation can only have disastrous ends. Sometimes insecurity is a result of genuine incompetence, and the only solution then is for the leader to develop a mastery in his field through adequate job training.

GRUDGE-HOLDING

The problem of holding a grudge is merely a partial implementation of either defensiveness or insecurity, or both. Through some petty misunderstanding the leader has had his "feelings hurt" and now distrusts or even dislikes the other person involved. Getting "hurt" is too often used by Christians as a substitute for getting angry. The overt reactions may be less pronounced, but the inner results are the same. Such a distorted self-concept results from having one's gaze fixed upon man rather than upon God and His Word. The psalmist has written, "Those who love Thy law have great peace, and nothing causes them to stumble" (119:165).

JEALOUSY

Another result of insecurity may be jealousy. When one is not satisfied with his own position he casts a covetous eye at the positions of others and begins to question the sovereignty of God in choosing the best for his life. Even Peter was not beyond such an attitude when he questioned Christ's prophecy of his martyrdom: "And what about this man?" His concern with John's life was invalid, however, and Christ's reaction was to repeat the call to discipleship, "You follow Me" (John 21:21-22).

Developing a Healthy Self-Concept

The healthy self-concept is one that is free from the above problems and many more like them. Not only is it in regular contact with reality but it is also growing and maturing continuously. In his fine article "The Power to See Ourselves" Brouwer has suggested several steps in the proper recognition of oneself in relation to the organization.[2]

SELF-EXAMINATION

The ancient Greek philosophers speak down through the halls of history to the modern-day leader when they say, "Know thyself." Such empirical introspection is not easy, for total objectivity is virtually impossible. Nevertheless, the leader is responsible for being as accurate in his self-appraisal as is possible.

SELF-INSIGHT

Determination provides information which is then put through a differentiation process which shows a more proper perspective on relationships. The leader who examines himself and discovers that he seems to have bitter feelings against another person moves on to the "insight" step to attempt some definition of the source of those feelings.

SELF-EXPECTATION

Great leaders have always been men who have been hard on themselves. Their aspirations to perfection in their own work were rarely, if ever, achieved, but the driving force of those aspirations rendered a work of far greater quality than if self-expectation had given way to apathy.

SELF-DIRECTION

At this stage of development, one is ready to broaden his horizons and extend his sights to wider and more advanced arenas of achievement. No longer hemmed in by his own limited abilities, the Christian leader sees himself as an instrument in the hands of a mighty God who can achieve supernatural results through a yielded servant.

SELF-REALIZATION

The concepts of self-actualization and self-realization are spoken of often by psychologists and even more often by social psychologists. The psychologist looks at man within the framework of himself, while the social psychologist is more concerned about that man's relationship with other people in the wider social context of family, organization, and society in general. Self-realization means fulfillment of one's personal goals and expectations.

The building of a healthy self-concept for Christian leadership is a long-term process. It begins with the calm assurance of one's placement by a sovereign God in a position of leadership and the enabling which that security will provide for the exercise of the duties required by the position. The process moves along through self-discipline, which brings control of the leader's heart and life under the lordship of Jesus Christ. A healthy self-concept identifies with the Holy Spirit as His channel and temple through whom the third Person of the triune God carries on the work of the church.

IMPLICATIONS FOR THE CHRISTIAN LEADER

Most of the above has been an attempt to define the role of the individual leader in relation to the organization as it is represented by other people. The principles are applicable to management and administration on almost all levels, secular or Christian. Before examining the leader's relationship to the organization as a collective monolith, what can be said further about the distinctively Christian aspect of working with other people in the church? Perhaps the following statements can serve as guidelines:

CHRISTIAN HONESTY CONTROLS AMBITION

Whether Caesar was ambitious or not is an argument for historians. What is of interest to administrators is that his colleagues *thought* he was ambitious and that his ambition would be the ruin of the organization. Consequently, they put him to death.

Doubtless the temptation to ambition visits men of ability who have committed their lives to Christ. Only when that commitment supersedes the desire for personal gain can sacrificial service result. The apostle Paul is the biblical example of such devotion to Christ and His church. "I have been crucified with Christ;

and it is no longer I who live, but Christ lives in me; and the life which I now live in the flesh I live by faith in the Son of God, who loved me, and delivered Himself up for me" (Gal. 2:20).

CHRISTIAN COURTESY CONTROLS RELATIONS WITH OTHER PEOPLE

Jesus Christ was full of grace and truth. Though He never allowed error to overwhelm truth, He did not defend the truth at the sacrifice of His graciousness to other people. Only to the Pharisees in their blatant denial of His Person and message did He direct clear-cut words of condemnation. His disciples were often wrong and at times very foolish, but He always dealt with them in a patient and gentle way, helping them to better understand themselves and their ministry.

CHRISTIAN CONFIDENCE DISPELS CONSTANT FEAR OF REPRISAL

Part of the reason for the insecurity among leaders in a worldly context is their dependence upon humanistic means to succeed. They cast their entire destiny upon their own shoulders and then stagger beneath the realization that their own abilities are insufficient to guarantee the security they desire. At best it is a constant performance of one's duty for the approval of other people.

The Christian leader ought not to be encumbered with thoughts of his own importance nor even with the attitudes of other people. This is not to say that one never listens to the evaluation which others offer of his own ministry. It merely emphasizes that the Christian recognizes his immediate dependence upon an answerability to his God concerning the way he exercises his own ministry. The apostle Paul wrote it this way:

> Let a man regard us in this manner, as servants of Christ, and stewards of the mysteries of God. In this case, moreover, it is required of stewards that one be found trustworthy. But to me it is a very small thing that I should be examined by you, or by any human court; in fact, I do not even examine myself. I am conscious of nothing against myself, yet I am not by this acquitted; but the one who examines me is the Lord. Therefore do not go on passing judgment before the time, but wait until the Lord comes who will both bring to light the things hidden in the darkness and disclose the motives of men's hearts; and then each man's praise will come to him from God. [1 Cor. 4:1-5]

For the Christian there is a genuine difference between ability and power. The former may be either man-developed or God-given and is usually a little bit of both. The latter, however, is entirely from above and works out through the life of the Christian leader through the instrumentality of the Holy Spirit of God.

The Christian's confidence is not in himself but in that power which God exercises in his life. Again two passages from the pen of Paul are strategic as he writes, "Not that we are adequate in ourselves to consider anything as coming from ourselves, but our adequacy is from God" (2 Cor. 3:5). And again, "But we have this treasure in earthen vessels, that the surpassing greatness of the power may be of God and not from ourselves (2 Cor. 4:7).

Relationships in Individual-Institution Interaction

Research in the mid-twentieth century has produced some interesting studies of the relationships between an individual and the organization in which he works. Although most of it has been developed within the context of industrial management, the principles can well be adapted and refined by biblical theology to fit relationships in the church. Generally speaking, most of the research concludes that the history of management has been too organization-centered without sufficient concern for the individual. Decentralization of authority and decision-making is a current reaction to the centralization of the past.

A paradox develops here for the Christian leader as he attempts to apply this information to his work in the church. On the one hand, there must be an overwhelming concern for the progress of the institution since it represents the extension of Christ and His ministry upon earth. On the other hand, no one was more concerned than the Savior that people in relationship to each other never let the organization become so powerful that it squelches the individual for whom He died.

The illustrations in Figure 4 demonstrate how the relationship of emphasis between the institution and the individual can take form within any organization, including the church. Rectangle *a* describes a level of relationship which might be operative in a general business concern. Rectangle *b* depicts any highly autocratic organization; for example, the Russian proletariat or even the monolithic structure which has grown up in the American democracy. Rectangle *c* represents a highly flexible situation in which the institution serves only to further the ends of the individual; perhaps a research laboratory would be a good example.

Which one of these best describes the church? No doubt all are represented in a broad cross section of the church, but a proper

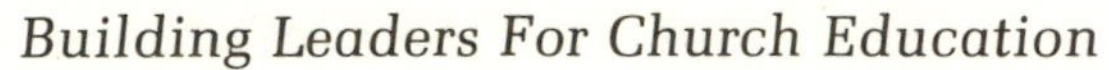

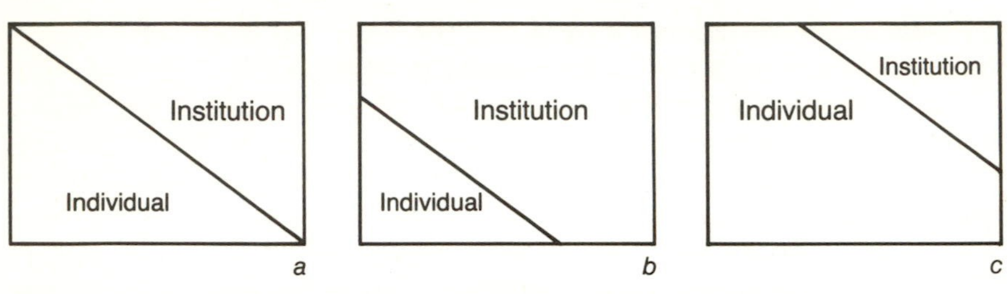

INSTITUTION-INDIVIDUAL RELATIONSHIP
Figure 4

relationship between the individual and his institution is best shown by rectangle *a*.

An entire jargon has developed to describe studies in the relationship between the individual and his organization. Organizations which are person-centered are described as "idiographic," with emphasis on decision-making, initiation of structure, and organization achievement. Organizations which are bureaucratic are described as "nomothetic," placing their emphasis instead upon group leadership, consideration, and organizational maintenance.

Blau describes some of the problems of bureaucratic organization but goes on to conclude that though bureaucracy may threaten democracy both in an organization and on the general social scale, it cannot be abolished because of the benefits derived from it. Bureaucracy according to Blau is "organization that maximizes efficiency in administration, whatever its formal characteristics, or as an institutionalized method of organizing social conduct in the interest of administrative efficiency."[3]

No doubt larger churches tend to be more bureaucratic and smaller churches less bureaucratic. The goal is to achieve administrative efficiency without losing sight of the importance of the individual in the organization.

Causes of Distorted Individual-Organization Relationships

DISORGANIZATION

When the church's organizational state is in disarray, the personnel working in various roles do not correctly perceive their roles and, as a result, confusion and frustration develop. The individual can only properly relate to the institution when its organizational factors have demonstrated clarity of purpose and specification of responsibility for all personnel. Two reasons for defeat and discouragement on the part of Sunday school teachers are the lack of job descriptions defining their roles and the lack of clear-cut objectives which can be measured to evaluate achievement.[4]

BUREAUCRACY

As indicated above, bureaucracy is here to stay and becomes a problem only when it infringes upon a biblical view of the individual's worth. Argyris defines four characteristics of bureaucracy: task specialization, hierarchy of position, unity of direction and span of control. He says the self-actualizing person has trouble with these facets in a bureaucracy because they tend to suppress the significance of the individual. The self-actualizing leader is characterized by activity rather than passivity, independence rather than dependence, flexibility instead of limitations in behavior, deep rather than shallow interests, longtime perspective instead of shortsightedness, and awareness of oneself as an adult rather than as a child.

Is there room in the church for the self-actualizing person? Certainly there is, and history has demonstrated it over and over again. The apostle Paul was that kind of man. St. Augustine was a self-actualizing thinker. Martin Luther's creativity is the mark of his genius. All of these men had some difficulties with the existing ecclesiastical system, but none found difficulty serving Christ within the confines of the New Testament church.

INSTITUTIONALISM

Institutionalism is bureaucracy taken one step further. Rather than utilizing the abilities of the individual for the smooth functioning of the organization as in bureaucracy, institutionalism completely subordinates the concerns of the individual to the goals of the institution. The institution expects and the individual performs. The needs of the person are not in consideration; and his own personal development—that which Argyris calls "self-actualization"—has to result from some other contact, for there is no room for individual priesthood in the institutionalized church.

It was against institutionalism that Martin Luther so strongly objected. This same spirit threatens now in the 1970s to choke out the spiritual life of many formerly dynamic denominations and church groups. The most obvious ecclesiastical example of institutionalism on the church scene today is the ecumenical movement.

According to Douglas McGreggor, "the traditional view of direction and control" must be abandoned if we are going to develop a satisfactory theory of management.[5] The traditional view assumes that the average human being has an inherent dislike of work. Because of this human characteristic, people must be pushed, controlled, and threatened with punishment to get them to put forth adequate effort toward the achievement of organizational objectives. Finally it assumes that the average human being prefers to be directed, wishes to avoid responsibility, has relatively little ambition, and wants security above all.

McGreggor challenges this viewpoint, arguing instead that external control and the threat of punishment are not the only means for bringing about effort toward organizational objectives. *Man will exercise self-direction and self-control in the service of objectives to which he is committed.* Furthermore, commitment to those objectives is a function of the reward associated with their achievement.

Again the application to the local church is obvious. In most cases the work of the church is carried on by an unpaid voluntary lay leadership. What keeps these people on the job? What leads them to commit their time to this kind of ministry when the earthly rewards are obviously lacking? Even the secular theorist has noted it. It is a commitment to the objectives of the church and the reward which will ultimately result.

The wise church leader *will* abandon what McGreggor calls "the traditional view of direction and control" in favor of a policy of drawing people into commitment to Christ and to His work through the church. If it can be done in totally secular industry, it can surely be done in the church as God moves in the hearts of people who "press toward the mark" for Him. All of this has enormous implications for worker recruitment, leadership training and recognition of service through the church.

Harry Levinson suggests that loyalty of people to their organization is secured in different ways today than in the past. It is no longer a question of higher salary, better working conditions, and the security of the position. Since these things are becoming increasingly more common, additional motivation is necessary to secure the satisfactory relationship of leaders to their organizations. How is this to be done?

According to Levinson, it is done "when, in addition, they feel they are being recognized, that they are achieving their goals and are making good use of their capacities, they give more of themselves in the form of innovation, creativity and investment of energy."[6] What suggestions are offered then to church leaders to both understand their relationship to the church's organization and to work more effectively with their subordinates in such a relationship? Levinson suggests the following:

1. Be open with subordinates.
2. Make it possible for people to meet together as responsible adults to solve mutual and common problems.
3. Offer people both the opportunity and the challenge to be responsible both for their work and the fate of the organization.
4. Recognize that loyalty is no longer to be equated with blind obedience.

Is it possible to treat people like this in the church? It is not only possible but mandatory if we wish to achieve harmonious relationships for the glory of Christ and the extension and expansion of the gospel. None of this for one moment replaces the centrality of the Word of God and the Christian's obedience to it and to Jesus Christ. It merely describes the context of human relations in which that obedience and the resulting service take place.

FOR FURTHER READING

Graendorf, Werner C., ed. *Introduction to Biblical Christian Education.* Chicago: Moody, 1981.

Kilinski, Kenneth K., and Wofford, Jerry C. *Organization and Leadership in the Local Church*, Grand Rapids: Zondervan, 1973.

Schaller, Lyle E. *The Pastor and the People.* Nashville: Abingdon, 1974.

NOTES

1. David Riesman, *The Lonely Crowd* (New Haven, Conn.: Yale U., 1967), p. 6.
2. Paul J. Brouwer, "The Power to See Ourselves," *The Harvard Business Review* (November 1964).
3. Peter M. Blau, *Bureaucracy in Modern Society* (New York: Random House, 1956), p. 60.
4. Chris Argyris, "The Individual and Organization: Some Problems of Mutual Adjustment," *Educational Administration*, Walter Hack, et al., eds. (Boston: Allyn & Bacon, 1965), pp. 159 ff.
5. Douglas McGreggor, "Theory X: The Traditional View of Direction and Control," *An Introduction to School Administration* (New York: Macmillan, 1966), p. 166.
6. Harry Levinson, "Whatever Happened to Loyalty?" *Think* (January-February 1966), p. 10.

PART III

Roles and Responsibilities of Church Leaders

10

The Leader as Administrator

ADMINISTRATION is getting things done through people. The study of administration from a scientific point of view has received more attention in recent years than perhaps in any other single period of history. The emphasis now is on the development of a theory of administration which will be operable in all aspects of administrative work, including business, education, industry, and church work.

James D. Thompson, writing in *Educational Administration*, says:

> There appear to be four primary sources of theory for administration: the comments and reports made by practicing administrators, the survey research of teachers, the deductive reasoning of teachers, and the adaptation of models from other disciplines. These are listed in the order in which they have appeared on the scene. The first two are long established and traditional; the last two reflect newer developments.[1]

But Thompson, of course, is writing purely in the secular domain. With a Christian leader, the most essential source of theory for administration is the Scriptures, and in chapter 21 we shall look more closely at what the Bible has to say about the gift of administration.

DEFINITION OF ADMINISTRATION

What is administration? Tead gives a couple of workable definitions. He says that administration is "the direction of people in association to achieve some goal temporarily shared" And again, administration is "the inclusive process integrating human effort so that a desired result is obtained."[2] Both definitions are obviously based on the democratic concept of leadership, since administration cannot be divorced from leadership technique. On the other hand, when compared with an understanding of leadership, administration seems to put more of an emphasis on the task, whereas leadership puts the emphasis on the person. A transactional approach of this dualism is that proper administration involves leadership of *persons* toward a given *task*.

For purposes of this volume, the concept of administration is considered almost synonymously with the concept of management. Both are concerned with the formulation and execution of policy. Perhaps it will be of some help here to designate two other words which relate closely to the concept of administration.

The word *organization* has to do with the setting up of the total task in its various aspects, particularly denoting an emphasis on planning and structuring the activities of the program. *Supervision* places the emphasis upon the leader's guidance of persons within the framework of the task which they hold in the organization. Therefore, it might not be improper to say that a leader organizes the task then supervises group members in the function of that task.

Administration and/or *management* are words of more general character which describe the total process of the leader in relationship to the organization which he serves. Along with Tead's definition stated above, other approaches to describing the administration-management process have been offered. Here are some samples:

> The stewardship of the talents of the people God has entrusted to the leader's care.
>
> The purpose for bringing together of the means and the end.
>
> Not the direction of things, but the development of people.
>
> The work a person does to enable people to work most effectively together.

Creative administration is the opposite of custodial management. The creative administrator seeks new solutions and does not base his decision-making on tradition, or on present or standard controls. He steadfastly resists slogans and clichés which destroy initiative and bog down ideation. He applies himself to the total task, in full recognition that most people in the organization already view administration as a necessary evil to be tolerated but never liked. He combats this misconception with the dynamic of his own leadership and a full awareness that administration is not only a necessary task for the organization's functioning but also a glorious ministry to which God has called him. The creative administrator makes sure that all church workers recognize that the administrative task is a supplement to, and not a substitute for, the supernatural working of the church as organism and organization.

Qualities of the Administrator

From the many characteristics which could be named, Tead selects five which, in his opinion, most clearly define the necessary elements of administration as personal performance.

> My own studies of personal administrative qualities stress the need for (1) sheer physical and nervous vitality and drive, (2) ability to think logically, rationally, with problem-solving skill that "gets the point" more quickly than average, (3) willingness to take the burdens of responsibility for executive decisions and acts, (4) ability to get along with people in a sincerely friendly, affable, yet firm way, and (5) ability to communicate by voice and pen in effective ways.[3]

Notice how Tead's emphasis resurrects the significance of leadership qualities in a focus on the importance of the individual in the administrative process.

Along with the personal qualities defined by Tead, the administrator must recognize the enormous amounts of time which will be spent in what often appear to be the more mundane aspects of this task. He must have time to talk to people about problems which are of great concern to them but may seem very small when compared to the responsibilities which he bears. He must be prepared to serve on and lead committees which play an important functioning role in the organization. Above all, the administrator must have time to think. The importance of initiation and ideation is foundational to creative administration; and since the first law of brainstorming indicates that quantity of ideas breeds quality in ideas, the administrator must have time to produce the quantity.

The emphasis on creativity in administration suggests the value of listing some characteristics of administrative creativity, most of which can be developed by those church leaders, seeking to be better administrators. The following ten are generally recognized qualities:

Sensitivity to One's Surroundings

The wise administrator will be one who notices people, places, events, and the little things that the average person will pass over.

CURIOSITY

The effective administrator was probably the kind of boy who continually wanted to investigate a cave or take apart a machine. Curiosity is the handle on the pump of ideation.

PERSPECTIVE

Unlike the child who can draw a dog larger than the house in which its owners reside, the focus of the administrator has to see things in proper relation to each other.

MENTAL FLEXIBILITY

The progressive administrator is an open-minded person. He listens carefully to other viewpoints and considers their value.

AN ORGANIZED MIND

This is the emphasis Tead is making when he talks about "ability to think logically and rationally." The organized mind can outline well. It sees things in symmetry and parallels.

TOLERANCE FOR AMBIGUITY

The untrained person in the lower echelons of the organization can afford to jump to quick conclusions and be satisfied with simple answers. The executive, however, must not make matters categorical and concrete too soon. A willingness to let one's mind dwell in the abstract consideration of difficult problems is essential to satisfactory decision-making.

INDEPENDENT JUDGMENT

The creative administrator is willing to buck the crowd. Often he stands alone on his nonconformity, bolstered only by the dreams of what he believes can happen in the progress of the organization.

PRIDE OF WORKMANSHIP

A willingness to assume responsibility carries with it the willingness to tack one's own name to a job when it is completed. Pride of workmanship demands giving one's best on any job simply because it will reflect upon the one who did it. In church leadership the further implications of this include a commitment to advance or deter the name of Christ by the outcome of one's work.

ABILITY TO SYNTHESIZE

Because of his mental flexibility and the organizational ability of his mind, the administrator can boil down and summarize both problems and answers. He then, of course, must be able to communicate the conclusions verbally to subordinates and peers in the organization.

ABILITY TO REASON AND ABSTRACT

At heart the administrator is a philosopher as well as a pragmatist. Though he may always appear to be caught up in the mechanical running of the organization, the administrator spends a great deal of time in abstract reasonings as preparation for the nitty-gritty decision-making and supervision which are a part of his everyday task.

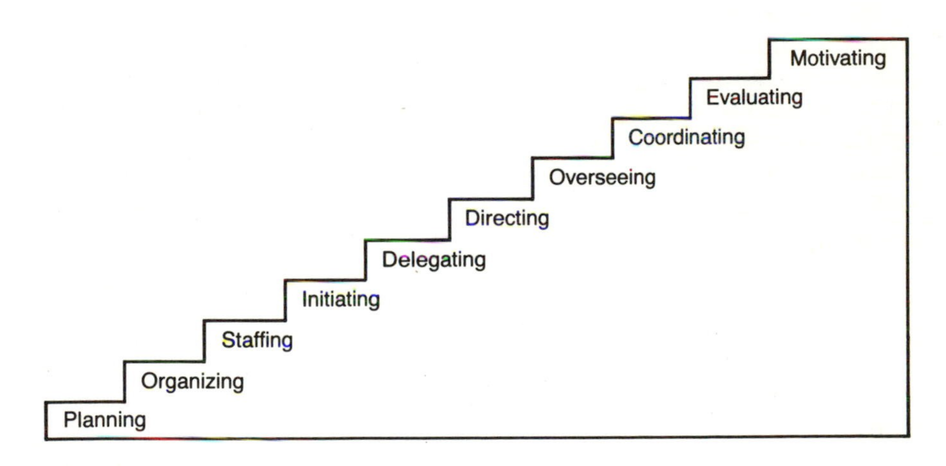

ADMINISTRATIVE FUNCTIONS
Figure 5

Aspects of Administration

Tead suggests ten elements of administration which are generally recognized by students in the field: (1) planning, (2) organizing, (3) staffing, (4) initiating, (5) delegating, (6) directing, (7) overseeing, (8) coordinating, (9) evaluating, and (10) motivating.[4] These elements of administration are backed by biblical examples. Consider their implementation in the administrative tasks of such God-used leaders as Joseph involved in economic administration with the problems of the famine in Egypt; Moses, employing religious administration in the giving of Levitical laws and ordinances; Joshua, a general involved in military administration in the conquest of Canaan; and Solomon, called of God to the task of architectural administration in the building of the Temple as recorded in the book of 1 Kings.

As indicated in Figure 5, the ten aspects of administration are sometimes viewed as stepping-stones in the total administrative task.

There is some confusion inherent in the diagram, however, since it seems to imply that one accomplishes these aspects one at a time almost as if they were developmental tasks. Actually, the administrator is involved in most of the ten most of the time. While directing one project, he may have another on the planning board and still another in the evaluation stage.

Also, the order is not quite as neat as it appears. The motivation stage of the given project may have to precede the staffing stage, and coordinating and directing may go hand in hand. Perhaps it is safest just to say that these are ten categories into which most of the administrator's work can be placed. It becomes essential then for him to understand each of them and how they relate to his particular ministry, whether pastoral or departmental superintendency.

The Administrator in an Instructional Role

The Christian leader as administrator is not only concerned with the smooth functioning of the organization but also with the development of all personnel under his authority. He constantly works with people; and though he may not have a specific classroom situation (of course, many administrators do), he is involved from day to day in an informal instructional process which makes him in reality a teacher. How is it possible to have the responsibility for the achievement of tasks within the organization and yet still maintain a satisfactory relationship with the personnel to serve them in an instructional capacity?

This pinpoints one of the difficulties of leadership, namely, the achieving of desired results while still retaining hedonic tone and individual satisfaction and initiative within the group. It is particularly difficult in Christian leadership since almost all workers are voluntary in the local church.

This problem of a satisfactory authority without authoritarianism is a common one when the leader finds himself in this role of teacher. Tead considers this role so important that he devotes an entire chapter in *The Art of Leadership* to this particular approach. In a terse paragraph near the beginning of the chapter, he states:

> The good leader, one has to conclude, is a good teacher. His role is like the teacher's in helping followers through experiences which bring a changed mind and motive. Emphasis upon this view of his task would be helpful if for no other reason than that it keeps to the front the complete difference between leading and bossing. A good teacher is never a boss. He is a guide helping to start and hold the students' interest toward mastery in a particular field. And this is no less true of the leader.[5]

Tead's chapter further delineates quite specifically the principle that followership will be forthcoming when the led have been brought through experiences like those of the leader which cause them to develop some of the same basic conclusions that he has. Here again, the picture is one of the leader representing a consequence of the needs of a group of people. The leader is no longer some kind of symbol or myth but rather one who can function in response to group goals.

FOR FURTHER READING

Allen, Louis, A. *The Management Profession.* New York: McGraw-Hill, 1964.

Bower, Robert K. *Administering Christian Education.* Grand Rapids: Eerdmans, 1964.

Drucker, Peter. *The Effective Executive.* New York: Harper & Row, 1967.

Engstrom, Ted W., and Dayton, Edward R. *The Christian Executive.* Waco, Tex.: Word, 1979.

Gangel, Kenneth O. *So You Want To Be a Leader!* Harrisburg, Pa.: Christian Publications, 1973.

Johnson, James L. *The Nine-To-Five Complex, or the Christian Organization Man.* Grand Rapids: Zondervan, 1972.

Schaller, Lyle E., and Tidwell, Charles A. *Creative Church Administration.* Nashville: Abingdon, 1975.

NOTES

1. Walter G. Hack, John A. Ramseyer, William J. Gephart, James B. Hack, eds., *Educational Administration* (Boston: Allyn & Bacon, 1965), pp. 86-87.
2. Ordway Tead, *Administration* (New York: Harper, 1959), p. 2.
3. Ibid., p. 59.
4. Ibid., pp. 30-42.
5. Tead, *The Art of Leadership* (New York: McGraw-Hill, 1963), pp. 140-41.

11

The Leader as Organizer

ORDWAY TEAD refers to the organizing aspect of the leader's task as "executive work" and says,

> It remains true that in every leadership situation, the leader has to possess enough grasp of the ways and means, the technology and processes by means of which the purposes are being realized, to give wise guidance to the directive effort as a whole.[1]

The emphasis here is on a coordinating responsibility which works itself out in the construction of charts, the planning of approach, the formulation of working principles, and the integration of all working groups.

Satisfactory administration depends upon effective organization. The organizing phase of the leader's work precedes other administrative duties such as staffing, supervising and delegating. When properly organized, these aspects of the work are facilitated and administrative performance is positive.

PRINCIPLES OF ORGANIZATION

It is important to recognize certain principles of organization which should be followed by the leader as he conducts himself within this realm of his responsibility. Though worded differently by different writers, the following principles are generally accepted: Organization—

IS NOT AN END IN ITSELF

To develop organizational charts and to plan programs for the church's educational program just to delight in the result of one's labors is a distortion of the role of organization in leadership. One of the stultifying diseases which can be contracted by leaders is "drawing boarditis." The symptoms are quite common. The patient spends a great deal of time in his office poring over books, charts, plans and programs which have marvelous aesthetic value but never find their way into an actual ministry with people.

SHOULD ALWAYS GROW OUT OF A NEED

The whole educational program, including objectives, emanates from a recognition of the needs of the people which the program serves. It is obvious, therefore, that the organizational development is inseparably related to those needs. By the same token it is important to say that the organizational structure should be designed to accomplish established objectives.

SHOULD CONTAIN MAXIMUM PARTICIPATION IN DIVISION OF LABOR

The educational program of the church does not belong to the pastor, the director of Christian education or the official board. It is a program "of the people, by the people, and for the people." The wise Sunday school superintendent, for example, will utilize the departmental superintendents by involving them in any planning sessions for the Sunday school. This division of labor relates specifically to the process of delegation which is taken up in a later chapter.

SHOULD BE FLEXIBLE

The church should not be interested in the development of spiritual robots. There is no need for the leader to lay down the mantle of his own thinking nor take off the shoes of individual initiative before he enters the church. Since the program of Christian education set up ten years ago will probably not meet the needs of today, organizational flexibility should allow for necessary changes in that program to achieve more satisfactorily and adequately the goals which are laid out for it.

SHOULD BE DEMOCRATIC IN PROCEDURE

All that has been said previously regarding styles is applicable in regard to the organization's democratic procedure. Autocracy hands down orders from the top and expects that they will be obeyed, whereas democracy allows for open discussion of the issues and a genuine choice by the people involved.

SHOULD DEVELOP CREATIVITY IN THE INDIVIDUAL WORKERS

Far from stifling the individual initiative spoken of above, proper organization finds ways and means of drawing out the creativity of the individual worker. Most churches need all the ideas they can get, and the contribution of every worker to the ideation process is not only desirable but necessary.

SHOULD INCLUDE JOB ANALYSIS AND DESCRIPTION

A job analysis asks the how, why and what of all tasks in the organization. There are five general methods of gathering information for a job description.

Interviews. The leader sits down with the person who is performing the job and discusses the various aspects of it with him.

Questionnaires. The questions must be constructed so as to produce accurate information about how the job is performed.

Observation. The person charged with the developing of the job description watches the individual worker on his task and records his observations of job function.

Job diary. The worker keeps a daily, time-structured record of what he does, how he does it and the results achieved.

External research sources. Job descriptions in education are becoming more numerous, and various sources can be consulted for information and assistance in construction of job descriptions for the church's educational program.

SHOULD INCLUDE RECOGNITION AND UTILIZATION OF PROPER ORGANIZATIONAL CHANNELS

A violation of organizational charts, line-staff relationships and span of control can never produce satisfactory functioning of the program. In order to utilize proper channels, all the personnel in the organization must be aware of the relationship which they sustain with other workers, both above them and below them in line of authority.

SHOULD INCLUDE REQUIREMENT OF RECORDS AND REPORTS

The superior is always accountable for the actions of his subordinates and each person should be accountable to only one superior. The superior is responsible to secure from his subordinates a written report of their achievements and activities as described elsewhere in this volume. Such reports must be regular, complete, specific and neatly prepared.

SHOULD INCLUDE CLEAR CHANNELS OF COMMUNICATION—ORAL AND WRITTEN

When communications in an organization are functioning properly, all personnel receive the information they need in order to do their jobs. Effective communications include provision not only for the sending of the message from the top down but also for the reception of feedback from the bottom all the way up. Faxenian places the responsibility for such communication on the leader himself.

> You encourage your people to communicate effectively first by setting the *example*—by being a good communicator yourself. The second step is to set a *policy* which will draw attention to good communications. The third is to back up your policy with an efficient *management reporting system.*[2]

Note that the emphasis on many of the above is again on the leader's relationship with his group and their reciprocating behavior. Tead argues that "the principle underlying success at the co-ordinative task has been found to be that every special and different point of view in the group effected by major executive decisions should be fully represented by its own exponents when decisions are being reached."[3]

Kilinski and Wofford emphasize that church objectives must be accomplished through the various organizational bodies that make up the structure of the congregation.

> These goals may be influenced in some degree by a formal, systematic approach, such as job descriptions and organizational charts. However, most of the activities of a dynamic organization cannot be programmed or even anticipated. They occur informally. Formal means of building the organization are important; however, they must be viewed as only a first step which inclines a person to fall flat on his face unless other steps keep him in balance.[4]

The Leader Organizing His Time

Every efficient administrator has learned to invest time in order to save time. By spending a certain amount of time organizing and planning his work, the carrying out of his plan achieves his goals much more satisfactorily than if he plunged into his work in a haphazard fashion, taking whichever task happened to be nearest to him rather than following selective priorities. This obviously places the effective leader on a regular schedule whereby he carries out the day's work by moving from task to task. All Christian leaders know that their work is never finished. They may have days which are more productive than others, but the day never ends with the job completely finished. The question of selecting and achieving priorities should properly be scheduled before others in the administrative process.

Numerous simple helps are important to operate on such a schedule. The desk calendar close to the telephone, the master calendar which establishes all the events in an organization, and a pocket notebook serving as a reminder of appointments and commitments are indispensable in the work of the church leader.

Every Decision Has Significant Consequences

The effective leader pays very careful attention to each choice that he makes, realizing that present choices will limit his future actions. The college student, for example, who upon graduation decides not to go on to graduate school may be only verbalizing an immediate preference for cessation of studies. What he is really doing, of course, is placing definite limitations and forms upon his entire future life and ministry. There will be some things which he can do without such education, and other things which he cannot do. The consequences of his initial choice, therefore, are far more extensive than they may appear in the immediate situation.

Another facet of the importance of decisions is the necessity of selecting priorities carefully, a matter which was touched on lightly above. To procrastinate performance of a certain task or even to procrastinate a decision about a certain task may lead to a chain of events which will injure the performance of the administrator. Though it is impossible to generalize a set of criteria here, it is important for every leader to apply an adequate set of criteria to decision-making so that he selects priorities intelligently and logically. Choosing tasks because they are either more difficult or more to the leader's liking is reminiscent of the child who either eats his peas first so that he can follow them with a more pleasant taste in his mouth or the child who pushes them to the side of the plate and procrastinates the tedious agony of swallowing them until everything else on the plate has been eaten. Either approach represents a juvenility which the mature leader cannot afford.

Organization Means Progress Toward a Goal

Just as organization is not an end in itself, so its activities do not function in a vacuum. As the teacher must have specific objectives to be achieved as the result of the teaching-learning situation in the classroom, so the organizer selects for himself and his organization definite goals toward which he moves. One concludes safely, therefore, that a large part of the process of organization is given over to planning which, when properly carried out, produces the realization of goals for the organization and its personnel. A more careful examination of organizational planning is in order at this point.

PRINCIPLES OF PLANNING

An event occurs in ratio to its planning. In other words, the expectation in the organizational process may be that a slovenly approach to the planning for some specific event will reduce the chances of the occurrence of that event. Consider, for example, the college student who goes on from day to day in a little dream world of basketball, student centers and coeds. His chances of graduation grow dimmer with each passing week that he remains in such a state.

Another example of this principle more closely related to the context of this volume is the attitude which many churches have toward vacation Bible school. Assuming that the objective is not only the existence of VBS but also the productive achievement of some specific goals in its operation, the church needs to begin early to lay plans for the vacation Bible school. The first step is an evaluation conducted within a month after the school closes. Then careful groundwork is laid for next year's school with specific planning beginning no later than January or February and increasing in intensity as the spring months draw near. Such an approach has a much better chance of realizing the possibility of an effective school than the church which wakes up to its planning needs in mid-April.

Planning must increase in specificity as the time of occurrence approaches. This principle really states two facts about organizational planning. The first emphasizes that there is such a thing as long-range planning which, in its flexibility, must deal in generalities, but nevertheless does exist. The second is more obvious in the verbalization of the principle; namely, that planning becomes more intense and more specific as the time of the event draws near. Perhaps Figure 6, which is related to the vacation Bible school situation above, will help to clarify the concept.

The effort applied should be commensurate with the result desired. The young man who is just casually dating a young lady does not go out of his way to charm her with flattering words and win her with gifts of flowers and candy. If, on the other hand, he sees in her a potential bride and life partner, he makes a genuine effort to please her, to win her confidence in him, and ultimately to make her his own.

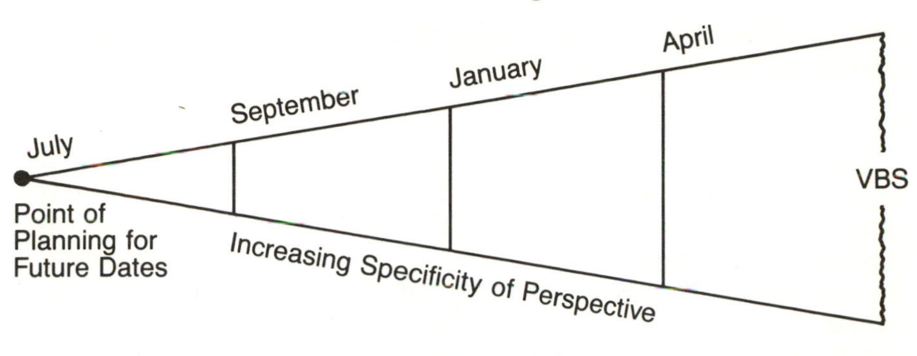

PLANNING SCALE
Figure 6

Planning takes work. The development of a ten-year plan for the educational program of a local church is not something dashed out on a napkin while the pastor and director of Christian education have coffee some Tuesday morning. Nevertheless, if these leaders want certain events to occur and certain goals to be achieved within the church by a defined date, their planning efforts must be directed to that end.

PROCESS OF PLANNING

Planning, like anything else, can be done properly or improperly. The effective process includes the following of certain guidelines which offer the leader a pattern for his planning activities. Though many could be delineated, the treatment here is limited to just three.

The planning process is based on an evaluation of past performance. To continue with the illustration of the vacation Bible school, all that went on in planning from January through the carrying out of the actual school in June had been predicated on the basis of the evaluation procedures of the previous July. If last year's school was quite satisfactory, there may be few changes in the planning for this year. If, on the other hand, last year's school was grossly inefficient, change will be a constant factor in the planning process for the school currently in the organizational development.

The planning process depends upon the setting of realistic goals. Once again it is necessary to emphasize clear and specific objectives. Another adjective has been added here, however, in stating that organizational goals must be "realistic." The creative leader may live in a dream world with his head in the clouds, providing his feet always remain on the ground. For the small, rural church of one hundred to set an attendance goal in another year of one thousand or more is probably grossly idealistic. When realistic goals are set and then accomplished, they provide reinforcement and impetus for the setting of more ambitious goals in the future.

The planning process involves people. This chapter has proceeded succinctly from the statement that "organization involves maximum participation" to the statement that "maximum participation is also important in the specific task of planning." Planning is not an ivory-tower operation. It proceeds through effective interchange of ideas between peer leaders within the organizational structure. Woodrow Wilson once said that efficiency in organization results from "the spontaneous cooperation of a free people." The American Management Association clearly identifies the relationship of people to organizational planning in the following list of "ten commandments of good organization":

1. Definite and clear-cut responsibilities should be assigned to each executive.
2. Responsibility should always be coupled with corresponding authority.
3. No change should be made in the scope or responsibilities of a position without a definite understanding to that effect on the part of all persons concerned.
4. No executive or employee occupying a single position in the organization should be subject to definite orders from more than one source.
5. Orders should never be given to subordinates over the head of a responsible executive. Rather than do this, management should supplant the officer in question.
6. Criticisms of subordinates should, whenever possible, be made privately; and in no case should a subordinate be criticized in the presence of executives or employees of equal or lower rank.
7. No dispute or difference between executives or employees as to authorities or responsibilities should be considered too trivial for prompt and careful adjudication.
8. Promotions, wage changes and disciplinary action should always be approved by the executive immediately superior to the one directly responsible.

9. No executive or employee should ever be required, or expected, to be at the same time an assistant to, and critic of, another.
10. Any executive whose work is subject to regular inspection should, whenever practical, be given the assistance and facilities necessary to enable him to maintain an independent check on that work.

FOR FURTHER READING

Bower, Robert K. *Administering Christian Education.* Grand Rapids: Eerdmans, 1964.

Dayton, Edward R. *Tools of Time Management.* Grand Rapids: Zondervan, 1974.

Dayton, Edward R., and Engstrom, Ted W. *Strategy for Leadership.* Old Tappan, N.J.: Revell, 1979.

Kilinski, Kenneth K., and Wofford, Jerry C. *Organization and Leadership in the local Church.* Grand Rapids: Zondervan, 1973.

Schaller, Lyle E. *Parish Planning.* Nashville: Abingdon, 1971.

NOTES

1. Ordway Tead, *The Art of Leadership* (New York: McGraw-Hill, 1963), p. 116.
2. Hrand Faxenian, "Effective Communications in Small Plants," *Management Aids* (April 1964).
3. Tead, p. 118.
4. Kenneth K. Kilinski and Jerry C. Wofford, *Organization and Leadership in the Local Church* (Grand Rapids: Zondervan), p. 151.

12

The Leader as Decision-Maker

SOME CONTEMPORARY SCHOLARS within the area of management theory have developed the concept that the leader's principle task is not basically concerned with decision-making. They would see him rather structuring conditions which serve as a context in which subordinates and others within the organizational structure make decisions. It would appear to the author that this is not only an idealistic proposal but is actually undesirable.

Since the responsibility for much implementation rests ultimately upon the leader himself (though he may not be involved in actually carrying out the task), the decisions which brought about that implementation should also be traceable to the person who bears the responsibility. It is possible, of course, for the leader to delegate the authority for decision-making, and a future section of this book is given to a treatment of the process of delegation. Suffice it to say at this point that decision-making is here to stay in almost any realm of leadership, and yet it is consciously and/or subconsciously feared by many who hold places of responsibility in the church's educational program.

Certainly the process of decision-making does not occur in a vacuum. It is, indeed, a part of administration and organization. Nevertheless, because of its importance, it is viewed here as a separate function of leadership.

CAUSES OF INEFFECTIVE DECISION-MAKING

Indecisiveness has ruined the effectiveness of many leaders. What produces it? What causes a person who seems to have the ability to perform a given task to stop short of shouldering the responsibility for making decisions? Ineffective decision-making consists basically of two problems: the hesitancy to make any kind of a decision, and the making of an inferior decision. Both of the negative results can be traced to several basic causes.

LACK OF CLEAR-CUT OBJECTIVES

Sometimes leaders don't act because they don't know what to do. Socrates is reported to have said, "We have a much better chance of hitting the target if we can see it." Consider, for example, the case of a Sunday school superintendent faced with the responsibility of structuring a staff meeting for his workers. When should it be held? How often should the workers meet? What should be the content of the meeting? Unless he determines in his initial planning stages the kind of results he wishes to achieve through the staff conference, such questions will be difficult to answer. When objectives are clarified and specified, decisions generally are made in such a way as to achieve those objectives.

INSECURITY OF POSITION OR AUTHORITY

Sometimes a leader is afraid to act for fear of the consequences. Perhaps he is a director of Christian education whose relationship with his pastor is shaky. He is not sure that the pastor understands his ministry and at times gets the impression that the pastor considers his work inferior.

Because of this situation, insecurity develops in the director's mind, and he has difficulty making decisions which might in any way demonstrate his authority in a manner distasteful to the pastor. This problem is complicated when a decision already made is set aside or criticized severely by the superior.

LACK OF INFORMATION

Decision-making is a difficult process when no alternative seems clear or when all alternatives seem equally clear. Sufficient information must be brought to bear upon the problem to narrow the alternatives. Decision-making is inseparably related to the process of selection among alternatives. Dr. H. Edward Wrapp emphasizes this fact:

> Cyert and March contend that in real life managers do not consider several possible courses of action, that their search ends once they have found a satisfactory alternative. My sample of good managers is not guilty of such myopic thinking. Unless they were mulling the wide range of possibilities, they could not come up with the imaginative combinations of ideas which characterize their work.[1]

The obvious purpose of limiting information is to demonstrate that some of the possible decisions which could be made are less valid than others. Sometimes such information will immediately focus on one of the courses of action as the best. At other times the limitations will chop away at the possibilities until only one respectable alternative remains. The leader who does not actively seek all the information he can get before rendering his decisions is crippling himself in the decision-making process.

FEAR OF CHANGE

Whether or not they admit it, many leaders actually desire to retain the status quo. Since most decisions produce some kind of change, they represent a constant threat to present modes of operation. The more radical the decision, the more change will result in the form of subordinate reactions. In other words, what will people say? The attitudes and opinions of people are of great significance, particularly in church work. But when these expected attitudes or opinions become detrimental to effective decision-making, they must be brought into proper perspective.

DECISION-MAKING AND THE PROBLEM-SOLVING PROCESS

When decision-making is viewed basically as a process of problem-solving, certain steps can be delineated which describe the mental activity through which the leader passes to solve the problem. This activity can be outlined in different structures, and the following is only one proposal. The first three steps represent the process of *studying the decision;* the next three steps relate to *making the decision;* the seventh and final step has to do with *testing the decision.*

ORIENTATION TO THE SITUATION

How does the leader get familiar with the background of the problem and the context under which the problem has arisen? First of all, we might assume that he has some general experience in the area. In fact, his experience and knowledge are the very factors which have elevated him to the position of leadership.

A director of Christian education, for example, is confronted with a problem. "Mr. Smith is threatening to resign from his Sunday school class. Will you speak to him and see if you can talk him into keeping the position?" The trained director of Christian education brings to the solution of that problem an understanding of adult psychology, an appreciation of the factors that motivate Smith's action to either stay or leave, and some notion of what he will do if Mr. Smith does leave the class.

In addition to this experience and general knowledge, there is the perceptive analysis of the situation which provides a quick mastery of the facts and attitudes involved. This is much more characteristic of the seasoned leader than it is of the novice. The pastor who has been working with his people for fifteen or twenty years can size up a situation rather quickly before making any decision concerning it. The process of orientation involves administrative intuition, intelligence and training.

One important feature is that during the first step of problem-solving decision-making, deferred judgment is practiced. This is the study stage, not the acting stage. It is not necessary yet to know exactly what one will say to Smith or who will take the class if he would leave. What is important is to attempt to understand why he is threatening to leave, why the informant happens to be the one telling the story, and what other variable factors are operative in the whole climate of the problem.

IDENTIFICATION OF THE KEY FACTS

It is important for a leader to realize that he probably will never have all of the facts in any given decision-making situation. It is necessary for him to sift through the information which he receives in order to isolate and study the *key* facts. To this particular step of the process he brings acute observation of the problem and a careful sifting of the information which he has gathered.

One facet of this second step is effective questioning of people involved. Such questions should be *open rather than closed;* in other words, they should be questions which allow the respondent to tell what he knows rather than answer yes or no as if he were in a witness box at a trial. They should be *leading rather than loaded* questions. Instead of "gunning" for answers which he thinks he may want, the leader should ask as a catalyst, hoping to stir important facts loose as people reply to the questions.

Such questions must always be *cool rather than heated.* Some problem situations may aggravate the leader. Parents will often reply to children, "Why did you do that?" using that question almost in the act of scolding rather than really attempting to get a legitimate answer. Effective questions are also *planned rather than impulsive.* It may be necessary for the leader to think by himself for a while before actually plunging into the problem that has been brought to him. Whom should I ask? How should I approach him? When would be the best time to raise the issue?

These and similar questions he will ask himself as he prepares to identify the key facts.

One additional criterion might be added to the evaluation of problem-solving questions. They must be *window questions rather than mirror questions.* That is, they should be geared to allow the administrator to look through clear glass into the problem rather than to reflect any opinions or prejudices that he may be tempted to bring to the problem (e.g., "Old Smith always has been a hard fellow to get along with, and I almost hoped he really would quit this time.").

IDENTIFICATION OF THE MAJOR PROBLEM OR PROBLEMS

Of course, not all decisions are problem-solving decisions. Some merely relate to the selecting of a course of action. When an identifiable problem is present, however, it *is* essential to identify that problem before it can be solved. How does one go about such identification?

Look for causes rather than symptoms. The leader must assume that all behavior is motivated. Sometimes the motivation may be internal, such as sin in the life; sometimes it may be external, caused by friction with other people in the organization, difficulties and discomforts at home, or some physical malady of which the particular worker may be unaware. The whole process of counseling may enter the decision-making situation at this point.

Isolate the sections through deductive reasoning. Deductive reasoning proceeds from the general to the specific. If the general problem is that Smith might quit his Sunday school class, the specific problems might be that he is not getting along with his wife and is therefore disgruntled about almost everything, that he dislikes the adult-department superintendent, or that some other matter has been a consistent problem for him week after week.

Open-mindedly weigh all the evidence. It is näive to assume that all of the evidence which presents itself in response to any given problem is accurate in its relation to fact. Even evidence provided by his superiors must be weighed by the leader as he considers the identification of the real problem.

PROPOSAL OF POSSIBLE CAUSES AND THE IDENTIFICATION OF ONE OR MORE

The emphasis in the first part of step three was in the identification of causes. Now we focus on the delineation and specification of those causes. The leader should be able to verbalize the problem and the proposed solution. Edge's criteria for good teaching objectives can well be applied to the proposal of problem causes in the decision-making process. The solutions offered should be "brief enough to be remembered, clear enough to be written down, and specific enough to be achieved."[2]

Sometimes a specific problem will never appear as the leader works his way through steps three and four of the decision-making process. When that is the case, he proceeds to generalize on past successes, applies the process of inductive reasoning, and makes his decision in the light of the accepted principles of sound administrative theory.

LISTING OF PROBABLE SOLUTIONS

The listing of probable solutions in the problem-solving process consists of engaging in creative brainstorming, the rules of which are simple and the rewards usually quite satisfactory if the process is carried out properly. Note the following guidelines:

In brainstorming, quantity breeds quality. This is another way of saying that the more ideas a person has, the more likely he is to come up with some good ones. The process of ideation is basic to the process of problem-solving, and the leader must approach this task with sufficient openness of mind to allow many and varied possibilities to present themselves.

In brainstorming one solicits as many ideas from others as possible. This is a throwback to the questioning process of step two. Here, however, the goal is not merely to identify the facts involved but to procure suggested solutions from people who may have something solid to offer. It is, in effect, a continual asking of the question, What would you do in this situation?

Brainstorming does not allow for evaluation at this point. Should the leader ask for the opinion of a co-worker regarding a situation, receive a reply, and then react by saying, "Well, that wouldn't work in this situation," he is rendering insignificant some information which may be of help to him in the next step, and also stifling future contributions from his colleague. At this point in the process, the assumption is made that almost anything will work to solve the problem. When the list of possible solutions is as long as it can be made, one begins to evaluate the solutions.

TESTING, SELECTION AND APPLICATION OF THE BEST SOLUTION

In the testing of possible solutions, the leader asks such questions as, Will it work? Will it be accepted? Is cost a prohibiting factor? Is this solution permanent or merely a stopgap action? On the basis of his testing process, he selects the solution which best seems to fit the case. A Christian leader makes this selection in the context of prayer, an understanding of biblical principles of Christian leadership and church work, and the sovereign leading of the Holy Spirit in his life.

Wrapp suggests that the selection of proposals requires a high tolerance for ambiguity. He defines three evaluatory questions which can be applied in the testing and selection of a solution.

> In considering each proposal, the general manager tests it against at least three criteria: First, will the total proposal, or more often will some part of the proposal, move the organization toward the objectives he has in mind? Second, how will the whole or parts of the proposal be received by the various groups and subgroups in the organization? Where will the strongest opposition come from, which group will furnish the strongest support, and which will be neutral or indifferent?
>
> Third, how does the proposal relate to programs already in process or currently proposed? Can some parts of the proposal now in front of him be added on to a program already under way or can they be combined with all or parts of other proposals in a package which can be steered through the organization?[3]

When the solution has been decided upon and a decision has been made to move in a certain direction, the leader must avoid vacillation or obvious apprehension about the decision. Very often such a reaction will exist within his own mind, but confidence toward colleagues and subordinates is important in the implementation of the decision. Also it is essential that all affected parties be informed immediately.

EVALUATION OF THE DECISION

In the threefold process, the decision has been studied, made and now must be tested. Did the problem disappear? If not, was the failure due to the decision itself or to some fault in the implementation? At what point did the flaw enter the application process?

Should the leader ever change his mind after a decision has been made and implemented? The answer is both positive and negative.

When the decision should not be changed.

1. Obstacles are blocking progress but it is possible that, in time, implementation will be successful and the problem will be solved.

2. Some people are reacting negatively, but there is no reason to believe that their actions in any way represent error in the decision.

3. Implementation is difficult but possible. Difficulty can be expected, and there is no reason for turning back.

When the decision should be changed.

1. New facts are available which alter the identification of causes or specification of solutions for the problem.

2. The situation has changed and the context in which the decision was made has been sufficiently altered to render the former decision inadequate under the new conditions.

3. Faulty reasoning becomes apparent in the decision-making process. The leader will make mistakes but, if he is wise, will recognize and correct them even if it means withdrawing a decision previously made.

Evaluating Oneself as a Decision-maker

Decision-makers are made and not born. The process of leadership evolvement described elsewhere in this volume indicates that there are traits and gifts which may be an aid in some persons to enable them to function effectively as leaders in certain situations, but that most of management behavior is a process of adequate training.

The following checklist can be used by the reader to evaluate himself and others in his organization relative to the adequacy which they bring to the decision-making process. Questions may be answered "yes," "no," "most of the time," or "rarely."

1. Are the objectives of the organization clear to me?
2. Are the objectives of the organization clear to my subordinates?
3. Do I carefully consider the overall goals of the organization when making decisions?
4. Am I able to specify individual goals for myself as well as general objectives for the organization?
5. Do I tend to shrink from decision-making or do I face each decision with the courage and conviction necessary to handle it competently?
6. Am I able to analyze my own problems clearly?

7. Do I generally have difficulty in analyzing the problems of others for whom I am responsible?
8. Am I able to distinguish the cause properly?
9. Am I able to verbalize understandable statements about organizational and individual problems?
10. Do I have sufficient rapport with colleagues and subordinates to effectively gather information for the decision-making process?
11. Does decision-making occupy an inordinate amount of time, that is, do I spend too much time gathering information and procrastinating the actual decision itself?
12. Am I consistent regarding the accuracy of the facts in every decision-making situation?
13. Do I face the issues open-mindedly, honestly considering the various alternatives?
14. Do I generally achieve good acceptance of my decisions by the personnel in the organization?
15. Are people agreeing to implement my decisions because of fear of my authority or respect for my judgment?
16. Do I tend to get unduly involved in my decisions to the point that I react emotionally if someone challenges the wisdom of the decision?
17. Am I too unilateral or dictatorial in decision-making (i.e., do I fail to delegate decisions that can be delegated)?
18. Do my decisions show a logical pattern of consistency over a period of time or does each one relate only to itself rather than to the whole?
19. Am I able to help other people make decisions as well as make them myself?
20. Am I able to evaluate the wisdom and correctness of the decision?

It is important for the leader to realize that decision-making is a process which lacks permanency; that is, decisions made today which may be entirely correct and profitable for the improvement and progress of the church's educational program, may need to be rethought and revised within the next five years, if not sooner. It is necessary to build into the decision-making process a feedback which will provide a long-run, continuous testing with options for revision as the events brought about by the decisions fall into place. Drucker pinpoints this necessity:

> Decisions are made by men. Men are fallible; at their best their works do not last long. Even the best decision has a high probabil-

ity of being wrong. Even the most effective one eventually becomes obsolete. . . . One needs organized information for the feedback. One needs reports and figures. But unless one builds one's feedback around direct exposure to reality—unless one disciplines oneself to go out and look—one condemns oneself to a sterile dogmatism and with it to ineffectiveness.[4]

FOR FURTHER READING

Bower, Robert K. *Administering Christian Education*. Grand Rapids: Eerdmans, 1964.

Schaller, Lyle E. *The Decision-Makers*. Nashville: Abingdon, 1974.

NOTES

1. H. Edward Wrapp, "Good Managers Don't Make Policy Decisions," *Selected Paper Number 26* (Chicago: University of Chicago Graduate School of Business, 1967), p. 8.
2. Findley B. Edge, *Teaching for Results* (Nashville: Broadman, 1956), pp. 92-93.
3. Wrapp, p. 8.
4. Peter F. Drucker, *The Effective Executive* (New York: Harper & Row, 1967), pp. 139, 142.

13

The Leader as Group Facilitator

As I indicated in the Introduction, the 1970s have produced a greater volume of literature on the subject of Christian leadership than any other decade in the history of the church. Most of the books have been somewhat general, attempting to help Christian leaders in a broad range of work situations, but some have dealt with specific aspects of church leadership and even the administration of church education. The work of Engstrom and Dayton has been notable in the first category (general Christian leadership), and the ready pen of Lyle Schaller has contributed a great deal to understanding church leadership. Because Schaller is more specific and tends to take a more group-oriented approach in leadership philosophy, his works are more useful in helping us understand the role of the leader as group facilitator.

Focus on Group Dynamics

People behave differently at different times because their perception of things to which they react differs. Changed perceptions then lead to changed behavior. The individual feels satisfied when he realizes that his perception and consequent behavior is considered correct in the eyes of the group to which he belongs.

The concept of group dynamics is certainly not new, but the scientific research which now brings an organized focus on the concept is a recent emphasis in the total field of the study of leadership. Andrew W. Halpin, a prominent social scientist, speaks clearly to this issue in one of his most important books on administration.

> This dilemma of definition emerges from the fact that we have incorporated into the term "leadership" both descriptive and evaluative components, and have thus burdened this single word (and the concept it represents) with two connotations: one refers to a role and the behavior of a person in this role, and the other is an evaluation of the individual's performance in the role. We have

compounded this confusion even more by conceptualizing leadership as an essentially innate capacity of the individual manifested with equal facility, regardless of the situation in which the leader finds himself. Yet Stogdill has shown that the trait approach to leadership, as it has been used in most studies reported in the literature, has yielded negligible, and often contradictory, results. Sanford has aptly summarized the situation.

From all these studies of the leader we can conclude, with reasonable certainty, that: (a) there are either no general leadership traits or, if they do exist, they are not to be described in any of our familiar psychological or common-sense terms, (b) in a specific situation, leaders do have traits which set them apart from followers, but *what* traits set *what* leaders apart from *what* followers will vary from situation to situation.[1]

In these paragraphs, Halpin gives clear expression to the dominant attitude of the "establishment" in leadership studies today. When one has recognized this emphasis, there are several questions that immediately come to the fore and to which attention must be given. For example, one wants to know what is a "group"; and further, how can a good leader relate himself to his group?

Defining the Concept of "Group"

According to one management specialist, Bernard Bass of Louisiana State University, "A group is a collection of individuals whose existence as a collection is rewarding to the individuals."[2] In other words, according to Bass, a collection of moths around a light bulb is not a group, for the plurality is not important. On the other hand, the lamb and its mother, though only two, do represent a group, for the sucking of the lamb satisfies both.

Bass goes on to indicate that his concept of a definition for the word *group* is shared by others. Cattell, for example, defines group as "an aggregate of organisms in which the existence of all is utilized for the satisfaction of the needs of each."[3] And Gibb, like Cattell, views groups as mechanisms for achieving individual satisfaction through interaction.[4] Other elements which contemporary research shows are usually found in groups include such things as perceived unity, common goals and face-to-face interaction.

People have always worked in groups throughout the history of the world, but thorough studies of their collective behavior have only been conducted in the midtwentieth century. Malcolm

Knowles, who was the executive director of the Adult Education Association from 1951 to 1959, has cooperated with his wife, Hulda, in a very helpful book introducing the concept of group dynamics.

The book indicates that the phrase "group dynamics" can be used in four different ways. It can refer to the complex forces which are at work in all groups at all times, consciously or unconsciously; it can refer to a field of study and becomes then "a branch of the social sciences concerned with using scientific methods to determine why groups behave the way they do"; it can refer to that body of basic knowledge about group behavior that has accumulated from past research; or it can refer to that body of applied knowledge of technology which translates into practical methods of group work.[5]

As the concept of group dynamics is being used in these paragraphs, it is most closely linked with the first of Knowles' suggestions and focuses on such things as personality interchange, the process of becoming, and the general dynamic of atmosphere when people who are interested in the same thing and motivated toward the same goals confront one another in the process of moving toward those goals.

Variables in Group Work

Another very helpful book representing a reflection of contemporary research in leadership is an Association Press publication by Ross and Hendry entitled *New Understandings of Leadership*. One of the emphases of this book is on group variables and the authors point out that the major group variables which relate to the work of the leader are *size, attitude of members,* and the *nature of the task.*

Among the minor variables relative to group work are *background of the members,* the *life-span of the group,* and whether *participation is required or voluntary* on the part of the members. The point here is that the leader, whether emerging from the group, elected by the group or appointed by a higher authority, must constantly take into account these variables which to a great extent condition the results of group activity.

Effectiveness and Interaction

"Group effectiveness" is a term describing the extent to which groups reward their members. "Group attractiveness," on the other hand, refers to the extent to which they are *expected* to reward their members.[6] Contemporary research tells us that the "effects" in a group are accomplished in direct relationship to interaction or noninteraction. In other words, interaction is an essential ingredient for effectiveness. Satisfactory interaction by the members of the group will result in behavior which changes both sooner and to a greater extent than if such interaction had not taken place.

Interaction also brings reinforcements which encourage the group to progress. If only isolated, individual activity takes place in the absence of external reinforcement, the tendency to change behavior will be reduced instead of increased. Consider for an example the Christian teenager who is not allowed to think for himself. All of his convictions and conclusions about Christian living are the results of the teaching of parents and pastors. The growth in maturity of such an individual will be considerably more retarded than the growth of one who has been taught to develop his own convictions within the light of the Word of God and at the prompting of the Spirit of God.

An obvious conclusion here is that the more forcible and maximum the effectiveness of a group becomes, the less formal leadership is needed to reach the group goals. Immediate effectiveness increases interaction, and interaction increases effectiveness.[7]

If effectiveness is so important, the leader must recognize the obstacles to effectiveness and know how to combat them. It is also important that the leader see that he is not *building* effectiveness as much as *unleashing* something probably already inherent in the group. This is the basic meaning of group dynamics.

Some of the more common obstacles to effectiveness include such things as favoritism toward one or more members of the group, inadequate reward for participation or services rendered in and to the group, lack of recognition of an individual either by the leader or by the group, meaningless tasks (sometimes called "busy work") given to group members, and inefficient procedural practices in group activity.

Group Climate and Identity

Another important concept of group work is called "group climate." This refers to the atmosphere that exists within the group. Current research reveals that the ideal group climate is a permissive, noncritical atmosphere in which each member is fully accepted in the group and feels free to speak his own personal opinions and ideas. In this climate, contributions are accepted and evaluated on the merit of the idea and not on the status of the individual.

"Group identity" is also deserving of mention at this point. Ordway Tead, long a leader in the study of leadership, in one of his earliest books says that a leader ought to capitalize in every way possible on the conscious awareness of each member that he is in the group. Members also must recognize their relationship to other members of the group upon whose support and cooperation they can rely. Tead argues that "the deep psychological need of identification, of being known as one of those following an admired leader in a worthy cause—this remains as a genuine need without which there is real loss of a sense of group unity."[8]

Leader-Group Relations

Earlier in the chapter a question was raised relative to the leader's position in relation to group activity. It is important to return to that question at this point. If, indeed, leadership is not some kind of an innate trait with which some people are born and some are not but is rather a series of services which a member of a group performs for and in that group, the traditional concepts of leadership need to be reexamined. Traditional authoritarianism needs to be replaced by a move toward shared leadership, which encourages member participation and responsibility.

Such leadership consists of coordinating efforts toward group goals rather than dominating group activities. If the leader acts as a boss, he plans, controls, directs and decides. The group submits and conforms with some kind of passive assent. On the other hand, when the leader acts as a guide, he seeks to allow and to encourage the *group* to plan, control, direct and decide. A guide is one who leads or directs another in any path or direction, showing the way by accompanying or going on in advance.

Leadership Styles

Some writers define three leadership-followership styles. The *nomothetic style* places emphasis upon requirements of the institution, its role and its expectation rather than the needs of the individual. The *idiographic style,* on the other hand, concerns itself with the requirements of the individual. The third is a balance between these two and an attempt to bring them together into some kind of a synthesis. It is referred to as the transaction or *transactional style*. Such a leader would attempt to bring into harmony the rationales of an institution or organization and the human needs of its workers.

Other designations of leadership styles in relation to group behavior describe authoritarian leaders, laissez-faire leaders, and democratic leaders. The first represents an extreme emphasis on the organization or perhaps even the leader's own interests. The second describes the kind of leader who refuses to give any help at all.[9]

Preference is indicated in most of the literature today for the democratic type of leader who states the issue clearly, refrains from always stating his own opinion, makes sure that everyone has an opportunity to participate, keeps the discussion on the subject, summarizes when necessary, and guides the group toward agreement by consensus. The result is a group decision rather than an individual decision which is ratified actively or passively by the group.

Stages of Group Growth

The nature of a group largely determines the type of leader needed to lead that group. Groups are rarely static but rather possess changing needs and interests to which a leader must be sensitive. Two phases or levels of group growth have been identified.

THE CENTRIC GROUP

Centricity marks a group at its immature or infancy stage. The individuals in the group are more concerned about their own needs and goals than those of the group. Group attractiveness may have been somewhat high, but effectiveness is very low because members of the group are not "pulling together."

Such a group is characterized by wide heterogeneity in objectives and interests. Incompatibility with each other and sometimes with the leader is quite obvious. There is a general resistance to authority, lack of uniformity, and a minimum of personal freedom. A domineering leader is sometimes necessary for a group like this until the group itself can pressure the individual out of his preoccupation with personal needs and goals.

THE "RADIC" GROUP

"Radicity" marks a group as concerned with more than just its group activities. Such a group exhibits a conscious altruism and receptive teamwork which are actually contagious to new members coming into the group. There is some conformity in *behavior* in a radic group but certainly not in *ideation*. Selfishness may be surrendered to the achievement of group goals, but individuality is not sacrificed on the altar of collectiveness.

A group progresses from centricity to radicity through careful leadership which takes the emphasis off of force and authoritarianism and extends the limits of freedom as the group is able to effectively use that freedom. Sometimes self-inspection on the part of the group, and evaluation of its motives and objectives, are valid procedures.

The local church ought to be a *radic group* rather than a *centric group*. New members coming into the congregation ought to feel the dynamic of the people who are already working together there in the bonds of Christ and the fellowship of the Holy Spirit. Such a group ought to be both attractive and effective in carrying out its ministry.

It is important to recognize that the church is a group which contains within it many subgroups. An analysis and understanding of group dynamics and behavior is therefore essential for any church leader who desires effectiveness in his ministry. The flexible definitions and scope of this chapter pinpoint the conclusion that almost any contact with people comes under the wide category of group study recognized today.

FOR FURTHER READING

Bass, Bernard M. *Leadership, Psychology, and Organizational Behavior*. New York: Harper, 1960. (Reprinted 1973, Greenwood.)

Johnson, Douglas W. *The Care and Feeding of Volunteers*. Nashville: Abingdon, 1978.

Schaller, Lyle E. *Assimilating New Members*. Nashville: Abingdon, 1978.

———. *Effective Church Planning*. Nashville: Abingdon, 1979.

NOTES

1. Andrew W. Halpin, *Theory and Research in Administration* (New York: Macmillan, 1966), pp. 82-83.
2. Bernard M. Bass, *Leadership, Psychology, and Organizational Behavior*, p. 39 ff.
3. Ibid., pp. 40-41.
4. Ibid., p. 41.
5. Malcolm and Hulda Knowles, *Introduction to Group Dynamics* (New York: Association, 1959), pp. 11-13.
6. Gordon L. Lippitt and Edith Seashore, *The Leader and Group Effectiveness* (New York: Association, 1962), pp. 11-25.
7. Bass, pp. 128-32.
8. Ordway Tead, *The Art of Leadership* (New York: McGraw-Hill, 1963), p. 177.
9. Bass, pp. 126-28.

14

The Leader as Board or Committee Chairman

SOMEONE ONCE FACETIOUSLY REMARKED that an elephant was a horse put together by a committee. The obvious intended criticism of this remark is that committee work is notoriously slow, needlessly laborious and hopelessly confused. Unfortunately, many boards and committees in local churches fit the image. Though the image resembles reality, however, it does not have to be so. Committee work can be extremely profitable and even enjoyable if it is approached properly.

The values of committee work should be obvious. Certainly it is significant that group ideation is greater than the thought processes of one man attempting to solve a problem. Second, in Christian circles the fellowship of God's people working together to accomplish God's work in God's way should make committee activity a monthly highlight for church educational leaders. Third, the presentation of joint-thinking on a controversial issue has more authority and can develop more respect than the attitude of one man, even if he is the pastor or director of Christian education. It is high time in the organizational patterns of the evangelical church for us to stop throwing stones at the utilization of committees and recognize instead the great contribution they can make toward achieving the objectives which the local church sets out to accomplish.

Perhaps it is necessary at this point to distinguish between a board and committee. For purposes of this chapter, a board will be considered a higher level, policy-making group; and a committee will be viewed as a recommending group, usually appointed by and responsible to a board.

The newest edition of *Webster's New World Dictionary* designates a board as "a group of administrators." A committee is defined in the same volume as "a group of people chosen, as from the members of a legislature or club, to consider some matter or to function in a certain capacity." In a college one generally finds a board of trustees or curators and administrative committees which are responsible to that board. In the church the board of Christian education could have several subcommittees as in Figure 7.

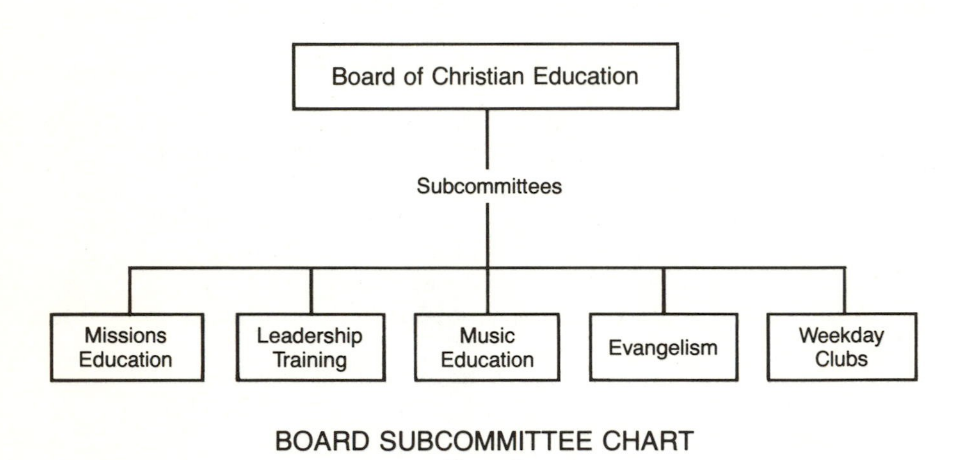

BOARD SUBCOMMITTEE CHART
Figure 7

Various Functions of Boards

The first step to proper function as a board or committee chairman is to recognize the essential nature of the board and its objectives. The second step is to convey this information accurately and adequately to all of the board members. A misconception of one's role on a board leads to inferior performance and possibly even to a distortion of the ministry which church board work should be.

No doubt the various functions of boards could be categorized in any number of ways, but one of the clearest would be to specify the board's relationship to the policies of the organization. In a local church situation, the official church board (deacons, elders, trustees, etc.) has the responsibility for total church policy. At the board of Christian education level, responsibility for policy narrows to authority over the educational aspects of the local church work.

BOARDS DETERMINE POLICY

A very familiar example of this aspect of board work can be observed in the function of any school board at any level. Operation of the school, its objectives and goals, enlistment of personnel, long-range planning for the institution, and all other aspects of policy-making are the board's responsibility. Recommendations may come to the board from faculty and administrative groups, but in the final analysis the board is responsible for setting the policy.

A number of steps should be followed in determining institutional policy, whether in school or church. A review of past policies and present procedures is necessary to analyze where the institution stands at any given time. Confirmation of goals and objectives and the gathering of information about various aspects of the program are essential to arrive at intelligent decisions regarding the direction that the institution should take. This is one reason boards should be securing thorough reports from all administrative officers in the organization.

When a decision is reached by the board regarding policy determination, the negotiation phase sets in, and it becomes necessary to communicate the decision and how it will be implemented through the personnel in the organization. Generally speaking, it is not the role of the pastor to determine church policies any more than it is the college president's responsibility to determine the direction of an institution of higher education. Both are obviously influential on and to the board, but the board itself is the policy-making body.

BOARDS IMPLEMENT POLICY

Actually the statement that boards implement policy is not entirely true, since much of the policy set by boards is implemented by staff throughout the organization. Nevertheless, the necessity of setting in motion the wheels of implementation rests on the board; and sometimes in certain aspects of board work, the policies will actually be executed by the board. It is at least consistent to say that the board is responsible for seeing that the policy which they have predetermined is satisfactorily implemented. Blumenthal refers to Celso and Pratt in dealing with the relationship of the board and staff in the organization:

> Considerable progress has been made by many organizations in achieving a satisfactory balance between board and staff functioning. We have come a long way from an earlier day when it could be

said about boards that "they are usually the product of consistent effort of a well-entrenched secretary, to place about him a group of ornaments who will never fail to say yes"; that the "board runs the whole works. . . . This kind of a board, when conducting a case work agency, for instance, insists upon disposing of every individual or family by solemn vote"; or that boards have been preoccupied with drawing up by-laws "frequently so worded that the authority of the professional worker is carefully curtailed while the actual functioning of programs involved is delayed and hampered."[1]

BOARDS ADVISE POLICY

The board may, in effect, delegate its policy-making functions on occasion, passing down to others in the organization the responsibility for carrying out to a decision certain issues under study by the institution. In such a case the policy itself is formulated by a lesser body, but that formulation is a result of authority delegated by the board.

Consonant with transmitting the authority may very well be some counsel regarding how the authority should be used and how the decision should be made. The board then makes it own influence felt in the decision, even though not exercising its policy-making function directly.

BOARDS ASSUME LEGAL RESPONSIBILITY FOR POLICY

A church congregation is really a legal nonentity which must be represented in some legal way. Generally these representatives take the form of some sort of board, such as a board of deacons or trustees. Legal documents (i.e., land deeds, incorporation papers, etc.) are signed by the board members, who are thereby assuming the legal responsibility for the organization's proper functioning. Should difficulties arise, the court cannot render judgment against the entire congregation, nor against the pastor, but against those representatives whose names are affixed to legal documents.

Board and Committee Membership

Although innumerable technical differences are found in church and institution constitutions, it is probably safe to say that boards secure their membership in three basic ways:

1. Self-perpetuation. A self-perpetuating board may or may not have a limiting-tenure clause; that is, board members may remain indefinitely or the constitution governing the board's ac-

tivities may call for a limited stay on the board. What is characteristic of such boards, however, is that when a vacancy occurs it is filled by election among the board members themselves. They add to their own ranks those whom they wish to serve. Many college boards operate in this way, as do some church boards, particularly in churches with a noncongregational polity.

2. Popular election. This is probably the most common approach and is represented by the Congress of the United States. Congress certainly is a policy-making body, and its members hold office by the choice of their constituents. There is almost always a tenure limit on board membership which is secured by popular election.

3. Ex officio status. Members who serve on a board by virtue of their office are neither appointed nor elected to that role. The pastor, for example, should be a member of every board and committee in the church. He holds that membership because he is the pastor, not because any of the boards or even the congregation have invited him to do so.

Proposals given earlier for constructing a board of Christian education lead toward that board being composed almost entirely of ex officio membership. The superintendent serves because he is superintendent, not because he is elected. Now, in a sense, there is a combination of these in the church which elects its superintendent popularly by congregational vote. He would then become superintendent first and, by virtue of being superintendent, assume his role on the board of Christian education. His membership then consists of a combination of election and ex officio status.

Limited tenure is certainly a valid and recommended procedure for almost all boards. Board members tend to become entrenched in policy-making roles if no boundaries are placed on the time of serving. Several obvious problems can occur when lifetime board membership is practiced. First of all, the board members tend to grow old together, and a stagnancy in terms of creative thinking and aggressive planning will develop at the highest level. Board members tend to develop vested interests when they know that they can protect them over a long period of time.

Still another problem, particularly for the church, is the extrication of a board member when such radical action is deemed necessary by the church. If, for example, a lifetime deacon falls into immorality, it becomes incumbent upon the church to exercise discipline and to remove him from his office. If, however, he has held the office for some twenty or twenty-five years and has developed a following among the congregation, such action may split the church and cause extreme difficulty.

Unlike boards, most committee memberships are appointive in nature. It is not impossible to have a permanent committee, but again most committees are up for review and change of personnel periodically. Appointments to committee membership are generally made by the chairman of the board from which the committee emanates. Membership may be approved at some other level, such as the entire board or even the congregation as a whole, but usually it is not elective. Committees, therefore, are responsible to the boards from which they have been drawn. They study, discuss and make recommendations, but rarely operate in a policy-making role. Sometimes committees are brought together only for a specific task which is obviously short term. Such a committee is referred to as ad hoc.

One characteristic of a competent board chairman is his ability to assess the interests and abilities of various board members as he places them on strategic committees. Once a committee has been formed, it also needs a chairman; and that position can be filled again by appointment from the board chairman or by an election among the committee members themselves.

Productivity of any committee is largely related to the aggressiveness and thoroughness of its chairman. He bears the responsibility of calling the meetings, helping the committee to analyze the problem on which it is working, motivating the committee members and drawing them into the ideation process, and assisting the committee in formulating an accurate and thorough report for the board. The chair is the strategic position of any board or committee, and most new educational leaders will soon occupy that chair, and continue to do so many times through the years of their ministry.

THE CHAIRMAN'S ROLE IN BOARD AND COMMITTEE WORK

The board chairman is usually not the chief executive of the organization. Though some pastors may chair their own church boards, it is probably not good policy. It is almost unheard of, for example, for a college president also to be the chairman of the board of curators of that institution. Blumenthal writes about executives and subexecutives, pinpointing three different levels of authority in relation to the board's work: the executive or subexecutive, the president and the chairman. For the sake of simplicity in the following paragraph, consider the pastor as the executive and the director of Christian education or Sunday school superintendent as subexecutive:

> The subexecutive's relation to the committee at its meetings is generally similar to that of the agency executive to the board at its meetings. He is a partner with the committeemen in dealing with the business of the committee. There is mutual consultation, free and critical discussion, a wholesome process of give-and-take, and a recognition by the worker and the committeemen of their complementary roles. The subexecutive exercises indirect leadership: he too acts as stimulator, information giver, and interpreter. He also uses when necessary the direct approach: he is adviser, recommender, advocate, interpreter, and information giver. As in the relationship of the agency executive to the president, the subexecutive at committee meetings works primarily through the committee chairman, reinforcing the chairman where the need for so doing develops.[2]

Perhaps it would be helpful to delineate the chairman's work in six major categories of function which would be applicable either to a board or a committee chairman.

PLANNING

The chairman is responsible for structuring board or committee meetings and gathering any necessary information to be disseminated there. The most strategic aspect of the planning function is the construction of the meeting agenda. This should be prepared in mimeographed or printed form and distributed to committee members, and should contain sufficient information so that they know in advance of the meeting what they will be expected to decide upon when they arrive.

A good suggestion for agenda preparation is to use action verbs which genuinely define what the committee will be doing. Examples might include "discuss," "decide upon," "propose," and so forth. Ample announcement should be given in advance of the meeting so that every member of the board or committee is fully aware of his responsibility to attend. Time limits should be set and kept. The announcement of the next meeting should appear either on the agenda or be clearly stated at the meeting itself and then appear in the minutes.

PRESIDING

The committee chairman is not a dictator but rather a catalyst for group discussion and action. Normally he would not vote on an issue unless his vote was necessary to break a tie. His task is to state the business clearly, keep the discussion moving, secure necessary motions from the floor and, as much as possible, refrain from influencing committee members with his own opinion.

It may be assumed that the very fact that he is chairman indicates his influence over the thinking of his colleagues. If a persuasive personality is added to the authority of the chair, the chairman's influence can actually overwhelm the committee situation. However, this is not his role, and to do so is a perversion of the office. Bennett's comments relative to leading a conference group are helpful here:

> Now, start the general discussion with an overhead question. Make certain that, at this point, you don't encourage the "head starter," the man who has the solution already for you without further discussion. Try to have the group develop factors bearing on the problem: facts, assumptions, definitions, criteria. Get group consensus for a plan of attack, how all conferences will proceed toward a solution. Your list of matters for discussion, the agenda, will probably be accepted for this purpose. But don't force it upon the group. Group approval on a plan of attack is essential.[3]

APPOINTING

As indicated above, it is often the responsibility of the chairman of the board or committee to appoint other officers, committee members or subcommittee members. This task must be carried out with the full realization of the goals of the institution in mind. Within the context of a local church, it cannot become a political feather-bedding operation.

Such appointments should generally be made publicly in the meeting and recorded accurately in the minutes. With the appointment should be a complete description of what is expected of the individual or committee.

REPRESENTING

The board chairman is spokesman for the entire board. In some situations this may require a great deal of public speaking, in others a certain amount of writing. It is essential that the chairman be, to some extent, a communicator able to express accurately the board's policies and attitudes to the organization's larger public.

In the case of the age-group committee structure shown earlier in regard to the board of Christian education, the chairman of the age-group committee represents all the church functions regarding that age group. The information which he must have for this task is expansive, and his ability to represent his people and their work accurately is a major criterion by which his effectiveness as a chairman is to be judged.

COUNSELING

The counseling role of a board or committee chairman leans more toward the function of advising than personal counseling. He may (and should) on occasion attend meetings of those committees which he has appointed. On those occasions he offers some words of counsel as to how the committee can best achieve its objectives and carry out its functions. He may meet personally with the chairmen of the committees or subcommittees, encouraging them in their work and guiding them in the fulfillment of their tasks.

The chairman is also responsible for spending some counseling time with lesser officers of the committee, that is, the vice-chairman, secretary, treasurer, and others. Once again it becomes apparent that his knowledge of the total committee structure and function must be thorough if he is to perform his role as chairman satisfactorily.

REPORTING

Although committee reporting will not be done by the chairman, he is nevertheless responsible for that reporting since the meeting minutes are the official record of what the board or committee is doing. The chairman will be very careful in the choice of a secretary. When the secretary has been appointed or elected, the chairman will give careful guidance to make sure that the minutes are recorded accurately and in proper style.

Since there is no virtue in spending a great deal of time in board or committee work just for the sake of having long meetings, a distribution of printed or mimeographed minutes in advance alleviates the drudgery of reading through the minutes at the beginning of every meeting. It is also necessary to make sure that the minutes are prepared in a concise fashion so that committee members do not need to wade through an enormous amount of material to find out what really went on in the meeting.

Along with this oral reporting and the keeping of meeting minutes, the chairman is responsible for the preparation of written reports describing the work of his group. These reports should pinpoint the policy issues and make them intelligible to the larger group served by the board or committee. Oral reports must be studiously avoided, but condensations in written form can be successfully used when carefully prepared. The image of the board and its work is developed and maintained by the reports given to the public. The necessity for accuracy and clarity in such reporting is obvious.

The Responsibility of Board and Committee Members

The chairman should assume some responsibility for teaching the membership of his group to function properly in their roles. This proper functioning begins with regular and faithful attendance at all meetings. It continues with some kind of preparation for the group meetings which may take the form of study of issues, careful perusal of the agenda, or even the preparation of reports or items for which the individual has been made responsible.

As the meeting progresses, the members should be involved in asking discerning questions about the policy isues that are on the floor. Constructive participation in the deliberations of the committee is essential on the part of every member. Of course, every committee has its negative members; and they usually exhibit one or more of the following characteristics:

1. Ability to see only one side of an issue. This is the person who rides the hobby horse and makes sure that the committee realizes the dominant importance of his position. There may be several views on the subject which are apparent to other committee members, but the only way this fellow can see to go is the direction in which he is headed. He is like a horse with blinders.

2. An emotional fixation on some issue or side of an issue. This describes the man who throws aside an empirical approach to the committee's examination of problems and operates from an emotional rather than a volitional concern for the issues at hand. He is most likely to be offended and perhaps even walk out of a committee meeting if things are not going his way.

3. The tendency always to vote with the chairman or majority. Even though the chairman may exercise careful discretion in not

offering his own opinion on the issues, this "rubber stamp" member will seize upon a position which he thinks the chairman prefers and vote that way. On the other hand, if he sees the majority building up for a certain vote, he will immediately jump on the band wagon and be counted with the larger group when the vote is taken.

4. Nonparticipation in board or committee discussion. This member may have a heart of gold and a head full of ideas regarding the issues that the committee faces, but neither can serve the committee in its work since their proceeds can't make an escape through a closed mouth. He may attend committee meetings regularly, listen carefully on all issues and vote diligently. But in the very necessary part of committee function, which requires a dissection of issues and review of various options, he is of no value simply because he does not contribute.

5. A tendency to monopolize the conversation. This is the opposite problem from that described above. Overloquaciousness can reap one of two possible results for this committee member. Either his arguments are persuasive and he draws support, or his much talking builds enmity among the other committee members. Even if they favor a given issue, they might vote against it because of his enthusiastic support. In the final analysis he may be easier to control than the person who never says anything, but the chairman must be careful not to allow such a member to dominate the meetings.

6. A begrudging expenditure of time. Every committee has clock watchers who are more interested in a motion for adjournment than they are in the business at hand. They probably are serving on the committee for the prestige that may be involved and are very little concerned with genuinely effective participation. If this attitude is displayed only once or twice in a year of committee work, it can be quickly excused; for all members of the committee will have occasions on which it will be necessary for them to watch a time schedule carefully. If, however, it characterizes a member's attitude at every meeting, he probably should not be asked to serve again.

Certainly voting on issues is a significant part of the responsibility of board and committee members. That voting must not be a careless affirmative, nor should it be a constant negative just to make sure that nothing passes unanimously. It is a voting according to conviction based upon a thorough understanding of the component parts of the issue. Anything less is a perversion of the significance of committee membership.

Perhaps, in closing this chapter, attention could be called to the fact that participation in a board or committee provides not only for contribution of the individual to the work of the group but also for the influence of the group on the individual member. Blumenthal suggests that

> the behavior of the board member is influenced not only by his own background, motivations, and attitudes. It is influenced also by the behavior of the board as a group. As has been indicated, man—by his very nature—is a social being; he is not independent of his environment. The attitudes of the group tend to modify his behavior, and few persons will behave in ways contrary to that of their group. (It is not implied that the board member's behavior is entirely controlled by the board group.)[4]

The hedonic tone of the group is largely set by its chairman. He is responsible for developing a satisfactory climate in which a free and open discussion of controversial issues can be carried out without any loss of love among the board or committee members. He is responsible not only for the attractiveness of the group but also for its effectiveness. Board and committee work is not a pedantic, mechanical vestige of bureaucracy. It is a challenge in group dynamics of the highest order.

FOR FURTHER READING

Apps, Jerold W. *Ideas for Better Church Meetings.* Minneapolis: Augsburg, 1975.

Madsen, Paul O. *The Person Who Chairs the Meeting.* Valley Forge, Pa.: Judson, 1973.

Sutherland, Sidney S. *When You Preside.* Rev. ed. Danville, Ill.: Interstate, 1969.

NOTES

1. L. H. Blumenthal, *How to Work With Your Board and Committees* (New York: Association, 1954), pp. 12-13.
2. Ibid., p. 36.
3. Gordon C. Bennett, "How's Your Conference I.Q.?" *Manage* (1967), p. 4.
4. Blumenthal, p. 60.

15

The Leader as Counselor

PROFESSOR HOWARD HENDRICKS of Dallas Theological Seminary suggests that counseling is the ministry of one individual seeking to help another individual to recognize, understand, and solve his own problems. Several things immediately greet one in scanning the definition. First of all, counseling is a ministry. Second, it is a *personal* rather than a *group* ministry. Third, if properly conceived, it is not something which one individual does *for* another individual but consists rather of the enlistment of the counselee in drawing conclusions for his own life.

Note also that the general threefold division of problem-solving as counseling identifies three distinct steps in the process:

1. The counselor must first of all recognize the problem himself. Often a counselee will talk about many issues in a conscious or subconscious attempt to obscure the real problem with which he is most bothered. It becomes the responsibility then of the counselor to thread his way through the cloudy maze of confusion and delineate the actual problem at hand.

2. The second step is to help the counselee to recognize his own problem—and understand it. This is a process of drawing out. In fact, a proper handling of this second step in the counseling process marks the distinction between directive and nondirective counseling. The directive counselor sees the answers and gives them to the counselee. The nondirective counselor attempts to lead the counselee to helpful solutions which he can select for himself.

3. For the Christian counselor, the solving step in the process is based on both biblical and realistic solutions to the counselee's problems. This is not a proof-text or a prayer-promise kind of ministry but a solid thorough understanding of what God in His Word has to say about the varied and many problems of human existence. When a counselee has seen the proper direction which he should take in a given situation, the actual application of a biblical solution to a human problem takes place when the Holy

Spirit manipulates the human will placed at His disposal to actually perform in accordance with the commands of God's Word.

Some will encounter this chapter with a degree of skepticism. "What," they will ask, "is a chapter on counseling doing in a book on leadership and church education?" The answer is simple. Very few church workers will be professional counselors. Almost all, however, will sooner or later have to engage in the ministry of "helping." In a very real sense, every Sunday school teacher is a counselor if he or she is performing satisfactorily in the teaching role. Certainly every pastor, whether he is trained for it or not, must devote a significant proportion of his ministerial time to the work of counseling. Indeed, his effectiveness in the pulpit may very well be related to whether or not he can help people on a person-to-person basis in their daily living. The reader is urged to go well beyond the bounds of this chapter in preparation for his counseling ministries. Even the books listed at the end of the chapter are just a beginning.

General Qualifications of the Counselor

When people are in trouble, they turn to certain kinds of people for help. Is there anything to be learned from an observation of the characteristics of the people who seem to have successful ministries in helping others through counseling? Obviously there is, and the resulting qualifications are not profound personality traits found only in very special types of people. As a matter of fact, they are rather common things which almost any of us can really offer with the help of God's Holy Spirit. Consider whether the following items describe you.

MUST HAVE CONTROL OF HIS OWN EMOTIONAL DIFFICULTIES

It has been the author's observation that many times students who have pronounced neurotical trends are the very ones who wish to specialize in a study of psychology and perhaps psychiatry. Whatever the implications of that observation (if it is valid), one thing is foundational. If such people are going to be used of God to minister to the problems and needs of others, it will only be after they have been able to control the pecularities and deviations of their own personalities.

MUST BE A GOOD LISTENER

The listening process of counseling is therapeutic in itself, but its purpose is even greater. Listening enables the counselor to identify and understand the counselee's problem. It helps him to know the counselee as a person. It indeed lays the groundwork for all and any help that will result from the counseling interview. Like teaching, counseling is more than telling; it depends on thorough and adequate feedback.

MUST SHOW HIMSELF A FRIEND

Friendship between the counselor and counselee is even more essential in lay counseling than in professional psychiatry. A person who pays forty or fifty dollars an interview to go to a professional psychiatrist realizes that it is a business proposition. Even though the psychiatrist may be warm and friendly, there is probably very little delusion that he is anything more than a professional doctor whose interest in the patient is less than personal. A Sunday school teacher or youth sponsor, on the other hand, counsels because he has demonstrated himself to be a trusting confidant of the persons to whom he ministers. Obviously this involves the keeping of confidences and the warm receptivity that encourages the people to seek out the leader for help with their problems.

MUST LEARN TO ASK CATALYTIC QUESTIONS

The questioning process is crucial to effective counseling. It is, in effect, a part of the listening process and will be discussed as such in later paragraphs. The counselor dare not appear overly inquisitive or even just plain "snoopy." The purpose of his questioning is to uncover the real issues involved in the problem and to direct the thought of the conselee in considering his own problem.

MUST LEARN TO SEE THINGS IN TOTAL PERSPECTIVE

Thought fragmentation is characteristic of emotionally disturbed people. They develop fixations on one event or idea and do not seem to be able to bring it into proper relationship with other matters. In short, they do not see the whole picture. This is why it is sometimes difficult for a counselee to identify his own problem properly, though it may be quite obvious to many of his friends and family. The particular problem at hand may have a history that is deeply rooted in the relationships and interrelationships of a very complex society.

MUST RESIST THE TEMPTATION TO BECOME AN ADVISOR

This temptation is complicated by the fact that the counselee may very well wish him to be so. At times it may seem like the logical action is simply to tell a counselee what he ought to be doing. Such telling, however, takes the burden of thinking through the problem off the shoulders of the counselee and makes him even more dependent upon his new-found "adviser." Should the solution be effective, the counselee will return again and again for answers to other problems of ever increasing complexity. If the advice proves inadequate, however, the blame for any negative results can always be passed along directly to the adviser by simply saying, "I was only doing what he told me to do."

MUST REMAIN A FRIEND REGARDLESS OF THE COUNSELEE'S DECISIONS

In the nondirective process, the counselee may very often yield to the voice of Satan and the influence of the sin nature within him, choosing paths which are obviously opposed to the will of God. The counselor faces the temptation of discouragement. He wants to turn away from one who has so clearly rejected the will of God for his life. But to turn away from the counselee at this time only guarantees that he will never again come for help. There are many such disappointing moments in the ministry of counseling, but the counselor must live with them and through them and seek to be of help to the counselee another day as God gives the opportunity.

The Process of Christian Counseling

Counseling is most effective when the interview is initiated by the counselee. Therefore, the leader who wishes to function effectively in this role should recognize some of the basic principles involved in the process.

Narramore in *The Psychology of Counseling* answers the question "To whom do they turn?" when speaking of the possibility of functioning in the counseling role within a Christian context. He suggests seven "drawing characteristics" of successful counselors:

> People usually turn to someone they know.
> People take their problems to someone they like.
> People take their problems to someone they respect.
> People are most likely to seek help from Christian leaders who indicate their interest in counseling.

People turn for counseling to someone whom they feel is competent.
People take their problems to someone who observes professional ethics.
People turn to the counselor who knows God.[1]

THE COUNSELOR MUST BE AVAILABLE

The counselor should be available to the counselee. This involves more than a geographical location; it represents an entire attitude toward other people. The "available" counselor is not *too* eager to initiate interviews with people whom he thinks need help. He may use an appointment system, but he is not so bound to it that his relationships with other people take on the sterile atmosphere of a medical office.

Availability also implies an allowance of sufficient time for each person so that his problem can be satisfactorily handled. Most interviews should not run over a half hour to forty-five minutes. The place of counseling should be reasonably quiet and certainly private enough to allow conversation without a third party listening in.

THE COUNSELOR MUST ESTABLISH RAPPORT

The leader who has operated his leadership role within a democratic framework, who has involved people and related to them satisfactorily from day to day, will be the leader who stands in a satisfactory position to counsel them. Other leaders, students, and people in the church will have already felt the attitude of confidence toward the ability and commitment of the properly functioning leader. Nevertheless, in the actual counseling interview it is necessary to allow the counselee to relate to him in an informal way. This he does by being relaxed and natural during the interview, by avoiding professionalism in attitude and jargon, and by attempting to speak in the counselee's language at all times.

THE COUNSELOR MUST LISTEN CAREFULLY

Certainly the greater amount of the counselor's time is spent in the listening process. The act of talking is, in itself, cathartic to the counselee, and his comments provide information which should lead the counselor to ascertain the real problem. Occasionally it may be necessary to question the counselee for clarification and additional information on certain crucial points.

Some counselors find it helpful to take notes, unless, of course, this procedure is particularly offensive to the counselee.

The wise counselor will never minimize the problem which the counselee describes, and he will never show shock at anything the counselee tells him. Throughout the listening process he is constantly alert for underlying causes of the problem, such as physical exhaustion, emotional distrubances, financial difficulties, and evidence of sin in the life, which might be causing a guilt complex.

Psychologists and professional counselors are somewhat divided on how much the counselor should actually direct the counselee's thought. A certain amount of this is not only desirable but necessary. Some counselees tend to excuse their rebellion, problems, and sin because of the way others have treated them in the past. Throughout the listening process, the counselor should be allowing the Holy Spirit to develop biblical answers to the problems before him.

THE COUNSELOR MUST WATCH CAREFULLY

How does the counselee approach the counselor's desk or person? Is he demonstrating timidity or courage in his approach? How is the counselee dressed? Is there evidence of carelessness and sloppiness in personal care? If there are various chairs in the room, where does the counselee choose to sit? What is his general behavior and reaction to the counselor's presence? Does he appear unduly nervous? Does he appear to be covering up a fear with blatant, yet false, self-confidence?

Rollo May suggests that facial expressions are extremely important and contends that the ends of the mouth on a neurotic person inevitably turn down. While the counselee is speaking, there may be occasional "Freudian slips" which serve as clues or glimpses into what is really going on in his mind. Since the subconscious remembers outstanding events of life, the events can occasionally break through the conscious control of what one is saying. When they do, they may represent important insights that the counselor cannot afford to overlook.

THE COUNSELOR MUST KNOW WHEN TO REFER

It is important that every lay counselor understand something about the nature of mental illness as a parallel to physical illness. There are many kinds of counseling which the church leader can, and should, involve himself in. Vocational counseling for young people, general educational counseling, problem-solving, and therapeutic counseling to a degree are all areas in which he will probably be working at one time or another. The area of psychotherapy, however, is best left to the psychologists and psychiatrists who have special training in this work. Referral at the proper time and to the proper person is as important a part of counseling as any other step in the process.

There is no hard and fast line between normality, neurosis and psychosis. It is rather a question of degrees, determined by whether the individual can manage his emotional conflicts or whether functional personality disorders become not only unmanageable but actually take control of the person himself. Blessed is the church leader who can refer someone who is mentally ill to an effective Christ-centered Christian psychologist or psychiatrist in or near his city.

Does the church leader really have a responsibility for counseling? Must he really take the enormous amount of time that is necessary to render an effective counseling ministry? Knowles writes that counseling is always a part of a supervisor's role.

> You as a supervisor have the responsibility for the productivity of your work group. Whenever any problem arises which interferes with productivity or affects the morale or cooperation of your group, you are authorized to attempt to eliminate the problem.
>
> However, every problem does not require counseling but all problems do have one thing in common—a cause. Your responsibility is to investigate the problem to determine the cause and then decide whether counseling may be of help.
>
> Remember—counseling is used to eliminate causes of behavior rather than to eliminate the problem. If the problem is solved but the cause remains you can be sure that you will be faced with the same problem later. You have everything to lose or much to gain depending on how you handle a counseling situation—if you aren't sure or don't know—get help.[2]

Success in counseling is determined by a number of things: the degree of rapport which is obtained, the effectiveness of the technique used by the counselor, and the willingness of the counselee to be helped. In Christian counseling, of course, there resides a supernatural ingredient, both in the life of the counselor and the counselee, which introduces a dimension that can never play a role in secular counseling. The Christian leader must capitalize upon this plus factor as he applies the power of the Word of God, the supernatural dynamic of prayer, and the vitality of the Holy Spirit in every counseling situation that he enters.

FOR FURTHER READING

Brammer, Lawrence M. *The Helping Relationship.* Englewood Cliffs, N.J.: Prentice-Hall, 1973.

Collins, Gary R. *How To Be a People Helper.* Santa Ana, Calif.: Vision House, 1976.

———. *The Joy of Caring.* Waco, Tex.: Word, 1980.

Crabb, Lawrence W. *Basic Principles of Biblical Counseling.* Grand Rapids: Zondervan, 1975.

Drakeford, John W. *People to People Therapy.* New York: Harper & Row, 1978.

Miller, P. H. *Peer Counseling in the Church.* Scottsdale, Pa.: Herald, 1978.

Tournier, Paul. *To Understand Each Other.* Richmond: John Knox, 1967.

Welter, Paul. *How To Help a Friend.* Wheaton, Ill.: Tyndale, 1978.

Wright, H. Norman. *Training Christians To Counsel.* Denver, Colo.: Christian Counseling and Enrichment, 1977.

NOTES

1. Clyde M. Narramore, *The Psychology of Counseling* (Grand Rapids: Zondervan, 1960), pp. 14-17.
2. Malcolm E. Knowles, *Training and Development Journal* (April 1967), pp. 4-5.

PART IV

Administrative Process In the Church

16

Organizing the Educational Program of the Church

More than twenty years ago Vernon R. Kraft wrote, "The church should learn from the business world the value and efficiency of unity in activity."[1] Yet thousands of churches are still satisfied with slovenly organized church programs and obvious disunity among the various branches of the educational ministry.

Two key words that represent the sine qua non of local church Christian education are "correlation" and "unification." Unification, in relation to local church Christian education, might be defined as "the adequate functioning of the various aspects of the program in their respective areas toward a single goal." Correlation has reference to the relationship that those various agencies or ministries sustain to each other. Hence it is obvious that correlation and unification are practically inseparable, and yet they focus on two different aspects of organization in educational programming. Perhaps the illustration below can clarify their relationship.

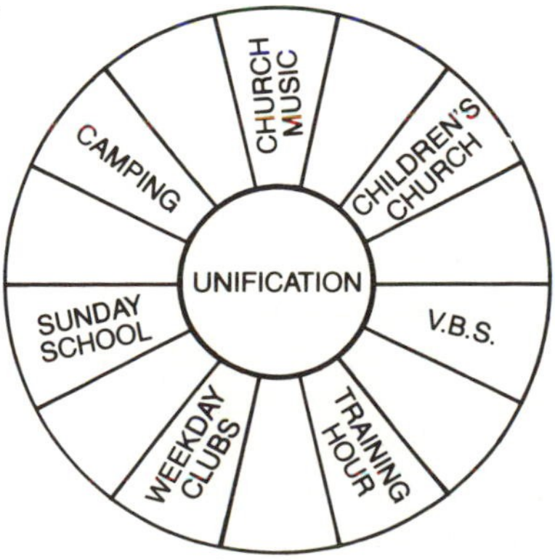

UNIFICATION—CORRELATION WHEEL
Figure 8

In the diagram the various spokes of the wheel represent the agencies of education in the local church. The hub of the wheel represents *unification* in that it is the center point from which all of the agencies emanate and which they share as their common base. The wheel would not be complete without the rim, which here illustrates *correlation*. It joins all the agencies together, causing them to function as the program whole.

One's theory of Christian education organization depends on what he believes in the fields of philosophy and theology. Only after the issues covered in chapters 1-4 have been honestly met, will we be ready to face the issue of organization. Even then, before we get to the specifics about aspects of organization, a word about theory is important. Wyckoff, for example, suggests three questions which must be answered: "How and by whom shall the program be planned and organized? How and by whom shall the program be managed? How and by whom shall the program be supervised, that is, standardized, evaluated, and systematically improved?"[2]

Any organizational framework palatable to evangelical church leaders must be theologically accurate, educationally adequate, and yet simple enough for all participating workers to understand.

The Primacy of Unification

Unity is a characteristic of good organization, whether in the large corporation or the small local church. As Vieth has reminded us, "It is not enough that the various programs in which our boy participates should each make a vital contribution to his education. These several contributions must be worked into a single pattern which has unity."[3] Unification is not to be confused, however, with uniformity. A variety of programming must meet the needs and objectives of the local church and therefore must be indigenous rather than handed down categorically from some ivory-tower planning center.

Too often the various educational agencies of the church spring up in a more or less spontaneous manner as the church's ministries expand. The Sunday school is usually the first, followed by evening youth groups, vacation Bible school, or some type of club program. The order is insignificant but the result is what causes trouble.

Such a church prides itself on a full program of educational activities for all age groups. Actually the church has a multiplicity of programs because the purpose and pattern of such programs have never been tied together in a single whole. Of this type of situation Heim says, "There is much overlapping of objectives, duplicating of programs, overstimulating of pupils and workers, neglect of certain areas and groups, fragmentariness and disunity of experience and, at times, conflicts in and rivalry for loyalty."[4]

The concept of unification is not new. Cummings was writing about it over twenty-five years ago. He spoke prophetically when he said, "The church will not truly be unified educationally, until all of its official family is united in a common educational purpose, and are willing to submit their problems of program and administration to the educational method."[5] Nevertheless, it is necessary for Christian education officers to continue emphasizing the principle until the local church catches the vision and implements the values.

ANALOGY TO THE BODY

The apostle Paul in 1 Corinthians 12 compares the church as Christ's spiritual body to man's physical body. The theological significance has obvious application to the church program of Christian education. Such a program can also be considered a "body," with the educational units as members of that body. As the spiritual body of Christ is singular, so the educational program draws its oneness in the church from the process of unification. (Review chapter 4.)

UNIFICATION AND THE CURRICULUM

The traditional definition of curriculum, now accepted by very few, focused only on the content or actual material used in education. D. Campbell Wyckoff defined curriculum as "selected educational procedures used to further the achievement of the aim of Christian education."[6] Lois LeBar suggests that "the term denotes the *activity of the student* as he runs through various experiences which involve content."[7] An important part of curriculum then is an organized effort on the part of teachers or leaders to relate truth to the lives of students.

The traditional battle over curriculum theory wages between two rather extreme positions. One is the pragmatic approach which centers the curriculum in life and pupil experience. The other is the more traditional Herbartian concept which focuses on content with accompanying application.

The traditional system begins with known Bible facts, presents new material, associates the new with the old, generalizes, then seeks to apply the matter to life. Pragmatism, in contrast, focuses on a problem, suggests a solution, gathers data, accepts the solution, and then seeks to relate the matter to God's revelation. The problem with the traditional system is that it too often does not reach the point of application. The problem with the twentieth-century emphasis is that it often omits the authority of the Scripture.

The evangelical educator will immediately lean toward the traditional system because he is evangelical, and yet he recognizes the value of relating to pupil needs because he is an educator. Lois LeBar, therefore, concludes that

> An authentic curriculum of Christian education incorporates insight from both these extremes. A curriculum is not Christian unless it involves interaction with the Word of God; it is not educational unless this interaction results in spiritual growth for the pupil.[8]

Curriculum coordination becomes part of the task of organizing the church's educational program. The church's task is to meet needs because it is constantly in relationship to life. The child must have instruction in obedience to parents, cooperation in groups, reactions to circumstances, adjustment, and many other areas of development. The young person needs to see the Word of God related to problems of the Christian in the world, life in the public school system, social development, future plans and service for Christ. Adults should hear God speaking on issues of parenthood, community life, current social crises and his individual personal problems.

All of this cannot be achieved through any single agency such as Sunday school or training hour but must be carefully built into a satisfactory relationship between the various organizations or agencies servicing any given age group. Effective coordination not only provides for the meeting of objectives and the filling of needs but also avoids duplication while developing a progressive and challenging program of education which can meet the increased levels of education and technology in contemporary society.

UNIFICATION AND THE STUDENT

Students should be led to recognize the church as a unit and all the parts of the educational program as branches of the same tree—not as separate organizations. Of course, not all individuals will support the same aspects of the program because interests and time will control participation. This does not, however, give license for distinction and even enmity between the Sunday school and evening youth groups or among any other agencies in the church.

Children, youth, and adults must be offered a single educational program. Vieth correctly complains that "all too often the church has permitted a two-fold or even a three-fold appeal, urging them to 'join the young people's society' and to 'come to Sunday school' and to 'join the church.' Often the programs themselves have overlapped."[9]

UNIFICATION AND THE CHURCH'S TOTAL MISSION

Christ loved the church and commissioned it to evangelize the world and educate its believers. Such a program must include systematic training, biblical nurture, and lifelong learning. The church's task is greater than any one agency, even if that agency is as large and popular as Sunday school. Total nurture experiences require multiple and varied learning situations constructed to meet needs at all age levels.

Paul charged Timothy to educate others as he had taught Timothy. On another occasion he told the Ephesian elders that he had not shunned to declare unto them the whole counsel of God (Acts 20:27). Paul had held intensive training for these church leaders over a period of three years.

Perhaps it's not too imaginative to suggest that Paul's program of Christian education operated on a unified basis to accomplish the teaching of the whole counsel of God in three years. If the church today would emulate its early leader, it must set about to accomplish its task through a careful process of organization, curriculum selection, and procedure adaptation which represents total Christian nurture.

DEVELOPING AN ORGANIZATIONAL CHART

A perusal of books on administration will uncover a variety of approaches to charting any organization. But a familiar pyramid of lines and boxes arranged in ascending or descending order of importance is the standard format of an organizational chart.

Byrne suggests several different kinds of charts, each dealing with the subject of organization at some length.[10] Some church leaders think the cold and empirical pyramid of boxes is an unspiritual approach to the church's spiritual problems. Nevertheless, order and proper function are characteristic of the omnipotent God and therefore ought to mark His church.

According to Winks,

> The true purpose of the Orgchart today is a reversal of the Bauhaus *obiter dictum* that form follows function; it is designed and distributed to induce function to follow form, being—in itself—an instrument of change. If this were not so, it would be no more worthy of study than the corporate telephone directory.[11]

The following four charts were prepared by me for various churches and are presented here because each one illustrates a different facet of charting Christian education in a local church. Chart No. 1 is a simple four-function program in a church which operates with an official board as the ruling body. Chart No. 2 represents a congregationally governed church with seven functions all represented on the board of Christian education. Chart No. 3 demonstrates government through presbytery and session and also shows an emphasis on age-group committee organization rather than functional organization. Chart No. 4 is similar to No. 2 but includes a full-time director of Christian education in the organization.

In developing an organizational chart, two major steps are important in the process. The first step is to chart the organization as it presently exists. On the basis of this information, knowledge can be brought to bear upon change (improvement). Winks notes:

> C. A. Efferson, an Orgplanner of national renown, has lucidly described the genesis of an Orgchart: "First," he said, "you study the work to be done, the functions, the long-range goals, and then draw the ideal organizational structure, forgetting personalities. The next step is to take the ideal structure to top management and determine what compromises have to be made—mainly because of personalities. However, the ideal structure is not thrown away when the official chart is published. It is kept and continually updated so the future planning does not run counter to the ideal structure, compounding mistakes and necessitating further compromises."[12]

Obviously Winks was talking about a business enterprise rather than a church; nevertheless, the principle of relationship of the organization to personality is a valid one. One thing might be added here. The organizational chart when finalized should be circulated completely among all the teachers and workers in

Chart 1

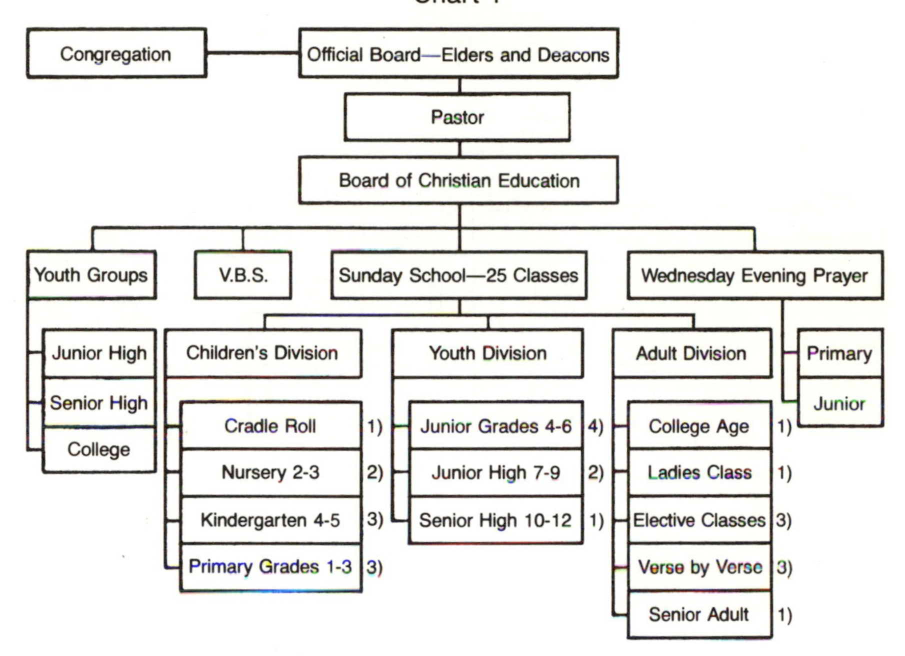

FUNCTIONAL CHART—BOARD CONTROL
Figure 9

Chart 2

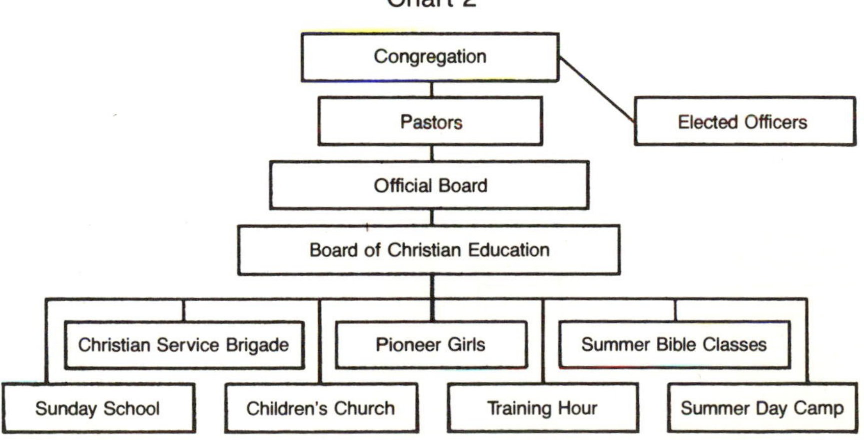

FUNCTIONAL CHART—CONGREGATIONAL CONTROL
Figure 10

Chart 3

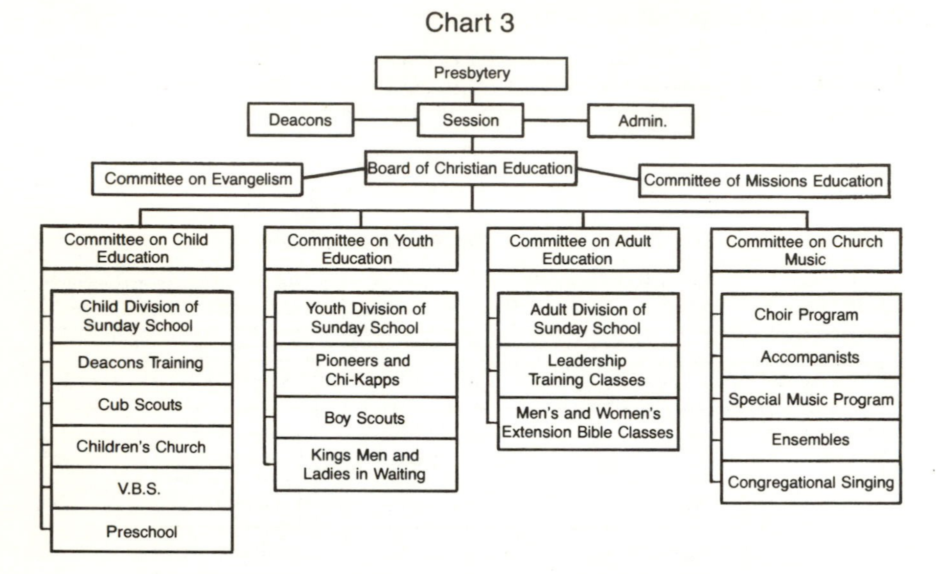

AGE-GROUP ORGANIZATION—PRESBYTERY CONTROL

Figure 11

Chart 4

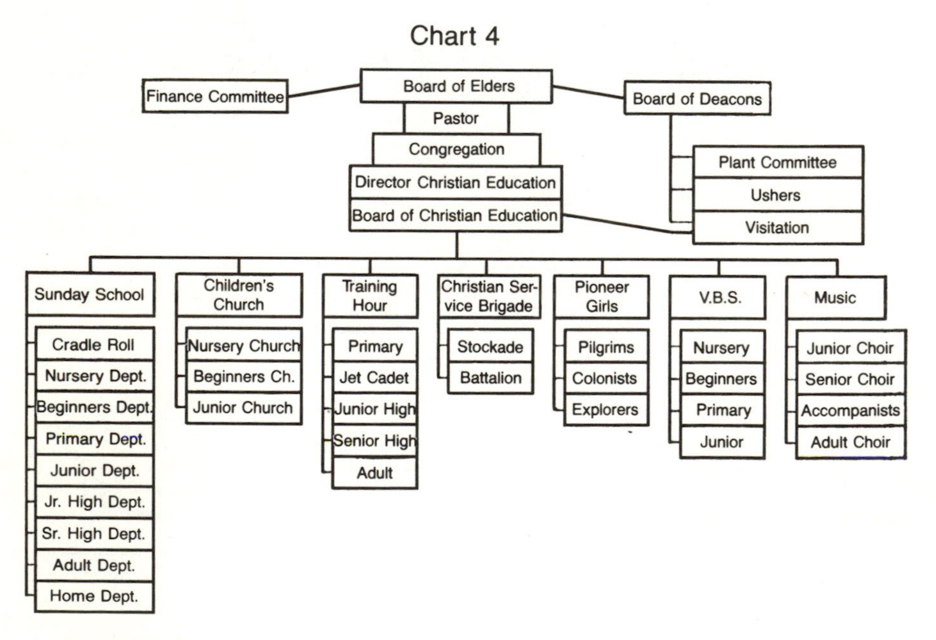

FUNCTIONAL CHART—DIRECTOR OF CHRISTIAN EDUCATION

Figure 12

the eduational program of the church. This will give each one a complete picture of where his particular class or group fits into the church's total program of Christian education. It will also clearly define the span of control, supervision received, supervision given, etc.

DEPARTMENTALIZATION

Departmentalization follows rather general forms throughout the Christian education program in the local church, with the exception of various programs which have certain prescribed departmentalization principles structured into their own programs. The following principles are therefore applicable not only to Sunday school but also to almost any local church agency such as vacation Bible school, children's church, training hour groups, and others. For a more thorough discussion of departmentalization, the reader is referred to Chapter 24 in *An Introduction to Evangelical Christian Education*, a chapter carefully prepared by James DeForest Murch.

THE PURPOSE OF DEPARTMENTALIZATION

The concept of departmentalization is very closely related to the importance of age-group characteristics. Children and young people learn differently and exhibit different needs at different levels. As a general rule, departmentalization during the school years follows the principle of grade allotment rather than age differentiation. In a small church, departmentalization may find all the primaries from grades one, two, and three in a single class, therefore making the class and department virtually inseparable in that kind of organization.

More commonly, however, departmental organization provides for correlated worship sessions in which various grades of the department meet as a unit, and then closely graded classes in which children of a specific age or a specific grade level are taught together. Still another approach is closely grading the students at every level so that worship sessions and class sessions divide on a closely graded basis and departments have virtually little effect on the organizational plan.

Departmentalization also relates to proper allocation of space. Provision of a content for effective learning experiences carries with it the responsibility of placing students in a proper room of a proper size. These kinds of decisions relate to departmentalization. Murch well says, "The organizational approach to the problem of effective teaching and nurture becomes one of providing a graded structure through which unity of purpose and program can be achieved and educational progress can be measured."[13]

THE PATTERN OF DEPARTMENTALIZATION

For years standard departmentalization allowed for three general divisions and approximately eleven departments. Many churches still operate under this system so the pattern must be included here. In the 1980s, however, a great deal of experimentation is going on with respect to how best to organize the church's educational ministries. Group electives including senior high, college, and all adults; intergenerational learning experiences spread across all ages; short-term units of study focusing on biblical answers to current issues are just a few of the variations presently in use.

There are still some time-honored guidelines, however, which normally defy change. One is that age specification is no longer used once a student has entered school, at which time we begin placing him in classes or groups by grade. Another is the recognition of developmental task units, which identify certain interests and needs for special groups (young marrieds, senior citizens, single adults). More attention must be paid to these groups as we think of new patterns. But for the sake of tradition, here is the generally accepted format:

Children's Division
- Cradle Roll, birth-1
- Nursery, 2-3
- Beginner, 4-5
- Primary, grades 1-3
- Junior, grades 4-6

Youth Division
- Junior High, grades 7-9
- Senior High, grades 10-13
- College and Career Class (Young People's Department)

Adult Division
- Young Adults, marriage to 30
- Middle Adults, 30-50
- Senior Adults, over 50

THE PROBLEMS IN DEPARTMENTALIZATION

One of the common problems already implied is the lack of standardization in local church organization. In a sense this is a built-in problem that may never be solved and, indeed, one we may not wish to solve. The desirability of adaptation to a local situation takes precedence over rigidly prescribed organization.

A second problem is the emotional age barriers that constantly present themselves in the adult division. Age differentiation presents a menace in most churches, and out of the confusion many have chosen to adopt the elective system for the adult division. Certainly this more recent curriculum development provides for educational grouping rather than social grouping and probably provides an additional academic thrust to the educational program of the church.

The third problem involves misused terminology. The word *intermediate*, for example, has virtually lost its usefulness through suffering divergent interpretations. A fourth problem has to do with sexes in the church's educational program. Should boys and girls be taught together or should they meet only in classes of their own sex? Many believe that mixed grouping through the primary department and again beginning in the senior high department is the desirable way to handle the situation. As this indicates, the junior department and the junior high department should meet in classes which are segregated according to sex.

Other problems concern difficulties in finding personnel and meeting space for various departments in the agencies. New trends in secular education must also be considered: open classroom, increased specialization, and team teaching. All of these issues must be faced when deciding upon departmentalization.

In the process of departmentalization, unification, correlation, construction of organizational charts and all the rest, we dare not lose sight of the fact that in the final analysis we are dealing with an *organism* and therefore must allow the church's spiritual aspects constantly to permeate the organizational process.

FOR FURTHER READING

Bower, Robert K. *Administering Christian Education*. Grand Rapids: Eerdmans, 1964.

Church Educational Ministries. Wheaton, Ill.: Evangelical Teacher Training Assn., 1980.

Westing, Harold J. *Make Your Sunday School Grow Through Evaluation*, Wheaton, Ill.: Victor, 1976.

The Key to Sunday School Achievement. Rev. ed. Chicago: Moody, 1980.

NOTES

1. Vernon R. Kraft, *The Director of Christian Education in the Local Church* (Chicago: Moody, 1967), p. 25.
2. D. Campbell Wyckoff, *The Gospel and Christian Education* (Philadelphia: Westminster, 1959), p. 80.
3. Paul H. Vieth, *The Church and Christian Education* (St. Louis: Bethany, 1963), p. 97.
4. Ralph D. Heim, *Leading a Sunday Church School* (Philadelphia: Fortress, 1968), pp. 81-82.
5. Oliver D. Cummings, *Christian Education in the Local Church* (Philadelphia: Judson, 1951), p. 31.
6. Wyckoff, p. 130.
7. Lois E. LeBar, *Education That Is Christian* (Westwood, N.J.: Revell, 1958), p. 203.
8. LeBar, "Curriculum," in *An Introduction to Evangelical Christian Education*, J. Edward Hakes, ed. (Chicago: Moody, 1964), p. 86.
9. Vieth, p. 108.
10. Herbert W. Byrne, *Christian Education for the Local Church* (Grand Rapids: Zondervan, 1963), pp. 33-44.
11. Donald Winks, "How to Read an Organizational Chart for Fun and Survival," *Harper's* (January 1967), pp. 38-39.
12. Ibid.
13. James DeForest Murch, *Christian Education and the Local Church* (Cincinnati: Standard, 1958), p. 308.

17

Evaluating the Educational Program of the Church

EVALUATION IS THE PROCESS of getting answers to the question, How are we doing? The educational cycle presented in Chapter 3 requires that educational leaders must engage in effective evaluation if the cyclical approach to the development of learning experiences is to be valid. Such evaluation is, of course, inseparably related to the clarity and specificity of objectives which are stated at the outset of the educational process.

The evaluation step is a measurement of the success or failure and the degree of success or failure in the achievement of educational objectives. Information gained as a result of evaluation lays the basis for changes in the program which may result in re-identification of needs, reclarification of objectives, and restructuring of forms and methodology.

Improvement is a biblical concept. The Scriptures continually remind the Christian to put his life to the test of God's holy standard. Note the emphasis of the following passages from *The Living Bible:*

> That is why a man should examine himself carefully before eating the bread and drinking from the cup (1 Cor. 11:28).
>
> Check up on yourselves. Are you really Christians? Do you pass the test? Do you feel Christ's presence and power more and more within you? Or are you just pretending to be Christians when actually you aren't at all? (2 Cor. 13:5).
>
> Dear brothers, if a Christian is overcome by some sin, you who are godly should gently and humbly help him back onto the right path, remembering that next time it might be one of you who is in the wrong. Share each other's troubles and problems, and so obey our Lord's command. If anyone thinks he is too great to stoop to this, he is fooling himself. He is really a nobody. Let everyone be sure that he is doing his very best, for then he will have the personal satisfaction of work well done, and won't need to compare himself with someone else. Each of us must bear some faults

> and burdens of his own. For none of us is perfect! (Gal. 6:1-5).
>
> Before they are asked to be deacons they should be given other jobs in the church as a test of their character and ability, and if they do well, then they may be chosen as deacons (1 Tim. 3:10).
>
> Dear brothers, what's the use of saying that you have faith and are Christians if you aren't proving it by helping others? Will *that* kind of faith save anyone? If you have a friend who is in need of food and clothing, and you say to him, "Well, good-bye and God bless you; stay warm and eat hearty," and then don't give him clothes or food, what good does that do? So you see, it isn't enough just to have faith. You must also do good to prove that you have it. Faith that doesn't show itself by good works is no faith at all—it is dead and useless (James 2:14-17).

Definition is important here since at least three terms are commonly used almost interchangeably within the framework of education evaluation. One is the term *testing,* and in the present study it is considered the most narrow of the three. It refers to information about a given student, a group of students or an educational program, the information usually being obtained through objective and written means.

A second word is *measurement.* Perhaps one could say that measurement over a period of time is the gathering of a body of information through the process of testing. It still has its major emphasis, however, on the procurement of data rather than the formulation of conclusions about the data.

A third idea employed in this chapter centers in the word *evaluation.* It is the broadest of the three terms. When we evaluate we move from the process of objective data-gathering to the process of the interpretation of that data and develop conclusions which will ultimately result in change.

Much of evaluation is subjective. Every honest educator would admit that he is subjectively evaluating most of the time. The teacher evaluates his students continually as he is in contact with them. The director of Christian education or pastor evaluates his teachers and church workers to a much greater extent through subjective observation than through objective testing. When the results of both the subjective observation and the objective measurement are brought together and decisions are made about the education process, evaluation is taking place.

This book, however, does not deal with the individual learner, but rather with the total educational program of the church. The principles of evaluation are the same for both, but the implementation of the process is somewhat different. Both types of evaluation are obviously necessary in a properly functioning church educational program. The focus on the individual pupil has been developed by the author in a different book.*

At first glance, program evaluation seems more simple than pupil evaluation. One can analyze the size of facilities and the functionability of the educational plant much more easily than he can analyze the behavioral changes in the life of a young Christian. Continual emphasis in program evaluation, therefore, must be directed toward the fact that all facilities, programs and methodology are geared toward the production of behavioral changes, bringing the individual student to "total Christian maturity." The inseparability of program evaluation should be obvious to even the casual student.

The analysis of the process of evaluation in this chapter takes the form of a series of categorized annotated questions which can be applied by the church administrator to the program for which he holds or shares responsibility.

Evaluating the Organizational Structure

IS THE CHURCH EDUCATIONAL PROGRAM PROPERLY UNIFIED?

Evaluation should demonstrate the singleness of purpose which exists in the minds of the workers and in the overt functioning of the program itself. Do all teachers and workers really feel themselves a part of the spiritual organism? Is the whole really greater than the sum of its parts? What built-in organizational structure is apparent which can produce the desired unification of the program?

IS THERE A PROPERLY FUNCTIONING BOARD OF CHRISTIAN EDUCATION?

The evaluator here will look for proper representation of the agencies on the board, clear-cut specification of responsibilities of board membership, productive meetings, evidence of vision and long-range planning, and an awareness on the part of the congregation of the significance of the ministry of his board.

WHAT PERSON OR GROUP OF PERSONS IS RESPONSIBLE FOR PLANNING AND SUPERVISING THE CHRISTIAN EDUCATION PROGRAM?

This question is inseparably linked with the previous one and the desirable answer is "the board of Christian education." A

*The reader is directed to the Evangelical Teacher Training Association text, *Understanding Teaching*, chap. 12. (Wheaton, Ill.: ETTA, 1968).

refinement of the reply should uncover proper principles of delegation to agency officers, a healthy ex officio involvement on the part of the pastor, and some evidence that the board of Christian education is achieving its objectives.

IS THERE AN ORGANIZATIONAL CHART WRITTEN AND AVAILABLE FOR ALL WORKERS?

Such a chart should be accurately drawn, showing proper line-staff relationships, and should be a part of some official document such as the church or Sunday school constitution. Each worker in the program should have a copy and be able to perceive the basic issues involved in organizational relationships, line-staff authority, and span of control.

IS THERE PROVISION FOR A CORRELATED CHURCH CALENDAR?

Here again responsibility should be shouldered by the board of Christian education. A calendar kept in the office of the church secretary is better than no calendar at all, but correlation of activities is best achieved through clearance at board level. Long-range planning necessitates calendar coordination.

ARE REPORTS REQUIRED FROM MINISTRY LEADERS?

Such reports may be at times verbal but should more frequently be written. The superintendent of the primary department, for example, should be responsible for some kind of written quarterly report to the general superintendent of the Sunday school. The report would include such items of information as children who come to know Christ during the quarter, those who dropped out of the department, needed additional equipment, equipment repair, and plans and programs for the coming quarter. Such data aids the board of Christian education in its planning responsibilities.

HOW, BY WHOM, AND HOW OFTEN ARE WORKERS APPOINTED?

Most Christian education leaders would like the following response to such a question: All workers are appointed annually by the board of Christian education for terms of one year after which time they are evaluated and either reappointed for another year or counseled toward another type of ministry in the church.

ARE JOB DESCRIPTIONS AVAILABLE FOR ALL TEACHERS AND WORKERS?

The answer should be affirmative and such job descriptions

should be brief, effectively utilized in worker procurement, and demonstrative of the responsibilities of both the worker to the church and the church to the worker.

ARE EDUCATIONAL OFFICERS BEING USED EFFECTIVELY?

Using the Sunday school as an example, the evaluator will be looking for evidence of an effective administrative ministry on the part of the assistant Sunday school superintendent, departmental superintendents, secretaries, and clerks. Is the assistant superintendent sharing responsibilities which are enabling him to be in actuality a "superintendent-in-training"? Are departmental superintendents effectively utilizing the teaching time to observe and assist teachers in their departments?

WHAT CHRISTIAN EDUCATION MINISTRIES ARE PRESENTLY BEING CARRIED ON BY THE CHURCH?

If the church being evaluated has a properly written organizational chart, the answer to this question can be obtained at a glance. If not, the evaluator must write down exactly what the church *is* doing now and compare that information with what the church *should* be doing now and in the future. It is important to remember here that no particular form of Christian education, that is, no specific agency, is of general necessity to all local churches. Conceivably in one given locality it may not be within the proper educational objectives of the church to conduct an annual vacation Bible school. The educational leader must be careful not to force agencies upon a church program just because they seem to be traditional or because most other churches have them.

WHAT RELATIONSHIP DOES EACH OF THE MINISTRIES SUSTAIN TO THE BOARD OF CHRISTIAN EDUCATION, AND WHAT RELATIONSHIP DO THEY SUSTAIN TO EACH OTHER?

The issue here again is one of correlation. Is there clear communication of goals, curriculum and programming between the teacher of junior boys in the Sunday school, the captain of Brigade Stockade, and the director of the junior-level training-hour group on Sunday evening? Do they realize that they are all affecting the life of the same boy and should be contributing harmoniously rather than competitively to his growth in Christ?

DOES EACH CHRISTIAN EDUCATION MINISTRY HAVE ITS DISTINCTIVE OBJECTIVES?

These objectives should be written and followed. A mere random verbalization on the part of the agency leader is inadequate. Exactly why does First Church conduct a Sunday school at 9:45 A.M. each week? If all the Sunday school teachers were asked separately what the objectives of their collective work were, would their responses be identical? Would they be even similar?

ARE THE VARIOUS MINISTRIES PROPERLY DEPARTMENTALIZED AND/OR GRADED?

Evaluation should be made of the criteria which are used in determining groupings in the educational program. This involves an analysis of all groups within the Sunday school, training hour and other agencies, and an explanation of any unusual grading devices presently in operation. Watch for such antiquated terms as "intermediate" which may represent a rather nebulous approach to grouping.

Some organizations such as Christian Service Brigade and Pioneer Girls recommend different groupings than those usually used in the Sunday school, and the evaluator should see that such recommendations are adequately followed. Proper relationship between age grouping and grade grouping is a primary consideration in the question of departmentalization.

ARE CLASS AND DEPARTMENT ENROLLMENTS PROPERLY LIMITED?

The old Sunday school maxim "divide and multiply" still applies to most of the education ministries in the local church. For example, the Sunday school class that gets too large and unwieldy will tend to stagnate rather than move ahead in growth and vitality. Although the Christian education literature available offers several different approaches to class and department enrollment limitations, the following may serve as a general standard for evaluation.

Nursery Department	15
Beginner Department	25
Primary Department	50 (classes 6 to 8)
Junior Department	50 (classes 6 to 8)
Junior High Department	50 (classes 8 to 10)
Senior High Department	50 (classes 10 to 15)
College and Career Department	No limit (classes under 20)
Adult Department	No limit (classes under 25)

The above figures obviously represent an ideal. Nevertheless, they provide a basic standard toward which a church can work if facilities and personnel will allow.

EVALUATION OF CURRICULUM AND INSTRUCTIONAL PROCEDURE

ARE TEACHERS USING A VARIETY OF METHODOLOGY IN THE CLASSROOM?

The focus here is upon effective communication. From whatever information he can obtain—utilizing written reports, suggestions from students, and counsel with supervisors and teachers themselves—the evaluator attempts to determine the degree of achievement in the actual teaching process. Variety is only one of the characteristics of good teaching, but it is an *important* one and the teacher who approaches his task week after week with the same format is suspect in terms of dynamic communication.

ARE AUDIO-VISUAL AIDS BEING USED EFFECTIVELY IN THE CLASSROOM?

Good teaching methodology assumes good teaching media. Is there evidence that chalkboards, teaching pictures, projected still or motion pictures, and other accessible teaching aids are part of the instructional process in the church's education program? Note that the evaluation must be made not only of the *fact* of use but also the *effectiveness*. If such materials are available and yet are not being used, the logical conclusion in evaluation is to ask why. The answer might lie in the area touched by the next question.

ARE THE TEACHERS BEING TRAINED TO COMMUNICATE EFFECTIVELY IN THE CLASSROOM?

Questions about leadership training in general are raised in a later paragraph. But insofar as lack of training has a direct detrimental effect upon the achievement of learning, an analysis of the instructional process requires some inquiry into the teacher's competence for the task.

ARE STUDENTS PARTICIPATING IN THE CLASSROOM PROCEDURE?

Another basic principle of instruction is the principle of involvement which states simply that the student will learn better if he is a part of the teaching-learning process rather than just a passive spectator to the teacher's performance. Evaluation discovers whether the student is being involved by his teacher and whether the teacher is being trained to implement this principle of valid instruction.

ARE BIBLES BEING USED EFFECTIVELY BY TEACHERS AND STUDENTS?

As earlier chapters have shown, every educational agency of the church is primarily engaged in biblical instruction. Part of that instruction is directly tied in with the student's ability to utilize the Word of God for himself rather than just listening to information transmitted to him by his teacher or leader. Do the various agencies evaluated give evidence of such education in "technique" as well as content?

Closely akin to the proper use of the Bible in the classroom is the misuse of quarterlies or other curriculum items. The Sunday school class in which the student sits throughout the hour with a closed Bible on a chair next to him and an open Sunday school quarterly in his hands is demonstrative of negative habituation in biblical education.

ARE TEACHERS DEMONSTRATING CHRISTIAN LOVE AND ENTHUSIASM IN THE CLASSROOM?

Someone has said that "teaching is contagious enthusiasm." The student cannot develop an excitement for his biblical studies unless such excitement has been communicated to him by his teachers. A genuine *agape* love should be evident in the classroom as teacher and student share alike in the Spirit-controlled atmosphere of Christian education.

ARE ALL REGULAR TEACHERS AND WORKERS MEMBERS OF THE LOCAL CHURCH?

To some churches this will be an irrelevant question since membership rolls are not a part of their policy. However, when membership rolls are kept and when fellowship in a local church is considered not only demonstrative of a place in the universal church but also obedience to Christ, its Head, then the teachers and leaders employed in the church's educational program should be examples of that obedience.

Some churches located near Christian colleges have found it desirable to develop an "associate membership" which enables a student to affiliate temporarily with the church in which he serves without losing or relinquishing his permanent membership in his home church. Such an associate membership ordinarily allows for all the privileges and responsibilities of regular membership with the exception of voting.

ARE CURRICULUM MATERIALS THEOLOGICALLY ACCURATE, EDUCATIONALLY ADEQUATE, AND ADAPTABLE TO LOCAL NEEDS?

Curriculum evaluation is very important and should be conducted probably about every three years. Consistency in the use of curriculum is a requisite to proper educational programming. Only confusion can result when the junior department uses material produced by one publisher and the primary department uses another publisher's curriculum. Wide flexibility can be allowed in the adult department, but curriculum should be standardized through senior high.

ARE CURRICULUM MATERIALS BEING PROPERLY USED BY TEACHERS AND STUDENTS?

Instructional poverty can result when the church allows budgetary considerations to negate the use of helps and aids available as a part of curriculum. Here again it is important not only to purchase such items but also to train classroom teachers to use them properly.

HOW EFFECTIVE ARE THE DEPARTMENTAL WORSHIP SESSIONS?

Are the first fifteen minutes of Sunday school time wasted, or are genuine worship experiences taking place? How about effective utilization of presession time (before the Sunday school actually begins)? Is valuable teaching time being consumed by ineffective "opening exercises" at the beginning of the Sunday school hour?

EVALUATION OF RECORDS, EVANGELISM AND OUTREACH

ARE PERMANENT RECORD CARDS OR FILES KEPT ON EVERY STUDENT?

Permanent record cards include more than just weekly attendance figures. Notes on counseling interviews, progress in spiritual maturity, Christian service experience, and general home and background information would be a part of a thorough permanent record card. Such a card serves pastors and leaders in years to come in providing answers to inquiries regarding young people in the church. Effective records also enable the church leadership to more effectively teach and counsel students presently enrolled in the program.

ARE THE WEEKLY RECORDS USED TO IMPROVE AND ENLARGE THE CHRISTIAN EDUCATION PROGRAM?

One of the problems many churches have with the record program is that records are only *kept* and not efficiently *used*. Competent record-keeping serves evaluation processes but also should lay the groundwork for a productive visitation and prospect follow-up campaign. Such records must contain adequate information on prospects, visitation procedures, calls made, and the results of those calls. Practically speaking, the record-keeping system serves two major groups of people: the people who are not a part of the church but perhaps should be, and those who are but do not attend regularly.

ARE THE VARIOUS CHRISTIAN EDUCATION MINISTRIES SHOWING CONSISTENT GROWTH?

This is a good example of how an adequate record system can help in evaluation. A comparison of the attendance records for the first quarter of this year with those of the first quarter of last year will indicate not only whether there is an overall growth or decrease but also in what areas growth (or lack of it) is most pronounced. To illustrate: if the total Sunday school showed an attendance increase of 5 percent but the adult department showed a decrease of 3 percent, a delineation of cause and effect must be interpreted.

The dynamic local church in the last third of the twentieth century must be constantly growing because static apathy can produce death. Growth does not necessarily have to be defined in terms of one building or one congregation. A church of three-hundred which over the years organizes three other churches which eventually grow to one hundred each, has doubled its ministry in that time just on the basis of simple arithmetic.

ARE PEOPLE CONFESSING FAITH IN CHRIST AS A RESULT OF THE CHURCH'S CHRISTIAN EDUCATION MINISTRIES?

Such an evaluation question assumes that evangelism is at least a part of the objective of almost all of the church's educational agencies. Some agencies such as club programs, home Bible classes, and vacation Bible schools have also demonstrated their effectiveness in reaching people with the gospel. If this is one of the objectives and there is no evidence that it is being realized, the issue of training the workers to present the gospel clearly and give students opportunities to receive Christ may lie at the root of the problem.

IS THE CHURCH PAYING AT LEAST AS MUCH ATTENTION TO RETENTION AS IT IS TO EXPANSION?

A subtle trap which has caught many is the effort of genuine attempts to bring people in the front door while those who have been there for a time are going out the back door. Visitation of presently enrolled students is every bit as important to the growth and ministry of the church as concentrated energy to reach new people in the community. Either emphasis to the exclusion of the other represents imbalance in the program.

ARE MISSIONS PROMOTED EFFECTIVELY THROUGH THE EDUCATIONAL MINISTRIES?

Promoting missions "effectively" means more than the annual missionary conference and the occasional reading of a missionary letter in church or Sunday school. It means a constant awareness on the part of the teachers of their role in world evangelization and their responsibility to communicate that burden to their students at every opportunity. It means a total world view of the cause of Christ and the gospel without undue emphasis on geographical areas and the crossing of oceans. It means exposure of all the people in the church to dedicated and productive missionaries rather than collection of missionary funds given to an ethereal budgetary item totally unrepresentative of flesh-and-blood discipleship.

EVALUATION OF PERSONNEL RECRUITMENT AND TRAINING

ARE WRITTEN STANDARDS AVAILABLE AND ARE THEY FOLLOWED IN THE PROCUREMENT AND UTILIZATION OF TEACHERS?

When the board of Christian education meets to decide prayerfully upon workers for the church program, the members should have before them clear-cut objective criteria by which those workers are chosen. Such criteria or standards may be a part of the church constitution or may be developed in connection with other documents which represent the official position of the church on various matters. Within legitimate bounds of flexibility these standards become the basic guidelines for worker procurement.

Like a job description, the worker's standards may deal with what the worker should *do,* but primarily they are concerned with what he should *be.* Such a list of standards may be passed down from the deacon board or board of Christian education but is better developed by the teachers and workers themselves.

IS THERE A PROPERLY FUNCTIONING WORKER'S CONFERENCE?

The words "properly functioning" mark the legitimate worker's conference as more than a Sunday school business meeting. It should probably be a monthly conference which emphasizes professional growth and development as well as group and departmental programming. The worker's conference should represent the minimal level of leadership training being carried on by the local church. Its format is under the direction of the board of Christian education and may be administered more specifically by the director of Christian education or other individual church leaders.

IS THERE A REGULAR PROGRAM OF ADULT LEADERSHIP TRAINING?

Such a program might take place during the Sunday school hour, Sunday evening training hour, or on week nights. The evaluator will want to know not only whether such a program is in existence but also whether it is doing the job for which it was set up. A Sunday evening Bible class before the church service may have obvious value in instructing people better in the Scriptures but is of dubious help in producing competent church leadership.

EVALUATION OF CHURCH-HOME RELATIONSHIPS

ARE TEACHERS EFFECTIVELY SECURING PARENTAL SUPPORT OF THEIR MINISTRIES?

The public school PTA has long been an established contact point between parents and the program of education in which their children are involved. In public education the parental voice may be growing increasingly dim. But in church education a revival is under way, recapturing the importance of church-home relationships. It is unfortunate that the evangelical church ever allowed itself to drift away from the very biblical concept of parental responsibility. The alert teacher will involve parents of her students through open-house sessions, parent-teacher conferences, written communication to the home, and frequent home visitation.

DO TEACHERS VISIT A LARGE PERCENTAGE OF ENROLLED STUDENTS DURING EACH YEAR?

The emphasis here is not on prospect visitation but on the retention ministry mentioned earlier. When a student is almost always in his seat on Sunday morning, it is difficult for the teacher to see the necessity of spending time that might be given to absentees or prospects. Such contact is important, however, if church-home relationships are to be strengthened.

Evaluation of Facilities and Equipment

ARE CLASSROOMS ADEQUATE IN SIZE?

Acceptable standards for room size in relation to age group are readily available in numerous sources. A church which puts younger children in a smaller room simply because their bodies are one-third the size and weight of adults is missing the whole point of the relationship of learning procedure to facilities. Part of the interpretation of evaluation reporting is an analysis of which classes and/or departments are deficient in space and how the deficiency can be alleviated.

ARE DEPARTMENTS AND CLASSES PROPERLY USING THEIR ALLOTTED SPACE?

Sometimes the issue is not absence of space but improper utilization. A classroom in which chairs are set in rows, for example, might provide for better learning experience if those rows were turned into a semicircle or full circle. A large departmental room given over to two small classes during the teaching time might be more effectively used by six small classes, a change which would not only provide more room for growth but cut down on distraction rather than increase it.

DOES EACH ROOM CONTAIN SUFFICIENT EQUIPMENT FOR ADEQUATE TEACHING?

Are the chalkboards large enough? Are the chairs the right height for the size of each child? Are the tables approximately ten inches above the chairs? Are the bulletin boards attractive and do they present a constantly changing message? Is the color and atmosphere bright and cheery? Are shelves and cupboards sufficient to handle the materials utilized in the teaching process? Are lighting and heating comfortable and adequate for educational purposes? Are pictures and visual boards placed at a proper height on the walls for correct viewing by students in that particular room? Such are the questions of equipment evaluation. The problems they uncover are not so easily remedied because there is almost always a financial factor involved. Nevertheless, the church that is genuinely concerned about effective Christian education will be willing to budget for it.

IS LONG-RANGE PLANNING TAKING ADDITIONAL BUILDING AND FACILITIES INTO PROPER CONSIDERATION?

Some churches have the idea that the time to build is when the congregation is pushing out the doors and walls of the present structure. Even after concern develops, several months or years may go by before building plans are drawn up, contracts are let, and the building is actually ready for use. During that time inferior education may take place in our classrooms, and many whom we might have reached in the interval will have gone to some other church which had room for them, or worse yet, decided not to go at all.

GUIDELINES FOR EVALUATION

The evaluative process will always be subjective at best, but after more than twenty years at the task I think a few general guidelines might be drawn from experience:

1. The evaluator must know what he is looking for if the evaluation is to culminate in a competent report. The seasoned educational administrator can sit in on a class for ten minutes and feel the temper of what probably goes on in that class most of the time. The nonprofessional visitor could sit in the same class several periods and not be able to identify the positive and negative factors which make up the dynamics of that teaching-learning situation. Knowing what to look for, however, is not to be construed as a priori conclusion-jumping before fair observation is made.

2. Evaluation is sometimes best made by a person not involved with the church. The director of Christian education is no doubt qualified to analyze the program which he has set up and is actually evaluating all the time. It is nevertheless "his program" and, therefore, something must suffer in the objectivity of evaluation reporting. The stigma of "a prophet in his own country" would also argue for evaluation from without.

3. When a written evaluation report is prepared, it should contain specific recommendations for improvement. These recommendations are presented in a manner which clearly states that

their implementation is to be carried out over a period of months and probably even years.

4. An evaluation report should be presented to the total working constituency of the church rather than just to a board or committee. In the final analysis it is the teacher in the classroom and not the chairman of the board who will have to make the program effective. As the evaluation report is presented, each worker should have opportunity to ask for clarification and to become involved in whatever generalization will be necessary as a result of the evaluation.

5. Proper evaluation always keeps the basic nature of the church central in its focus. An analysis of the church that views the church more or less as a secular corporation can never provide the spiritual guidance for growth and improvement that a heavenly, supernatural organism needs.

FOR FURTHER READING

Church Educational Ministries. Wheaton, Ill.: Evangelical Teacher Training Assn., 1980.

Rusbuldt, Richard E.; Gladden, Richard K.; and Green, Norman M., Jr. *Local Church Planning Manual.* Valley Forge, Pa.: Judson, 1977.

Westing, Harold J. *Make Your Sunday School Grow through Evaluation.* Wheaton, Ill.: Victor, 1976.

Wyckoff, D. Campbell. *How To Evaluate Your Christian Education Program.* Philadelphia: Westminster, 1962.

18

Principles and Practice of Church Growth

A number of new terms have come into the vocabulary of evangelical Christianity in the last ten years. One such term is *church growth*. At first glance, church growth seems to be an obvious concept having to do with an increase in attendance and/or membership of the congregation. But when used technically, the idea is extremely complex. It is based on years of research now spreading into a number of areas around the world but stimulated primarily at the Institute of Church Growth at Fuller Theological Seminary.

Initially the work of Donald McGavran was directed primarily toward church growth on the foreign mission field, and only more recently has the Institute for Church Growth focused on the United States.

To be sure, what follows is an oversimplified analysis of the church growth process. But for some readers it may be at least an introductory primer.

MOTIVATION FOR CHURCH GROWTH

The indispensable condition for a growing church is that *it wants to grow.* That principle is found at the base of all the research done by the people at the Institute for Church Growth and other organizations.

But just "wanting to grow" does not speak to the whole matter of motivation. The church must ask itself *why* it wants to grow. Is our motivation to beat that other church across town in the annual Sunday school contest? Do we want to grow so that we can write on our Sunday school buses "Largest Church in Town"?

Motivation is obviously the key to involvement. Although we may agree that the minister sets the pattern for growth, true church growth only takes place when the members of the local congregation see their own collective and individual responsibilities within the broad impact of the Body of Christ in the world.

Diversification for Church Growth

There are certainly some basic underlying principles that relate to the growth of all churches, but it is imperative to recognize and understand that different methods and techniques are needed for each individual church. Each congregation is ministering *with* different kinds of people and *to* different kinds of people.

One example of church growth would be the extremely large churches we see in our day, the ones we have even begun to call "super churches." At first glance it appears that their techniques and approaches surely provide the proper answers to church growth: strong pulpit evangelism, with long and regular invitations; wide-ranging Sunday school bus ministry; huge programs offering everything from nursery day care to seminary degrees right on the church campus; and an attempt through sheer size to make an overwhelming spiritual impact on a community. But Dr. Charles Chaney of the Southern Baptist Convention challenges that philosophy:

> To begin with, [it] is based on faulty information. In terms of evangelism, big churches are not nearly as effective as little churches. Churches of over three thousand members in the SBC last year (1974) averaged 122 baptisms. Churches with 49 or less members averaged 2 baptisms. The average membership of these little churches was 34. That is one baptism for every 17 members. The average membership of churches over three thousand was 4,340. That is one baptism for every 35.5 members. Tiny, baby, struggling churches with 49 members or less baptized at a ratio twice as good as large churches. If we want to win the North Central states for Christ, 1,000 churches with 30 members would win twice as many as 10 churches with 3,000 members.[1]

So there you have two completely different philosophies and techniques. One is to develop a huge, *centralized*, monolithic congregation that reaches out to bring in as many people as it can to its widely diversified, multiple programs. The other suggests that *decentralization* is the best approach, with as many small churches as possible. Somewhere in between those two views is the idea of the strong (possibly quite large) church developing, at regular intervals, mission churches or *extension congregations* in other parts of the same area.

SPECIFICATION IN CHURCH GROWTH

Here the field really gets technical as we begin to identify various kinds of church growth. The reader needs to be prepared to encounter letters and numbers, which designate kinds of growth and kinds of evangelism (T1, T2, E1, E2, etc.). Here are four generally recognized kinds of growth and three kinds of evangelism.

T1—INTERNAL GROWTH

Internal growth describes growth within the body. Included would be such things as church renewal, body life ministries, training of believers, and other "in-house" growth functions. Richard Ottoson refers to *"celebreation, congregation,* and *cell"* as balanced functions that have brought his church to a position of satisfactory growth. By *celebration* he means the Sunday morning worship experience. *Congregation* emphasizes fellowship in small groups. In this particular case they take the form of house churches.

The term *cell* refers to small clusters of two to four people who meet regularly to share and pray about personal needs. Ottoson evaluates this balance:

> I cannot say that our church is a prime example of evangelism and dynamic growth. But I do see people becoming genuinely alive in their faith through *celebration, congregation,* and *cell* experiences. This I feel is a balance of functions essential for spontaneous and continuing church growth. People who are experiencing change and fulfillment in Christ will inevitably reach others and contribute to the growth of a local church.[2]

T2—EXPANSION GROWTH

Here we are referring to the adding of new members to a local congregation. There are multitudinous ways to experience expansion growth, but it is important to notice that expansion growth follows internal growth. Only the congregation that is healthy in its church life can be expected to attract outsiders.

T3—EXTENSION GROWTH

Extension growth, when viewed in a simple format of the North American church, is a reference to church planting or "branching." My own opinion leads me to prefer this kind of growth over some others. Of course, it is really a combination of internal, expansion, and extension growth, which makes for a well-rounded total church growth program.

The New Testament pattern, however, seems to indicate that Jerusalem gave birth to Antioch, which, through the ministry of Paul and Barnabas, gave birth to all of the churches started on the first missionary journey. But it is also obvious in the New Testament that the "mother-daughter" relationship did not continue. Jerusalem never became the Rome of New Testament Christianity.

To be sure, the Council at Jerusalem in Acts 15 does record a decision of importance to some of the outlying churches, but the umbilical cord was cut as quickly as possible, and Antioch made decisions on its own without the necessity of contacting Jerusalem to get an official policy statement.

It has been demonstrated again and again that a healthy, growing church can "slice off" extension congregations without damaging its own program or cutting back on its own normal growth patterns. If we take seriously the argument of Dr. Chaney described in early paragraphs, a "mother church" of four or five hundred people giving birth to five branch churches with the congregation of about two hundred each is much to be preferred over a single church of fifteen hundred members. Quite obviously, that argument takes on even more strength if we compare fifty congregations of two hundred with a single church of ten thousand.

T4—BRIDGING GROWTH

Here the emphasis is on cross-cultural growth, and this leads us to an examination of the three kinds of evangelism I alluded to earlier.

E1 —Reaching people of the same cultural background. A basic principle of the church growth movement involves the "homogeneous unit." L. Ted Johnson quotes church growth expert Donald McGavran:

> If there is one thing that worldwide research in church growth continues to confirm it is that churches grow best when they concentrate on only one homogeneous unit. Unfortunately, largely as a consequence of the blemish of racism that we Americans have written into our social history this principle, which as nearly approaches a "law" as anything in church growth, is difficult for some Americans to accept. So heavy has been the burden of guilt because of inhuman treatment given to blacks, American Indians,

> and other minority groups, that some contemporary interpretations of biblical problems such as Jew—Gentile relationships have been distorted.[3]

Sociological studies show us that Episcopalian and Presbyterian homogeneous units tend to be upper middle class people with higher educational levels than are found in Baptist or independent church groups. This is not a matter of prejudice or discrimination but a demonstration of McGavran's homogeneous principle. E1 evangelism is therefore reaching "our kind of people" with the understanding that they are most likely to respond to a church in which they feel at home.

E2—Reaching people of slightly different cultures. The key word is "slightly." Perhaps the easiest barrier to cross is the income barrier. Upper middle class people could reach out to lower middle class people in the same church and evangelize quite successfully. Not as easy as E1 to be sure, but the barriers here are not very great. A white church reaching out to blacks or an English-speaking church reaching out to those whose mother tongue is perhaps Spanish, or some other language not indigenous to this country, will have a much more difficult time at evangelism. They are practicing E2.

E3—Reaching people of vastly different cultures. Obviously we are talking here about foreign missions. A missionary in West Irian who seeks to bring the gospel to interior tribesmen there crosses much more than an ocean in his efforts at evangelism. He crosses monumental language and cultural barriers. It should be clear, therefore, that the best approach to reaching such people is the immediate *training of nationals* to reach their own countrymen with the transcultural message of the gospel. That is why a board like Greater Europe Mission has immediately established training schools in most of the countries in which it serves in an effort to train national leadership as quickly as possible. That is also the reason that most progressive mission boards now concentrate on urban centers with a view to reaching the largest number of people where they are, anticipating that they, in turn, will spread out from the cities and reach their relatives and acquaintances in the villages and hamlets all over the country.

So, our concerns in the North American church are primarily E1 with a bit of E2. With respect to kinds of church growth, we want to balance T1, T2, and T3 without getting T4, because T4 represents our whole thrust of foreign missions. Perhaps the statistic that should challenge us most as we think about the growth of our own local congregations is that *80 percent of the population of the world will have to be reached through E2 and E3 kinds of ministry.*

Visitation for Church Growth

In the local congregation, church growth is not to be equated with traditional visitation, but visitation is certainly one kind of outreach that represents a strategy for church growth. Perhaps we have used the term too long and your church may prefer different ways to speak about an outreach program, but whatever we call it and however we do it, visitation must take place.

TYPES OF VISITATION

There are basically three types of visitation, and they must be accurately distinguished one from another. In *absentee visitation* we are dealing with people who are regular members of the Sunday school or some other church educational agency. They may or may not be Christians, but they have been exposed to the church's message for a period of time and were regular attenders.

Now for some reason they are gone. They may be gone temporarily or permanently. This is one of the questions the church must answer. A second question asks, Why? and a third, What can be done about it? Absentee visitation obviously goes forward on the shoulders of an accurate and up-to-date record system. It is essential for us to know who is not there and to put into motion the program of absentee follow-up which will secure the best redemptive results.

There is also *prospect visitation.* Here we are concerned about the person who is not attending our church but could be, and perhaps should be. We've learned about him through one of the usual methods used to procure the names of prospects. He may be new in the community or the relative or friend of someone who is already attending our church. The point is, now we must go to him with the message that the church has to offer. He must know that we are interested in him, and he must feel welcome at the church. Here again the prospect visitation records are important.

The third and perhaps most important type of visitation is *evangelistic visitation*. Evangelism is the proclamation of the gospel of Jesus Christ. It is not "soul-winning" since the actual drawing of people to Christ for salvation is the ministry of the Holy Spirit. The messenger presents the gospel and perhaps an opportunity to respond volitionally to the invitation of the cross. When the witness attempts to make the person's decision for him, he is encroaching on a work that is nonhuman.

Evangelistic visitation has been the most neglected type in spite of its New Testament quality. In the early church there were no church buildings as we know them now. Any kind of drive or program to get people to come to church was out of the question. The early Christians considered it their responsibility to communicate the gospel to those who were on the outside. The New Testament takes the view that the church is the place for building up Christians so that those Christians can go out and proclaim an evangelistic message among the unsaved.*

Joe Bayly, noted author of *The Gospel Blimp,* suggests that there are eight hindrances to evangelism.

1. Lack of planning
2. Substitution of "come to church" as major drive, instead of taking the gospel to people in their homes, etc.
3. Spirit of indifference
4. Judgmental attitude toward sinners
5. Failure to train laymen for evangelism
6. Lack of prayer
7. Lack of friendship with nonchristian people
8. Our self-centeredness[4]

As Bayly suggests, our task in the church is to effectively equip people to go out and speak the gospel in the homes of the community. The people may never come to church. If they do, well and good. If they come and hear the message there, respond and are saved, we can rejoice. Should they *not* come, however, and *not* hear and *not* respond, the church has not fulfilled its *responsibility* to its community. People deserve the opportunity of hearing the message of Christ where they are. This is not something that can be done more effectively by the pastor; rather, it is something that belongs properly in the hands of every layman in the church.

STEPS TO ORGANIZING A VISITATION PROGRAM

Visitation programs (absentee, prospect, or evangelistic) do not just happen—they are carefully planned. The visitation program that is doing the job consists of more than cards, calls, and visits. It thrives on total involvement of God's people in a program of outreach.

*See chapter 1, "The Nature of the Church."

Preparation—What Do We Want to Do? There is the very important preparation of people. This is done through Sunday school classes, pulpit preaching, counseling, training programs, and a great effort of prayer in behalf of the growth program. People must awaken to the responsibility for communicating the gospel and caring for those who are not in the church.

There is also preparation of *program*. As indicated above, we must be ready to attract and retain, lest we merely bring people in to foster further absenteeism.

There is also the preparation of a *procedure*. What kind of visitation program is most effective for our church? No doubt we will want to involve ourselves in all three types of visitation as we follow up absentees, reach out after prospects, and attempt to communicate the gospel in the community. How this will actually be structured is another question.

Motivation–Why Do We Want to Do It? There are improper motives for Christian service. Like Ananias and Sapphira, people in the church can do good things with ulterior motives, and God cannot accept the results. Christians in the church should not visit because it is a requirement; nor should they visit because it is the traditional thing to do. They should not visit because it may make them appear more spiritual than those who do not involve themselves in the program of outreach. These are improper motives and we might be better off not to have a program than to have involved in it people who are trapped in the error of "Galatianism"—an effort to secure spiritual status through the energy of the flesh.

There are biblical motives for visitation. Of prime importance is *love for Jesus Christ*. When our Lord sought Peter to bring him to complete commitment, He asked first, "Simon, son of John, do you love Me?" The feeding of the sheep and the lambs was to be Peter's service, but the raft of service had to float forward on the waves of genuine love for the Savior.

A second satisfactory motive is a *recognition of responsibility*. Somewhat different than requirement, responsibility represents a voluntary acceptance of the duty of the Christian. It is not correct in the light of the New Testament to say that we are "saved to serve." It is correct, however, to say that the Christian who is living in proper relationship to Jesus Christ will genuinely desire to serve Him, especially in communicating His message to other people.

A third important motive is *love for the lost*. This must follow in its proper place. It can never precede love for Christ since it is based upon it. Indeed, love for the lost is really love for Christ operative through the Christian, rather than some high degree of human love alone.

Participation–Who Will Do It? Effective visitation takes a full team; everyone must do it. Certainly it is the pastor's job. It is also the responsibility of church leadership from the official board right down to every teacher and helper in the Sunday school. In the final analysis, God must do it.

Some churches have found a special visitation night most effective. Others provide teachers and workers with addresses, asking them to make a certain number of calls during the week. The actual methodology is only important to the extent that a well-organized program seems to be much more successful than a program which rests too heavily upon the initiative of the individual worker.

One church has had great success at making departmental superintendents in the Sunday school responsible for having a certain number of workers on the job each Thursday evening for visitation. If there are eight workers in the department and the department quota on visitation night is two, no one worker would be required to come more than one night a month. Yet, an effective visitation would be carried on by the church.

Evaluation–Have We Done It? Here again records are essential. They tell us whether the calls have been made. They tell us something about the results of those calls. And they help us plan for the future of our outreach program.

DIFFICULTIES IN THE VISITATION PROGRAM

There are four problems that plague the church in its attempts to carry out a successful program of visitation. All four are represented by figures appearing in the great "seeking the lost" chapter, Luke 15.

Aimlessness. This word best describes the lost sheep. Off he wanders without care or concern. He was out there because he didn't know any better. He was lost because he didn't know how to stay with the sheep and did not know how to care for himself. His aimlessness is characteristic of the whole spirit of society today. Yet the shepherd took the responsibility upon himself and actively sought the lost sheep to bring him to the fold.

Uselessness. What good is a coin that is lost? It cannot be spent; it cannot be invested. It can bring no good to its owner. In the parable the owner makes every effort to find the coin. When it is found, uselessness is replaced by usefulness. So it is with people who are apart from God.

Godlessness. Here is the prodigal son. He turns his back on all that is righteous and good, involving himself in sin and worldliness until it overwhelms him and engulfs his starving soul. Nevertheless, when he returns home the father meets him with open arms, delighted at his arrival.

Lovelessness. The older brother was a self-righteous Pharisee. He cared neither for the prodigal son nor for his father, but only for himself. It is the "older brothers" in our church who stifle our attempts at outreach. Spiritual immaturity is exemplified by his kind of attitude toward other people.

One of the most familiar names associated with church growth in the American context is C. Peter Wagner. In looking back, Wagner labels the last thirty years by indicating that "the 50s were a decade of church growth, the 60s of transition and the 70s of reassessment." He is most optimistic about church growth for the 1980s and writes,

> In the final analysis, all church growth takes place in local churches. While many find themselves in areas of low potential for growth with some even suffering from terminal illnesses, many others—probably the majority—can grow if they have determination and are willing to pay the price. Churches belonging to denominations need not wait for denominational programs to come along: a large and growing number of resources is available to them. So many institutes and agencies geared to helping local churches grow have emerged that they are forming a professional society called The Academy of American Church Growth. They produce films, books, home study programs, seminars, games, Sunday school curricula, computerized surveys, long-term planning models, and many other aids. These combine with an increasing number of denominational resources to make church growth a possibility for most local churches.[5]

FOR FURTHER READING

Belew, Wendell. *Churches and How They Grow.* Nashville: Broadman, 1971.

Hauck, Gary L. *Is My Church What God Meant It To Be?* Denver: Accent, 1979.

Kelly, Dean. *Why Conservative Churches Are Growing.* New York: Harper & Row, 1972.

Longenecker, Harold L. *Building Town & Country Churches.* Chicago: Moody, 1973.

McGavran, Donald, and Arn, Win. *How To Grow a Church.* Glendale, Calif.: Regal, 1973.

McGavran, Donald. *Understanding Church Growth.* Grand Rapids: Eerdmans, 1970.

McQuilken, J. Robertson. *Measuring the Church Growth Movement.* Chicago: Moody, 1974.

Wagner, Peter. *Your Church Can Grow.* Glendale, Calif.: Regal, 1976.

———. *Your Spirit Gifts Can Help Your Church Grow.* Glendale, Calif.: Regal, 1974.

NOTES

1. Charles Chaney, "A New Day for New Churches." *Church Growth Bulletin*, March 1976.
2. Richard Ottoson, "Functions and Balance for Church Growth." *The Standard*, December 1974, pp. 25-26.
3. L. Ted Johnson, "A Unit for Church Growth," *The Standard*, December 15, 1974, p. 25.
4. Joseph Bayly, "Our Evangelistic Commitment." *NADCE Digest*, 1968, pp. 2-4.
5. C. Peter Wagner, "Aiming at Church Growth in the Eighties." *Christianity Today*, 21 November 1980, p. 27.

19

Christian Education in the Small Church

HERE'S A STRANGE THING: the church that most needs good Christian education is often the church with cramped space, few helpers, and outmoded programming. It is sometimes difficult to convince leaders in small churches that the same principles which function adequately in large churches can also function in small churches. It seems to be so easy for the small church to shrug off organizational innovation with that time-worn, hackneyed phrase, "It just won't work here."

Thousands of small churches across the United States face the crisis of the 1980s with the prospects of either growing or dying out altogether. For purposes of this chapter, a "small church" is defined as one having one hundred or fewer active members participating in its program. Most of these churches are rural, but not all of them. The fact that a church is rural does not necessarily compound the problem which it already has by being small. Secularization is as big a problem for the urban church as urbanization is for the rural church.

No specific church size is in view at any point in the writing of this book. The information contained herein is just as relevant and significant for the small church as for the large church. This is true because universally valid principles of Christian education need only adaptation to a local setting. It may be necessary for a foreign missionary to revise freely in the application of the ideas of this book and others like it to a *culture* totally different from that of North America. *Culture* is a considerably stronger variable than *size*, however, and it *is* possible for a small local church to have an effective Christian education program. The following pages consist of ten principles which can serve as guidelines for the small church in developing its Christian education program and securing the leadership for it.

The Small Church Must Learn to Scale Principles down to Size

Almost every aspect of Christian education advocated by specialists in the field today can be adapted to any local church in one form or another. Unification and correlation provide a ready illustration because of their frequent mention in these pages. Fragmentation of ministries is as much a problem in the small church as in the large church even though there are not as many agencies involved. Therefore, it follows that the principle of unification is a necessary and valid one for the development of a total church program in a church of any size. The small church and educational leader who reads books on Christian education or attends conferences or conventions needs to develop a frame of mind which will always take the *constructive stance* (How can we use this idea in our church?) rather than the destructive stance (That will never work in our church, it's too small.).

It is surely obvious that the small church must always think positively. Defensiveness and defeatism are the constant enemies of the small church program. How easy it is to give up when one sees the same fifty or sixty people in attendance week after week for a number of years. What a temptation it is to determine that it will always be this way—that growth or change will be unknown factors in such a church. Many small churches stay small because they have convinced themselves of this fate. Rather than aggressively spreading the gospel in the community and reaching out for Christ, they are engaged in a "holding action," desiring only to keep the doors open as long as possible.

Such an attitude is surely to the delight of Satan and can never be glorifying to God. The book of Proverbs reminds us that "where there is no vision the people run wild" (29:18, Berkeley). The New Testament corollary is found in 1 John 5:4 where the apostle reminds us, "This is the victory that has overcome the world—our faith." God's people in small churches need to take their eyes off of what *is* and cast them upon what *can be* if they work together empowered by the Spirit of God to make an impact for the gospel upon their community.

The Small Church Must Engage in Long-Range Planning

In chapter 1 of his second epistle, Peter talks about Christians who are "blind, and cannot see afar off" (v. 9, KJV). This wording seems strange to the English reader since the person who is blind cannot see at all and the words "afar off" seem to be superfluous to the statement. The Greek word for blind, however, in this passage is the word from which our English words *myopic* and *myopia* are taken. Peter's argument is that the immature Christian (i.e., one who has not added to his faith the various Christian virtues through the ministry of the Holy Spirit in his life) has a tendency to see only those things which are immediately before him, so he does not take a long-range view of the Christian life.

The problem of myopia is widespread, but nowhere is it more disastrous in consequence than in the small local church. It is important for such a church to view itself as small only because it is on the way to becoming larger. A realistic view of the community and surroundings may clearly indicate that the church will never have a membership in the thousands or perhaps even three hundred. Rarely, however, is it necessary to abandon the ship completely or to try to keep it afloat indefinitely with a skeleton crew.

The Small Church Must Clarify its Objectives

Do pastor and people alike genuinely feel that God has brought the church into existence for specific purposes? Are the purposes today different from when the church was first organized? If not, has the need which brought about the initial development of the church disappeared in the community? Delineation of objectives may provide a solution to the apathy which seems to grip many congregations of lesser size.

Perhaps the answers to the above questions will lead to the conclusion that the church should indeed close its doors and encourage its people to put their influence and support into some other church for which justification of existence can be given. If, on the other hand, the church clearly has a continuing ministry, if it is fulfilling a job for God in its community, if it does represent a meeting of needs, a clear realization of this dynamic may bring about the vision needed for renewal and progress in its work.

The Small Church Must Emphasize Its Advantages Rather Than Its Disadvantages

This concept is akin to thinking positively about the total church program. The focus earlier was a general one which leads to a recognition of what can be done in a small local church if vision and the power of God take control. Here we are thinking about planning and promoting the educational program itself. What are some of the features which are indigenous to the small church which can be capitalized on for a more successful educational program? Adams suggests several:

In a small church members can know one another.
The home becomes a natural meeting place for many groups.
A small church can use the out of doors for teaching.
A small church can use its total environment for teaching.
There is concern across age lines.
The family unit is more easily identified and nurtured in the small church.
The values of small group participation are more easily achieved.
Creativity can be stimulated in the use of facilities, personnel and resources.[1]

Some of the above "advantages" seem genuine, and others are questionable. For example, emphasis on outdoor education is surely not related to the size of the church as much as it is the geographical location. Surely there are other advantages which do not appear on the above list. Each church must decide what it *has to offer* because of its size rather than concentrating on what it *cannot do* as a result of its size.

One of the most helpful books I have seen in recent years pertaining to the matter of emphasizing strengths in small churches is part of the Creative Leadership Series, edited by Lyle Schaller. It is entitled *Preaching and Worship in the Small Church* and in the foreword Schaller writes, "Approximately 60 percent of all Protestant churches in the United States and Canada contain fewer than 200 members each, and two-thirds of them average less than 120 at worship. In other words, at least one-half of all Protestant congregations on the North American continent can be classified as small."[2]

The Small Church Must Seek Cooperative Ministries With Other Small Churches

The two biggest drawbacks to effective education in the small local church are inadequate facilities and lack of leadership. If, therefore, two or more small churches can join forces on a given project, the combined strength of their facilities, personnel and finances can probably bring about a more satisfactory program than that developed by any of the churches operating alone. The principle of consolidation in public schoolwork is an example of the strengthening of educational programs through cooperative endeavor.

Many churches of varying sizes are already doing this in joint camping programs. It would be extremely difficult (if not impossible) for one local church to purchase and operate a camp on its own. But the combined efforts of several churches provide sufficient counselors, facilities and campers for an effective program. Couldn't this principle be applied to educational agencies other than camping? Perhaps a vacation Bible school could be conducted as a cooperative effort. Certainly leadership-training classes could profit from joint sponsorship by several churches. Cooperative youth fellowship meetings and socials bring into contact young people of the same age group for wholesome fun and fellowship with other Christians.

Such cooperation in education depends upon theological harmony between the churches. This is true because the church's educational program is absolutely grounded in its theology. Geographical proximity would be a desirable product, but it is not absolutely necessary. There must be flexibility among the leaders in structuring mutually profitable Christian education programming.

The Pastor of the Small Local Church Must Concentrate on Leadership Training

Leadership training is an essential in every church. In the small church it is a necessity. Since lack of personnel is one of the major detrimental factors in the small church, it is at this point that genuine effort must be made to alleviate negative factors. Again, the long-range view comes into focus as the pastor thinks in terms of the kind of workers he might have in five or ten years if he begins now to prepare them for service responsibilities.

Leadership training in the church of one hundred is significantly different from what it would be in a church of five or six hundred. For one thing, the training will be headed by the pastor rather than some other full-time staff member. In the large church, leadership training will tend to be more group centered—special classes for teachers, leadership retreats, seminars—but the small church may be forced to a one-on-one discipling process. Furthermore, the small church is less likely to utilize the Sunday school hour for such training because it will need all of its available workers to staff the regular functioning of that ministry.

The really crucial difference arises when one discusses leadership training for the church of thirty to thirty-five members. Can anything really be done by a pastor who has just *one man* in his entire congregation? This experience enunciates a principle which can be generalized to all very small churches. Leadership training may have to begin with the "Timothy approach!"

The "Timothy approach" to training consists of the pastor building his life one by one into the men of his church. The pastor's wife can do the same thing with the women. It may take six months or a year to prepare one worker for Christian service in this way. The worker is probably better prepared in the final analysis, however, than if he had gone into a mass program of leadership training consisting only of large group study.

In such a program the pastor and his wife spend many hours in the homes of the prospective leaders. They study the Bible together with them and discuss principles of church programming, youth work, teaching, and effective Christian witness. It should be obvious that if the task is effectively carried on with the first couple, a ministry of multiplication can set in. When the pastor moves on to someone else, the initially trained workers begin to communicate what they have learned to others. The danger of this approach is expecting glamorous results in too short a time. This is a long-haul ministry and years may go by before it produces sufficient workers for the growing church.

The Small Church Must Be Departmentalized as Accurately as Possible

Because of the lack of space and personnel, there is a temptation in the small church to abandon the sound principles of departmentalization which are promoted by all reputable Christian education specialists. It is difficult to conceive of the need for a junior-high department if the church has no place to put it, no one to teach it, and no students to be in it! Nevertheless, the principle of "divide and multiply" is still valid in terms of Sunday school growth; and the small church should try to grade its classes as closely as possible to the accepted format.

The minimum number of class divisions for the Sunday school should be three, plus adults. This applies even to the church which must hold all of its activities in one room. If such space restriction is the case, a general family worship session can be held involving all ages; and then four classes can be conducted in the four corners of the room. If only one room is available, it is best to have folding chairs rather than pews so that flexibility can allow for educational grouping. The four basic groups would be as follows: Preschoolers—from two years of age through kindergarten; primary and junior class—grades 1-6; young people's class—grades 7-12; adult class—all adults from marriage through senior citizens.

The above departmentalization may not be desirable, but it may on occasion be necessary. Among the many obvious deficiencies is the fact that young parents will have to hold babies and toddlers on their laps in the adult class if any effective teaching at all is to be carried on in the preschool class. It follows, furthermore, that if the church has one additional small room in connection with its main sanctuary room, it should be made into a nursery for the care of babies.

There are two departmentalization principles which should never be violated even in the smallest of churches:

1. Never group children who are in school with children who are not in school (except in intergenerational classes).
2. Never allow young people to stay in the teenage class after they are married.

As the church grows, classes and departments should be consistently divided until the full complement of departmentalization is achieved.

The Small Church Must Widen and Vary Its Educational Activities

Surely the Sunday school will always be the largest and most visible educational ministry in the smaller church, but it is precisely because of the Sunday school's limitations that such a church must seek new and creative means of congregational nurture. These will be uniquely related to the needs and objectives on the local scene and may take the form of house churches, homes Bible classes, or numerous other ministries, some of which may not be commonly known among other churches in the area. Sunday school is important but the leadership of small churches must examine other agencies of Christian education which might meet specific community needs and provide a wider range of ministry for the church.

This argument applies epecially to those agencies which are carried on during the week, thus relieving the overtaxing of the church facilities on Sunday. Why would weekday clubs work just as well (or maybe better) in small rural church as in the large urban church? Is it possible that a summer day-camp ministry could effectively supplement or even substitute for a vacation Bible school? In the rural church, outdoor education may be an effective means of teaching children and young people the things of the Word of God through creative methodology that could not be employed in an inside classroom.

The traditional approach to Christian education in the local church has made the Sunday school the dominant agency. Many are wondering now whether it is worthy of this high a place as one takes the total church program in view. The small church is in a unique position to supplement its Sunday school with a wide variety of activities and ministries which contribute to the nurturing process.

The Small Church Must Press for Increased Home Cooperation

This is not tantamount to saying that the small church needs to have a family emphasis. *Every* church, regardless of size, should be concerned with the development of the Christian family and its relationship to the local church. The rallying point here is an attempt to transfer the burden of providing educational facilities from the church to the home. This is in keeping with the New Testament pattern since it is questionable whether there were any church buildings at all until after the first century. People who attend small churches may find themselves confronted with smaller buildings at church, but they do not necessarily live in smaller homes.

What kinds of church activity can be transferred to the home? Since the groups are smaller, many more activities of small churches will fit into homes than could be accommodated in a larger program. Consider the following list. Which of these activities might be carried on in the homes of your congregation?

prayer meetings
youth meetings
club meetings
parties
special Bible classes
leadership training classes
musical group practice
weekday clubs

Getting people to open their homes for such activities will not always be an easy task. Bringing families to a recognition of the ownership of Christ over all possessions is, in itself, a process of education which must be carried on over a period of time in pulpit and classroom before the desired fruit will be seen. The blessing to those who participate will be guaranteed, however, both through the joy in being host to whatever group may meet in the home and also in the blessing which God will bestow upon those who serve Him through sacrificial use of their possessions.

Christian education in the smaller church can be of high quality!

The quality necessitates flexibility and creativity on the part of those who have the responsibility for its leadership. If God calls you to a small church ministry, do not let discouragement and pessimism destroy the effectiveness which can result if the task of education is taken seriously and willingly.

FOR FURTHER READING

Adams, Rachel Swann. *The Small Church and Christian Education.* Philadelphia: Westminster, 1961.

Carroll, Jackson W., ed. *Small Churches Are Beautiful.* New York: Harper & Row, 1977.

Dudley, Carl S. *Making the Small Church Effective.* Nashville: Abingdon, 1978.

Foster, Virgil E. *How a Small Church Can Have Good Religious Education.* New York: Harper & Row, 1956.

Madsen, Paul O. *The Small Church–Valid, Vital, Victorious.* Valley Forge, Pa.: Judson, 1975.

Mavis, W. Curry. *Advancing the Smaller Local Church.* Winona Lake, Ind.: Light & Life, 1957.

Willimon, William A., and Wilson, Robert L. *Preaching and Worship in the Small Church.* Nashville: Abingdon, 1980.

NOTES

1. Rachel Swann Adams, *The Small Church and Christian Education* (Philadelphia: Westminster, 1961), pp. 14-16.
2. Lyle E. Schaller, ed., *Preaching and Worship in the Small Church* (Nashville: Abingdon, 1979), p. 7.

20

Personnel Selection and Supervision

THERE IS, in Christian ministry, a dynamic tension that must be maintained between the concepts of *gift* and *call*. We know from the New Testament that the Holy Spirit sovereignly gives to every Christian a spiritual gift which He intends for that individual to use in the service of Christ through the church. Some Christian leaders are given multiple gifts, and there seems to be evidence that these are the persons then called into positions of professional leadership in the various ministries of the church, both in its local congregations and in its outreach in education, literature, and world mission. An individual properly understands his relationship to the whole concept of Christian service only when he understands his spiritual gift and develops its capacity for implementation.

But the other dimension, the concept of call, is rather like the rudder that steers the ship. None of the spiritual gifts delineated in the New Testament has any geographical connotation. No one, for example, has the gift of "missionary work in Africa" or "ministry to inner city youth." The gift, rather, describes the what of ministry, and the call then designates the where of ministry. That is why we should not be upset when a missionary who has been ministering, let us say, in Germany, may decide at one point that it is within the will of God for him to switch to a ministry among German-speaking people in Argentina.

It is quite obvious that those who have the responsibility of supervision and administration of people in collective ministry must recognize both of these crucial ingredients as biblical components. Sunday school superintendents must consider the necessity of the gift of teaching in their staff members, and also impress upon them the issue of being called to that specific kind of local-church ministry rather than to club work, music ministry, or youth leadership. Both Peter and Paul had multiple gifts for Christian ministry, certainly including the gift of proclamation (prophecy). But Paul was distinctly called to utilize his gift as an itinerant missionary-evangelist establishing new churches among the Gentiles, whereas Peter was given the responsibility of leading congregations of Jewish Christians.

The concepts of *gifts* and *call*, if taken seriously, have profound implications for the way we recruit workers in the church or Christian organization, the way we supervise their activities, and the way we evaluate their performance. It is the intent of this chapter to explore some of those implications.

Developing a Christian Concept of Work and Ministry

One of the most interesting books I have ever encountered on the subject of leadership and administration is Abraham Zaleznik's *Human Dilemmas of Leadership*. Zaleznik's concern is the relation of an individual to his organization, and he writes out of a purely secular, industrial-management context.

Perhaps the key concept of the book has to do with the author's acceptance of human tension and conflict as a condition of existence and an opportunity for change and progress in the interrelationships between the individual and his organization. His psychoanalytical framework, with emphasis on Freud and Piaget, drifts far from a biblical frame of reference. Nevertheless, he explores some of the crucial issues, such as conflicts in work, authority and self-esteem, subordination, equality, rivalry, status, group formations, and other problems common to the relationship between an individual and the institution in which he serves.

What we have often failed to recognize in the church is that these problems do not exist only in the management-labor relations of the UAW or Teamsters. These same issues are among the cardinal points of difficulty in interpersonal relations in a Christian publishing house, an evangelical college or seminary, and a local church.

Interestingly enough, Zaleznik attacks what he calls "the Utopian View" of man's nature, denying that man is inherently good and rejecting the idea that the natural course of human life is toward personal growth or self-actualization. He substitutes his own position, which he dubs "the Individualistic View," emphasizing man's capability and the necessity for assuming responsibility in the work relationships. According to Zaleznik, the historic model of work is threefold: tension represents a need, activity results from the tension, and a discharge results

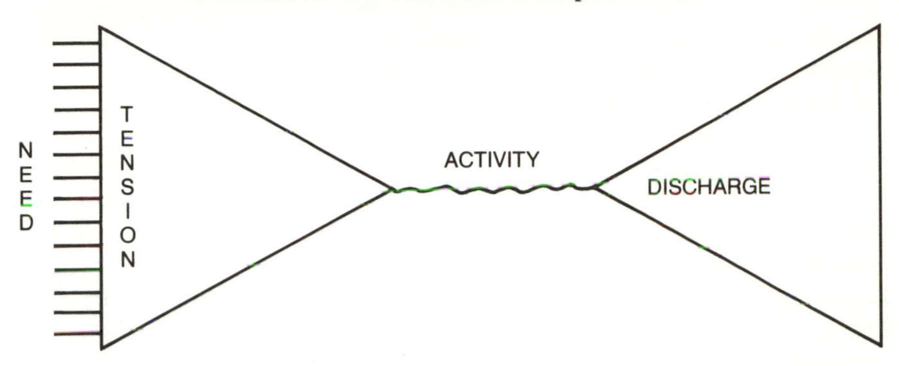

from the gratifications of the action. Both rivalry and equality are developmental crises for the individual.

It is impossible for an organization to solve this problem, but it can "foster the ideas that make the developmental gains worth pursuing." Perhaps the most significant sentence in the book is the author's perceptive analysis of the key problem in personnel relations:

> The unsolved problem in understanding man in organization centers around the inability of existing theory to grasp the essential dynamics of the individual, and from this understanding to formulate a true psychosocial theory of organization and leadership.[1]

Now what does all of this have to do with a Christian view of work and ministry? Simply this. Zaleznik has identified the crucial problem as *a misunderstanding on the part of all existing, secular theories in analyzing the nature of man, his understanding of himself, and his relationship to other people.* Unfortunately, Zaleznik, with his neutral view of human nature, also misunderstands the issue, and, as in all rejections of revelational truth, ends up with a perverted concept of reality. The fact of the matter is that man is neither good nor neutral, but essentially evil in his moral nature, as an abundance of biblical evidence clearly demonstrates.

The Christian view of man, so often characterized as being a *low* view, is, rather, in its totality a very *high* view of man. The Bible teaches that man was created in the image of God, and Christians are bona fide members of His family. Even the Christian administrator who is involved with personnel supervision in a secular organization must understand that the persons under his leadership are *potential* restored images and are therefore deserving of a genuinely Christian treatment (Col. 4:1).

There is another important factor in a Christian view of work and ministry. In Christian service there are no menial jobs. Many contemporary psychologists have shown us (even though their views are most frequently not based on a biblical philosophy) that the foundation for a sense of well-being and meaning in life is not so much a matter of external circumstances, as it is a person's deep-down belief that he is indeed a worthy human being. In other words, rather than the menial job thrusting its impersonal clutches of despair upon the individual, the person recognizes the dynamics of gift and call and responds in a totally renewed way to whatever job he might have (Col. 3:22-25). Call it a Christian work-ethic if you will, but do not identify it with Puritanical capitalism, for in contemporary society that is the kiss of death.

But there is more at stake than just the worker's attitude toward himself. That attitude is influenced by the administrative style of his supervisor. The Survey Research Center at the University of Michigan conducted a national survey of more than 1500 workers. This survey was analyzed in the January 1972 issue of *Manpower,* a publication of the U.S. Department of Labor. Some of the findings are most interesting. For example, construction workers and the self-employed were at the top of the contentment scale, with only about one in twenty registering dissatisfaction with his job. In technical, professional, and managerial occupations, the dissatisfaction rate was about ten percent but it climbed to twenty-five percent for workers in service occupations and in the wholesale-retail industry. Among workers with low incomes, college experience was a real handicap to attaining job satisfaction.

Generally in the survey, women were shown to be more dissatisfied with their jobs than men, and age did not seem to be a significant factor in that dissatisfaction. Marriage, however, was a strategic component, since unmarried young people were twice as likely to be dissatisfied with their lives as their married counterparts.

Perhaps the most significant finding, for those of us concerned with church ministries, was the seeming lack of emphasis on the matter of salary. Of the five work features rated "most important," only one had to do with tangible or economic benefits. Indeed, ranked higher than salary levels were "interesting work," "enough help and equipment to get the job done," and "enough authority to get the job done." Church leaders who constantly work with volunteer personnel should pay attention to the inherent message of those statistics.

To hark back for just a moment to chapter 4, the emphasis of the twelfth chapter of 1 Corinthians reinforces the concept that there are no menial jobs in Christian service. Given the human value-system and the cultural priorities of our society, certain ministries, like certain jobs, appear to be more important and prestigious. But in God's value system, all parts of the body are equally important, and all must be functioning at acceptable levels if unity and collective health are to be maintained.

In the helpful volume, *Counseling in an Organization,* Roethlisberger and Dickson identify what they call "five basic concerns" of employees:[2]

1. Keeping a Job
2. Friendship and belonging
3. Felt injustices
4. Authority
5. Job and individual development

These concerns, the authors tell us, stem from three sources: company requirements, group values and norms, and individual needs. If we can "Christianize" the Roethlisberger and Dickson research by recognizing spiritual needs and sin as a part of that third concern, we may have a workable model by which to analyze our understanding of a Christian view of work and ministry. Such a model can help us identify the kind of managerial attitudes and administrative styles church leaders bring to their important tasks.

Securing and Serving Volunteer Workers

Notice the double emphasis in the heading above. We know that the responsible Christian administrator has the task of recruiting workers. But as I have tried to show in chapter 6, a New Testament style of leadership requires that he see himself as their *servant* rather than their *lord* once they have become members of the ministry team. Surely the difference between paid employees and volunteer workers is an irrelevant factor here. It seems to me that there is a distinctive kind of managerial technique which one employs if he is committed to both successful functioning of the organization and biblical norms.

Perhaps the following four guidelines represent a mixture of competent administrative science and Christian philosophy of leadership.

EVALUATE YOUR RECRUITMENT PROCESS

How are you going about the matter of securing workers? Is your leadership largely dependent upon what Andrew Halpin calls "initiating structure"? Or do you emphasize the other end of the continuum, consideration? According to research in administration, the most effective leaders are those who score high in *both* dimensions of leadership behavior.

We must avoid being so intent upon getting a job done that we forget we are dealing with human beings, not cogs in the machine. At the same time, we want to steer away from the leadership style which may ooze with the milk of human kindness but contributes little to effective performance because there is no commitment to the initiation of structure and the pursuit of objectives in the organization.

In a real sense, a local-church board of Christian education functions as a personnel department in the recruitment and maintenance of workers. Board members are fallible and therefore must evaluate their recruitment activities in conjunction with certain basic questions: Are we recognizing gifts and calls? Are we emphasizing the meeting of individual needs? Are we avoiding the creation of concerns that trouble workers?

EMPHASIZE STRENGTHS IN JOB PLACEMENT

If Peter Drucker's book *The Effective Executive* is not the best book on management, it is certainly among the best. And one of the most significant chapters in that volume is the one entitled "Making Strength Productive." The initial paragraph warrants reproduction here:

> The effective executive makes strengths productive. He knows that one cannot build on weakness. To achieve results one has to use all the available strengths—the strengths of associates, the strengths of the superior, and one's own strengths. These strengths are the true opportunities. To make strength productive is the unique purpose of organization. It cannot, of course, overcome the weaknesses with which each of us is abundantly endowed. But it can make them irrelevant. Its task is to use the strength of each man as a building block for joint performance.[3]

One of the rubrics Drucker offers in the chapter is the suggestion, "Effective executives know that they have to start with what a man can do rather than with what a job requires."[4] That implies getting the right man for the right job in staffing any organization, including a Sunday school or youth society in the local church.

In terms of the worker's response, we are faced again with the important factor of a positive self-concept based upon a biblical understanding of one's gift and call. The creative Christian in a world of challenge can never be content with the desires of Sancho Panza, in *Don Quixote,* who wished to be lord of an island if it were offered to him "with little trouble and less danger." Nor, of course, does he wish to follow the frenetic neuroticism of Sancho's lord and spend his days of service tilting at windmills. Somewhere between lies that happy, median ground of sane and scriptural ministry as the utilization of divine power through a human instrument.

APPRAISE POTENTIAL LEADERS

Good leadership always breeds leadership—that is the thrust of what we have come to call the "Paul-Timothy approach." The effective Christian administrator has the task of assessing and recording how well each worker performs in his present position, and what kind of ability he demonstrates for other tasks. To be specific, which of the teachers in the primary department has the potential of becoming a departmental superintendent? Which of the departmental superintendents would make a competent general superintendent? Who are the potential deacons who will give leadership to the congregation?

Effective appraisal of potential leadership is only possible when three basic, managerial functions are properly operating:

1. Individual workers have a clear-cut knowledge of their roles in the organization.
2. Objectives and goals (including reasonable time lines) are established for measuring orderly results.
3. Regular, personal interaction is available for the discussion of mutual problems and progress.

DEVELOP ADEQUATE PERSONNEL POLICIES

The term *personnel policies* is simply a handy label to describe the guidelines affecting the dealings which supervisors have with subordinates in an organization. Positive personnel policies (if the presuppositions of this book are valid) center on a biblical view of man, a biblical understanding of the importance of the individual in the institutional framework, and a biblical commitment to the strategic position of the "gift-call" analysis of ministry. Such policies should be clearly defined and understood by the workers, so that they will not suffer from that organizational disease sometimes called normlessness—an expectancy that socially unapproved behaviors are required to achieve given goals.

In the volunteer organization, we are not dealing primarily with pay raises, promotions, and attractive retirement benefits. We are, however, dealing with the problems of isolation, self-estrangement, and the inability of an individual to achieve his own goals while helping his organization to achieve *its* goals. Positive personnel supervisors will emphasize development of meaningful relations, competent administration, encouragement of employee participation at all points in the decision-making process, and a high level of flexibility in the organization's roles and expectations.

Functioning in the Role of Supervisor

Supervision is the directing of the activities of other people toward the accomplishment of organizational goals. As an administrative function, supervision is linked with "staffing" and delegation. All are distinct people functions and will account for success or failure in leadership and administration.

Byrne suggests that "at the heart of supervision lies improvement. The administrator gives himself to organization and management, whereas the supervisor strives for better quality."[5] In a large business organization, supervisors (foremen) may hold completely different posts in the organizational framework than administrators (executives). In a local church, however, the pastor and the director of Christian education are indeed administrators; but they must spend a great deal of their time in the role of supervisors. In this latter role they are constantly dealing with people.

Joining the pastor and/or director of Christian education in the important ministry of supervision will be the general Sunday school superintendent and all departmental superintendents, as well as the directors and coordinators of all of the other Christian education agencies. It is the responsibility of these leaders to oversee those sections of the total church program that have been assigned to them. Supervising the program means supervising people in the program. Whether one's span of control is wide or narrow, the leadership role almost always includes some form of supervision.

Ben M. Harris in his book *Supervisory Behavior in Education* gives the following definition of supervision:

> Supervision is all efforts of designated school officials directed toward providing leadership to teachers and other educational workers in the improvement of instruction. It involves the stimulation of professional growth in development of teachers, the selection and revision of educational objectives, materials of instruction, and methods of teaching, and the evaluation of instruction. Supervision is what school personnel do with adults and things for the purpose of maintaining or changing the operation of the school in order to directly influence the attainment of the major instructional goals of the school. Supervision has its impact on the learner, then, through other people and things.[6]

Note that Harris calls attention to the fact that supervision deals with both *maintaining* and *changing* the educational structure in which the supervisor finds himself.

THE SUPERVISOR MUST PRACTICE ADEQUATE ADMINISTRATIVE PROCESS

There are certain universally recognized essentials to efficient management and administration. These are applicable not only to the executives at General Motors but also to Sunday school superintendents, directors of Christian education, or pastors:

1. A clear and well-understood chain of command.
2. Clearly defined lines of authority and responsibility.
3. Elimination of overlapping authority, overstaffing, and duplication of function.
4. Delegation of responsibility, including sufficient authority to carry out that responsibility.
5. Simplification of executive function and procedure.
6. Ability to make the optimum decision in the shortest possible time.
7. The ability not only to get things done, but to do the right things.

The implementation of these guidelines in the church should not lead us to the hard-nosed kind of executive power that is exhibited among "the kings of the Gentiles." When practiced in love, they may very well produce a blend of spiritual fervor and administrative competence that is precisely what we need in order to be the church in the contemporary world.

PLACEMENT

The supervisor usually has a voice in the initial appointment of the worker to his task. In the context of the properly functioning Sunday school, the authority for the appointment probably comes from the board of Christian education. But the Sunday school superintendent makes the personal contact and asks the person to accept the task. He thus becomes involved right from the very first in a supervisory capacity.

OBSERVATION

One of the reasons effective Sunday school teachers are alerted to the importance of their task is that their supervisors make a specific point to observe every teacher in his classroom at least twice a year. The Sunday school records and offering can be taken care of adequately by the Sunday school secretary, assisted if necessary by the assistant superintendent.

A good Sunday school superintendent has properly analyzed his job as one of direct observation of the teacher in his classroom situation. Of course, if the church has a professional director of Christian education on its staff, he would also be involved in the task of observation.

EVALUATION

Evaluation is an objective, written measurement of the teacher's classroom performance. The supervisor's evaluation may be supplemented by written evaluation by students in that class. This would be largely limited to classes of at least junior-high age and above and would be carried out with the knowledge and agreement of the teacher.

FEEDBACK

It is an established fact of management research that high achievers in almost any task characteristically *want* evaluation of the results of their actions. When applied to church education, this simply means that the effective teacher will probably become more effective because he wants to know his weak points for purposes of correcting them.

The problem sets in when the reverse is also recognized; namely, that the poor teacher is characteristically *afraid* of the results of an evaluation of his teaching. Nevertheless, feedback is a necessary step in proper supervision.

RESOURCE

In addition to counseling with the teacher regarding his strong and weak points, the supervisor also has the responsibility of being a resource person for teacher improvement. He should be ready with ideas and helpful books and be prepared to assist in any way the efforts which a teacher will make toward improvement.

THE SUPERVISOR MUST FOLLOW SOUND PRINCIPLES OF SUPERVISION

In the final analysis, supervision must be related to specific tasks and specific personnel. Nevertheless, certain principles of effective supervision, when followed, may not guarantee success but will most likely lead the supervisor to perform his tasks more satisfactorily.

The effective administrator is completely open with his workers regarding his concept of the supervisory role. He does not prowl around in the dark looking for things to complain about. He explains to the entire Sunday school staff (preferably at the monthly workers' conference) that he considers the above steps part of his task as a supervisor and seeks cooperation and prayer support in his attempt to carry them out.

But what if someone reacts negatively, either in the public meeting or in private conversation with the supervisor? That situation requires more time, more prayer, and more personal counseling with the individual worker. It may be necessary for a time to leave that worker and others like him out of an observation and evaluation system. Eventually, however, one should achieve his goal of complete supervision that includes all of the workers in the program.

The alert supervisor will also predetermine what to look for in a worker. This is necessary if he is to be objective and clear in his written and verbal evaluation. It does little good to go into a classroom and sit in the back of the room during the period unless one has an organized format for the observation and evaluation. It may be necessary for the supervisor himself to seek some training in proper evaluation procedures before beginning the suggested program.

In the personal interview the wise supervisor will be as positive as possible. It is never legitimate to be dishonest with the teacher by telling him that he is satisfactorily doing the job when the supervisor well knows that he is not. Surely though, there will be some note of praise that can be given; and the interview should dwell on such commendation as much as possible. Weaknesses can be described as "areas that need improvement" rather than "faults" or "things that you are doing wrong." Keep the interview on a spiritual plane and share some prayer time with the worker.

Finally, the successful supervisor will emphasize the *team* nature of the task and the important role that each teacher has on the team. He communicates to the worker his genuine desire to see the worker improve. He assures the teacher that he has not the slightest intention of taking his class away from him but seeks only to serve the worker and assist him to become the best teacher that he can possibly be.

THE SUPERVISOR MUST CUT DOWN ON RESIGNATIONS

This is obviously the next level of responsibility in the matter of dealing with grievances. *I quit* are words heard too frequently in Christian service, and particularly in the local church. Yet the words of Jeremiah the prophet haunt us in our contemporary situation: "His word was in my bones like a roaring fire, I was tired of trying to hold back, and I simply could not quit" (Jer. 20:9, author's paraphrase).

We are told that in the secular employee-market, the rate at which employees resign or are dismissed from jobs in some companies and locations is more than 100 percent a year. Perhaps an even more pressing problem is the people who do not leave the organization but continue at their jobs disgruntled, unhappy, and making themselves and everyone about them constantly miserable.

This entire book is an attempt to answer the problem of resignations. To be specific, the key to retaining good workers may be summed up in three words: *challenge, recognition,* and *reward.* We must recognize that the worker needs opportunity to pursue *individual* goal achievement as well as to assist in *institutional* goal achievement. He needs participation in decision making, and a recognition that he is an important part of the organization. To put it another way, he must understand that his gifts and call are very much a part of the functioning body, and that the role which he is fulfilling is a strategic one.

All of the information provided from administrative science needs to be filtered through a theological sieve if it is to be applicable in the life and ministry of the Christian administrator. Perhaps the key concept of a genuinely biblical work ethic, to be followed by supervisors and subordinates alike, is found in the words of the apostle Paul in Ephesians 6:6-7, TLB: "Don't work hard only when your master is watching and then shirk when he isn't looking; work hard and with gladness all the time, as though working for Christ, doing the will of God with all your hearts."

FOR FURTHER READING

Allen, Louis A. *The Management Profession.* New York: McGraw-Hill, 1964.

Black, James Menzies. *Developing Competent Subordinates.* New York: Amer. Management Assn., 1961.

Bower, Robert K. *Administering Christian Education.* Grand Rapids: Eerdmans, 1964.

Edwards, Mary A. *Leadership Development and the Worker's Conference.* Nashville: Abingdon, 1967.

Gangel, Kenneth O. *You Can Be an Effective Sunday School Superintendent,* Wheaton, Ill.: Victor, 1981.

Ford, George L. *Manual on Management for Christian Workers.* Grand Rapids: Zondervan, 1964.

Harris, Ben M. *Supervisory Behavior in Education.* New York: Prentice-Hall, 1963.

Heyel, Carl. *Organizing Your Job in Management.* New York: Amer. Management Assn., 1960.

Kepner, Charles, and Tregoe, Benjamin. *The Rational Manager.* New York: McGraw-Hill, 1965.

NOTES

1. Abraham Zaleznik, *Human Dilemmas of Leadership* (New York: Harper & Row, 1966), p. 207.
2. F. J. Roethlisberger and William J. Dickson, *Counseling in an Organization* (Boston: Harvard, 1966).
3. Peter Drucker, *The Effective Executive* (New York: Harper & Row, 1966), p. 71.
4. Ibid., p. 73.
5. Herbert W. Byrne, *Christian Education for the Local Church* (Grand Rapids: Zondervan, 1963), p. 109.
6. Ben M. Harris, *Supervisory Behavior in Education* (New York: Prentice-Hall, 1963), p. 39.

PART V

Administrative Personnel in the Church

21

The Gift of Administration

THE NEW TESTAMENT CHURCH has two dimensions to its existence. It is both an *organization* and *organism*. Because of its dual nature, the church faces two kinds of problems—*administrative* and *spiritual*. Too frequently, church leaders attempt to give spiritual answers to organizational problems and organizational answers to spiritual problems. The difficulty is compounded by some unfortunate misunderstandings of the nature of administration. Consider, for example, the following three myths:

1. Administration is nonessential. Some pastors think that the work of the local church will be carried on purely by an emphasis on pietistic endeavors, without a concern for the dreary, paper-shuffling tasks frequently associated with the work of administration.

2. Administration is uninteresting. After all, the real glory of Christian leadership is in preaching, teaching, counseling, and similar interpersonal ministries. Most people who hold this view would grudgingly agree that somebody has to handle the administration, but they have no inclination to offer an Isaiah-like "Here am I; send me" (Isa. 6:8).

3. Administration is not spiritual. Perhaps this is the most dangerous myth of all, for it attempts to drive a wedge between crucial ministries of the Christian leader. It suggests that some ministries are "sacred," and others are "secular." People who think this way tend to gravitate toward unbiblical views of church leadership because they misunderstand the crucial, New Testament function of administration as a spiritual gift.

ANALYSIS OF BIBLICAL BACKGROUNDS

The word used in the New Testament to describe the gift of administration is *kubernētēs*. It is the noun form of *kubernao*, which literally means, "to steer a ship." Although one passage in the New Testament is distinctive in helping us understand the gift, other passages in both the New Testament and the Septuagint (the Greek version of the Old Testament) provide significant, parallel information. Since the word appears only three times in the New Testament, it is not impossible to examine briefly each usage in this biblical analysis.

NEW TESTAMENT USES

Acts 27:11. The context of *kubernēsis* here is Paul's trip across the Mediterranean Sea to Rome. Although Paul predicts danger from the coming storm, the centurion pays no attention to the words of the prisoner but listens to the suggestion of the master of the ship. Here the emphasis is clearly on the idea of a helmsman. It was the responsibility of this ship administrator to know times of the day; the nature and direction of storms; the habits of air currents; the process of steering by the stars and sun; and, because of his knowedge, to correctly direct the ship.

Revelation 18:17. I have deliberately skipped over the passage that would appear second in chronological order, because the Revelation reference is so similar to the usage in Acts. Here, in a condemnatory poem spoken against historic and eschatological Babylon, John talks about the tremendous wealth of the city as viewed by tradesmen and "every shipmaster."

Perhaps one point about the above description should be clarified. The helmsman is not to be thought of just as a man who obeyed orders and kept his hands on the wheel. He is, rather, the responsible decision-maker on the ship. He has complete charge of the vessel's activity, in behalf of the owner. As Kittel notes, "Sometimes he [the owner] engages only the *kubernētēs* and the *kubernētēs* the rest of the crew."[1] In effect, then, the *kubernētēs*, or *kubernēsis* (the words are virtually synonymous), is the captain of the ship.

1 Corinthians 12:28. It is this passage which clearly marks administration as a spiritual gift. Although the word *governments* is used in the text of the Authorized Version, our understanding of the process of administration is the most fitting concept of the word in present vocabulary. Kittel has a most helpful, descriptive paragraph, which relates *kubernēsis* to the other gifts which appear in the same passage.

> The reference can only be to the specific gifts which qualify a Christian to be a helmsman to his congregation, i.e., a true director of its order and therewith of its life. What was the scope of this directive activity in the time of Paul we do not know. This was a period of fluid development. The importance of the helmsman in-

> creases in a time of storm. The office of directing the congregation may well have developed especially in emergencies both within and without. The proclamation of the Word was not originally one of its tasks. The apostles, prophets and teachers saw to this. . . . No society can exist without some order and direction. It is the grace of God to give gifts which equip for government. The striking point is that when in v. 29 Paul asks whether all are apostles, whether all are prophets or whether all have gifts of healing, there are no corresponding questions in respect of *antilenpseis and kubernēsis*. There is a natural reason for this. If necessary, any member of the congregation may step in to serve as deacon or ruler. Hence these offices, as distinct from those mentioned in v. 29, may be elective. But this does not alter the fact that for their proper discharge the *charisma* of God is indispensable.[2]

OLD TESTAMENT USES (SEPTUAGINT)

Proverbs 1:5. Interestingly enough, most of the Old Testament uses of *kubernēsis* are in the book of Proverbs. The emphasis is closely related to the concept of wisdom, and denotes the ability of the leader to offer proper direction to his group. In this passage, Solomon suggests that the wise man will increase his knowledge, and one who has understanding will find proper direction to perceive the truth and act accordingly.

Proverbs 11:14. Where there is no proper administration, the people will fall. The dependence on clear-cut direction from a competent leader is a frequent theme in Solomon's writings.

Proverbs 24:6. This is a military context. Only with wise administration can one win a war, for, in the final analysis, wisdom rather than might prevails.

Ezekiel 27:8. This is similar to the Revelation passage, in that it speaks of the helmsman, the administrator of a ship.

SECULAR CONCEPTS OF ADMINISTRATION

There are at least three components in all administrative situations, and some leaders in the field recognize four. There is, of course, a person who brings to the administrative task his own personality and ability (or lack of it) as a decision maker, motivator, organizer, and leader of others. Such an individual will have a distinctive self-concept, which will greatly affect the work of administration which he handles. The administrator's self-concept of leadership will significantly determine his approach to almost every duty.

There is also the *work group*. This term is always a reference to the people with whom the administrator interacts on a regular basis. It may be a congregation; it may be a professional staff of subordinates; it may be a faculty; or it may even be students over whom one has a "helmsman" responsibility. It is toward the work group that the focus of this book will be directed, under the umbrella term *human relations.*

The third ingredient is generally described as the *situation* itself, but some writers derive a total of four components by dividing the situation into the *task* and the *organization. Task* is a reference to the organizational goals established by others, usually a board of directors. Occasionally the word *problem* is used to describe the task as the administrator sees it. The concept of *organization* may have two slants. At times it refers to the institution itself, describing constitution, bylaws, and lines of authority. It may also refer, in a more general sense, to the standard procedures of behavior and function within the institution, although these might not be prescribed in formal, written documents.

One of the best definitions of administration is also the simplest: *administration is getting things done through people.* Interaction among the three or four elements is a constant mixture of the carrying out of administrative tasks in any institution. We may be talking about a pastor, a Sunday school superintendent, a mission board executive, or a managerial consultant for General Motors. Since administration is a single science, each of these men faces similar tasks in attempting to achieve organizational goals by directing the activities of its people. Obviously, such a conclusion has some rather basic assumptions:

1. The organization has goals. These goals may not be written and may, indeed, not even be clearly understood by the constituency. Many Christians have distorted concepts of what the church is supposed to be and do in contemporary society. If the administrator is really a helmsman, the way he perceives organizational goals dare not be fuzzy.

2. The organization has some structure to facilitate goal achievement. It is this issue of structure which has become such a battleground for the church in the 1980s. How much structure is really prescribed for a Christian organization? Where are the fences between form and freedom? Here again, the administrator, whether pastor or bookstore manager, Sunday school superintendent or college dean, must thoroughly understand, if not initiate, structures and forms for the achievement of his organiza-

tion's goals. At times these may be handed down to him from policy-making bodies, such a boards. At other times, those bodies will look to him to not only carry the water but first construct the pail.

3. The organization requires effective administration if goals are to be reached. Effective administration is not an option for the church any more than it is for AT & T. The administrator's position as a decision maker and group leader will either facilitate or hinder institutional goal-achievement.

Some writers in the area of management science attempt to make specific distinctions between the concepts of leadership and administration. James M. Lipham, for example, writing in *Behavioral Science and Educational Administration,* suggests that although leadership and administration have many factors in common, they are really mutually exclusive. Leadership, according to Lipham, has to do with changing organization goals. But administration is concerned with maintaining established structures.[3]

Such a narrow concept tends to further confuse already foggy notions about administration. All Lipham is doing is describing different administrative styles. It ought to be quite obvious that many administrators are very creative leaders, and the role of bringing about change is welcomed and competently handled. On the other hand, many administrators are "custodial managers" whose only concern is to "keep the lid on." In Lipham's own words, "Leadership functions and administrative functions are usually combined in a single role incumbent."[4]

The grouping of Lipham and other writers to pinpoint the distinctives of administration is indicative of research which emerged in the wake of the human relations movement in management science. Following the Hawthorne studies, the emphasis in the second quarter of the twentieth century was a rather extreme reaction to the failure of the "trait approach" to isolate significant leadership personality. Administration in those early years became almost exclusively the ability to work with one's group.

In the sixties and seventies, however, contemporary research is recognizing that those who emphasized certain leadership traits as the basis for identification of administrative roles may have had more of a point than the human relations people allowed them to retain. Present emphasis, then, is one of balance, recognizing the validity of individual traits (gifts in the biblical sense), goal achievement and situational adaptation of leadership style.

Drawing Some Practical Implications

What help is there for harried administrators in an analysis of the relationship between secular research and biblical exegesis? Certainly, several themes emerge which properly fit both the biblical and secular patterns:

1. The Christian leader's administrative style will depend upon what he considers administration to be. If *kubernēsis* is nothing more than paper shuffling, a necessary evil to the continuing existence of the organization, then administration will always appear unessential, uninteresting, and unspiritual. If, on the other hand, the leader can view himself as a biblical captain of the ship handling its course and cargo in stewardship for the heavenly owner, he certainly can approach his task with a dynamic and a spiritual enthusiasm not often attached to the role of administration.

2. The blending of spiritual gifts and leadership roles has evolved considerably since the days of the New Testament. Kittel, in the lengthy paragraph quoted earlier, notes that in the early church, administration was clearly essential. But it was not usually the work of the apostles and prophets. Even by the time of Timothy and Titus, however, Paul was giving direction for activities which are basically administrative in function such as widow rolls, leadership training responsibilities, and organization of congregational activities. It is probable that several men in any given congregation or organization will have the gift of administration. One of them may be the multigifted pastor who serves as main "helmsman." But if the pastor does not possess the gift of administration, he must seek out other men who do, and trust their judgment in matters of management.

3. The gift of administration is a capacity for learning executive skills, not a package of already developed skills. Of course, this is true of any spiritual gift. No sensible pastor would argue that he has no need to study, because he has the gift of teaching, and the Holy Spirit simply gives him things to say when he stands in the pulpit. Yet, while many pastors and other Christian leaders train extensively for preaching, teaching, and counseling ministries, most of them spend very little time in formal training (or even informal reading) to develop the capacity for adminis-

trative oversight. The gift of administration therefore suffers from "benign neglect."

4. The gift of administration is inseparably bound up with the process of working with people. Christian leaders must know how to get along with people. Developing and polishing human relations skills is a basic ingredient of successful administration. It will lead to understanding of the innate conflict between individual personality and institutional role. It will recognize the necessity for matching personnel utilization, in the church and other Christian organizations, with human interests and needs. Above all, it will emphasize a leadership style and concept of administration which focus on the community and *koinonia* of Christian groups not as a desirable approach, but as the crucial guideline by which biblical administration can be effectively judged.

INVOLVEMENT

The supervisor's ultimate goal is to secure such complete cooperation from the worker that self-evaluation and self-improvement become a part of the teacher's regular teaching process. Another axiom of management is that workers perform more adequately in tasks that they themselves have helped plan. Rather than just telling the teacher to improve in certain aspects or, even worse, expecting that somehow he will automatically do so, the supervisor should sit down with the teacher and plan specific improvement schedules.

THE SUPERVISOR MUST MAINTAIN QUALITY IN WORKER PERFORMANCE

How do you as supervisor evaluate and rate your workers? By their personality? By their past performance? By the amount of work which they can accomplish in a given amount of time? By their faithfulness? By their loyalty to the institution?

Most professional, employee-measuring programs depend upon an annual interview, the filling out of forms, and a general, subjective judgment on the part of supervisors. Although it is supposed to help the employee develop his skill and ability, the system usually does not work, because it is too often focused on the trait approach of leadership. The problem of adequate measurement of traits becomes almost insuperable.

Furthermore, most supervisors dislike the appraisal interview system, are hesitant to observe employees while they are performing their jobs, and do not like to sign their names to permanent records which might offer negative information about a subordinate. Frequently the forms are filled out and then forgotten.

What, then, is a satisfactory system of analyzing and enhancing worker performance?

Perhaps the best answer is not to forget these traditional factors of performance appraisal, but rather to improve the timing factor, which is what complicates the process. In other words, rather than an annual report, in which we try to reach back to analyze what a teacher or editor was doing ten or eleven months ago, constant communication between supervisor and subordinate should be the standard procedure in any administrative system. Immediate praise is a reinforcing factor, and prompt correction may keep the worker from habituating an erroneous practice. Discuss achievement when achievement occurs, and shortcomings when shortcomings occur.

THE SUPERVISOR MUST LEARN HOW TO HANDLE GRIEVANCES

In today's revolutionary society, it is not difficult to imagine workers at the local factory marching on strike, and carrying placards which read:

> We demand meaningful work.
> We want to be plugged in.
> We demand responsibility.

Such a situation is not likely to occur among Sunday school teachers in an evangelical church, but they may very well be *thinking* things which they would never write on signs. What *is* happening is that teachers and workers tend just to give up when they become disenchanted with the institution or their work in it.

A supervisor's response to worker grievances may very well retain the employee or alienate him completely. He must understand precisely what the worker's complaint is, if there is a satisfactory basis for the complaint, and if there is any precedent, in the organization, for handling this kind of complaint. It is important to assure the worker that prompt attention will be given to the issue and that corrections will be made if the organization is wrong.

Frequently it may be a matter of misunderstanding, which can be cleared up by a careful explanation of institutional policy. On other occasions, it may be a clear-cut policy disagreement, which must be understood in the light of the worker's emotional and social context. In the Christian organization, a grievance may very well stem from spiritual immaturity or sin in the life of the worker or the supervisor. The sources of grievances may be organizational or organismic, and we should not make the mistake of giving organizational answers to organismic problems and organismic answers to organizational problems.

FOR FURTHER READING

Engstrom, Ted W. *The Making of the Christian Leader.* Grand Rapids: Zondervan, 1976.

Gangel, Kenneth O. *You and Your Spiritual Gifts.* Chicago: Moody, 1974.

Lindgren, Eldon J. *Foundations for a Purposeful Church Administration.* Nashville: Abingdon, 1965.

Richards, Lawrence O., and Hoeldtke, Clyde. *A Theology of Church Leadership.* Grand Rapids: Zondervan, 1980.

Wagner, C. Peter. *Your Spiritual Gifts Can Help Your Church Grow.* Glendale, Calif.: Regal, 1974.

NOTES

1. Gerhard Kittel, Theological Dictionary of the New Testament, s.v. "Kubernēsis," p. 1036.
2. Ibid.
3. James M. Lipham, "Leadership and Administration," in *Behavioral Science and Educational Administration*, ed. Daniel E. Griffiths (Chicago: U. of Chicago, 1964), pp. 121-22.
4. Ibid.

22

The Pastor's Role in Church Education

LARGE CORPORATIONS often speak of men holding distinctive positions within the organization as "top executives." Such a designation could be used to describe the pastor's role in the educational program of the church. He may have little training for the task. He may not desire a close relationship with the church's educational agencies. He may consider some of the organizational aspects of church programming unimportant.

None of these things changes the fact that the pastor is the key to the properly functioning program of church education. Even in churches which require the services of a professional director of Christian education, the success of the ministry still rests upon the shoulders of the pastor.

The Ephesians passage (4:11-16) mentioned earlier shows that the ministry of the biblically oriented pastor is distinctively educational. It is not to be construed as just "preaching the gospel" if by that is meant a constant ministry of evangelism. The pastor as shepherd and teacher is constantly concerned for the nurture of the flock, including both the lambs and the sheep. The ultimate goal of the true pastor is that people come to a mature relationship with Jesus Christ. This kind of maturity implies spiritual growth which, in turn, implies instruction. The fact that the body edifies itself indicates that the ministry of "building up" is not one of pulpit alone. It consists rather of constant confrontation among the various members of the body under the ultimate control of its Head and the immediate supervision of the local shepherd.

The apostle Peter knew something about this shepherding ministry because he was distinctly called to it by our Lord Himself, a call recorded in John 21. Looking back upon his own ministry in Christian nurture and exhorting others toward their ministries, he says, "Shepherd the flock of God among you, exercising oversight not under compulsion, but voluntarily, according to the will of God; and not for sordid gain, but with eagerness; nor yet as lording it over those allotted to your charge, but proving to be examples to the flock. And when the Chief Shepherd appears, you will receive the unfading crown of glory" (1 Pet. 5:2-4).

All church leadership is largely concerned with relationships with other people. Certainly this is multiplied in the ministry of the pastor. It is the purpose of this chapter to view the pastor's role in Christian education at the local church level as a ministry of continuing relationships. How he meets this demand will serve to produce a shoddy ecclesiasticism or a properly functioning program of spiritual edification.

The Pastor's Relation to the Total Christian Education Program

A word that is helpful here is *oversight.* Looking upward in some churches, the pastor sustains a relationship of responsibility to a church board, a denominational headquarters and, ultimately, to God Himself. Looking downward in another type of church structure, he may be responsible to a church board, to his staff of workers and teachers, and to the congregation as a whole.

Some years ago I visited with a pastor who had some problems in his Sunday school. His solution for the problem was to concentrate more on his pulpit ministry and to avoid attending Sunday school himself. He almost gave the impression that if he ignored the problem with sufficient determination, it would go away. But no amount of ignoring or even pleading of ignorance can change the fact of responsibility and relationship that the pastor has to the program of education in his church. How then can he effectively relate himself to that program?

By Knowing What Is Going On—Inspection

The entire congregation must know that the pastor has definite interest in the educational program. Every teacher and worker must see that the pastor's ministry is an example for his own, and that, far from being wrapped up in his own ministry exclusively, the pastor has a great deal of concern for each worker, no matter how "insignificant" his or her task may appear in comparison with the church's total task. He involves himself in the training hour and engages in a constant observation of what the church is doing in Christian education.

This ministry does not have to be accompanied by a critical attitude which leads him constantly to correct the work of other people. Rather, it can be a helpful source of information to which the people of the church will frequently come when they need assistance in developing their own ministries for Christ.

BY SETTING AN EXAMPLE OF ACHIEVEMENT AND PROGRESS—INSPIRATION

The progressive pastor cannot always develop a first-rate educational program in the local church. There may be many variable factors which stand in the way of such attainment. One thing is sure: a satisfactory program can *never* be developed if he does not lend his support and influence to constant improvement. Other workers need to see the pastor in the role of a pacesetter, a man of purpose and action whose dedication to Christ and the work of the church is constantly demonstrated through contagious enthusiasm.

Such enthusiasm will not only accrue to the benefit of those who are involved in serving Christ through the church, it will also be caught by young people who watch the life of their pastor quite carefully. Their scrutiny will lead them to the place where they can respond positively to God's calling in their own lives regarding vocational Christian service. Most young men studying for the ministry have had contacts at one time or another in their lives with a pastor whose ministry influenced them positively.

BY COORDINATING THE EFFORTS OF THE CHURCH STAFF—INTEGRATION

Organizationally, unification and correlation of the program takes place through the efforts of a board of Christian education. Symbolically, however, in the church which does not have a director of Christian education, the pastor must assume the status of integration. He mediates between workers who find themselves having differences over some facet of the program. He encourages the board of Christian education by his regular attendance at board meetings and his frequent consultation with board members as individuals. He becomes to his church what General DeGaulle and Prime Minister Churchill were to their respective countries during World War II—the rallying point at which the troops gathered to press the battle against the enemy. At once he is the active leader and the symbol of unity.

THE PASTOR'S RELATION TO LEADERSHIP PERSONNEL

The staff of a local church might well be compared with a football team. Workers have varying responsibilities, but in the final analysis all are contributing to the same overall objectives. The coach does not own the team but works for the man who does. As far as the active participation in the game is concerned, the coach is the final authority and his influence reaches to every player on the team.

THE PASTOR AND THE DIRECTOR OF CHRISTIAN EDUCATION

Since the pastor has been selected in the football analogy as the coach, the director of Christian education must be the quarterback for the instructional team. The next chapter explores the role of the director of Christian education and what he should do in securing a satisfactory relationship with the pastor. What are some guidelines for the pastor in effectively working with the director of Christian education?

1. He should meet frequently with his director, praying with him and discussing plans with him for the church's educational program.
2. When a plan has been selected and approved, he must give his director *full* support in the implementation of that program. This support must be obvious to the congregation. He must be a flexible listener to the ideas and innovations of the director of Christian education, especially if he himself has not had professional training in the field.
3. He must encourage the members of the congregation to adopt a satisfactory attitude of respect toward the ministry of the director in their midst.
4. He must remember at all times that though they are colleagues in the work of the church, he exercises a very definite pastoral ministry toward the director and cannot let that degenerate into a "buddy-buddy" relationship.

THE PASTOR AND THE SUNDAY SCHOOL SUPERINTENDENT

In the church which has no director of Christian education, the pastor's relationship to the general superintendent will not be dissimilar to that described above for the pastor and the director. The span of control of the superintendent is not nearly as large, but the personal relationship with the pastor is desirable if the Sunday school is to be effective. One Midwest pastor takes his superintendent to lunch every Monday noon, at which time they discuss the results of the day before and the plans for the week ahead. A rapport is being built that will enable the layman to be much more spiritually productive in his ministry.

In the church where a Christian education director is ministering, the pastor must be careful to follow organizational lines in relation to the Sunday school. It is not proper for the pastor to bypass the director in discussing Sunday school plans directly with the superintendent. Just as a college president goes through the dean to discuss matters with his faculty, so the pastor approaches teachers and workers through the personal instrumentality of his Christian education director.

THE PASTOR AND THE BOARD OF CHRISTIAN EDUCATION

One church program I evaluated had a rather elaborate system of education presided over by a board of Christian education effectively directed by a layman. Though the constitution called for the pastor's ex officio relationship to this board, he never attended its meetings and, consequently, could not respond to even the simplest questions about what was going on in the church's educational program. A ministry of positive relationships was being hindered by the pastor's failure to participate in the church's educational program at its hub.

In some churches it may be necessary for the pastor to chair the board of Christian education, though such a dominant role has the danger of allowing too much of the implementation responsibilities to fall on his shoulders. A satisfactory posture for him to assume is that of an interested participant in all of the board's activities. In this way he stands ready to offer counsel and guidance to the board but does not give the picture of dominance.

THE PASTOR AND ALL CHURCH WORKERS

If every pastor knew how important it is to the Sunday school teachers and educational workers in his church to have some verbal or visible indication of his love and support, he would spend more time in a relationship ministry. The very concept of *koinonia* carries with it a dramatic appeal to fellowship *together* in the work of the gospel. Lay workers need to feel this unity and to experience a feeling of significance in what they are doing for Christ. They must know that in proper perspective, whatever their ministry might be, it is as important to the total church program as the pastor's pulpit ministry.

The pastor constantly is involved with motivation and encouragement. He must bear the burdens of his staff without carrying his own on his sleeve. His spiritual relation to Christ must be sufficiently strong to sustain not only his own ministry but the bleak moments that will come in the ministry of his lay workers. In a proper relationship role, he becomes not only shepherd and leader but also counselor, confidant and friend.

THE PASTOR'S RELATIONSHIP TO SPECIFIC MINISTRIES

Because he is a trained Christian worker, the pastor faces the same temptations as the director of Christian education in regard to involving himself in specific agencies of the church. Like the director, he must avoid as much as possible such specific involvement. In a sense it is probably quite realistic to say that in the smaller church the pastor can better afford such involvement than he can in the larger church. This is true because the pastor's ministry is one of administration, and the task of administration grows with the size of the organization.

The source of the temptation is basically twofold: the need for trained workers and the pastor's superior ability. The *problem* sets in when the pastor allows his superior ability to perform many and varied functions of the church so that trained leadership never really emerges. Sometimes it will be necessary for the pastor to stand by and watch lay workers do tasks that he obviously can do better.

Poor is the church, however, in which the pastor and his wife teach Sunday school, direct the youth group, superintend the vacation Bible school, carry on the ministry of music, and head the camping program. When these talented people leave, gaping holes are immediately apparent in the church's educational program. Furthermore, confusion besets the pulpit committee and the congregation in trying to find a pastoral replacement who can effectively function in all of these areas.

The wise pastor is not on the job very long before he discovers that one of the finest goals of his ministry is the developing of Timothys. When an effective pastor leaves the church, he leaves behind a trained leadership that is more competent and stronger in force than it was when he came. Rather than involving himself in specific ministries, therefore, the pastor should set about the task of leadership development as he becomes—along with his director of Christian education or, in lieu of a director—a teacher of teachers and a leader of leaders.

In many churches across the country the local pastor functions as his own director of Christian education. Many times he has no training for the task, but the necessity is there and so he carries on as best he can. Is it possible for such a man to learn some

Christian education in a more satisfactory way than just by trial and error? Yes, it is! Here are some suggestions:

1. Take classes whenever possible. The urban pastor, no doubt, will be close to an evangelical seminary or Bible college in almost any major city in the United States. One or two courses a year in Christian education will ultimately save many more hours than they will consume, so the sacrifice of the time is well worth the investment.

Education courses at a secular college or university are a very poor substitute. In such courses the pastor may learn something about the educational process and gain some good information about administration procedures. It will be up to him, however, to relate this information to the church's educational program. The philosophy, perspective, and orientation of the courses will be vastly different from the task that he faces.

2. Attend Christian education conferences. Such conferences are still being conducted at city, regional, and state levels. In most places they have broadened their horizons to take in more than just the ministry of Sunday school. Several publishers now conduct regional training seminars in different parts of the country. Denominational conferences provide specific information since they are generally under the sponsorship of a denominational publishing house.

3. Read the literature being produced in the field of Christian education by almost every evangelical publisher. The list of books at the end of this chapter is exemplary of the kind of literature that speaks specifically to the pastor in regard to his responsibility for education in the local church. In addition to books, many periodicals regularly carry articles which are geared to facilitate improved instruction in the church's program of nurture.

FOR FURTHER READING

Adams, Jay E. *Pastoral Leadership.* Grand Rapids: Baker, 1976.

Caemmerer, Richard R. *Feeding and Leading.* St. Louis: Concordia, 1962.

Gangel, Kenneth O. *Lessons in Leadership from the Bible.* Winona Lake, Ind. BMH, 1980.

Getz, Gene. *Sharpening the Focus of the Church.* Chicago: Moody, 1974.

Judy, Marvin T. *The Multiple Staff Ministry.* Nashville: Abingdon, 1969.

Greenleaf, Robert J. *The Servant as Leader.* Cambridge, Mass.: Center for Applied Studies, 1973.

Schaller, Lyle E. *The Pastor and the People.* Nashville: Abingdon, 1973.
Taylor, Marvin J. *Foundations for Christian Education in an Era of Change*. Nashville: Abingdon, 1976.
Wolff, Richard. *Man at the Top.* Wheaton, Ill.: Tyndale, 1969.

23

The Director/Minister of Christian Education

THE IMPORTANCE of the director of Christian education in the total church program is not questioned by many today. Twenty-five or thirty years ago the vocation scarcely existed, but now a significant emphasis is being placed on the training of directors of Christian education in both undergraduate and graduate Christian education programs. In spite of increased production, the demand continues to outrun the supply.

Unfortunately the work of the director of Christian education is largely misunderstood in most local churches today. This is true for two major reasons: the newness of the vocation, and the total lack of training in Christian education on the part of the majority of church membership.

In my classes I often liken the relationship that a Director of Christian Education has to the church educational program with that which the academic dean in the college has to the curriculum and educational structure of the institution. He is a specialist in "church academics." Growing educational programs in many churches are actually larger than corresponding educational programs in some secondary schools and colleges. They therefore involve more teachers and more students in the total enterprise. It should not be surprising that such programming needs professional direction at the top.

THE CALL OF THE DIRECTOR OF CHRISTIAN EDUCATION

A strategic point in the study of the ministry of the director of Christian education is the recognition that this is a unique ministry to which men are called just as other men are called to the pastorate or professional missionary service. A directorship of Christian education in a local church is not a stepping stone to some other kind of ministry. Since it is a distinctive kind of ministry, it must be prepared for in a distinctive fashion. Unfortunately, because of the great demand, many churches yield to the temptation to draft directors who are not properly trained for the task.

The National Association of Directors of Christian Education (NADCE), largest evangelical group in the professional organization of the vocation, recommends that the title "minister of education" be applied to one who is ordained or commissioned by the church. The title "director" applies to one who has not received ordination.

It is probably best that the director of Christian education not be viewed as an assistant pastor. The traditional image of the assistant pastor is that of the young man standing by waiting for the regular pastor to retire or move so that he can assume that post. At best it carries with it a very transitory and temporary responsibility, except in a few churches where the ministry of the associate pastor has become a regularly established function of the entire church program. Even then the title "assistant pastor" does not convey the specialty of function which characterizes the ministry of the director of Christian education.

It is extremely important for students training in the area of Christian education to specify for themselves whether God's call for their lives is to the pastorate (a preaching, shepherding ministry) or to leadership in the field of Christian education (with emphasis on educational programming and leadership development).

To say that the director of Christian education is not "called to preach" is not a petty technicality. It is a basic philosophy of the vocation. He may on occasion fill the pulpit, but his calling is different from regular pastoral preaching.

Twenty years ago the majority of directors of Christian education were women. The trend has changed during the 1960s and 1970s, however, and the present membership of NADCE is largely composed of men. Nevertheless, women do function most adequately in the field of Christian education as directors, coordinators, and sometimes as denominational superintendents. Dr. Paul Finlay indicates that there are advantages connected with a woman functioning in this position.

> Many of the advantages of a female director are parallel to the disadvantages of the male. If there is much work in connection with the younger children's departments, then a female director frequently has the advantage. She usually takes to detail work better than a man and is better able to live on the salary offered.

> There is a reduced chance of professional jealousy. She will not be using the office as preparation for the ministry: therefore, a career in the directorate may be more appealing to a woman.[1]

There are some disadvantages, too, but most of them can be overcome by a prayerful and biblical approach to the leadership role of women in the church. That role is changing significantly in the last quarter of the twentieth century and, though all the old prejudices may not be broken down, a much wider ministry is now open to women in the field.

THE DUTIES OF THE DIRECTOR OF CHRISTIAN EDUCATION

The general task of the director of Christian education is to organize and conduct, under the pastor and official church board, a unified, comprehensive program of Christian nurture and training for the whole church. His executive authority is delegated through constitution, job description or directly from the pastor and/or official board.

In a very real sense the director of Christian education functions as an individual in the same way that the board of Christian education functions as a group. This does not mean that the presence of either one negates the necessity of the other, but that when the church's educational program is sufficiently large to merit both, they complement each other in their various functions. The director is a necessary resource person for the board of Christian education, which is composed mainly of laymen.

The director, as the professional educational leader of the church, has the necessary information to make intelligent educational decisions and is therefore influential in determining policy. He provides initiative, resourcefulness, skill and supervision in cooperation with the board of Christian education and individual educational leaders.

The director formulates and interprets policies and standards for the total program, helping the leaders of the Sunday school, youth group, vacation Bible school, and other groups to develop their programs. Since he is responsible for the training of educational leadership throughout the total church program, he must keep abreast of the latest trends and methods in local church Christian education, endeavoring to bring them to the attention of the pastor and the entire congregation.

A very helpful brochure entitled *Guidelines–The Church and the Director of Christian Education*, produced by the NADCE, offers a suggested list of "What a Director of Christian Education will do for a Church."

1. He will help the church develop an educational viewpoint in all its work.
2. He will provide executive leadership to the board or committee of Christian education.
3. He will assist the pastor by relieving him of administrative responsibilities relative to the educational program.
4. He will bring into focus the educational objectives of the church program.
5. He will unify the educational thrust of the church.
6. He will train lay leadership to serve the program.
7. He will introduce and develop new ideas and ministry with the church.
8. He will explore and interpret trends in the field of Christian education.[2]

The director is the educational executive of the local church and therefore spends a great deal of his time planning. The December 1967 issue of *Church Management* magazine contains an article which deals with the resources of planning. In the article, author Carroll Fitch indicates that there are seven basic steps which constitute the planning process:

1. Survey
2. Diagnosis
3. Prognosis
4. Policy Formulation
5. Design of Action Program
6. Effectuation
7. Read Back and Review[3]

Certainly the new director will follow Fitch's suggestion and assume as his first task the achieving of total familiarity with the existing educational structure. Another writer suggests a fivefold approach.

1. Make a thorough study of the needs and interests of the people whom he is to serve.
2. Make a study of the needs of the community.
3. Find out what extent other agencies in the community are meeting public needs.
4. Evaluate the present program of the church organization.
5. Then make plans for a new year.[4]

Responsibilities of organization fall ultimately to the director of Christian education. Along with the necessary program ingredients of unification and correlation, the proper functioning of various agencies and ministries again become the director's ultimate concern. It is essential that he give sufficient time to see that the machinery of the program is well oiled and efficient. The director helps leadership in the various agencies to crystallize objectives and then to identify programs and procedures which will meet these objectives. In a large church a well-trained director may very well be the key which unlocks the heavy door to success in a unified program of local church education.

SHOULD THE DIRECTOR OF CHRISTIAN EDUCATION TEACH, SPONSOR OR DIRECT ANY GROUPS PERSONALLY?

A very strong tendency for local churches is to employ a director of Christian education and then throw him immediately into the gap at the weakest aspect of their program. He becomes youth director, music director, or a Sunday school teacher rather than an executive officer of church academics. It may be idealistic to say that the director of Christian education should *never* personally direct a youth group or teach a Sunday school class. It is not idealistic to say that his primary responsibility is to be a teacher of teachers and a leader of leaders.

The secret of the church's program is in the use of volunteer workers. The average church uses at least ten percent of its people in ministry as teachers, visitors, youth leaders, musicians, and so forth, and should be using many more. These people need training to do their job well. According to Mason, "The employment of a trained pastor and a director provides sufficient leadership in education to train and maintain an adequate staff of workers."[5]

WHAT IS THE DIRECTOR'S PUBLIC RESPONSIBILITY TO THE ENTIRE CONGREGATION?

Too little is said in church education books about the responsibility for public relations on the part of the church's educational program. A church which does not have a director of Christian education must rely upon its pastor, the church bulletin, various publications, and an occasional bulletin-board display to inform its constituency of the importance of nurture in the total church program. How much more valuable to be able to demonstrate to the congregation the concern that the church has for this nurture by exhibiting a leader who gives all of his time to caring for the educational program.

In a real sense much of the director's work takes place behind the scenes. In another sense it is important for him to be clearly visible to the congregation so that his presence reminds them of the importance of the program which he represents. One pastor insists that the director of Christian education be on the platform at every service, participating in some active way such as reading of Scripture, handling of announcements, or even chairing the entire service.

The NADCE brochure mentioned above emphasizes that the director must "be responsible for the organization, supervision and *communication* of the Christian education program." If his ministry of "communication" is handled properly, the corollary ministry of enlistment and training of workers will be less difficult to perform.

CAN THE CHRISTIAN EDUCATION DIRECTOR'S DUTIES BE GENERALIZED?

The key to the utilization of the director of Christian education is adaptation at the local level. The principles enunciated in this chapter and in other books and articles dealing with this subject certainly will be helpful in recognition of the strategic elements of this ministry. Nevertheless, each church will have to define for itself what it wants the director to do. He will be hired to do different tasks by different churches according to the decision of the church officials. In general, he will always be the chief administrator of the educational program. He will be just what his title implies: the one who directs Christian education.

THE DIRECTOR OF CHRISTIAN EDUCATION AND HIS CHURCH

Too many churches hire a director of Christian education out of desperation. Thus, he responds to a collective cry for help from a church which has not thought through a definition of duties or necessary qualifications to carry on the ministry. The question of status is quite important since it is directly related to the acceptance by the congregation of this distinctive, new kind of minister in their midst. Every director of Christian education who goes to a church which has never utilized a director's services before, knows immediately that part of his task will be selling himself and defining his role in the total church program. This may take most of the first year that he is on the job.

WHAT SIZE CHURCH SHOULD CALL A DIRECTOR OF CHRISTIAN EDUCATION?

Unfortunately the perception of many churches toward the

value of the professional worker for this ministry has been rather dull. Some feel that the pastor can handle this phase no matter how large the church becomes. Others are shocked at the idea of a "professional" in the church, never stopping to realize that the well-trained pastor is definitely a "professional man" in the good sense of that designation.

The educational ministry of the church is a full-time job apart from the pulpit ministry, the visitation and general pastoral duties. In the large church no pastor, regardless of how talented he may be, can successfully carry on a complete educational program in addition to his regular pastoral duties. One hesitates, of course, to identify "large church" since the relativity of such a statement is obvious. Nevertheless, a growing church which has sufficient financial solidarity, sufficient interest in its educational program, and promise of development of additional ministries and agencies, should seriously consider some kind of director of Christian education when its regularly attending membership approaches three hundred or more. Kraft boldly says,

> The church must take its choice. If it wants good preaching and faithful pastoral care, then it must give its minister time for this kind of work. The minister should then be relieved as far as possible from the work involved in the educational program. This work should be delegated to a director of Christian education who, in turn, places responsibility so that every person in the church has a part in carrying out these plans.[6]

A clarification of needs, an understanding of the objectives of his ministry, a specification of long-range objectives for the church, and the general financial condition of the congregation are all major factors in deciding upon whether or not to hire a director of Christian education.

WHAT QUALIFICATIONS SHOULD THE CHURCH LOOK FOR IN ITS PROSPECTIVE DIRECTOR OF CHRISTIAN EDUCATION?

Personal qualifications. The director of Christian education must like people. When directors on the job report back to their professors, the call most often heard is for more preparation in the art of working with people, since the exercise of that art can occupy ninety percent of the director's time. Meeting people continually and dealing with them in general matters is coupled with counseling and visitation in this ministry. The art of friendliness and comfort in the presence of people is not found in textbooks. Sincere, natural warmth will carry the director a long way in his dealings with the congregation.

Intelligence and good common sense aid in any occupation and especially the position of leadership. Mason calls the combination of these two gifts "the X quality which constitutes an educator."[7] Ability in making decisions, solving problems and handling new things in his program will be important to the director. The enterprising director will find that the past pattern is often the worst enemy of the present progress. In line with personal qualifications, Kraft includes humility, unselfish sharing, self-control, physical and emotional maturity, cooperativeness, and obedience to Christ.[8]

The director's appearance is also important since he often will be in the public eye. He cannot be too careful about matters of dress and personal grooming.

Spiritual qualifications. The prerequisite of a regeneration experience for any type of Christian work is assumed since any other conclusion would be spiritual suicide for the church. The director, just like the pastor, must know that he is a Christian, be walking with the Lord daily, and must be sure that God has called him to do this type of work. His spiritual life must be an example to the church and the community.

Educational qualifications. Ten years ago not many of us in the field were suggesting that the director of Christian education should have the same level of education as his pastor. That emphasis has changed. With increasing educational levels of church membership and the complexity of contemporary educational programs, solid undergraduate education followed by a graduate degree (almost certainly at a seminary) seems highly desirable if not necessary. In some situations a director could carry on an effective ministry with three or four years of specialized undergraduate training in Christian education, but that would now be the minority opportunity. A good background in Bible and theology is basic since the content that he will be training others to communicate rests in a solid understanding of exposition and theology.

In addition to his work in basic supervision, the director may also be responsible for research and statistical analysis of the educational program. It is imperative that the hiring church recognize that training in *education* is not training in *Christian education* since the context and philosophy of church education is considerably different from that of public education.

WHAT SALARY SHOULD THE DIRECTOR OF CHRISTIAN EDUCATION RECEIVE?

The question of salary causes great concern to many churches looking toward hiring a director of Christian education, primarily because it is difficult to develop criteria for decision. One objective criterion is to compare the salaries offered for teachers and administrative personnel in the local public school system. Consideration is given then to education and training, experience, local living costs, and the nature of the tasks the director will be asked to perform.

There may be fringe benefits such as insurance, car expense allotment, and some retirement program. If the director is really to produce results as well as keep on top of his professional field, it will be necessary for him to have access to secretarial service plus sufficient finances to attend necessary conventions and conferences which relate to the development of his ministry.

Salary guidelines can be obtained from the National Association of Directors of Christian Education which, in conjunction with the National Association of Professors of Christian Education, now publishes *In Focus*, a professional magazine released three times a year (Editorial Council, 810 South Seventh St., Minneapolis, Mn. 55415).

The following two lists have been used in placing directors of Christian education and consulting with churches that have done the hiring:

The church asks the director:

1. Describe briefly your call to be a director of Christian education.
2. What is your experience in local church ministries?
3. How do you conceive of the relationship between yourself and the pastor?
4. What is your formal training in Christian education? In theology? In psychology? In adult education?
5. Do you find yourself in accordance with the constitution and doctrinal position of our church?
6. What is your idea of what a director of Christian education should do for the local church? Can you name specific elements of your program? Specific goals? How do you propose to go about accomplishing these?
7. What is your position on such matters as salary, vacation, office space, secretarial help, and so forth?
8. Describe your relationship to the board of Christian educa-

tion. To the Sunday school superintendent. To the official board.

9. What definite plans do you have for the training of supervisors and lay leadership in this church?
10. What relationship do you expect to sustain with the young people of this church? To the musical program?

The director asks the church:

1. Why do you want to hire a director of Christian education?
2. What do you expect me to accomplish here? Is there a job description already formulated?
3. What is the church's position on the ordination of a director of Christian education and his relationship to the Christian ministry?
4. What provisions is the church prepared to make in terms of salary, secretarial help, housing, travel allowance, and other things?
5. Has the church employed a director previous to this and what were the results? May I ask why the former director left his position?
6. Is there an organizational chart for the church? Where will the position of the director of Christian education fit into this chart?
7. What other officers presently constitute the professional church staff?
8. Is the decision to hire a director of Christian education a decision of the total church or just the board? In other words, do you expect the majority of the people to cooperate in any programs which are introduced?
9. What will the church's attitude be toward my attendance at conferences, writing of articles, and involvement in other ministries not specifically related to the educational program of this church?
10. How does the pastor conceive of my role in relation to his?

Relationships of the Director of Christian Education

Since the director's work is constantly involved with other people, it obviously follows that his success or failure on the job will be directly tied in with his ability to work well with the other key people in the program. The "relationships" of the director of Christian education involve constant working contact with the pastor, the other church leaders, the official board, the board of Christian education, leaders of various agencies and ministries in the church, all teachers and leaders in the program, and the congregation as a whole.

THE DIRECTOR AND HIS PASTOR

The offices of pastor and director of Christian education in the local church may be of equal *importance*, but they are not of equal *authority*. The pastor is the chief executive of the church and carries the responsibility for coordinating and administering the total program.

The best way to describe the relationship between the director of Christian education and his pastor is to say that they must be an inseparable *team* in all that they do. Since an analogy was drawn earlier in this chapter between the director of Christian education and the college dean, the analogy might be expanded here to indicate that the pastor functions in the pattern of a college president. Just because the President is the chief executive officer of the college, no one would conclude that he had no relationship with the academic program. In like manner the pastor has a very distinct role in the educational program of the church.

The wise pastor will not only recognize but will actually promote the authority of the director of Christian education in all matters that concern instructional programs. The two work hand in hand and, although they may not agree entirely when they discuss things together in private, when they face the congregation publicly, they support each other without fail.

THE DIRECTOR AND THE BOARD OF CHRISTIAN EDUCATION

Some directors of Christian education prefer to chair the board of Christian education, but most prefer to have a competent layman handle that post. Whether or not he chairs the board, the director certainly will be its guiding light, providing resource information for all of its decisions. It is important for the director not to accept responsibility for all the work himself but rather to see that implementation is carried out through the leaders of the various agencies serving the church's educational program.

After the pastor's support has been secured, the board of Christian education is the next most important step in terms of selling the program.

THE DIRECTOR AND THE SUNDAY SCHOOL SUPERINTENDENT

One of the dangers in many church educational programs is

the overglorification of the Sunday school to the minimization of other agencies. Nevertheless, the Sunday school will continue to be the largest agency and that which employs the most workers in the educational program. It is important, therefore, for the director to assist the superintendent continually in the carrying out of his tasks as the chief administrative officer of the Sunday school. In those tasks he is responsible for general supervision, communication of needs and plans to the board of Christian education, serving as liaison officer from the board of Christian education to all facets of the Sunday school, and handling records and reports for the entire Sunday school. Yet, in all of this the director of Christian education serves as *his superintendent* and constant guide.

Writing in *Link,* Roy Crans suggests that there are four elements of curriculum concerning which the director of Christian education and the Sunday school superintendent must be in agreement, "namely, instruction, worship, fellowship, and service. In order to see these elements in action there must be organization of the total Sunday School program as well as the individual departments."[9]

THE DIRECTOR AND THE OFFICIAL BOARD

Most church organizational charts will show the official church board (whether it be session, elders, deacons, or some other organizational form) to be over the work of the director of Christian education and board of Christian education. It is extremely important that the director maintain open and effective lines of communication *upward* to these elected representatives of the congregation.

Many directors testify that their greatest difficulty in operating a Christian education program in a local church came from stagnating relationships with the board. Sometimes it will be wise to approach the board through the pastor; at other times to communicate to its members in writing. The wise board chairman will frequently request the presence of the director in board meetings to define and describe educational plans to the board members.

The subject of the chapter has hardly been covered in these few pages, and the student thinking seriously of pursuing a career as a director of Christian education is asked to study carefully all of the resources listed at the end of the chapter. At least two other items need mentioning here, however.

The first has to do with the tenure of the director in his church. Unfortunately this is one of the few negatives in the profession. At the time of one recent survey the average tenure of directors was less than two years! All mature Christian workers know that effective service for Christ cannot be developed in any kind of ministry in this short period of time. This problem must be solved, and it will take the cooperative efforts of pastors, teachers in Christian education departments of all evangelical schools, members of church boards, and organizations like NADCE to build a "long term of service" philosophy into present and future directors of Christian education.

The final question deals with the rapidity with which the new director is expected to bring about changes in the church program. Two extremes must be avoided: namely, the attempt to change everything in the first year, and an undue satisfaction with the status quo resulting in lethargy and apathy which will be too easily communicated to the people. The director who has his eyes on a long-range program can afford to wait a reasonable amount of time before seeing major changes in a church.

FOR FURTHER READING

Asper, Wallace J. *How to Organize the Educational Program of Your Church*. Minneapolis: Augsburg, 1959.

Beal, Will, comp. *The Work of the Minister of Education*. Nashville: Convention Press, 1976.

Bell, A. Donald. *How to Get Along with People in the Church*. Grand Rapids: Zondervan, 1960.

Bower, Robert K. *Administering Christian Education*. Grand Rapids: Eerdmans, 1964.

Harris, Maria. *The D.R.E. Book*. New York: Paulist, 1976.

Sisemore, John T. *The Ministry of Religious Education*. Nashville: Broadman, 1978.

Taylor, Marvin J. *Foundations for Christian Education in an Era of Change*. Nashville: Abingdon, 1976.

NOTES

1. Paul R. Finlay, "The Christian Education Director," in *An Introduction to Evangelical Christian Education*, J. Edward Hakes, ed. (Chicago: Moody, 1964), p. 228.
2. *Guidelines–The Church and the Director of Christian Education*, National Association of Directors of Christian Education, brochure No. 101.
3. Carroll Fitch, "The CBA as Director of Resources," *Church Management* (December 1967), p. 31.
4. Philip Henry Lotz, ed., *Orientation in Religious Education* (Nashville: Abingdon-Cokesbury, 1950), pp. 222-23.
5. Harold C. Mason, *Abiding Values in Christian Education* (Westwood, N.J.: Revell, 1955), p. 151.
6. Vernon R. Kraft, *The Director of Christian Education in the Local Church* (Chicago: Moody, 1967), p. 23.
7. Mason, p. 156.
8. Kraft, pp. 32-33.
9. Roy Crans, "The Relationship of the D.C.E. and the Sunday School Superintendent," *Link*, August 1965.

24

The Board/Committee of Christian Education

NOT EVERY CHURCH is of sufficient size and financial solidarity to hire a full-time director of Christian education. In some churches this has created a lack of coordination and organizational unity due to the fact that there is no single individual responsible for maintaining the correlation of the total educational program. This situation does not have to exist, however, for there is no church too small to have a properly functioning board of Christian education. The strategic centrality of such a board is clearly demonstrated in even a cursory observation of the charts in chapter 16. The board works at the heart of the program and assumes the important tasks of unification and correlation.

A church desiring to improve its Christian education program will begin by constructing or reconstructing the Christian education board. It is of the utmost importance that this board find its proper place in the organizational structure of the church and that it be functioning in proper relationship upward to the official board and higher echelons of authority, and downward to the various agencies and ministries of the local church.

Acting as the "school board" of the congregation, this body works with the pastor and other educational leaders to carry out the educational objectives which have been decided upon by the church. The Lutheran Church—Missouri Synod well describes the function of the board in its *Handbook for Local Boards of Christian Education:*

> Thus the Board of Christian Education is the agent of the congregation set up to deal with the educational needs and problems of the congregation. It concerns itself wih education for all age levels and suggests the policies for all the educational agencies and groups of the congregation. It considers and acts on the recommendations of the school staff, the Sunday school staff, and leaders of other educational agencies. It concerns itself with the call-

> ing or appointment of personnel. In short, the board seeks to advance the total educational program of the congregation for all age levels.[1]

The essential nature of this board is such that it will find itself at the control center of all educational programming in the church. It is essential, therefore, that the board be composed of people who can function competently as mature leaders working together to achieve specific ends.

The Purpose of the Board of Christian Education

It cannot be stated too often that the basic purpose of the board of Christian education is to serve as a body of unification and correlation for all the various Christian education activities carried on by the local church. Obviously, the larger the span of activities, the larger the board membership and the more detailed its responsibilities. In reality, the work of the board of Christian education will touch on every phase of the church's educational life. According to Dalton, "Its basic functions may be considered fourfold: *integration* of all activities toward a common objective; *correlation* of personnel, time, activities, and energies; *unification* of purpose; and *distribution* of responsibility."[2]

VALUES OF THE BOARD

A good board of Christian education provides an agency of guidance relative to Christian education abilities and planning both on the immediate and long-range scale. It will provide a channel for constant leadership training, a matter which is of extreme concern to many churches in view of the paucity of leaders and workers in the average church.

The presence of the board also gives all the church teachers and workers assurance that there is a thinking, praying and planning group which is responsible for the affairs of their particular ministries as well as the ministries of all other church workers. The recruitment of teachers and workers for the various facets of the total church program is one of the basic purposes of the Christian education board.

A properly functioning board also relieves the pastor or the Sunday school superintendent of the heavy load of executive responsibilities and decisions, many of which are best made by a group. The curse of a one-man ministry can be lifted if the pastor will effectively utilize this board in grappling with the decisions and problems directly concerned with the carrying out of the total church program of Christian education. Although he may have to invest time in the initial stages of its development, the busy pastor will eventually profit greatly by an adequately functioning board of Christian education.

The detail and decision, which are necessary parts of educational administration in any institution concerned with instruction, can be turned over almost entirely to this board. As in many things, so in administration, the whole is greater than the sum of its parts; and this board purposes to see all of the facets of the church's work in single perspective.

The board is itself an educational agency whose task is to constantly inform the congregation of the various needs and developments in Christian education which are being experienced in the church. Communication of the need for service and the opportunities for workers is a constant process which the board carries out through verbal announcement, bulletin boards, church publications, personal contact, small-group meetings, workers' conferences, special seminars and a host of other media. This board serves as a "Christian education conscience" for the local church.

SIZE OF THE BOARD

The size of the board will vary with the size and activity of the church. Generally speaking, under five is small and over fifteen may become unwieldy. Though size is certainly not the major factor in the selection of board members, it is important to construct a board that is of satisfactory proportions to do the job in a given church situation.

THE PERSONNEL OF THE BOARD OF CHRISTIAN EDUCATION

THE NECESSITY OF REPRESENTATION

The matter of representation may well be the crisis point of success or failure for the board of Christian education. It is not sufficient just to have a board; it is essential that that board adequately represent all of the agencies or ministries currently functioning in any local church program. Once again, an accurate organizational chart will immediately show its readers who should be on the board of Christian education.

Each agency is represented by its highest ranking leader: Sunday school by its superintendent; the Pioneer Girls organization or Christian Service Brigade by the committee chairman; training hour by a coordinator or director; vacation Bible school by a superintendent; church music by its director; children's church by a coordinating director; and other organizations by presidents or leaders. If for some reason the highest ranking representative of the group cannot be on the board of Christian education, someone else can take his place in that post.

In conjunction with representative membership, certain church officials should be on the board of Christian education in an ex officio capacity. These would include the pastor, the director of Christian education, and perhaps a deacon, elder, or member of the official church board. Some congregations also find it desirable to elect from the congregation a member at large whose primary mission on the board is to objectively represent the totality of the congregation.

AGE-GROUP ORGANIZATION

All of the above assumes that the church's organizational chart is structured in accordance with the functional plan, allowing a direct line from the board of Christian education to the various agencies. If age-group committees are preferred, the representation on the board of Christian education would most likely be through the chairmen of the age-group committees. Such a board might then include the following members: pastor, Sunday school superintendent, deacon, director of music, chairman of the adult education committee, chairman of the youth education committee, chairman of the committee on children's education, and a member elected from the congregation.

The obvious task of representative membership is to speak adequately for one's organization on the board of Christian education. A children's church representative, for example, would represent the needs for any budget requests, speak for personnel, and catalytically motivate other long-range planning for the various units of children's church conducted by that congregation.

ORGANIZATION OF PROGRAM OBJECTIVES

Some churches may wish to structure the board around the various aspects of the church's ministry. There would then be committees on worship, fellowship, instruction and service, with their chairmen constituting the core of the board.

SECURING OF BOARD MEMBERS

If the representative plan is used, members will take their places on the board because of their affiliation with another agency of Christian education within the church. There will be no need for either election or appointment to the board of Christian education except in the case of the representative from the official board or deacon board, and the election of a member from the congregation. All other members are "ex officio" in the genuine meaning of that term (i.e., by virtue of office).[3]

There are, of course, other ways to construct the board of Christian education. Election from the congregation at the annual church meeting is a possibility. The problems it brings with it, however, include the possibility of unqualified board members, less enthusiasm for the task on the part of elected members, and insufficient knowledge of the various church agencies. Electing members for the board of Christian education is akin to electing Sunday school teachers and workers in the church, a practice not generally recommended by leadership in the field of Christian education.

Still a third possibility of board composition is the appointment system whereby members will be appointed by the official church board, subject perhaps to congregational approval. Their terms of office can rotate on a two- to three-year basis so that approximately one-third of the board will be replaced each year.

QUALIFICATIONS OF BOARD MEMBERS

People serving on this board ought to be dedicated Christians who are spiritually mature, have some amount of leadership ability themselves, and preferably some training or practical experience in Christian education. They must be able to pray earnestly and speak honestly about problems and people as the board carries on its work. There is no room here for argumentative persons or those who have no courage for frank discussion when a given name is presented to the board for a leadership position. It becomes necessary at that point for the board members to speak out very clearly if any of them know of reasons why the suggested person is not capable of carrying on the duties of the job for which he is being considered.

It is obvious that the keeping of confidence is an important qualification for board members. Add to these qualities faithfulness, willingness to work, and a generous amount of vision and flexibility to allow for elasticity and innovation in a long-range planning of the educational program.

THE STRUCTURE OF THE BOARD OF CHRISTIAN EDUCATION

Regular board offices should be effectively utilized, including a chairman, vice-chairman, secretary and any other office necessary for proper executive performance. If a competent layman can be found to chair the board, such an arrangement is preferable to chairmanship by the pastor or director of Christian education (though the latter is extremely tempting to expedite the board's operation). A large evangelical church in St. Louis has a very satisfactory plan whereby the Sunday school superintendent, after having served three years in the office, automatically becomes the chairman of the board of Christian education for the next three years. He comes to that post with a wide knowledge of the church's educational program. It might also be said that the board chairman should hold no other post during the time he is serving in that capacity.

The formation of committees and subcommittees will probably be a common board responsibility. Professor David Bell, writing in *Link* magazine, suggests several subcommittee services may be necessary on occasion: personnel, job, library, budget, and program.[4]

One question I am often asked in conferences and churches relates to how often the board should meet. Ultimately, of course, this has to be answered on a local level since the board is attempting to fulfill the objectives and to meet the needs of a given congregation. A rather safe generalization, however, would be to schedule a regular monthly meeting for approximately two hours.

Such a time schedule assumes that a satisfactory agenda is kept, responsibilities of implementation are shared by the board's membership, and minutes are mimeographed and distributed in advance, alleviating the necessity of reading them in the actual meeting. The individual responsibility of each board member and the expectations of the group as a whole should be clearly understood.

Regular reports to the church are an essential part of any functioning board. These reports will most likely take the form of written and/or verbal communication to the total congregation at the time of quarterly and annual business meetings. However, informal reporting through church bulletins and other publications can keep the congregation constantly aware of what the board is doing and how it is serving the total church program.

THE PERFORMANCE OF THE BOARD OF CHRISTIAN EDUCATION

What does the board of Christian education do at its meetings and between its meetings? That question has been partially answered by many of the things said earlier in this chapter. The Lutheran handbook, referred to earlier, identifies twelve "chief concerns of the board of Christian education":

1. provision for all age levels
2. objectives
3. curriculum
4. agencies
5. teaching staff
6. administrative staff
7. leadership training
8. plant and equipment
9. home relations
10. evaluation
11. finances
12. coordination.[5]

The student of Christian education will find almost as many lists of duties for the board of Christian education as books which he reads on the subject. For purposes of simplicity, here are three general areas of performance which can be identified.

THE BOARD OF CHRISTIAN EDUCATION IS A PLANNING BODY

The board evaluates the present situation, then it projects the needs of the church into the future in a continuing program of planning and developing toward an adequate total church program. This, of course, includes what the church will be doing in the immediate future and the distant future, how it ought to be done, and who will be responsible for actually getting the job done.

Such planning implies provision for worker recruitment and training plus the gathering, filing, and utilization of information regarding prospects for the various church tasks. The board must have at its fingertips a complete listing of every task of the total church program and an indication of who is responsible for fulfilling that task at a given time.

In its planning work the board is also a policy-making group. It decides matters of curriculum, organizational procedure, establishment of record systems, and the determination of standards in all phases of the educational program. If the board is adequately doing its job, it will forsee needs and develop the personnel to meet those needs through adequate leadership-training programs. Job descriptions will be written so that everyone who is asked to participate in service for Christ through the church will know exactly what is expected of him.

Planning for curriculum and personnel also includes board performance as a purchasing agent. The budget of the church's educational program can be unified under the care of this board. If a Sunday school teacher needs a piece of equipment, he can make the request through the Sunday school superintendent to the board of Christian education. If the request is a reasonable one and the budget will allow such a purchase, the board can handle it in the best and most businesslike manner. This procedure will avoid "piece purchasing," which is often done by various workers in the Sunday school or church with no careful record of what is spent and for what purpose.

THE BOARD OF CHRISTIAN EDUCATON IS A SUPERVISING BODY

Collectively in its meeting discussions, and at the grassroots level through its membership directing the various agencies which they head, the board is constantly supervising the total church program. It is the supervision coupled with the planning that produces the unification and correlation so desired in the church's educational program.

Supervision includes the provision of all curriculum materials and teaching aids necessary, guidance for all workers in the total church program, and the constant representation of those workers to the congregation as a whole. Matters of instructional improvement, proper plant and facility utilization, and achievement of objectives are all the concern of this board and its ministry of supervision.

THE BOARD OF CHRISTIAN EDUCATION IS AN EVALUATING BODY

Evaluation is inseparably related to planning. The board of Christian education is constantly engaged in the process of asking itself the question, How are we doing? Needs change, and our understanding of them must be refined. Such refinement brings about new objectives and a clarification of previously stated objectives. Potential is compared with the present to determine where we are able to go in the development of the total church program. Performance of each Christian education worker in the church is carefully watched to see if his appointment will be made for another year. Evaluation thus turns into planning, planning is followed by supervision, supervision by evaluation, and the cycle constantly repeats itself as the board carries out its duties in connection with the program of Christian education in the local church.

The Problems of the Board of Christian Education

Most books on Christian education point up the bright side of the work but fail to confront the future director of Christian education or pastor with the pitfalls to avoid and the problems to expect when he engages in his all-important task of nurture through the church. The following list is limited, but it represents some of the problems which the author has encountered in working with boards of Christian education in churches throughout the United States:

Reaction Against Innovation

The construction of the board of Christian education in many churches is a "new thing" on the horizon. Generally there will be some traditionalists in the congregation who will oppose it just because it is new and they do not understand it. Sometimes it will be necessary to work in and with the situation for several years before a properly functioning board of Christian education will really result and achieve the work attributed to it in this chapter.

Fear of Unwarranted Power

Occasionally members of an official board or a deacon board will be afraid that the younger brother will usurp the authority of the older brother in the organizational church family. Since an overwhelming percentage of what the church does is educational, it is more than appearance when the board of Christian education is observed to be involved with the entire church life. It is organizationally unsound to conclude that the board of Christian education has authority over the official church board, and an understanding glance at the organizational chart can immediately alleviate the confusion.

Failure to Achieve Objectives

Few attitudes are more difficult to combat in leadership than the smog of repeated failure. Often this stems from setting unclear or unrealistic objectives at the beginning of the church's educational year. Christian education boards and/or committees must be spiritually and organizationally precise in describing what the educational ministry seeks to accomplish and what procedures will be utilized to realize those goals.

LETHARGY ON THE PART OF THE MEMBERS

Laziness in the board will very quickly spread into the ranks of all of the church leadership and affect the troops. Enthusiasm for the total church program must filter down from the board of Christian education. One safeguard against lethargy in the board is not to load board members down with too many other responsibilities. Another safeguard is a genuine time for confession and commitment to Christ as a group at the beginning of each board meeting.

Since the New Testament teaches that nurture and edification represent a comprehensive goal, it is necessary for the church to have a comprehensive program of nurture and education. The achievement of satisfactory function, unification and correlation of such a program is certainly not guaranteed by a board of Christian education. Its fulfillment is certainly advanced, however, and made much more likely by such a board functioning properly. The board is the highest level of authority in all educational matters of the church. The relationships must be adequately developed between the board and the pastor, the director of Christian education, the other boards and committees in the church, and the total constituency.

Serving on the board of Christian education is not only a spiritual ministry, it is a rewarding one if one is willing to work faithfully over a period of years. Zuck concludes that there can be very significant results from the efficient work of a board of Christian education:

1. An organized total church program—keeping things running.
2. An efficient total church program—keeping things running smoothly.
3. A coordinated total church program—keeping things running together.
4. An advancing total church program—keepings things running ahead.[7]

FOR FURTHER READING

Bower, Robert K. *Administering Christian Education.* Grand Rapids: Eerdmans, 1964.

Church Educational Ministries. Wheaton, Ill.: Evangelical Teacher Training Assn. (Revised 1980).

Gangel, Kenneth O. *So You Want To Be a Leader.* Harrisburg, Pa.: Christian Publications, 1973.

Judy, Marvin T. *The Multiple Staff Ministry.* Nashville: Abingdon, 1969.

Schaller, Lyle E. *The Decision Makers,* Nashville: Abingdon, 1974.

Schaller, Lyle E., and Tidwell, Charles A. *Creative Church Administration,* Nashville: Abingdon, 1975.

Taylor, Marvin J. *Foundations for Christian Education in an Era of Change.* Nashville: Abingdon, 1976.

NOTES

1. The Lutheran Church—Missouri Synod, *Handbook for Local Boards of Christian Education.*
2. Dean A. Dalton, "The Board of Christian Education," *Introduction to Evangelical Christian Education,* J. Edward Hakes, ed. (Chicago: Moody, 1964), p. 235.
3. Edward L. Hayes, "The Board of Christian Education," *Church Educational Ministries* (Wheaton, Ill.: Evangelical Teacher Training Assn., 1980), pp. 89-90
4. David A. Bell, "The Board of Christian Education," *Link,* April 1963, pp. 8-11.
5. Missouri Synod, *Handbook for Local Boards.*
6. Dalton, p. 241.
7. Roy B. Zuck, "The Board of Christian Education" workshop outline.

25

The Church Business Administrator

Someone has suggested that if the present technocracy continues, the only vocations still available by the year 2000 will be law and accountancy. Hyperbole, of course, but indicative of the complexity that administration now carries. Business expertise is almost as important in a church today as it is in a college, mission board, or other Christian organization. Whether or not that should be the case is hardly a point for argument. We can talk all we want to about the church as organism, and we dare not ever forget that crucial dimension. But the local church is also organization and, as such, expertise in business management is a component more and more congregations are searching for in the 1980s.

Church business administrator is hardly a new office—it was described in print more than ten years ago by Marvin Judy. Judy addressed the question, When should a congregation employ a church business administrator?

> A CBA should be added when the congregation has grown to the dimension that the operational tasks of the church are too large to be handled by volunteer help and the paid staff. Here, however, there are problems, for the paid staff may be performing well in the operational tasks of the church, but failing to perform in the professional roles for which they have been employed, thus causing the major works of the church to be neglected.[1]

What is of great significance in a book like this is a reminder that *administration* and *ministry* are words formed from a similar root. We have already established the significance of the gift of administration and the service function it carries in the local church. More and more seminaries are beginning to develop courses in church leadership, administration, and management. Pastors are better trained now than ever before to handle these aspects of ministering, but, as Judy has noted, there comes a time when a specialist is required, and that is what this chapter is all about.

Office Administration

We will discuss the role of the church business administrator under four categories, the first of which is the most obvious, his role in the office complex itself. It is very tempting to take a broad view of the role without specifying the distinctive functions of the church business administrator. His work in office administration, for example, must focus on the work plan of the office facilities themselves (not to be confused with the overall plant and property administration to be discussed later). Engstrom and Dayton write: "What managers *do* everyday can best be described as leading, handling disturbances, acting as a figurehead, disseminating information, acting as a spokesperson, negotiating with people, monitoring how things are going, and allocating resources."[2]

All of this happens within the context of the church office, which is supervised by the administrator. Quite obviously he does not control the activities of his staff peers or superiors, but in a large church there will be numerous administrative activities, commonly carried out by members of the pastoral staff, which can now be delegated to the business administrator.

As a part of office administration, the church business administrator also deals with the master calendar. True, he may delegate control of this extremely important document to his secretary, but ultimately he is the administrator in charge, and everyone, including the senior pastor, clears events on the long-range calendar through this office. Careful administration of events is a time-saving ministry performed by the business administrator, and it develops people as well. One is reminded of the words of Jesus,"For which one of you, when he wants to build a tower, does not first sit down and calculate the cost, to see if he has enough to complete it?" (Luke 14:28). A passage like this is reminiscent of budget as well as calendar, but we must defer that important aspect of the business administrator's function for just a moment or two. Skelton captures the ministry aspect of something as mundane as scheduling and calendar administration when he writes, "Church administration may be defined as the sum of the processes of leadership engaged in for the purpose of guiding the work of the church. It includes the essential activities by which congregations and leaders seek to achieve the church's total God-given ministry."[3]

A third aspect of office administration is the care of the records—membership records, financial records, prospect records, and just about anything that needs to be kept with accuracy and ready accessability. As Bill Shackelford puts it, "The church office is an information bureau. . . . Although some may not find the answer to their questions, the church office is a place where any person can call and find a counselor and friend."[4]

Finally, there is the matter of publications that come out of that office. The administrator presides over mailouts, bulletin preparation, newspaper advertising, personal letters, monthly or quarterly newsletters, devotional booklets, and anything else the church produces for the use of its members or outreach to the total community. Quality control is the key here as the administrator makes sure that the representation of the church in print is both attractive in form and spiritual in content.

Financial Administration

Noted researcher and author Lyle Schaller argues that a *church budget* is a theological document. He suggests that the budget "identifies the gods that are worshipped in that organization, and the ranking of those gods in that organization's hierarchy."[5] Certainly the budget of a church is a theological document because a great deal of prayer and sensitivity to the Holy Spirit's leading have presumably gone into its construction and utilization. The handling of the budget is one of the key facets of financial administration.

In my opinion, the only logical conclusion regarding a financial plan for today's church is the unified budget with special restricted accounts for designated giving and possibly an alternative missions budget. Ellis develops his entire chapter on the church budget around the basic assumption that the unified budget plan is the only one that really makes sense.

> A unified or single budget represents the estimated receipts and disbursements of all organizations, committees, and projects of the church and combines such estimates into one budget for the year. In this way, a single budget reflects plans and estimated financial transactions for the entire church program. Each organization does not raise its own money or make its own separate disbursements. All receipts and disbursements are handled through one treasury or General Fund. Members understand that their contributions are used for the overall operations and programs approved by the church membership. It is also assumed in this chapter that a budget is prepared only for the General Fund. Furthermore, designated gifts are not estimated and budgeted.

> Special funds may require separate budgets occasionally, but these are relatively simple to prepare if one understands procedures for preparing the General Fund budget.[6]

I am inclined to place more emphasis on designated gifts and restricted funds than Ellis suggests, but that is a minor variance which can be decided in any given local church. The main point is that a budget is a projection for planning and a control for operations, and therefore its unification demonstrates in symbolic form the very unity of the body of Christ.

A church business administrator also has a responsibility for developing *biblical stewardship* in the congregation. He dare not become a "bottom line business tycoon" who can think of the Lord's work only in terms of dollars. Working on the principle of 2 Corinthians 9, he develops the foundational idea of that text; "Now this I say, he who sows sparingly shall also reap sparingly; and he who sows bountifully shall also reap bountifully" (v. 6). What it all boils down to, whether we are talking about "tithing," "offerings," "elections," "estate planning," or "stewardship," is that the people of God must understand the biblical necessity of their giving so that the work of the Lord can be carried out properly. There is hardly a dearth of biblical information on this subject, and if the budget is a theological document, then the church business administrator is the lay theologian whose task it is to interpret that document.

Schaller and Tidwell raise the question of values with respect to financial planning and suggest that when the annual business meeting comes around, instead of handing the congregation only a copy of the typical expenditures budget, we should also distribute a sheet that summarizes the proposed budget by percentages centered on the word *ministry.* The point is to force the congregation to recognize where it is spending its money and whether indeed that is the direction it intends the funds to go. Schaller suggests that "the format of the presentation causes the member to think in terms of proportions and to compare the expenditures for a ministry to the membership with the expenditures for a ministry to others. This tends to produce a more affirmative, although often critical, response."[7]

Also a part of financial administration is the role of *purchasing.* This is a hobgoblin of confusion in many churches as people in different facets of the ministry purchase what they wish and either charge to the church or submit all manner of bills to the harassed treasurer. In the excellent book by Ellis, referred to earlier, churches are warned against the failure to safeguard assets and provide adequate financial records: "Internal control is relatively poor in the church environment. Disbursements often are not authorized properly either by the budget or by specified officers. A limited number of personnel employed by many churches makes it difficult to segregate responsibilities such as receiving and depositing cash, posting to contributor's records, and maintaining other accounting records."[8]

Ellis is speaking of a much broader function than just purchasing, but internal control is impossible unless purchasing is controlled first. Klempnauer offers five values of the purchase order system for churches:

1. It allows authorization in purchasing.
2. Only a limited number of people are authorized to request purchases.
3. It saves time.
4. It allows a constant check on budget expenditures.
5. It affords a check to see that merchandise ordered is delivered.[9]

Closely linked to all of the above is the function of *accounting*. Accounts receivable and payable must be handled with the greatest exactitude and accurate reports must be filed. This again is the responsibility of the business administrator carried out in conjunction with the church board and other volunteer staff members directly or indirectly responsible for finances.

> A monthly report is needed for the official church board, with an annual report required for the total church body. These reports should be structured in accord with the responsibility areas. Each member of the official board should be able to make an easy comparison between his budget items and his expenditures. Where appropriate, the report should also be categorized according to the responsibility areas of each person under his direction. For example, suppose the elder in charge of evangelism has a visitation director, an evangelism training director, and an evangelism team coordinator working under his direction. Following the procedure mentioned above, he would have a budget for each of these three areas. The period financial report should list total expenditures for each of these areas. The board member should then give to his workers the financial report data of the area for which he is responsible, acquaint them with their standing, and discuss the expenditures with them.[10]

Personnel Administration

Four subcategories apply to the work of the church business administrator in personnel administration: procurement, relationships, supervision, and development. Perhaps the business administrator finds his greatest ministry in this part of his work. He has the opportunity of cultivating other leaders and sharing with them some of the expertise God has enabled him to develop. In his relationships with other people he observes the principles of Philippians 2:1-5 and follows the example of Christ in every way. Far from being a fiscal bloodhound who spreads fear throughout the congregation, he must be a warm, approachable servant of the Lord while at the same time maintaining professionalism and exactitude in everything that he does. Myers offers a pungent paragraph describing this people ministry of the business administrator.

> With the help of the personnel committee, the church business administrator plans, interprets, and administers church-approved personnel policies, vacation and salary schedules, staff benefits, and insurance programs. Much can be accomplished when a staff member feels he is a part of the team, with a feeling of support and cooperation. The task of developing a person's God-given ability to its greatest potential is an exciting and rewarding experience for the administrator.[11]

Plant and Property Administration

Although trustees or some other officers of the congregation may be the legal custodians of all property, it stands to reason that a full-time or even part-time church administrator will function in the capacity of property manager. In such a role, he is concerned with maintenance, the various legal issues of city and county regulation, inventory and control of any church-owned vehicles. Of all people in the church, he would be most familiar with Treasury Department regulations such as those issued on January 4, 1977, which describe how a church must handle what Internal Revenue Service calls an "integrated auxiliary." The competent business administrator is familiar with Form 990 and can speak intelligently about such Internal Revenue code regulations as section 6033 (a) and Section 501 (c) (3).

He deals with such matters as insurance of all kinds, supervision of the custodial staff, and expert care of the church building and grounds. This again is a ministry, because few evangelicals miss the significance of the building in which they meet as genuinely "belonging to God."

Food Service Administration

It is virtually impossible to talk about this aspect of church business administration apart from the other four discussed above. Indeed, we could take one function from each of the other four areas and describe what the church business administrator does in food service administration—*scheduling, purchasing, supervision,* and *maintenance.* In many places church food service programs are now big business, whether dealing just with the local congregation and special events or catering events for other churches and para-church organizations all through the year. Then, of course, there is the social service ministry to the community, such as "meals on wheels," which provides food service programs to the elderly and shut-ins.

In all of this the business administrator works closely with a food service committee and perhaps a church hostess. His role is not to direct kitchen activities but to make sure that the food service, like other aspects of service in his congregation, is carried out in accordance with appropriate business procedures and genuine biblical motivation.

It may be a long time before your church is large enough to hire a full-time church business administrator. Keep in mind, however, that many such officers are already on the job across the country. Park Street Church in Boston recently moved its minister of education to a position of church administration, and in the Key Biscayne Presbyterian Church of Miami, Florida, the minister of music doubles as church administrator. Sometimes staff members carrying other titles function as business administrators, and often that role will fall to the minister of education.

The link between this chapter and the rest of the book is surely obvious. Unification and correlation of the church's educational program requires leadership in the business and finance area as well as in church education, missions, evangelism, and music. God will call an increasing number of people to hold these positions in the future, and they must be viewed as ministry in the fullest and best sense.

FOR FURTHER READING

Ellis, Laudell O. *Church Treasurer's Handbook.* Valley Forge, Pa.: Judson, 1978.

Engstrom, Ted W., and Dayton, Edward R. *The Christian Executive.* Waco, Tex.: Word, 1979.

Judy, Marvin T. *The Multiple Staff Ministry.* Nashville: Abingdon, 1969.

Kilinski, Kenneth K., and Wofford, Jerry C. *Organization and Leadership in the Local Church.* Grand Rapids: Zondervan, 1973.
Schaller, Lyle E., and Tidwell, Charles A. *Creative Church Administration.* Nashville: Abingdon, 1975.
Schaller, Lyle E. *Parish Planning.* Nashville: Abingdon, 1971.

NOTES

1. Marvin T. Judy, *The Multiple Staff Ministry* (Nashville: Abingdon, 1969), p. 183.
2. Ted W. Engstrom and Edward R. Dayton, *The Christian Executive* (Waco, Tex.: Word, 1979), p. 52.
3. J. Roger Skelton, "The Meaning and Ministry of Administration in a Church," *Search,* Winter 1974, p. 24.
4. Bill Shackelford, "What's Different About a Church Office?" *Church Administration,* February 1978.
5. Lyle Schaller, *Parish Planning* (Nashville: Abingdon, 1971), p. 38.
6. Laudell O. Ellis, *Church Treasurer's Handbook* (Valley Forge, Pa.: Judson, 1978), p. 91.
7. Lyle E. Schaller and Charles A. Tidwell, *Creative Church Administration* (Nashville: Abingdon, 1975), p. 47.
8. Ellis, p. 99.
9. Lawrence R. Klempnauer, "Save More than Money with Purchase Orders," *Church Administration,* February 1978, p. 8.
10. Kenneth K. Kilinski and Jerry C. Wofford, *Organziation and Leadership in the Local Church* (Grand Rapids: Zondervan, 1973), p. 200.
11. F. Marvin Myers, "What's Involved in Church Business Administration?" *Church Administration,* February 1978, p. 6.

PART VI

The Leader Working With People

26

Human Relations in Christian Leadership

It should be clear by now that the problems facing educational leaders in the local church are largely related to getting along with people. One hesitates to identify what percentage of ministerial failures trace back to this issue, but it is certainly a disproportionate amount.

As directors of Christian education look back on their college and seminary training, they do so with mixed emotions. Seemingly the schools have done quite satisfactory jobs in preparing them to analyze the church's educational structure, determine needs, clarify objectives, draw up organizational charts, implement programs and evaluate the results. What is lacking is recognition of how to handle all of these tasks in a church carpeted with wall-to-wall people. Most pastors would agree that human relations is a constant and pressing problem in church work. The problem only emphasizes the fact that any form of the ministry of the gospel of Christ brings one in constant confrontation with other people.

The Word of God abounds in passages which teach specifically about the relationship between people, individually or within groups. Indeed, the very mark of the church was to be *love*, cherished mutually among the brethren. Christ speaks to the issue in Luke:

> But love your enemies, and do good, and lend, expecting nothing in return; and your reward will be great, and you will be sons of the Most High; for He Himself is kind to ungrateful and evil men. Be merciful, just as your Father is merciful. And do not pass judgment and you will not be judged; and do not condemn, and you shall not be condemned; pardon, and you will be pardoned. Give, and it will be given to you; good measure, pressed down, shaken together, running over, they will pour into your lap. For whatever measure you deal out to others, it will be dealt to you in return. [Luke 6:35-38]

One of the central ecclesiological messages in the Pauline epistles is that factionalism within the local assembly is of Satan and not of God. The apostle John makes very clear that the man who claims to love Christ and yet displays a hatred toward his brother is a liar.

The most significant factor in human relations is genuine interpersonal understanding. Most of the time when one thinks he dislikes another person it is because he has misunderstood or misjudged that other person's motives, abilities, attitudes or personality. Relating oneself to other people as a person is important for all Christians but essential for the Christian leader.

In his excellent book *The Meaning of Persons* Paul Tournier concludes that such relationship results in both freedom and satisfaction for the person who embraces it properly.

> Thus two diametrically opposite paths are open to us in our search for liberty—the effort of our own will, which simply means artificially making up a personage for ourselves and achieving a certain skill at the task; and the path of the trusting personal encounter. The first brings tension; the second, an easing of tension. One is a glorification of willpower; the other is self-abandonment. The first is the method of Stoicism; the second is that of modern psychology.[1]

It would appear that a book on church leadership ought to offer some practical suggestions which can be implemented by the leader in his relationship with other people in the church. There is, of course, a great deal of personality theory which serves as a foundation for the suggestions, but our objective is the simplest and clearest delineation toward a solution for the problem of human relations.

If, as indicated above, most of the problems in human relations stem from misunderstanding or misjudging of the other person, an alleviation of such misunderstanding lies at the root of successful human relations. Perhaps the following suggestions can be of some help toward this end.

Attempt to Be Open-Minded When First Meeting a Person

A practice extremely injurious to developing effective human relations is commonly referred to as "pigeonholing." This practice is so common that it is often carried on before we meet people for the first time. From discussions about him or a description offered by someone who knows him, images are conjured in the mind which fix his personality as "one of those kind" or "just like old Sam." At the time of meeting, first impressions are important. A wise leader, however, will make a great deal of first impressions when he is considering how he will impress the other person but will play down the significance of the first impression in his evaluation of others.

Try to Familiarize Oneself with Persons as Individuals

Records are valuable in church work but they can never substitute for personal contact with the people whom they represent. When that personal contact does present itself, the leader should cast himself in the role of a listener. Seeing the person in his own "natural habitat" is important, because people are rarely entirely natural or relaxed at church or in public. Obviously the best place for such familiarization is in the person's own home. This is one reason why Christian education leaders have been saying for years that a Sunday school teacher is not effectively equipped to teach any student until she has been in his home.

Try to View the Person in the Singular Rather than the Plural

All leaders work with groups, as earlier chapters have emphasized. Groups are collections of individuals, and it is tempting to be always comparing those individuals with their peers. Neurotic trends can be built into a child during his very early years by parents who insist on comparing him with an older brother who may or may not have had superior ability but whose manner of doing things was more suited to the parents' likes.

The same difficult situation can be created by the leader if he insists on always looking at and working with his people in groups. One helpful approach is to think of people "vertically" rather than "horizontally." The emphasis in such evaluation is to attempt to see the individual as God would see him.

Observe the Person in Varying Situations

During seminary days I became acquainted with a fellow student who was not particularly outstanding during the school year. During the following summer, however, the same student was observed in a camping situation in which his motivation, desire and ability distinguished him immediately as a leader. In the classroom and library he was an average person, but in a different context he appeared outstanding. Persons may possess and demonstrate considerable ability in an area which is rarely seen by the leader.

But how is it possible to carry on such a wide observation? Certainly the most significant way is by spending time with the person and listening to him talk about his own interests, concerns, and problems. It is also helpful to observe the people with whom he associates and, if possible, how he chooses to spend his leisure time.

Take Time to "Read Between the Lines"

The driving motivations of people are not always easily seen on the surface. In the case of some gregarious, almost extroverted persons, their conversation often will center on their own interests and concerns. Others will not so readily talk about what drives them. Nevertheless, every person has a philosophy of life; and if the leader would work effectively with his people, he should attempt to discover, understand, and appreciate that philosophy.

Understand the Psychological Factors that Motivate Behavior

Why does a person act the way he does? Actually, before it is possible for the leader to discover and understand that philosophy of life, he must learn where to look. Courses in general psychology and psychology of human development should have taught the church leader to distinguish and understand age-group characteristics. The Bible teaches us that people act largely from the motivation of their hearts. Jesus said, "For the mouth speaks out of that which fills the heart" (Matt. 12:34).

Psychologists tell us that heredity and environment condition value systems in a person, and value systems determine behavior. Then behavior becomes habituated until one acts many times in accordance with subconscious motivation which has been internalized through the years.

Strive to Avoid the Unpleasant Traits of One's Own Personality

Knowing oneself is prerequisite to knowing other people. Many characteristics of the old sin nature represent carnality in the life. When allowed to demonstrate themselves through the leader's personality, they create barriers between himself and those whom he would love, win, train, and recruit for Christ's service. Here is a partial list of common but dangerous negative personality traits:

Selfishness. The old nature is inherently selfish just as Satan is characterized by selfishness. Only through the control of the Spirit of God in the life of the leader can selfishness be turned to selflessness as he prefers others in his relationships with them. Such self-giving is rarely known in young people because they are accustomed to receiving. As marriage approaches, however, self-giving becomes more necessary. If marriage is to succeed, it becomes essential. Selflessness is a basic ingredient of effective parenthood.

Sarcasm. Satire and sardonic comments have been used throughout the history of literature and public speaking to emphasize critical points. No doubt there is an important place for the use of such literary devices in church work. Rarely, however, is sarcasm successful in building satisfactory human relations. Often meant in clever humor, it is taken with offense and drives a deep wedge between brothers.

Defensiveness. The leader can never afford a "chip on the shoulder" attitude toward other people. When he has become convinced that other people are out to get him and want to hurt him, his ministry will be seriously impaired. If such defensiveness is allowed to go unchecked, it will develop into full-blown neurosis and eventually psychosis.

Self-pity. There is a wonderful verse in a wonderful psalm, speaking to the offended child of God. David wrote, "Those who love Thy law have great peace, and nothing causes them to stumble" (Psalm 119:165). Someone has noted that church people never get "angry"; they just get "hurt." Unfortunately the effect is the same; and such an attitude both stems from and develops additional self-pity.

Moodiness. The person who must have time to brood silently over things which do not meet his approval will have an extremely difficult time in attaining and maintaining a leadership role. Consistency in personality is basic if one would relate properly to other people. Moodiness can be the result of any of the above but is most closely related to self-pity. It is genuinely characteristic of spiritual immaturity.

These are five self-indulgments which the Christian leader cannot afford. He will see them in many people throughout the years of his ministry, and at times they will seem like insurmountable barriers in his dealings with those people. Let them never, however, be a reflection of himself. Let him rather follow the words of the apostle Paul to another leader in the first-century church:

> Let no one look down on your youthfulness, but rather in speech, conduct, love, faith and purity, show yourself an example of those who believe. . . . Do not neglect the spiritual gift within you, which was bestowed upon you through prophetic utterance with the laying on of hands by the presbytery. Take pains with these things; be absorbed in them, so that your progress may be evident to all. Pay close attention to yourself and to your teaching; persevere in these things; for as you do this you will insure salvation both for yourself and for those who hear you [1 Tim. 4:12, 14-16].

The leader cultivates friendships based on genuine love—the *agape* of which the New Testament frequently speaks. It is sacrificial, focusing upon the value of the object loved. Moreover, it is God-given rather than engineered on a human level. Many times in the lonely life of a leader it is unilateral as he reaches out by the grace of God to love someone whose acts and words are unlovely and unloving in return. The poet has well captured the difficulty of such a task:

> So send I you to labor unrewarded,
> To serve unpaid, unloved, unsought, unknown,
> To bear rebuke, to suffer scorn and scoffing—
> So send I you to toil for Me alone.
>
> So send I you to bind the bruised and broken,
> O'er wand'ring souls to work, to weep, to wake,
> To bear the burdens of a world aweary—
> So send I you to suffer for My sake.
>
> So send I you to loneliness and longing,
> With heart ahung'ring for the loved and known,
> Forsaking home and kindred, friend and dear one—
> So send I you to know My love alone.
>
> So send I you to leave your life's ambition,
> To die to dear desire, self-will resign,
> To labor long, and love where men revile you—
> So send I you to lose your life in Mine.
>
> So send I you to hearts made hard by hatred,
> To eyes made blind because they will not see,
> To spend, though it be blood, to spend and spare not—
> So send I you to taste of Calvary.
>
> As the Father hath sent me, so send I you.
>
> E. MARGARET CLARKSON

Use Special Care in Reaching Difficult Cases

Who are the difficult people of church leadership? Sometimes they are young; sometimes they are old; sometimes they are timid; sometimes they are bold. Often they are discouraged and perhaps even disgruntled. They may be wealthy, or poverty may have driven them to a primitive fear of the public eye. Whoever they are and whatever their problems, they exist in every church. It is the responsibility of the pastor, the director of Christian education, the superintendent and teachers to reach out to these people and represent Jesus Christ in their lives. It takes tact and infinite patience, both the product of the infinite wisdom and mercy of the God of heaven.

Be Able to Pay the Price of Leadership

James offered wise, experienced counsel when he said, "Let not many of you become teachers" (James 3:1). The price of leadership is not a small one; it includes faithfulness and self-denial. The time, the privacy and the personal life of the average man are all left behind in the role of leadership. Study and preparation consume hours in a week, weeks in a year, and years in a lifetime. The responsibility of maintaining the office "where the buck stops" becomes heavy and never abates.

When the investment has been made, a return in the form of appreciation and thanks can be logically expected. Instead, there is often the offense of some who misunderstand and retaliate negatively for all of the efforts in their behalf. At moments like this the limelight dims, and the life of leadership becomes the life of loneliness.

The leader is often the dreamer, the idealist, the crusader for a cause. He finds himself bucking the tide of popular opinion and standing against the crowd. Since he is probably something of a perfectionist, the leader is his own most severe critic and tends to deal most harshly with himself.

This was the pattern of the life of the great leaders of the Old Testament, the disciples and apostles of the New Testament, and the example of our Lord Himself. Yet somehow in the midst of the pressing demands of ministry, He took time to carry on the most successful human relations that the world has ever seen. He discussed theology with Nicodemus and living water with an adulterous woman. He shared intimate moments with the young apostle John and prayed personally for impetuous Peter. He visited briefly with two disciples after the resurrection and took time to make a special appearance for the skeptical Thomas.

Perhaps His secret was that His relations with people were reflective of His relations with the Father. He did not deal in horizontal communication alone but was the constant representative of the Father to those with whom He came in contact. In return their lives were ever brought to the Father in prayer, perhaps never more significantly than in John 17. Such completely spiritual human relations marked the ministry of Jesus Christ. May those same markings be found in the ministry of His ambassadors who lead the church educational ministries of our day.

FOR FURTHER READING

Bell, A. Donald. *How to Get Along with People in the Church*. Grand Rapids: Zondervan, 1960.

Bennett, Thomas R. *The Leader and the Process of Change*. New York: Association, 1962.

Berne, Eric. *Games People Play*. New York: Grove, 1964.

Blumenthal, Louis H. *How to Work with Your Board and Committees*. New York: Association, 1954.

Buchanan, Paul C. *The Leader and Individual Motivation*. New York: Association, 1964.

Dobbins, Gaines S. *Learning to Lead*. Nashville: Broadman, 1968.

Elliott, Grace L. *How to Help Groups Make Decisions*. New York: Association, 1959.

Gangel, Kenneth O. *So You Want To Be a Leader*. Harrisburg, Pa: Christian Publications, 1973.

LeBar, Lois. *Focus on People in Church Education*. Westwood, N.J.: Revell, 1968.

Peachey, Laban. *Learning to Understand People*. Scottdale, Pa.: Herald, 1965.

Prime, Derek. *A Christian's Guide to Leadership*. Chicago: Moody, 1966.

Sanders, Oswald. *Spiritual Leadership*. Rev. ed. Chicago: Moody, 1980.

Tournier, Paul. *The Meaning of Persons*. New York: Harper & Row, 1957.

———. *To Understand Each Other*. Richmond: Knox, 1967.

Wedel, Leonard E. *Building and Maintaining a Church Staff*. Nashville: Broadman, 1967.

NOTES

1. Paul Tournier, *The Meaning of Persons* (New York: Harper & Row), p. 224.

27

Communicating with People in the Church

COMMUNICATION is the transmission of ideas between persons in a language that is common to both. Such communication is a basic ingredient of sound leadership and administration in the church's educational program. In recent years church leaders have become increasingly aware of the significance of sound communication theory in developing satisfactory witnesses for the gospel (either in terms of the individual Christian or the collective assembly). Bird and Dean, writing in *Christianity Today,* express the significance that the field of communication has for the church:

> These theories and others like them hold new insight for all Christians who will study and apply them. Not only the intended meanings of the words used but also the meanings which the hearer's experience gives to them are essential to communication. Attention to communication theory can be the basis of greater effectiveness in witnessing to the gospel of Christ.[1]

The goal of this chapter is to deal broadly with the principles and problems of communication as they are found in almost all phases of Christian relationships. The communication process is a dynamic one, always in operation when people are in confrontation with each other. These principles affect the relation between husband and wife and between parents and children. They are operative in every classroom situation in Christian church or school. The dynamics come into play when a Sunday school superintendent consults a church member about the possibility of teaching a class, or when the church board meets to discuss plans for the new building.

These are the things we do all the time without thinking about them. Like most things that become commonplace habituation, the process of communication can fall into erroneous usage and carelessness. Many of the problems we face today in the evangelical church are the result of a breakdown in communication between people. If this breakdown is to be repaired, it is essential that church leaders understand the communication process.

Development of the Communication Process

Donald Ely writes, "There is nothing quite so wonderful as a good idea; there is nothing so tragic as a good idea which cannot be communicated."[2] From his vantage point as director of the audio-visual center at Syracuse University, Ely has developed a model for the understanding of communication which is reproduced in Figure 13 because of its simplicity and effectiveness.

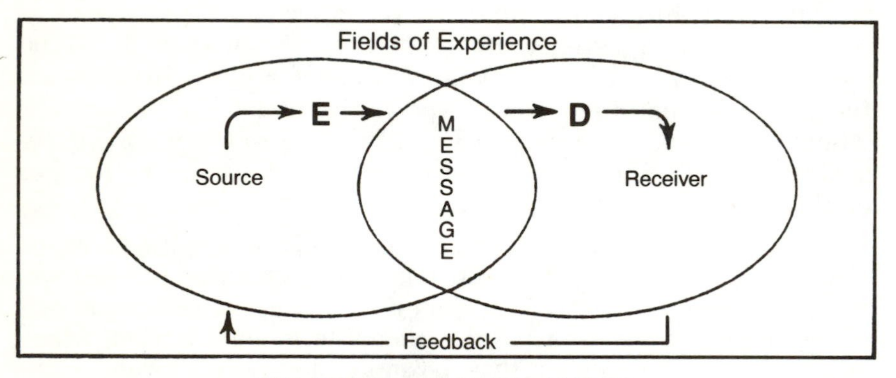

ELY COMMUNICATION MODEL
Figure 13

Notice that at the center of Ely's diagram is the message which is to be communicated. The centrality of the message in the process of communication ought to be of significant interest to evangelicals. What ought also to be of significance is that the message does not travel the entire route from the source to receiver unless the process of communication is operating properly. The model is a general one and can fit one's understanding and perception of almost any aspect of communication.

Source

The source of an idea in person-to-person communication is the mind of the communicator. This is where the thought or idea originates and receives its motivation to be transmitted to the thought patterns of another person. In the teaching situation, of course, the source is the mind of the teacher and the message is the Bible, teaching what the teacher wants to communicate to his students during a given class period.

In a very real sense the ultimate source of the Christian's message is not the mind of the teacher but the mind of God. He has revealed Himself through His Word, the Bible. The teacher has studied the Bible and been illuminated in his study by the Holy Spirit. Now he must go on to communicate those revealed and illuminated ideas to his students.

It should be obvious even to the casual observer that an idea which exists only in the mind of the source is of no value to anyone else. The Christian who knows the gospel and does not share it is not fulfilling Bible commands to witness and is not permitting his unsaved friends to know God through his verbalization of the truth.

ENCODING

When a message has been decided upon, it must be verbalized or symbolized in some way so it can be communicated to other people. Encoding is not all verbal, as every good teacher knows. In most forms of human communication it will consist largely of verbalization, but good communication will also include visualization. People who are deaf and dumb can communicate quite effectively through sign language. No word is spoken, yet ideas are encoded so that they can be transmitted from a source to a receiver.

A basic problem in communication is that people do not always say what they mean nor mean what they say. Sometimes it is even thought impossible by some to encode their ideas verbally. A common statement which well demonstrates the difficulties in encoding sounds something like this: "I know what I want to say, but I can't explain it to you." As long as one persists in that attitude, he is nipping the communication process in the bud.

Nothing can be achieved in the transmission of information unless it is first encoded. The young man who is "too in love for words" had better find some words fast lest his fair love wander off to another young man who may not have as much love but knows better how to express it to its object.

DECODING

Encoding is futile unless it is accompanied by an adequate process of decoding. When decoding is operative the message is received and comprehended by the receiver. The decoding is inseparably related to the encoding in terms of reception. A word must be heard; a picture must be seen. The succulent aroma of sizzling steaks must be smelled. Note that the sensory experiences of man are extremely important in both the encoding and decoding process of communication.

Two things are significant here. First, if the orginator of the message wishes the receiver to decode properly, he must take pains to encode his message clearly in a form that will be understandable to the receiver. Furthermore, he must be somewhat confident that the receiver has the wherewithal to carry on the decoding process.

How foolish, for example, to speak to a young child in Russian if one knows in advance that he understands no other language than English. One could encode most distinctly; and yet, since decoding would be an impossibility, no communication could take place. The navy flagman standing on the deck of his ship speaks no words verbally to his colleague on another ship in the convoy. The positions of the flags are encoding by symbolization; and if *both* men have been properly trained, the reception decoding and feedback of the message are handled by flag positioning as well.

Defective decoding can result from other problems than the failures of encoding and the receiver's inability to understand the language of the message. A common flaw is the introduction of a negatively charged emotional element into the communication process. A husband who wishes to speak seriously with his wife about some matter does not begin the conversation by complaining about his supper and condemning his mother-in-law. Conceivably, whatever he might say after such a beginning would possibly be heard but the understanding grossly perverted by anger which would distort the decoding.

RECEIVER

It is plain by now that the receiver is the person for whom the message is intended. It may be an individual, as in a counseling situation, or a group such as the pastor preaches to on Sunday morning. Desired results may be varied and the situations widely dissimilar. Nevertheless, the principles of communication do not change. If the pastor is going to motivate his hearers to action and behavioral change as a result of his sermon, he must go through basically the same process of encoding and decoding that the counselor does when seeking to help another individual understand and solve his own problems.

FEEDBACK

The major process distinction between the preaching and counseling situation described above is the introduction of the element of feedback. It is foolish to say that the preacher is not getting feedback. Every time a person smiles, offers a hearty "amen," yawns, looks at his watch, or gets up and walks out, the pastor is receiving feedback. The feedback may not be verbal, but it is nevertheless telling him something about what is happening in the communication process.

The purpose of feedback is to help the source to interpret whether or not the receiver is understanding and internalizing the message. In short, he needs to find out whether he is "getting through." When Mom says, "Johnny, didn't you hear me?" she is asking for feedback. When the classroom teacher asks for questions on the lesson, feedback is being solicited. An obvious conclusion relative to the importance of feedback is that the teacher who allows his class to do a good portion of the talking during the lesson time is going to be in a better position to use effectively the minutes which he spends in speaking.

The church leader who suggests an innovative idea and then keeps his ears open for the next two weeks to gather comments (negative and positive) regarding that idea is sensitive to feedback and will be rewarded for his efforts at improving and refining his idea. Ely reminds his readers that feedback can be both simple and complex:

> The degree of success which a given message has achieved can be determined by *feedback*. Feedback provides a teacher with information concerning his success in accomplishing his objective. The feedback may be covert or overt. A perceptive question stemming from the message is one of the simplest examples of feedback. The learner who asks a pertinent question indicates his degree of understanding. Most feedback is more complex, particularly in the case of value judgments and attitude changes which may not be as easy to process. A teacher should attempt to elicit feedback to determine how well he is achieving his purpose. Feedback assists in determining how future messages will be encoded.[3]

The desire which one has for feedback is directly related to his philosophy of leadership. The dictator speaks and expects everyone to listen and do what he asks without question. The democratic leader, on the other hand, is sensitive to what people think, and concerned whether or not his purposes and the reasons for his actions are properly understood by his constituency.

FIELD OF EXPERIENCE

The communication process does not take place in a vacuum. It is not simply a series of words encoded by a source and decoded by a receiver. There is a total context or environment in which any message is given and/or received. Communication is more than words and ideas; it is a veritable matrix of human relationships.

The field of experience may refer to how much the receiver understands. A Sunday school lesson in advanced eschatology would probably not be given to primary-age students because their background and learning level at that point would be insufficient to grasp it. The wife who wants ten dollars for a new hat may discover after only a few weeks of married life (if indeed she does not already know it by an intuitive sixth sense) that her husband's response to such a request may be more favorable after he has just enjoyed his favorite dinner.

Another way to speak of the field of experience is in terms of the ecological significance of communication. Man is both acting upon and being acted upon by his environment. That environment may refer to a room in which he is sitting when a certain message is transmitted to him. It may describe the social and cultural frame of reference in which he has been brought up. Considered broadly, it is the entire world situation in the last third of the twentieth century.

The effective communicator takes all of these factors into consideration in structuring the communication process. He realizes that the receiver's mind is a product not only of his internal life (sin, worry, frustration) but also of the mass communications that permeate society today. Whether one is a pastor, parent, deacon, youth sponsor, Sunday school teacher, or simply a person who wants to relate more effectively to other persons, he must recognize that that relationship cannot effectively take place without communication. Effective communication, furthermore, does not happen by chance.

The Messages of Communication

Someone has pointed out the wide diversity of information that can enter into the communication process as the various "messages" in the process progress from element to element. It is a cyclical pattern which repeats itself over and over again as the various distortion points in the process are passed.

WHAT THE SOURCE INTENDS TO SAY

The message originates in the mind of the speaker. Assuming he has some understanding of what he wants to convey to other people, he then frames a sequence of words or symbols which will serve as the transportation vehicle for his ideas. At this point the message is known only to him and exists only in this form.

WHAT THE SOURCE ACTUALLY SAYS

Unfortunately, what one intends to say and what one actually says may not accurately offer a glimpse at the reality of this problem. Who among us has not had to say on some occasion, "I didn't mean to say that," or, "That didn't come out just the way I wanted it to." Already in its second stage of communication, the message has been subjected to the possibility of distortion. The mouth is not always an accurate channel for the mind.

WHAT THE SOURCE HAS SAID

There is still a third version of the message. The source may not have taken into proper consideration the field of experience of the hearer, the emotional state in which he found himself at the time of the encoding, or deficiencies in the encoding process itself. Many arguments in the home begin on just this point. She argues that he said a certain thing, and he argues that he never said any such thing. Who was right? Unfortunately, unless there is some kind of written record or a third party witness, the argument must end in capitulation or a "draw." Thus the communication process exhibits again a vulnerability toward distortion of the message.

WHAT THE RECEIVER WANTS TO HEAR

The counselee, listening to the counselor offer some possible alternatives to his problem, may very well already have in his mind the kind of answers which he expects to hear. Indeed, they may be so firmly entrenched that whatever the counselor says, the counselee goes away thinking that he heard a certain solution offered. Two students may sit in a Sunday school class, later discuss the lesson, and be surprised to find that they each understood the teacher to say a completely different thing or offer seemingly divergent answers to the same question. The reason for these situations is that every hearer brings to a communication situation some expectation of what he is going to hear. This expectation is framed by one's own personal desires, the prompting of another, or the reputation of the speaker himself.

WHAT THE RECEIVER HEARS

It is possible and even not improbable the the original message in the mind of the source, what the speaker says, what the speaker thinks he says, what the receiver wants to hear, may all be different from what the receiver actually hears. It is easy to say that what the speaker says and what the hearer hears *must* be one and the same since only one set of words or set of symbols could be involved between the two. But such a conclusion fails to take into consideration the variable factors in the encoding-decoding process.

What the receiver hears is colored by what he wants to hear, what he understands about the subject being dealt with, and by the pattern and makeup of his own mind. Sometimes even the basic words themselves fail to get through. How much more distorted is the meaning which those words convey. Words are only vehicles to carry thoughts. The great prophet of the general semanticists, Alfred Korzybski, well reminds all communicators that "the map is not the territory." In other words, a word or set of words are to an idea what a road map is to a road—merely a picture or representation of the reality. The hearing of the word is relatively unimportant when compared to the understanding of the idea which is being conveyed.

WHAT THE RECEIVER THINKS HE HEARS

The same problem of confusion we discussed above enters here in terms of what a speaker thinks he has said. A young executive is being scolded by his superior for having routed a business order in the wrong direction. His response is, "But sir, I distinctly understood you to say that—" Again it is important to recognize that the receiver is acting not upon what the speaker thought he said, nor upon what the receiver heard, but rather what he *thinks* he heard.

If all of the six versions of the message mentioned above can be made identical, then the communication process is in good shape. The feedback element is the built-in control factor which lets the communicator know whether the messages have gone through on the same wave length. Teachers, preachers, parents, personal workers, counselors, and all church leaders must recognize the points at which misunderstanding may enter the communication process. It is essential to keep a constant vigil against distortions of the message if interpersonal relationships are to be carried on smoothly within the framework of the church.

Suggestions for Improving Communication

IN CHURCH ADMINISTRATION

Avoid verbal instructions. Use written memos and mimeographed reminders whenever possible.

Use informal settings to facilitate dialogue. Try to break down the barrier that naturally exists between an administrator and the people he is attempting to serve.

Use careful planning before any group presentation. A pastor confronting his board with a building project, for example, should have carefully thought through how he will make the presentation, what possible questions might be raised, and how he will answer them.

Try to speak to small groups whenever possible. Good audience contact is best assured by limiting the size of the group.

Know the audience. Be acquainted with those to whom you are speaking.

Know your subject matter well. Do not attempt to bluff your way through a presentation.

Attempt to establish rapport with your people. Spend time with them, knowing and understanding their problems and needs, and demonstrating interest and Christian love in them as persons.

Be sincere. Genuine sincerity can cover and atone for a multitude of technical errors.

IN THE CLASSROOM

Know the subject matter. This involves a depth of personal study in preparation for the classroom experience.

Know the persons whom you teach. This includes their age-group characteristics, their personal needs and problems, and their home situations.

Use visuals often and with variety. Try to open as many sensory gates as possible rather than always just spraying your class with words.

Learn the students' names, and use them often. Dale Carnegie has built a financial empire on the basic concept that every person is fond of his own name and wants to hear other people use it when addressing him.

Don't teach to impress your students; teach to communicate your message. It is possible for students to be overwhelmed by the teacher's erudition and still not understand what he is trying to say.

Use variety. Repetition may be the key to learning, but if misused it can also be the key to boredom.

Cultivate feedback. Learn to use feedback as an evaluation measurement of whether the communication process is succeeding.

Take time to explain any items that need explanation. Do not take for granted that your students have a clear-cut understanding of what you expect of them.

IN PERSONAL RELATIONSHIPS

Be friendly, polite, and considerate. Avoid being cold, overbearing, and offensive.

Cultivate the practice of listening. This is important not only for feedback but as a courtesy to the person with whom you are speaking. Like the praying of the Pharisees, the communicator is not heard because of his much talking.

Use positive words in speaking with people. Avoid offensive terms. Referring to teenagers as "children," for example, is the first sentence of the book on how *not* to teach teenagers.

Give praise whenever possible. Honest praise and not simply flowery speech is needed. Colorful expression and showy words are generally devices used by an insecure person to dress up what he feels may be an ineffective presentation.

Avoid jargon that may confuse. Do not try to overwhelm the other person with technical gobbledygook. In speaking to people either individually or in groups, the effective communicator is careful to see that his words are simple and sincere, and that they express in a clear, concise manner the thought that he is trying to communicate.

Avoid ambiguity. This problem is akin to the one above. The ability to live with ambiguity in thought process may be a mark of a philosopher, but speaking in ethereal and cloudy thought patterns is not the mark of a good communicator.

Demonstrate clearly your dependence on and expectation of some results from the person. When a Sunday school superintendent encourages a teacher to visit, she ought to understand that he is counting on her really to achieve the job. This is not a question of motivation. The teacher visits not for the sake of the superintendent, but for the sake of Christ and the student. In communication the receiver should never go away wondering what it was that the speaker was really asking of him.

Listen carefully to feedback. Watch for any indication that the receiver is saying or doing something that will help to understand him better and therefore to communicate with him more effectively.

Human Needs: Basis for Effective Communication

Because of the administrator's position in the organizational chain of command, he has the greater responsibility toward developing positive human relations through proper use of interpersonal communication. One outstanding psychologist has indicated that a person's usefulness is enhanced proportionally as his linkages with life multiply. The multiple relationships which a leader maintains are dependent upon his ability to keep tabs on all the variable factors which sustain those relationships. This is largely accomplished by means of face-to-face interaction during the working hours.

In the realm of Christian ministry, a proper vertical relationship, with Christ as the head of the church and the director of all of its leaders, is essential before satisfying and profitable horizontal relationships can be developed and maintained.

Understanding People's Needs

Part of the problem which many leaders have in developing effective human relations is the very driving nature of their own personalities. The effective leader is generally a person with a high level of personal accomplishment. He has learned ways to get things done, to achieve goals, to obtain results, and to maintain tight rein on his own time. Consequently, he frequently appears to subordinates and colleagues as a cold and calculating person who is quite unapproachable. Such an image immediately puts him at a disadvantage in developing satisfying relationships through interpersonal communications.

The basic needs of people in groups will be explored in Chapter 30. When we apply them to their relationships to the organization, we come up with such things as these:

Sense of belonging
Share in planning
Clear understanding of what is expected
Genuine responsibility and challenge
Feeling that progress is being made toward organizational goals
Intense desire to be kept informed
Desire for recognition when it is due
Reasonable degree of security for the future

Although research supports all of these items and more, most good leaders could become aware of human need without the research. The problem with most of us is that we become so entangled with our own problems and our personal, administrative overload, that we fail to recognize and deal with the things we really know are important.

INTERPERSONAL AND INTRAPERSONAL RELATIONS

There are dynamic forces operative within the personality of an individual worker which have profound effects upon his interactions with other people in his work group. *Intrapersonal relations* describes the phenomena existing within the individual as a feeling, thinking, and expressing person. *Interpersonal relations* focuses on his visible encounters and interaction within the organization.

In one sense, it is correct to say that there is no communication without the interpersonal dimension, since mutuality is a basic ingredient in the communications process. But it is also quite true that the inner factors of personal equilibrium influence the communication process. Meanings are placed upon words as an individual listens to another's communication through his grid of emotional, social, religious, and political prejudices.

Without subscribing to or even discussing psychoanalysis, we can note that its general theory views individual development as a complex interaction between instinctual processes, the evolving psychic structure, and the changing relations with persons in the environment. So, although interpersonal relations unfold in the present, many psychologists would argue that their meaning, particularly in emotional and symbolic qualities, is distinctly related to the individual's personal history.

One does not have to buy raw Freudianism to nod approvingly toward such an emphasis. If the leader genuinely wants to understand and relate to one of his colleagues, he recognizes that *the interpersonal communications he is attempting to establish are being greatly affected by two sets of intrapersonal factors, his own and those of the other individual.*

STRUCTURING FOR COMMUNICATION

The desirability of breaking up managerial responsibility into smaller units is related to the basic theory of communications and decision-making in administration. Such decentralization enables the administrator to "touch all the bases" in a more comprehensive and yet intensive fashion in his relationships with other persons in his organization. Good administration is multidimensional, and so there are always a number of diverse factors which must of necessity elude the autocratic leader who fancies himself one of the kings of the Gentiles.

One of the axioms of the PERT (Program Evaluation and Review Technique) system states that an event can occur only when all of the activities which lead up to it have been completed, and no succeeding activity may begin until the event is finished. As administrators, we do not have great difficulty applying a rule like this to the process of planning. Sometimes, however, we seem to expect positive communications just to happen, without laying specific groundwork to insure a continuing climate of open communication in the organization.

A Sunday school superintendent, for example, might decide that one of his general purposes for the year is to create a climate of openness and mutually happy interpersonal relations among the departmental superintendents and teachers. One of his objectives for the year might be regular staff meetings that follow a carefully prepared agenda to explore some of the areas of mutual concern. Another objective might be to spend time individually, with each of his departmental superintendents individually, attempting to build through those counseling sessions a spirit of rapport and mutual exchange of ideas. As he becomes more specific in delineating goals for the meetings, he will be considering his role as a listener, his response to questions, and his openness in providing thorough information at the staff meetings and in the personal counseling situations.

Some communications experts argue that communication is relative to the centrality of a person in a group. People in the periphery, they suggest, tend to be negative and contribute less to the solution of group problems. Obviously, in a highly centralized bureaucracy there are many more people on the periphery than is the case when decentralization secures an increasing involvement of personnel.

Part of the problem with peripheral people is that they are probably the least informed of the group, and they maintain a constant aura of suspicion regarding the plans and practices of the nuclear control group. So the structure of the organization, even when it is informal, provides for or minimizes the level of interpersonal communications.

Understanding Communication Channels

An individual's ability to communicate effectively with others depends upon the adequacy of his inputs, the accuracy and appropriateness of the way he treats those inputs, and the techniques he can utilize in composing and delivering a message.

So far, we have only touched upon the sending of the message. If the leader is impressed by the arguments of the symbolic interactionists, he recognizes that words are the basic building-blocks of all conceptual behavior, and he thinks of them as individual stimuli intended to arouse in a receiver the desired intellectual or emotional state. Consequently, words in sentences are the primary tool for the communication of ideas.

A sentence gives form to thoughts and serves as the vehicle for their transmission. Paragraphs represent the organization of sentences and ideas into larger forms of written communication. But in oral communication, the focus is obviously placed upon words and sentences, both of which can be recognized.

Communication channels in an organization are influenced by internal characteristics and environmental factors. As communications within an organization become stabilized, flows are differentiated, and message contents are affected by their relationships to authority, expertise, friendship, or status.

Think of a church in which a lay member responds with indifference when requested by a fellow lay member to carry out a certain task. The same person jumps immediately to the job if the request comes from the pastor. What has happened is that the content of that communication has been affected by the status of the second sender.

There are a number of different kinds of channels in any kind of institution. What we call formal channels are consciously established to carry messages up and down. A memo is a formal channel, as is a bulletin board, a church newsletter, and announcement time during the Sunday morning service. An informal channel is one which carries the information even though the organization has not specifically planned for it to do so. Mrs. Jones calling Mrs. Smith on Monday morning may very well provide a higher volume of information for either or both of the ladies than they had received during the formal communications the day before.

A channel of communication is *interpersonal* when it is informal and carried out for purposes of information, affection, or mediation of rewards or punishments, and based on personal interests between the communicants.

Sometimes the literature on management speaks about intragroup and intergroup channels. An intragroup channel is a leadership channel, formal or informal, which carries information pertinent to the group's operations. An intergroup channel, on the other hand, is a more formal process designed to convey messages pertinent to the interests of each group within the organization, its relationship with other groups, or its changes. A monthly meeting of the board of Christian education, for example, is concerned largely with intergroup channels of communication, because its responsibility is to coordinate the total educational program of the church.

In *Administrative Communication.* Lee Thayer talks about the uses of communication channels and suggests several guiding principles:

1. The more important, significant, or urgent a message, the more channels should be used.
2. When speed of transmission is the guiding factor, use informal channels. If the message is also an important one, it can be reinforced by also sending it through the slower formal channels.
3. To be authoritative, an official message must pass through formal, organization channels.
4. To be influential, the most advantageous are power and prestige channels, followed by intragroup and intrapersonal channels.
5. Policies are most effectively transmitted through organization channels, but practices are more effectively transmitted through interpersonal channels.

6. A channel which ordinarily "carries" a certain type of message may "carry" other types of messages less effectively.
7. Attitudes are best reached through intragroup, interpersonal, and value channels; knowledge is best reached through the formal and ideological channels.[4]

Communication and Motivation

If mutuality and simultaneity are really crucial factors in the communication process, then no two people can meet without transmitting and reacting to signals of some kind. The communication of A depends upon the response of B, and vice versa. In that kind of communication, the purpose should be to promote attitudes or action, or possibly to promote understanding without regard to motivation.

This concept is important, because sometimes administrators think only about the motivating role of communications. In other words, they see communication only as a one-way street down which they want to drive their trucks laden with information from the front office. As the trucks dump that information on a waiting populace, individuals and groups within the organization are supposed to respond in accordance with the intent of the executive leadership. When that does not happen, the leaders tend to become hostile, accuse the workers of lack of loyalty, and feel very threatened in their positions of control.

In their helpful book entitled *Interpersonal Communication and the Modern Organization*, Ernest Bormann and his coauthors talk about what they call "a new concept of communication."

> Since 1950 business executives have been peculiarly receptive to a revised concept of communication. For decades the word had conveyed one meaning only—the distribution of information. But in the post war years increasing numbers of thoughtful businessmen began to think of communication as a *two-way process*.
>
> True, management still consisted of getting other people to do things that had to be done. But simply telling others what to do was no longer good enough. Successful managers were those who listened to their employees as frequently as they instructed them. Even if a manager could do nothing immediately in response to an employee's complaints or wishes, he found it highly profitable to learn as directly as possible what his workers were talking and thinking about.[5]

But we are concerned primarily with the development of positive human relations in the Christian organization. Communication is only one of the dimensions of that relationship and environment. Therefore, it may be important to suggest here that whereas communication is still the most strategic factor in group or individual motivation, it ought not to be given over completely to that end. Speaking and listening are tools which the leader can use to build a climate of receptivity and warm, human interaction in the organization. When the organization is also an organism such as the church, the relations of body members one to another may be just as important as (some would suggest even more important than) the volume of productivity of the congregation in outreach, community witness, or world evangelization.

When one takes such a view of communication, *clarity* is no longer the only important factor. *Courtesy* now comes in, because the leader recognizes that all of his communication generates feelings, as well as conveys ideas. Although the Scriptures do say, "Those who love Thy law have great peace, and nothing causes them to stumble" (Psalm 119:165), it is obviously not to the administrator's advantage to push this passage to unwarranted extremes. Every leader must develop his capability to walk alone, if need be, but he must guard against making self-dependency an obsession.

On the positive side, communication and motivation are almost inseparable parts of the leadership function. One of the issues of the *Hillsdale College Leadership Letter* talks about this phenomenon and likens it to the "two parts of the complete wave of alternating current electricity. We are not always aware of electricity . . . but its presence may produce the results we want, or it may kill us. The same is true of communication and the motivation it does or does not produce."[6]

Churches are talking a great deal today about change, but are spending relatively little time creating the proper atmosphere for change. The questions are virtually rhetorical: how much time do seminary students spend learning the intricacies of administration in order to be agents of motivation in the congregation? What kind of leadership training are we offering lay leaders such as Sunday school superintendents, deacons, and board chairmen? Where are the denominational leaders who have been highly trained in communication and other administrative skills?

Avoiding Communications Breakdown

If communications breakdown also means a breakdown in human relations in the organization (and it does), then we must pay careful attention to the problems that we might encounter in the communications process. Experts tell us that the loss in communication can be measured primarily in factors such as foggy detail, distortion of words, retention of emotional concepts, and an attachment to the facts of innate prejudice. In the process, certain central ideas seem to hang on, whereas obscure or misunderstood concepts fade into even greater ambiguity.

The emphasis ought to be clear: *the centrality of the important ideas must be emphasized, and comprehension, not memorization, should be what we look for in the feedback.* Any good college teacher has come to grips with the relationship between *knowing* and *understanding* early in his career. A Sunday school teacher ought not to be as concerned that little Johnny can memorize huge portions of Scripture as she is that he can understand them and feed them back in his own words.

At this point, it is important to recognize again that John 17 concept of being in the world and yet not of the world. Because the church is in the world, it finds itself both doing battle with, and under the compulsion to use the systems of, the world's culture. Consequently, Paul could write to the church at Rome and warn its people against the pagan idolatry all around them, and yet claim his Roman citizenship in order to make a desired visit to that city. Perhaps this is what our Lord meant when He suggested to His disciples that they must be as "wise as serpents, and harmless as doves" (Matt. 10:16, KJV).

Living within the society without becoming a part of the society has been a difficult task faced by the church since its earliest days. What is obviously essential is a recognition that biblical separation is neither isolation nor insulation from the culture; therefore the church must recognize and utilize the very principles which Lacy has articulated.

Christian employers' and leaders' openness to the ideas and innovative suggestions of their employees and subordinates ought to characterize the flow of communication in any Christian organization. In an excellent article which appeared in *Personnel Administration* in 1967, John Anderson speaks about the blockades to upward communication. Without going into detail, it might be helpful at least to identify the factors delineated in Anderson's analysis of the problem:

1. It must occur to B that it matters whether he says anything.
2. Once aware that he has significant information, B must choose to pass it on.
3. B must have an opportunity to make his information available to A.
4. If B does speak, A must be able to receive his message.
5. Having listened to and understood B's message, A needs to act on it.[7]

If at any one of these points the communications process goes awry, it can destroy the attempts of a subordinate to communicate with his superior about matters that might be of extreme importance to both.

In the Bormann book mentioned earlier, the authors have delineated, from the many case studies with which they have worked, a profile of the communicating leader. In the profile, they have isolated six characteristics which supposedly mark the man who recognizes that communication with persons in the organization is especially crucial to the survival of his leadership and the ongoing productivity of his institution.

1. *Do not play the role of manipulator.* When a person in an organization constantly uses others to serve his own ends, or perhaps even the ends of the organization, he will soon find himself without a leadership role.

2. *Be willing to pay the price.* It is interesting that in their research, Bormann and his coauthors discovered that almost every person of the work group wanted to be a leader because of the obvious rewards of leadership, but few wanted to be leaders badly enough to assume the enormous responsibility and work load.

3. *Talk up.* The quiet, reticent member of the group is rarely chosen as leader because it does not appear that he has sufficient interest in the group. On the other hand, it is not the quantity of words which makes the difference, but the clarity of the group's objectives and the leader's seeming ability to carry the group toward those objectives.

4. *Do your homework.* "Members who emerge as leaders have sensible, practical ideas and state them clearly."

5. *Give credit to others.* Subordinates are not interested in working toward the glory of their leader, but they are quite willing to work for their own glory and perhaps even for the glory of the group, assuming they are in complete harmony with its objectives and directions.

6. *Raise the status of other members.* "People who emerge as leaders compliment others when the latter do something for the good of all. . . . In short, they are honestly disinterested in whether they emerge at the top of the pecking order or not—so long as the team does well."[8]

Perhaps one warning can be offered in closing. The development of an effective communication pattern is not something that can be achieved overnight. One must discipline himself to perform satisfactorily in all the various aspects and elements of the process. He must learn to listen rather than talk. He must learn to speak clearly rather than mumble. Rather than depending upon the other person's efforts to make sense out of what he is saying, he must learn to convey his ideas accurately.

Effective communication, however, is not an element that is desirable only for preachers and teachers in a church. It is essential for all Christians to learn how to speak to other people. Ely says, "Where does one start? Start where you are, with what you have. You can do no more, but as a Christian communicator, you can do no less."[9]

FOR FURTHER READING

Bell, A. Donald. *How to Get Along with People in the Church.* Grand Rapids: Zondervan, 1960.

Berne, Eric. *Games People Play.* New York: Grove, 1967.

Blumenthal, Louis H. *How to Work with Your Board and Committees.* New York: Association, 1954.

Bower, Robert K. *Administering Christian Education.* Grand Rapids: Eerdmans, 1964.

Dobbins, Gaines S. *Learning to Lead.* Nashville: Broadman, 1968.

Elliott, Grace L. *How to Help Groups Make Decisions.* New York: Association, 1959.

Frank, Lawrence K. *How To Be a Modern Leader.* New York: Association, 1954.

Gable, Lee J., ed. *Encyclopedia for Church Group Leaders.* New York: Association, 1959.

Hendry, Charles E., and Ross, Murray G. *New Understandings of Leadership.* New York: Association, 1957.

LeBar, Lois E. *Focus on People in Church Education.* Westwood, N. J.: Revell, 1968.

Peachey, Laban. *Learning to Understand People.* Scottdale, Pa.: Herald, 1965.

Tournier, Paul. *The Meaning of Persons.* New York: Harper & Row, 1957.

———. *To Understand Each Other.* Richmond: John Knox, 1967.

NOTES

1. George L. Bird and Lillina H. Dean, "Christians Can Learn from Communications Theorists," *Christianity Today,* 20 January 1967, p. 10.
2. Donald P. Ely, "Are We Getting Through to Each Other?" *International Journal of Religious Education,* May 1962, p. 4.
3. Ibid., p. 5.
4. Lee O. Thayer, *Administrative Communication* (Homewood, Ill.: Irwin, 1961), pp. 254-55.
5. Ernest Bormann et al., *Interpersonal Communication and the Modern Organization* (Englewood Cliffs, N. J.: Prentice-Hall, 1969), p. 175.
6. "For Those Who Must Lead . . .," *The Hillsdale College Leadership Letter* 9, no. 9: 1.
7. John Anderson, "What's Blocking Upward Communication?" *Personnel Administration,* January-February 1968.
8. Bormann et al, pp. 75-77.
9. Ely, p. 5.

28

Working with People in Groups

A PROPER PARTICIPATORY VIEW of leadership involves a maximum amount of group activity. In the local church, educational leaders are constantly involved with groups from the smallest Sunday school class to the pastor's confrontation of the entire congregation at a given time. Two factors are necessary in light of this demand. First of all, the present and continuing leadership of the church must understand how groups operate and be able to work well with people in groups. Second, the selection and training of future leaders should be geared toward the mechanics and dynamics of group operation.

A leadership handbook prepared by the Board of Christian Education of the United Presbyterian Church U.S.A. suggests that

> *the way in which leaders are selected has considerable effect upon the quality of leadership that prevails in a congregation.* Those who select and invite persons to serve communicate something of the concept of the church and attitudes toward persons that guide those who do the selecting and inviting. The manner in which a leader is approached may affect his attitude toward the church and his performance in his task.[1]

Developing satisfactory group leadership flows from the initial step of asking, all the way through the training program and the exercise of leadership in the educational program of the church. The leader's individual behavior interacts with the individual behaviors of all of the persons in all of the groups over which he has responsibility. In this sense, "group dynamics" describes those forces which are active at all times in all groups, even when group members and leader are not aware of them. Knowles maintains that this is indeed the most basic definition of the term:

> We can think of every group as having certain relatively static aspects—its name, constitutional structure, ultimate purpose, and

> other fixed characteristics. But it also has *dynamic* aspects—it is always moving, doing something, changing, becoming, interacting, and reacting. And the nature and direction of its movement is determined by forces being exerted on it from within itself and from outside. The interaction of these forces and their resultant effects on a given group constitute its dynamics. In this sense, "group dynamics" is to groups what "personality dynamics" is to individuals. It is a phenomenon that occurs naturally; nobody invents it.[2]

UNDERSTANDING GROUP BEHAVIOR

Business and industry have spent millions of dollars in researching the dynamic factors that make up and control a group's behavior. Their motivation in this expenditure is geared to additional profit. The church has virtually ignored group study and has rarely trained its leadership (either professional or lay) in even the elementary principles of group work. Yet we claim to be operating from a high motivation, the fulfillment of the objective of making people more like Jesus Christ. One can only lay the inexplicable difference in concern at the doorstep of ignorance or carelessness.

Someone has likened recent interest in group study to the parallel interest in the study of atomic and nuclear power. Both are basically neutral or amoral. Both can be used for good or ill. Both have significant power which is waiting to be seized by sinners and saints alike. Therefore inner motivation and commitment will determine whether the end result is used for Satan or for God.

In the helpful little booklet referred to above, Knowles details some of the "properties of groups" which must be investigated and understood if the leader is to fulfill satisfactorily his role in group dynamics. Theoretically, these are properties that all groups possess, though they may be present to a greater or lesser extent and in differing qualities in various groups.

BACKGROUND

No group operates in a vacuum. Its members are bringing to it certain attitudes and patterns of behavior which they have cultivated as individuals and from their contact with other groups. Some may feel essentially involved in the success and ongoing of the group (such as executives who have founded a large corporation); others may be participating only because of force (such as the draftees in a given unit in an army training camp). Some possess higher educational levels than others. Some may be wealthy, some almost poor.

PARTICIPATION PATTERN

How does the group function? This depends largely on the style of the leader involved. Is it basically dictatorial as the leader does all the talking and the various group members passively agree or silently disagree? Is it like the typical adult Sunday school class which proceeds from week to week with a monologue unaccompanied by active participation or perhaps even interest?

FREE COMMUNICATION

In this context the word *communication* describes how group members relate to one another, that is, how they transmit their idea, values, feelings, and attitudes toward matters which the group decides. It is important to recognize that the communication patterns in a group may be nonverbal.

COHESION

Knowles defines cohesion as that which shows how well the group works together as a unit, suggesting that "this property indicates the morale, team spirit, the strength of attraction of the group for its members, and the interest of the members in what the group is doing."[3] A good indication of cohesion can be observed in the way members talk about their group. Instead of "his class" it ought to be "my class" or "our class."

ATMOSPHERE

Atmosphere is the same as climate. How do the group members feel about the actual setting in which the group does its work? Is it relaxed, cold, hostile, informal?

STANDARDS

Every group operates with some code of acceptable type of behavior. This could describe everything from being quiet in church to shouting loudly and jumping high as a member of a cheerleading team. The standards are not always written, and they may not always be of high quality; but there is some mutually accepted determination of conduct that goes on within every group.

SOCIOMETRIC PATTERN

Within every group there are formal or informal subgroups. Group members react differently to some members than they do to others. Any church committee meeting will demonstrate the fact that group members tend to identify with and support people whom they like and disagree more frequently with people against whom they may have some prejudice or discrimination.

STRUCTURE AND ORGANIZATION

This may describe the various offices necessary to the group function: prestige levels, influence, seniority, and so forth. Knowles emphasizes that there are two kinds of organization.

> Groups have both a visible and an invisible organizational structure. The visible structure, which might be highly formal (officers, committees, appointed positions) or quite informal, makes it possible to achieve a division of labor among the members and get essential functions performed. The invisible structure consists of the behind-the-scenes arrangement of the members according to relative prestige, influence, power, seniority, ability, persuasiveness, and the like.[4]

PROCEDURES

Formal groups may use formal procedures, and informal groups, informal procedures; but all groups operate with some pattern of function. What is essential here is that the group and its leaders select and follow the procedure which will best facilitate the achievement of the group's objectives.

GOALS

The effectiveness of the group is inseparably related to its goal achievement. In turn, goal achievement is determined by goal clarification. Even a group of women gathered on Tuesday morning during coffee has its goal. It may be only to share the latest information about other families in the neighborhood, but their meeting, nevertheless, produces some effect in the direction of goal achievement. The centrality of goal clarification and achievement in the educational work of the church has been amply emphasized in earlier pages.

Unleashing Group Dynamic

If group dynamic is really inherent in the operation of all

groups at all times, then the role of the leader and the group members themselves is to *unleash* rather than *produce* this dynamic. Particularly is this true of Christian groups. Persons who pray for "the Holy Spirit to come and be with us" are dealing in theological error. The New Testament clearly indicates that the Holy Spirit is already resident within every Christian.

When Christians get together in groups, it is essential that individuals collectively allow the Holy Spirit to control and manipulate the activities of the group. This is an unleashing of a Christian dynamic. The question before us now, however, asks whether there are elements of group work which, by their presence or absence, *facilitate* the unleashing of that dynamic.

Obviously, from a supernatural point of view, the spiritual level and maturity of the group members is the factor which determines the control of the Holy Spirit in the group itself. Within this context there are still some natural (human) factors which clamor for attention.

CLARIFY THE GROUP'S OBJECTIVES

The objectives of the group must be clarified. Once again we focus on this absolute essential of educational effectiveness. It is necessary that the group not only *have* objectives but that these objectives be understood and subscribed to by all of the group members. The objectives are significant in the choice of a leader for a group, and they are the most significant collective factor which guides the group through its procedures and functions.

A group that is unleashing its dynamic is a group in which the objectives are determined by the members themselves through open discussion. Indeed, in a Christian group the objectives may be absolutes which come from the Word of God, but an understanding of the interpretation and application of the absolutes is brought about through the discussion of group members. Leadership in this situation becomes the process of coordinating group effort toward the agreed goals.

A stagnating group is one whose objectives belong to the leader only. Having pressured them on the group members, he now sees his task as one of making them conform to a behavior which will produce the fulfillment of *his* objectives.

CONSIDER THE GROUP'S HEDONIC TONE

Hedonic tone describes the way the members feel toward their participation in the group. Is this a happy experience? Do the group members like one another and spend time with each other even outside of group meetings? Is the atmosphere an informal one? Many factors determine whether a group will have hedonic tone, including how members are selected, the attitude of the leader, the conditions under which the group is meeting, the attractiveness and effectiveness of the group, and almost all of the properties described earlier in this chapter.

Suffice it here to say that the leader who wishes members and potential members to desire participation in the group must pay attention to the level of hedonic tone which the group offers. Like people in general, group members do well that which they like to do and like to do that which they do well.

CONSTRUCT PATTERNS FOR GROUP INTERACTION

As people interact, behavior changes and groups achieve. Effectiveness is inseparably linked to adequate interaction patterns. These patterns are never complete when any group minority (or even an individual in the group) is not effectively participating in group procedures. Though this is more easily achieved in small groups, it is no less important for larger groups. In a class handbook on group dynamics used at Dallas Theological Seminary, Grant Howard (now at Western Conservative Baptist Seminary, Portland, Oregon) has visualized twelve different "types of group interaction." The names and diagrams are worth reproduction here (see Figure 14).

CRYSTALLIZE THE GROUP'S ACHIEVEMENT

In the present context, achievement is just another word for effectiveness. The same quality might be described by the word *productivity.* Serving Christ in conformity to the Word of God is the ultimate objective of every Christian group. Its achievement is, therefore, measured by its allegiance to biblical patterns of service.

In a properly functioning group, the members have a security which comes from acceptance both by God and by the other members of the group. There is little need for dominance or intimidation to achieve one's own petty ends. To realize that one is a part of an achieving group can go a long way toward abandoning the crutches of self-preservation and a commitment of oneself to the service of others through the group.

CREATE A FAIR SYSTEM OF EVALUATION

Evaluation should not only be a looking at the past but a plan-

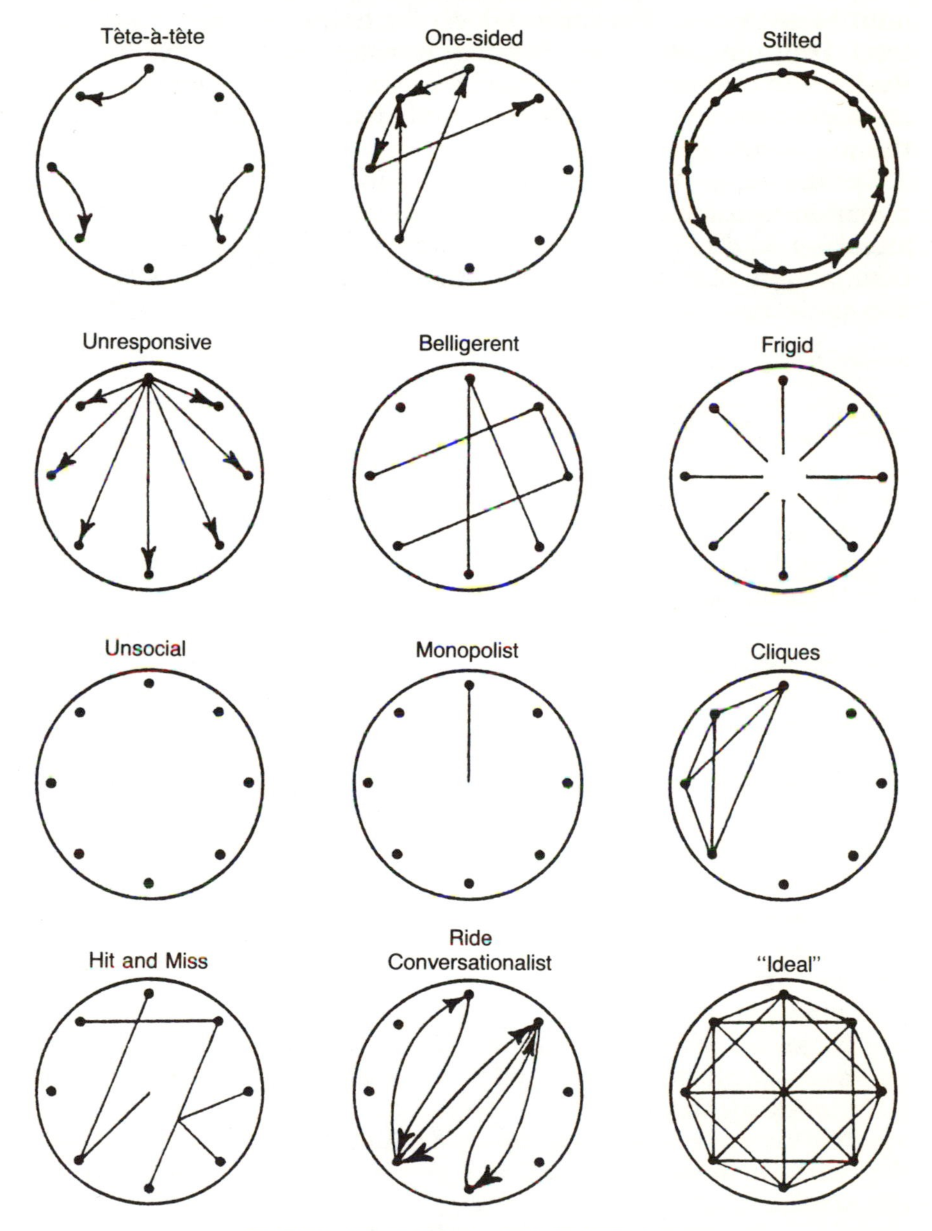

TYPES OF GROUP INTERACTION*
Figure 14

*Grant Howard, "Group Dynamics," Christian Education notes (Dallas Theological Seminary, 1963), p. 12.

ning of the future on the basis of the past. To this end, past failures as well as past successes can be helpful. Creative groups are trying out new ideas and defining a vision for the future. Evaluation process may very well be a recognition of whether the proper group dynamic has been unleashed in the group's activities during the past year.

Groups have been described as monolithic or idiographic; dynamic unleashing or stagnating; power inhibiting or power releasing; and in simplicity as healthy or sick. Douglass offers a comparison of twenty characteristics of healthy versus sick groups:

HEALTHY	*SICK*
A group is healthy when:	A group is sick when:
1. All the members speak up about what they think.	1. A few members do all the talking.
2. Decisions are worked through until a general consensus of agreement is reached.	2. Most members mumble assent.
3. Well-informed members contribute ideas in the area of their competence.	3. Competent people sit silently by.
4. A member's value is judged by the merit of his idea.	4. New people with good ideas are not listened to.
5. The whole group handles questions that concern the whole group.	5. Decision-making is quickly referred to committees.
6. Major issues get major time.	6. Minor issues consume the major time.
7. Major issues evoke mature approaches to change and "working through."	7. Minor and simple issues make people seethe and boil.
8. Minor issues are settled with the attention they deserve.	8. Major issues are passed over.
9. Decisions reached by thorough participation are final and satisfactory.	9. The same subjects, supposedly settled, keep coming up again.

10. Members really understand one another's ideas, plans and proposals.	10. Quick judgments are passed on issues people do not understand.
11. Members objectively center interest on goals and tasks.	11. Members subjectively talk about people in scapegoating fashion.
12. The group carries forward in the performance of tasks and the achievement of goals.	12. The group accomplishes little in absence of chairman.
13. The group works goalwise toward change.	13. The group is afraid to change.
14. Rewards and criticism are shared.	14. Rewards and criticism are concentrated in a few.
15. Initiative and responsibility are encouraged by growth in a sense of personal confidence, competence and worth.	15. Initiative and responsibility are stifled by dependence.
16. Search for help from all sources is continuous.	16. No resources outside the group are drawn upon.
17. Information is fed back into the group.	17. Little is told to the group.
18. The worth of persons is respected.	18. The person is squelched in his expression and stunted in his growth.
19. Experience is considered the occasion for growth in responsibility and love.	19. Action lacks altitude and depth, remaining on the horizontal plane without vertical relationships to God.
20. Action is God-related.	20. Action is self-centered.[5]

Helping Groups Make Decisions

Decision-making by a group looks backward toward goal formation and forward toward achievement or effectiveness. In a sick group a disgruntled minority may stand in the way of achievement, even though a majority had decided upon a particular course of action. No one is interested in compromise. It is simply a process of certain factions in the group blocking other factions. Participation in such a group is not much more than "choosing up sides."

A healthy group, on the other hand, emphasizes consensus. This is not necessarily unanimous agreement since honest, creative groups will rarely experience unanimous consent. It does mean that all group members are working together toward certain ends so that the majority takes into consideration the viewpoint of the minority, and the minority lends its support to the decisions of the majority. An opposing group member is respected by the total group for his opinions. Hedonic tone and respect for all individuals are maintained.

The major difference between decision-making by the individual leader and decision-making by the group is that various persons share in considering possible alternatives and selecting one. They share as well in the success or failure of the decision when it is implemented. This is one reason why group work in the form of committees or boards is, in the final analysis, a more satisfactory way of arriving at satisfactory decisions than is autocracy. In a helpful little booklet entitled *How to Help Groups Make Decisions,* Grace Elliott lays out an entire outline of the process through which the group moves in making a decision.

An Outline of Group Decision Procedure

1. *Seeing what the problem is*
   a. What is the situation? (What, who, why?)
   b. What factors in the situation are important and must be taken into account?
   c. What are the specific questions to be decided?
2. *Considering possible alternatives*
   a. Examination of possibilities:
      (1) To meet the situation and problem as outlined, what are the possible courses of action and the reason for each?
      (2) What bonds seem to unite the group? On what is there agreement in fact, principle, or objective?
      (3) What are the chief differences, if any (on matters of fact, objectives, principles, desires)?
   b. Exploration of differences as to facts and points of view:
      (1) What additional information is needed? How can it be secured?
      (2) Can the differing points of view be talked out?
3. *Reaching a conclusion*
   a. What decision will best take into account the relevant factors, the purposes and desires of the group, the various points of view?
   b. What are the reasons for this decision?

4. *Moving toward action*
   a. What are the ways and means of putting the decision into effect?
   b. What are the next steps? Whose responsibility? (What, where, how?)[6]

How can individual group members facilitate the proper decision making process on the part of their groups? Here are some suggestions:

1. Clearly understand the objectives of the group.
2. Evaluate your own motives for being in the group.
3. Spend more time listening than you do talking.
4. Make a genuine attempt to understand the viewpoints and opinions of other group members.
5. Raise honest questions about group procedure and problems and join the group in searching for answers. Do not be a mere "naysayer."
6. Accept and learn to handle verbal opposition. Sooner or later someone will verbally attack you in a group, and your reaction will be very important at that moment.
7. Avoid defensiveness. Express your own opinions honestly, expecting that the group members will receive them and consider them fairly, just as you receive the suggestions of any other group member when he speaks.
8. Observe group loyalty at all times. Do not appear to be vitally interested in the group at its meetings, only to talk about its shortcomings to outsiders.
9. Learn as much as you can about the responsibilities of the group. If the group, for example, is the board of Christian education, reading books on Christian education in the local church should occupy a significant proportion of leisure time while you are serving on that board.
10. Be willing to accept group and committee responsibilities. Do not let the leader do all the work himself.
11. Share in the failures as well as the successes of the group. Do not attempt to "pass the buck" when something which the group has decided does not reach a level of expectancy.
12. Try to understand more about group dynamics. Observe what is going on at each meeting of the group and consider what you can do to unleash the spiritual dynamic described above.

Roadblocks to Effective Group Work

Research in group dynamics has demonstrated that there are a number of dangers or difficulties which can arise in group activity to stifle the dynamic that can and should be the very lifeblood of the group's achievement. As these are controlled and alleviated from group work, the level of effectivenes will be raised.

FORGETTING THE INDIVIDUAL

The political system known as communism subordinates and sacrifices the individual to the interests of the group. This same mistake can be made in simple group process, particularly when one or two individuals always find themselves in the minority of a question. It becomes the responsibility of the leader and the group to safeguard and encourage recognition of each member and his viewpoint.

EXPECTING TOO MUCH FROM GROUP DYNAMICS

Because of the emphasis which has been placed on group process in sociology, psychology, and education in the past two decades, some people tend to think of group work as a panacea for all of the problems which may face an organization. This is simply not true, and it is essential to recognize the limitations of group work, as well as its benefits. The attitude of overexpectation may later give birth to that death knell of traditionalism, "We tried it and it didn't work."

WASTING TIME IN GROUP WORK

If the group's objectives are not clear and the problem which they are dealing with is not properly specified, the group work itself may be quite unfruitful and unsatisfactory. The group fumbles around with various approaches to the problem and finally bogs down in its own discussion.

IMPROPER PLANNING FOR GROUP SESSIONS

Unless the leader and other appointed group members plan for satisfactory group meetings by preparation of agendas, and so forth, it is possible that the group will spend a great deal of time only to arrive at no conclusion. This is very much akin to the problem of wasting time.

LETTING GROUP DYNAMICS BECOME AN ACTIVITY OF THE FLESH

This is a problem that is confined to Christian use of groups, but it is a real one. Just as the individual Christian yields to a control of the Spirit of God, so the entire group yields its collective mind to that divine control.

FOR FURTHER READING

Anderson, James D. *To Come Alive!* New York: Harper & Row, 1973.

Bergevin, Paul; Morris, Dwight; and Smith, Robert M. *Adult Education Procedures*. New York: Seabury, 1963.

Berne, Eric. *Games People Play*. New York: Grove, 1964.

Blumenthal, L. H. *How to Work with Your Board and Committees*. New York: Association, 1954.

Buchanan, Paul C. *The Leader and Individual Motivation*. New York: Association, 1964.

Dobbins, Gaines S. *Learning to Lead*. Nashville: Broadman, 1968.

Douglass, Paul F. *The Group Workshop Way in the Church*. New York: Association, 1956.

Elliot, Grace, ed. *How to Help Groups Make Decisions*. New York: Association, 1959.

Fallaw, Wesner. *Church Education for Tomorrow*. Philadelphia: Westminster, 1960.

Frank, Lawrence K. *How to Be a Modern Leader*. New York: Association, 1954.

Howse, W. L., and Thomason, W. O. *A Dynamic Church*. Nashville: Convention Press, 1969.

Howard, J. Grant. *The Trauma of Transparency*. Portland, Ore.: Multnomah, 1979.

LeBar, Lois E. *Focus on People in Church Education*. Westwood, N.J.: Revell, 1968.

Let's Look at Leadership. Handbook. Philadelphia: Bd. of Chr. Ed., United Presb. Church USA, 1962.

Luft, Joseph. *Group Processes: An Introduction to Group Dynamics*. Palo Alto, Calif.: Mayfield Publishing, 1970.

Prime, Derek. *A Christian's Guide to Leadership*. Chicago: Moody, 1966.

Tournier, Paul. *The Meaning of Persons*. New York: Harper & Row, 1957.

———. *To Understand Each Other*. Richmond: John Knox, 1967.

Wedel, Leonard E. *Building and Maintaining a Church Staff*. Nashville: Broadman, 1967.

Zuck, Roy B., and Getz, Gene A. *Christian Youth: An In-Depth Study*. Chicago: Moody, 1968.

NOTES

1. *Let's Look at Leadership*, handbook (Philadelphia: Bd. of Chr. Ed., United Presb. Church USA, 1962), p.35.
2. Malcolm and Hulda Knowles, *Introduction to Group Dynamics* (New York: Association, 1959), p. 12.
3. Ibid., p. 45.
4. Ibid., p. 48.
5. Paul F. Douglass, *The Group Workshop Way in the Church* (New York: Association, 1956).
6. Grace Elliott, ed., *How to Help Groups Make Decisions* (New York: Association, 1959), pp. 30-31.

29

Delegation: Key to Survival

It is probably impossible to suggest one aspect of leadership that is more important than the rest. For example, can we say that decision-making is more important than planning? Is organization a more significant ingredient in leadership success than human relations? Such value judgements are futile because functioning leadership is a seamless garment of variable activities, each of which is interwoven with the rest. But on the firing line, delegation comes as close to being indispensable as any leadership characteristic can be.

Delegation has to do with the leader consigning certain tasks, and authority for those tasks, to other persons in the organization. It is a process rather simple to define but exceedingly difficult to carry out. Bower, in his excellent chapter on delegation, speaks to the importance of the issue:

> The larger an organization becomes, the more important it is for an administrator to apply the principles of delegation. Those on the staff of a moderately large and growing church will of necessity concern themselves increasingly with more abstract operations, such as policy-making, supervision, counseling, and coordination. These more important activities can be adequately carried out, however, only if lesser important duties are delegated to Sunday-school superintendent, sponsors of youth groups, adult fellowship officers, and other leaders. As a matter of fact, the aim of the administrator ought to be that of utilizing the delegation process as frequently as possible so that duties and decisions of lesser significance will be transferred to those at the lower levels of the church structure. "The making of decisions," according to Pfiffner, "should ordinarily be delegated to the lowest possible level of the hierarch." This will then permit him to devote himself to those administrative operations which demand the presence and skill of a full-time, well-trained staff person and will assure a continuing expansion of the church program.[1]

Such delegation begins with a proper view of administration as described in an earlier chapter. It focuses attention on the achievement of group goals rather than the retaining of authority and power by the leader for himself. The autocratic leader will generally be ineffective at delegation. The free-rein leader, on the other hand, will tend to allow too much flexibility to achieve the desired results in the delegation process.

In the church the delegation process is complicated by the leader's constant dealing with unsalaried workers. In a very real sense, he can only *ask* someone else in the organization to take a task and carry it out even though authority may be consistent with such a request in terms of the organizational chart. But difficult though it may be, delegation is an essential part of the leadership role carried out by the pastor, director of Christian education, and other church educational officers.

The Necessity of Delegation

WHY SHOULD LEADERS DELEGATE?

One of the basic reasons for delegation within the context of the church is that *it is biblical.* Moses found himself strained almost to the breaking point under the responsibilities that were his as the single leader of the children of Israel in the wilderness. Such unilateral responsibility was unnecessary, however, and at the suggestion of Jethro it was divided among some of the other men who were capable of assuming the assignment of such duties (Exodus 18).

In the New Testament the Lord Himself certainly used a classic pattern of delegation. Even while He was on earth he consigned many of the tasks of His total ministry to His disciples, and at the time of His ascension He passed on to them the entire responsibility for the ongoing church. All biblical commissions (such as those found in Matthew 28 and John 20) are in a very real sense commissions of delegation first to the disciples and then, through them, to every Christian to carry out the ministry of Christ.

Another reason for delegation is *sheer necessity* in order to get the job done. The physical and mental weight of church work cannot be carried by one or even a few men. Their incapacity to move adequately under the burden should be an immediate indication to them that delegation is necessary.

A third but still valid reason for delegation is that it serves in the important task of *training future as well as present leadership* for the church's program. The leader who would bear heavy responsibility in some executive office must first learn to bear lighter responsibility in some subordinate role. The whole process of involving senior-high young people in the planning and execution of their own programs is an example of delegation which hopefully will result in more maturity and leadership responsibility on the part of those teenagers. People who have things done for them all the time never learn to do things for themselves. Consequently, they are never able to do things for others.

WHY DO SOME LEADERS FAIL TO DELEGATE?

Delegation is a ministry fraught with fear of the unknown. Without ever verbalizing it in so many words, many leaders would hesitate to delegate duties simply because they are afraid to give up authority which they claim as rightfully theirs. In a sense there is a certain amount of carnality involved here as selfish pride wins the day. Nevertheless, failure to delegate is also the result of ignorance of the administrative process.

It is quite true that most delegatees will not perform the assigned task to the same level of competence that the leader himself would have performed it. Hopefully, however, after exercising the responsibilities for a period of time, his level of competence will rise considerably and will even begin to approach that of his mentor. This in itself is both a blessing and a threat to the leader who might already be somewhat skeptical of the delegation process.

Some leaders fail to delegate because they do not want to spend the necessary time. In the initial stage, delegation *does* take more time than doing the task oneself. Making the consignment, issuing reminders, checking and double-checking results, possibly making some corrections, and other aspects of the delegation process tempt one to say, "I'd rather do it myself." But delegation is not an *expenditure* of time. It is an *investment*. Unfortunately, because the returns of the investment do not always appear immediately, discouragement can set in and lead some to forsake the process.

WHAT KINDS OF TASKS CANNOT BE DELEGATED?

At first glance it would appear that one delegates almost without limitation, but there are restricting guidelines which must be observed. Several can be noted:

Items assigned in a job description. If, for example, a church has hired a director of Christian education to plan and carry out an annual leadership-training retreat during the month of September, the planning and implementing of that retreat should not be passed on to someone else in the organization.

If the basis and authority of the delegation is not clear. The person who is asked to accept the assignment should know that the person who is asking him has the right to do so. This necessitates an understanding of the entire organizational structure by all of the workers concerned.

Something which belongs to someone else's area of authority. A Sunday school superintendent should not be delegating responsibilities relative to the operation of the training-hour program on Sunday evening. A director of Christian education should not be delegating aspects of the church music ministry if the church has employed a director of music on organizational par with the director of Christian education.

Generally the literature on delegation argues that the leader delegates everything that he does not absolutely have to do himself. This may be an overstatement, but it generalizes the enormity of importance placed upon delegation in sound administrative theory.

The Degrees of Delegation

In one sense delegation must carry with it the authority to carry out the consigned task. Certainly the task and its authority constitute a responsibility, and to that extent responsibility is delegated. In another sense, however, the leader can never delegate *ultimate* responsibility.

Assume, for example, that the pastor has asked the director of Christian education to plan the program for the February workers conference. The director, in turn, passes the responsibility on to the chairman of the board of Christian education. If at conference time no program is prepared, the director is answerable to the pastor for the error.

The concept of "degrees of delegation" has to do with the amount of authority passed on with the consigned task. The greater the authority given, the higher the degree of delegation. Bower speaks to the matter of authority when he says,

> Along with the delegation of responsibility there must be a delegation of authority, for without authority, subordinates will be seriously handicapped in the execution of their duties. This

> means that they will also be given the power to initiate and carry such plans through to their completion. Hence, the necessary authority must be delegated so that the decisions to be made in connection with the execution of plans will be possible at every organizational level. This implies, too, the delegation of responsibility for planning to delegatees, and of authority *sufficient* for the execution of plans.[2]

The trick in delegation is to realize that the leader can never give away ultimate accountability. He transfers tasks and even responsibility but ultimately he is accountable to his superiors for what he delegates to subordinates. That is why some managerial scientists talk about four different degrees of delegated authority.

EXECUTIVE AUTHORITY

The highest level is the executive level, and it carries with it the full authority to see the task through to its completion. The leader assigns to the delegatee some given responsibility and then no longer concerns himself with it. In the above illustration the pastor may have said to his director, "Please plan the February workers' conference," and never thought again about what the program would be.

The pastor's inattention to follow-up is a perversion of proper delegation process but serves also as an example of complete authority. In this illustration it would have to include the expenditure of funds, if such were necessary in the appointment of speakers and leaders for the conference.

REPORTING AUTHORITY

In a reporting type of delegation, the delegatee is responsible for undertaking the task but must report to his supervisor at predetermined points in the execution process. Reports may be single or multiple, but the supervisor is asking to be kept informed of what decisions are being made in the carrying out of the task.

MAKE DUTIES CLEAR

Clearly define the delegated duties. Generalization is the bugaboo of successful delegation. It is necessary to delineate specifically what is expected of the delegatee; what time or date the task is to be finished; and, if necessary, what form the finished product is to take. All necessary information to accomplish the task must be provided.

DO NOT ASSIGN METHODS

Delegate according to desired results and not according to methodology. The "how" of the task is usually not proper information to be communicated in delegation. It is possible that the delegatee will do things quite differently than the supervisor would do them. Assuming he achieves the same results, no complaint should be offered. Obviously at times it may be necessary to say that the end does not justify the means. In the simple mechanics of getting the task done, the delegatee should be allowed the freedom to choose his own methodology.

SET UP CONTROLS

Establish built-in controls to pinpoint difficulties at an early stage. It is really quite foolish to go all the way to the date of that February workers conference only to discover that no one has properly planned the program. Periodically from the point of delegation to the point of conclusion, the pastor could have reminded the director; and the director should have followed up on his delegation to the chairman of the board of Christian education.

Such reminders can be in the form of simple questions, such as, "How are the plans for the workers conference coming, Bill?" A more effective system of control is a regular reporting system such as that which should be required from every church agency leader by the board of Christian education periodically throughout the year.

GIVE PRAISE AND CREDIT

Offer praise and credit when the delegated task is successfully completed. This is the important step of reinforcement and is dealt with by Brethower and Rummler.

> Since behavior is influenced by its consequences, there are several things the manager or management can do to realize the optimum effect of this relationship:
>
> 1. Train only when the behavior trained will be reinforced on the job.
> 2. Design jobs so rewards for the desired behavior exceed punishment for failure.

3. Arrange conditions so an employee can see which of his acts are being reinforced.
4. Arrange the reinforcement so it is given time to be linked to the act.
5. Select reinforcers that are in fact reinforcing to the employee.[3]

Delegating in an Anti-Establishment Culture

I have frequently said that the New Testament does not support a leadership concept which is based on authoritarian attitude. Blau argues that the whole concept of authoritarian administration refers to a relationship between persons, and not to an attribute of one individual. It involves exercise of social control which rests on subordinates' willing compliance with certain directives from the superior.

The dilemma of bureaucratic authority, therefore, is that it rests on the power of sanctions (enforced controls) but is weakened by frequently having to use its sanctions to strengthen its authority. Consider, for example, a dean of students in a small Christian college. He wants to maintain a warm climate of rapport so that he can be a friend and confidant to the students in counseling situations. But he is hired to maintain discipline as well, and his authority rests on the sanctions he can impose upon violators. The more he must appeal to this authority, the less attractive he will be for personal counseling.

In a most helpful article on authority in the church, Bill Patterson points out the significance of the difference between human authority and divine authority, a recognition which forces an accompanying commitment to the limitation of objective authority in the church.

> No mere human being—be he leader, deacon, preacher, teacher, editor, professor or somebody's archbishop, cardinal, or pope—has any true religious legislative authority. Some operate as if they do have, as they attempt to change or even deny God's holy word or force their opinion upon others, but God is not mocked, and when His authority is usurped, let that usurping man or system remember that "whatsoever a man soweth, that shall he reap."[4]

Patterson identifies two extremes polarizing the abuse of power in the church. The extreme to the right is dictatorial, despotic, tyrannical, and coercively authoritarian; the extreme to the left is raw individualism and anarchy.

Once again, the practice of decentralized and participatory

democracy, centering in the body and resting upon the principles of universal priesthood, emerges as the only valid New Testament concept of leadership and administration.

One of the most exciting chapters in Alvin Toffler's *Future Shock* is the one in which he discusses what he calls "the coming ad-hocracy." After concurring with Bennis's predictions of the breakup of the pyramid and the demise of bureaucracy, Toffler tries to identify the administrator of the future.

> Executives and managers in this system will function as coordinators between the various transient work teams. They will be skilled in understanding the jargon of different groups of specialists, and they will communicate across groups, translating and interpreting the language of one into the language of another.
>
> Thus we find the emergence of a new kind of organization man—a man who, despite his many affiliations, remains basically uncommitted to any organization. He is willing to employ his skills and creative energies to solve problems with equipment provided by the organization, and within temporary groups established by it. But he does so only so long as the problems interest *him*. He is committed to his own career, and his own self-fulfillment.[5]

Such a picture may or may not be an accurate projection of the future in secular business and industry, but the church must once again avoid the problems of extreme reactionism. Increasing flexibility, yes. Decentralization of authority and decision-making, yes. But a situation in which all administrators work for themselves and turn their backs on institutionalized organizations, no. The old maxim calls for moderation in all things; we must be temperate in our knifing of bureaucracy and our welcoming of "ad-hocracy."

The question of authority and reaction to authority is crucial to the process of delegation. One cannot delegate without authority, and yet abusing authority can cripple the effectiveness of delegation. The gentleness and kindness of the leader filled with the Spirit of God stands against the contemporary conflict between labor and management and always emphasizes the team concept of the people of God at work together.

Delegation builds the future leadership of the church. Its elements include responsibility, authority, and accountability, all of which must be reckoned with in proper perspective in the delegation process. Someone has said that with all the evidence to commend it, failure to delegate is an emotional problem, not a rational one. The church leader who can effectively delegate tasks to people and then effectively supervise them in those tasks is demonstrating the gift of administration and is contributing much to the overall ministry of his local church.

FOR FURTHER READING

Engstrom, Ted W., and Dayton, Edward R. *The Christian Executive.* Waco, Tex.: Word, 1979.

The Chief Executive Office and Its Responsibilities. New York: Amacom, 1970.

Laird, Donald A., and Laird, Eleanor C. *The Techniques of Delegating.* New York: McGraw-Hill, 1957.

Likert, Rensis, and Likert, Jan Gibson. *New Ways of Managing Conflict.* New York: McGraw-Hill, 1976.

MacKenzie, Alec. *The Time Trap.* New York: American Manhood Assn., 1972.

NOTES

1. Robert K. Bower, *Administering Christian Education* (Grand Rapids: Eerdmans, 1964), pp. 75-76.
2. Ibid., p. 79.
3. Dale M. Brethower and G. A. Rummler, "For Improved Work Performance: Accentuate the Positive," *Personnel Magazine,* September-October 1966, p. 9.
4. Bill Patterson, "Authority—What is It?" *Christian Bible Teacher,* May 1972, p. 196.
5. Alvin Toffler, *Future Shock* (New York: Random House, 1970), pp. 129, 134.

30

Principles and Practice in Motivation

THE PURPOSE OF THE CHURCH'S EDUCATIONAL PROGRAM is to provide spiritual growth in the life of people, individually and collectively. The methodology utilized in the attainment of that objective is distinctly related to group activity and is "people-centered." It has been emphasized that the productivity and effectiveness of a group is directly related to the kind of leadership provided for that group. The authoritarian leader will press on with his ideas and concepts regardless of what the group thinks or feels regarding his procedures. If a vote is taken, dissatisfied minority members will either cause trouble in the group or leave it.

The "laissez-faire" leader, on the other hand, allows the pendulum to swing too far to the other side. He sees himself only as a catalyst and allows the group to wander aimlessly up and down the bypaths of their own discretion, usually with minimum productivity as the result. Group members may blame the leader for this lack of productivity, as well as being discontented with the group itself. The group's hedonic tone will obviously suffer in such a situation.

The democratic leader finds himself directly involved with the two crucial concepts which are the focus of this chapter. Rather than pushing on ahead with his own ideas and programs, he seeks to bring about individual motivation so that the members of the group themselves become productive. Not content with stagnation or apathy, he seeks a satisfactory approach to the process of change. Those who have held leadership positions in or out of the local church realize immediately that successful technique in motivating people and bringing about change is absolutely essential to effective leadership.

MOTIVATING PEOPLE

The essential factor that the leader must recognize in the

motivation process is that there is a cause (and usually an identifiable one) for the way people think and act. A person's behavior is the direct result of his value system. Secular sociologists would argue that one's value system is the result of environmental influence and has been produced largely from factors outside of himself.

The Christian responds by saying that a biblical value system emanates rather from what an individual believes in and has committed himself to. In a very real sense the constant task of the Christian leader is to help his group throw off the external influences that seek to motivate behavior and yield rather to internal motivations, such as obedience to Christ, commitment to the will of God, and a recognition of discipleship responsibility.

Buchanan sets forth five principles which, though secular in the context of his book, can be adapted in Christian leadership study. He identifies these five principles "as being particularly important in exploring why people behave as they do":

1. The way a person behaves depends on *both* the person *and* his environment.
2. Each individual behaves in ways which *make sense* to him.
3. An individual's *perception* of a situation influences his behavior in that situation.
4. An individual's *view of himself* influences what he does.
5. An individual's behavior is influenced by his needs, which vary from person to person and from time to time.[1]

Buchanan's emphasis is both simple and significant. He suggests that the leader dare not try to find only one cause of any given behavior but rather must recognize the complexity of factors which produce behavior. The obvious implication is that if the leader can recognize what makes a person do what he *does*, then he will be one step closer toward providing a kind of motivation which will help him do what he should do. The "should" can be defined either as "what the leader wants him to do" or "what is right according to biblical and spiritual standards of church work." The closer the motivation goals approximate this latter definition, the more effective the leader's ministry.

MOTIVATION IS INSEPARABLY RELATED TO PERSONAL GOALS

The name Carl A. Rogers is synonymous with the nondirective approach to counseling. In a very helpful booklet entitled *A Therapist's View of Personal Goals*, he deals with the basic ontological questions of life. Based on the experiences he has had with his clients, Rogers examines the matter of personal goals and how people set out to achieve them.

Five dimensions of value in human existence are borrowed from the research of Charles Morris:

1. A preference for a responsible, moral, self-restrained participation in life.
2. Delight in vigorous action for the overcoming of obstacles.
3. The value of a self-sufficient inner life with a rich and heightened self-awareness.
4. A receptivity to persons and to nature.
5. Sensuous enjoyment and self employment.[2]

Rogers is rather unhappy with these choices, however, and adds one of his own, using the words of Kierkegaard: "To be that self which one truly is."[3] In effect, self-actualization (according to Rogers) is the goal of human endeavor.

Rogers finds his clients drawing away from the "shoulds," away from the "oughts," and away from meeting expectations and pleasing others. The positive experience of these people is toward more openly "being a process," toward "being complexity," and toward "trust of oneself."

What are the implications of the above for the Christian leader? All church work today is carried on in the context of a society that is emphasizing the worth of the individual and his right to make decisions and choose courses of action without being influenced by standards of behavior, either internal or external. Carried to its extreme, such a philosophy can justify divorce, premarital sex, and the general relative morality and value system which has already established itself as a characteristic of this last third of the twentieth century.

To this kind of a climate, the Christian brings the necessity of appealing to biblical motives. A Sunday school teacher, for example, is asked to teach not because it is "self-actualizing" but because service for Jesus Christ through the church must be the normal experience of every Christian who wishes to obey his Lord. The absolute standards of Christian discipleship demand the "shoulds" and "oughts" that Rogers is so willing to cast aside.

The Christian leader agrees wholeheartedly with Rogers that personal goals are a major factor in the motivation process. He realizes, however, that part of his responsibility is to help his people bring their personal goals into conformity with the will of God rather than establishing personal goals which are predicated upon their own interests and desires.

MOTIVATION DEPENDS UPON INFORMATION

An obvious example of the impact of information (true or false) is the significance of political propaganda in the world society of the twentieth century. In any given organization the focus is on the necessity of keeping one's people informed with the expectation that the information, because of its accuracy and inherent activism, will serve as a motivating agent in helping the groups to achieve. The distribution of such information is often through use of impersonal large-group communiques, such as mimeographed memos, general letters and church bulletins. A more personalized approach might take the form of a telephone call or a personal interview.

Some say that every church leader (particularly the pastor) is engaged in public relations and/or propaganda. What is the difference between these two? Propaganda, which tries to influence public opinion by promoting a special interest, has predetermined ends and is engaged in a manipulation process. The propaganda is merely a means to an end. Generally, propaganda cares not whether the results obtained may be detrimental to some groups or to some members of the group.

On the other hand, public relations has a respect for truth and goes about its task with dignity and good manners, recognizing its responsibility to the various publics involved and engaging in cooperativeness at all points. No doubt there are propagandists in some churches, but the spiritual role of leadership is one that motivates through the communication of information to all the people who are involved. The needs are made known, the objectives are clarified openly, and the program proceeds on the assumption that an informed people will respond intelligently.

MOTIVATION IS INVOLVED WITH THE CHANGING OF GROUP ATTITUDES

There are three basic parts to the human attitude: the cognitive, the affective, and the behavioral. The cognitive has to do with mental recognition of facts; the affective with one's feelings, which are the result of knowing the facts; and the behavioral deals with resultant actions. Sometimes these three aspects are referred to as intellect, emotions, and will. The leader who wishes to produce motivation in his people must deal with all three of these aspects of attitude before he will see results.

Attitude changes increase with a decrease in ego involvement of group members. In other words, as one becomes less self-centered, he becomes more motivated toward participation in group activities and, therefore, toward satisfactory achievement. It should be noted also that an overt conforming behavior does not necessarily imply attitudinal change. Someone has wryly remarked, "A man convinced against his will is of the same opinion still." He may withdraw his verbal attack on the leader's program, but a sullen passivity does not signal cooperation.

Recent research on the area of attitudinal change has indicated that there are at least five principles involved in the changing of attitudes in a group:

1. Attitudinal change increases with the increase of contact and involvement on the part of a member of a group with the other members of that group.

2. Attitudinal change is more likely as the degree of similarity among members of the group decreases. Homogeneity in a group tends to stagnate, and thought patterns conform if all of the group members are of the same mind.

3. Attitudinal change increases as opportunities for interaction increase. A church member who has an overt dislike for blacks might have that attitude changed as he allows himself more thorough personal interaction with individual blacks.

4. Attitudinal change increases or decreases in response to events which take place outside of the group. A board member may be quite open-minded or rather hostile at a board meeting, depending on the kind of conversation he had with his wife just before he left home.

5. Attitudinal change is directly related to group crises. If the continued existence of the group is threatened by an outside force, a change of attitude on the part of some members may be necessary to defend the structure of the group itself. The Epicureans and Stoics were no friends of each other until they could unite against the common foe they saw in the supernaturalism of the apostle Paul when he visited Athens.

In the booklet mentioned above, Buchanan draws some final conclusions from the principles he states at the beginning of his work. Their succinctness and helpfulness justify reproducing them here:

1. Understanding one's motivation helps one to understand other people. It does so not through "doing unto others . . ." but by

reducing blocks which prevent one from listening to, and thus understanding the other person.

2. Motivation, like growth, is inherent within people. Hence, the task to the leader is not so much that of "motivating others" as it is of "unleashing" and helping to harness the motivation that is already there.
3. We all respond to a situation *as we see it*. Thus, one way to influence another person's behavior is to help him get a more accurate view of what is reality. (This also applies to our own behavior!)[4]

Maslow's Hierarchy of Human Needs

According to Abraham Maslow, man is a perpetually wanting organism.[5] His wants stem from five basic human needs, of relative predominance. The hierarchy concept stems from Maslow's belief that when a lower need is satisfied, it disappears and is replaced by a higher-order need. Thus, gratification is considered as important a concept, in motivating theory, as deprivation, since it releases the individual from dominance by a lower order and enables him to concentrate on more social, or higher-order, needs. Once a need has been satisfied, it is no longer considered a "need," since it exists then only in a potential fashion and may emerge again at any time to dominate the individual. It is the unsatisfied needs which dominate a person and organize his behavior.

The hierarchy of basic human needs, arranged in order from lower to higher, includes the following: physiological needs, safety needs, belongingness and love needs, esteem needs, and the need for self-actualization. Maslow would argue that the order is not fixed (there have been a number of exceptions), but that it nevertheless holds true for the overwhelming majority of persons encountered in his research.

Physiological needs are the issues of subsistence and, consequently, are the most dominant of all. They include such factors as hunger, thirst, and sleepiness. They are relatively independent of each other and of other issues in the motivational process, allowing a person to be completely dominated by a single physiological need, such as hunger.

When the physiological needs are satisfied, safety needs may emerge. It is quite possible that safety needs dominate only in emergencies such as war, disease, and natural catastrophe. When one has been shipwrecked, for example, it does not seem consequential to him that he might also be hungry.

Love, affection, and belongingness needs will emerge if the physiological and safety needs are fairly well gratified. They are demonstrated by a desire for affectionate relations with people in general, and manifested in a longing for group acceptance or group membership.

The next step upward in the hierarchy is the esteem-need level. Satisfaction of this need can be derived from self-respect or self-esteem as a feeling of adequacy accruing from achievements and accomplishments, prestige, status, or appreciation by others.

When all of these lower needs are satisfied, then the need for self-actualization emerges and becomes the significant factor in the motivational process. It represents a longing for self-fulfillment and a desire to become everything that one is capable of becoming.

Once again, an analysis of a secular theoretician in the light of the New Testament offers some striking insights. Surely we understand James to be saying that the communication of Christian theology to a man who is starving is sheer nonsense (James 2:14-20). His need for inner peace and eternal salvation is properly recognized by him only when physiological and safety needs have been met.

On the other hand, a company (or a church) does not motivate a man by offering him additional fulfillment of needs that have already been met. When a man has enough bread, he is not impelled to action by the offer of more bread, or even by the potential wherewithal to buy more bread.

What is there about Christian ministry that is self-actualizing? Is it possible that the discouraged pastor or a Sunday school teacher ready to quit finds himself in that position because no one has taught him to think of his service as self-actualizing? Has the Christian service dropout developed a distorted, slave-to-the-church concept of his task? Is it possible that the task itself has very little self-actualizing potential?

My brother-in-law tells hilarious stories of the days when he was a factory worker putting screws in refrigerator doors all day long—a task hardly calculated to produce self-esteem or a feeling of belongingness and importance. How are we helping our people to understand that teaching and leading in Christian ministry is not the theological equivalent of putting screws in a refrigerator door on some assembly line?

HERZBERG'S MOTIVATION-HYGIENE THEORY

Frederick Herzberg is professor of psychology at Western Reserve University and has also served as research director of the Psychological Service of Pittsburgh for several years. Primarily through his orientation toward mental illness and health theories, he has developed what is called the Motivation-Hygiene Theory and has detailed it in three books entitled *Job Attitudes: Review of Research and Opinion; The Motivation to Work;* and *Work and the Nature of Man.*[6] Actually the three volumes represent three stages in the development of the theory. They detail the gathering of scientific inquiry and data, new research and investigation, and actual construction of the conceptual theory. The interesting outcome of the Herzberg study is that the factors which make people satisfied with their jobs are *not* the same as those which make them dissatisfied, nor are these factors necessarily the opposites of one another.

Herzberg concludes that the presence of so-called satisfiers tends to increase an individual's satisfaction with his work, but their absence does not necessarily make a worker dissatisfied, only apathetic. Similarly, the presence of so-called dissatisfiers makes people unhappy or disgruntled about their work, but the absence of dissatisfiers does not necessarily make them happy on the job. Here are the lists which came out of the research:[7]

Satisfiers	*Dissatisfiers*
Achievement	Interpersonal relations (both with superiors and peers)
Recognition	Technical ability of the supervisor
Work itself	Company policy and administration
Responsibility	Working conditions
Advancement	Personal life off the job

It is interesting to note that the satisfiers distinctly relate to the work itself, whereas the dissatisfiers quite frequently relate to the job context, or the environment out of which the job emerges. Herzberg concludes that the presence of satisfiers leads to higher productivity, but the dissatisfiers, on the other hand, do not necessarily lead to lower productivity. Strauss and Sayles summarize the Herzberg findings well in a brief paragraph:

> The experimenters called the factors which lead to this rather sterile, non-involved attitude "hygienic factors" (since they are used to avoid trouble). We shall accordingly call management which emphasizes these factors "Hygienic Management." Such a "be good" policy may provide a pleasant environment in which to work and a considerable amount of around-the-job satisfaction, but little satisfaction through the job, and little sense of enthusiasm or creativity.[8]

Once again, we can be helped by the work of secular research. The Christian organization needs to emphasize the satisfiers of achievement, responsibility, and advancement. But surely our primary deficiency does not lie here, but in our failure to recognize the presence of dissatisfiers. The problem develops because we have frequently failed to recognize their existence and have concentrated our attention on mulitplying and enhancing the satisfiers, while the dissatisfiers may have been chipping away at the morale, and consequently the motivation, of our workers.

Surely it is thoroughly biblical for a Christian employer to be concerned with the life of his employees off the job. Surely it is consistent with Christian theology to recognize that the inner factors of a man's attitude toward personnel, himself, and his supervisors will represent a crucial role in his service performance.

Zaleznik and the Individualistic View

As I have indicated earlier in this volume, Abraham Zaleznik is one of the few management theoreticians who seeks to place responsibility upon the worker rather than constantly harping on changing the organization. His position emphasizes an internal view of man and attempts to show how men, by the strength of their character and personality, can remake organizations. The effect of their personality induces a contagious desire to perform that is considerably stronger in directing organizations than are depersonalized systems such as interlocking committee structures or shared management. The release of this individual energy and its contagion of desire to perform may well occur within organizational structures, but the impulse and inspiration are derived from individual personality. Zaleznik points out that even when we are interested in group and organizational problems as we should be, the ultimate "chooser," or decision maker, is the individual. Even when he performs within groups, he is still performing as an individual. Since this is the case, it is essential for leadership to understand the ways in which an individual personality is influenced by the attributes of the groups in which he works and lives, the other individuals with whom he interacts, the organization within which he and his group work, and the cultures in which they all live.[9]

The Christian leader will find himself nodding vigorously when he reads Zaleznik's emphasis on individuality starting in family life. Specific persons, and his relationships to them, influence each person and are in turn influenced by him. As his world and self broaden, he is increasingly concerned with the environment beyond his immediate, face-to-face groups.[10]

One of the reasons why Zaleznik's theorizing appeals to me is his concern for changing men rather than organizations. Or perhaps I should say, changing organizations by first changing the individuals which make up those organizations. In these days of enormous emphasis on change in the church, Zaleznik's focus ought to put cautious guidelines on the massive restructuring advocated by some renewal writers. According to Zaleznik, the social scientist who takes such a utopian positon (that organizations can consistently be conformed to suit the individuals) only exerts a new type of stress on individuals who still must act within the framework of their own personal developmental problems.

Zalesznik also emphasizes that while behavioral scientists like Maslow and Herzberg can be enormously helpful in providing theoretical constructs, the decision as to how to use that information must ultimately fall to the leader in the local organization. What disturbs me, with respect to churches and Christian organizations, is that the information of the behavioral scientists is meaningless unless leaders in those organizations make themselves aware of it, run it through a proper, theological grid, and seek a practical application in local problem-solving. I suppose it is precisely to that end that I am offering these chapters.

McGregor: Theory X and Theory Y

This is one of the better motivational theories, which again focuses on individual personality. McGregor argues, "Management has adopted generally a far more humanitarian set of values; it has successfully strived to give more equitable and more generous treatment to employees . . . *but it has done all of these things without changing its fundamental theory of management.*"[11]

The basic assumptions of Theory X, McGregor delineates in this fashion:

1. The average human being has an inherent dislike of work and will avoid it if he can.
2. Because of this human characteristic of dislike of work, most people must be coerced, controlled, directed, threatened with punishment to get them to put forth adequate effort for the achievement of organizational objectives.
3. The average human being prefers to be directed, wishes to avoid responsibility, has relatively little ambition, and wants security above all.[12]

McGregor argues that as long as management holds such presuppositions it can never develop a genuinely human-relations context for work motivation. He refers to Theory Y as "the integration of individual and organizational goals" and offers some basic assumptions in contradistinction to those held by practitioners of Theory X.

1. The expenditure of physical and mental effort in work is as natural as play or rest.
2. External control and the threat of punishment are not the only means for bringing about effort toward organizational objectives. Man will exercise self-direction and self-control in the service of objectives to which he is committed.
3. Commitment to objectives is a function of the rewards associated with their achievement.
4. The average human being learns, under proper conditions, not only to accept but to seek responsibility.
5. The capacity to increase a relatively high degree of imagination, ingenuity, and creativity in the solution of organizational problems is widely, not narrowly, distributed in the population.
6. Under the conditions of modern industrial life, the intellectual potentialities of the average human being are only partly utilized.[13]

Once again it seems that the alert reader can recognize some basically biblical undertones in the work of McGregor. He suggests, for example, a high view of man rather than the low view so often obvious in old "carrot-and-the-stick" approaches to leadership and administration. He also takes a high view of the nature of work, a position consistent with biblical rubrics as early as the twentieth chapter of Exodus, and perhaps as early as God's activity in creation recorded in the first two chapters of the

Old Testament (Gen. 1—2). He also recognizes the difficulties in achieving genuinely humane management in the complex democracy in which we all must function today.

Let us look at the end of the whole matter, some meaningful remarks about how to translate helpful theory into the practice of management. Motivation obviously has to do with motive, and motive can be simply defined as that which incites an individual to action, sustains the action, and gives direction to this action once the individual has been initially aroused.

In the *Master Plan of Evangelism,* Robert E. Coleman lists eight aspects of motivation used by Christ with his disciples: selection, association, consecration, giving, demonstration, delegation, supervision, and reproduction.[14] Note the personal emphasis in all of these. Christ's pattern was to build His life into a small number of men rather than to spend the majority of His time speaking impersonally to large numbers of men (Matt. 10).

So perhaps first in the matter of translating theory into action, is a *commitment to the discipleship approach in one's relationship to his workers.* That will obviously be more easy to attain in some supervisory situations than in others, but that does not make it any less important.

Another factor is *a significant program of education for all responsible employees.* A pastor should constantly be exposing his men to materials in the behavioral sciences and management research, as well as to what scant materials are available in a theological analysis of the field. Obviously we are talking here about a long-term process rather than a "fixed-point millennium" with respect to either organizational or individual change.

The third ingredient of implementation is the matter of *managing the motivation.* Two aspects of producing motivation seem to outshine all others in importance. First of all, communication must provide thorough information to all personnel. The communication flow should be two-way—down from management and up from the workers. Secondly, mutual agreement upon goals and standards should pervade all organizational processes. We must *know* together and *agree* together what we are going to *do* together.

Another factor is *the participation of as many personnel as can be comfortably handled in one's sphere of control.* We know that change occurs faster and is more lasting when it is accompanied by a high degree of interaction among the workers. This obviously forces an emphasis on people rather than program. It helps us to zero in on the matter of God's design through spiritual gifts, calls, and empowerings. Objectives and needs precede forms.

Above all, we must avoid the common sins of superficial motivation: guilt motivators ("If you are really a loyal church member you will do this"); plastic enthusiasm ("Everything is really great at our church"); and manipulation (using others against their will to obtain your own desired ends.).

FOR FURTHER READING

Buchanan, Paul C. *The Leader and Individual Motivation*. New York: Association, 1964.

Cavalier, Richard. *Achieving Objectives in Meetings*. New York: Program Counsel, 1973.

Engstrom, Ted W., and Dayton, Edward R. *The Christian Executive*. Waco, Tex.: Word, 1979.

Kilinski, Kenneth K., and Wofford, Jerry C. *Organization and Leadership in the Local Church*. Grand Rapids: Zondervan, 1973.

Maslow, A. H. *Motivation and Personality*. New York: Harper, 1954.

Rogers, Carl A. *A Therapist's View of Personal Goals*. Wallingford, Pa.: Pendle Hill, 1966.

Schaller, Lyle E., and Tidwell, Charles A. *Creative Church Administration*. Nashville: Abingdon, 1975.

NOTES

1. Paul C. Buchanan, *The Leader and Individual Motivation* (New York: Association, 1964), p. 15.
2. Carl A. Rogers, *A Therapist's View of Personal Goals* (Wallingford, Pa.: Pendle Hill, 1966), p. 5.
3. Ibid., p. 6.
4. Buchanan, p. 59.
5. Abraham H. Maslow, *Motivation and Personality* (New York: Harper & Row, 1954), pp. 80-106.
6. Frederick Herzberg, et al. *Job Attitudes: Review of Research and Opinion* (Pittsburgh: Psychological Service of Pittsburgh, 1957); Frederick Herzberg, Bernard Mausner, and Barbara Snyderman, *The Motivation to Work* (New York: Wiley, 1959); Frederick Herzberg, *Work and the Nature of Man* (New York: World, 1966).
7. Herzberg, *Work and the Nature of Man*.
8. George Strauss and Leonard R. Sayles, *Personnel: The Human Problems of Management* (Englewood Cliffs, N. J.: Prentice-Hall, 1960), p. 137.
9. Abraham Zaleznik, *Human Dilemmas of Leadership* (New York: Harper & Row, 1966), pp. 5-9.
10. David Moment and Abraham Zaleznik, *Casebook on Interpersonal Behavior in Organizations* (New York: Wiley, 1964), p. 2.
11. Douglas McGregor, "Theory X: The Traditional View of Direction and Control," in *An Introduction to School Administration*, M. Chester Nolte, ed. (New York: MacMillan, 1966), p. 175.

12. Ibid., pp. 167-68.
13. Ibid., p. 176.
14. Robert E. Coleman, *The Master Plan of Evangelism* (Westwood, N. J.: Revell, 1964).

31

The Leader and the Process of Change

A professor once told his class that he was about to place on the chalkboard the most important principle relative to the process of change. Thereupon, he turned and spent the next fifteen minutes etching out two words: GO SLOWLY. Good teachers of leadership technique constantly emphasize and reemphasize to their students a simple phrase related to the process of change: "Change nothing major during the first year."

People are afraid of innovation. They are particularly afraid of the young aggressive leader who comes dashing out of college or seminary with a briefcase full of ideas, casting about for a group of people to serve in an experimental capacity for his theories. Phrases such as "We've never done it that way before," "It will never work here" or "We tried it that way and it won't work" are characteristic of almost every church, and they are phrases which throw up roadblocks to the process of change.

Indeed, change is such a significant aspect of leadership that it has coined its own distinctive vocabulary, including such phrases as "sacred cow," "trial balloon," "innovation," "experimental design" and, of course, "it's not in the budget." One leader keeps a motto on his desk that reads, "Come weal or come woe, my status is quo."

People fear change because it undermines their security. Yet, change is inherent in progress, and every organization must be interested in progress. As someone has pointed out, the term *status quo* is merely a Latin expression describing the mess we are in.

Kinds of Change

Bennett has identified four kinds of change which confront the leader. The first is change in *structure*. This has to do with the changing of the organizational chart, the shuffling of positions in personnel, and the reworking of the organization itself. "Such a reorganization of a company or a committee is intended to change the relationship of persons so that work is done more effectively and efficiently."[1]

The second kind of change is in *technology*. The introduction of electronic processes, whether a computer or an electric typewriter for the church secretary, will be classed as technological change.

A third type of change has to do with the *behavior* of people. Bennett points out that the crucial question here is, "How can people be helped in the present to develop behavior which will enable them to be more effective and creative persons?"[2]

The final type of change is in *assumptions and values*. As indicated in the last chapter on motivation, the assumptions and values of people determine their behavior. Thus, the leader must know what these assumptions and values are before he can bring about change in his people. Indeed, he must have this information for himself. As Bennett points out, "The leader needs real insight into the assumptions and values guiding his behavior, and why he has made his judgments about the importance of the change he is seeking."[3]

Principles of the Change Process

CHANGING PEOPLE IS MORE IMPORTANT THAN CHANGING THINGS

I have referred in earlier chapters to Abraham Zaleznik's book entitled *Human Dilemmas of Leadership*.[4] Zaleznik's concern is the relation of an individual to an organization. Perhaps the book's key concept is Zaleznik's acceptance of human tension and conflict as a condition of existence and as an opportunity for change and progress in the interrelationships between the individual and his organization. He identifies four polarities of human existence relative to one's individual development: giving and getting, controlling and being controlled, competing and cooperation, and producing and facilitating.

The emphasis in personal development is on the individual learning to assume responsibility and to exercise choice. Zaleznik complains that the unsolved problem in understanding man and organization revolves around the inability of existing theory to grasp the essential dynamics of the individual, and from this understanding to formulate a truly psychosocial theory of organization and leadership.

Zaleznik claims that the act of choice, whether through conscious or unconscious mechanisms, places the individual in the forefront of organizational behavior. In the final analysis men think, feel, choose, and act.

If there is any organization in which an emphasis on the change of people ought to be basic it is the local church! General Motors and Western Electric may want to change the attitudes and behavior of their employees, but in such a process of change they are limited to natural means. The leaders in the local church, on the other hand, are able to depend upon and, indeed, bring to bear a supernatural force which changes human behavior from the inside out rather than from the outside in.

Why has it been so difficult to recruit leadership for youth groups in years past? Is it because the curriculum is inferior or because of a spiritual problem on the part of the people in the local church? If it is the former, then the task of the leader is to change *things;* if it is the latter, a change in *people* is what is needed.

Such a change is brought about through a dynamic prayer ministry by the church leadership and the faithful and thorough communication of God's revealed will through prophetic preaching and creative teaching. Furthermore, it is brought about by counseling and a personal relationship ministry on the part of church leaders. Sometimes such change is produced through group dynamics as people interact with one another. Surely it is obvious to even the most casual reader that the process of change is inseparably related to the process of motivation and is, indeed, the outcome of the latter.

THE PROCESS OF CHANGE BEGINS WHERE THE LEADER HAS THE MOST CONTROL

In a sense, no change in things or people is too hard for God; therefore any change is possible within the framework of the local church. But, in another sense, on the human level the leader must operate within his own span of control and must be able to make reliable predictions about the consequences of his action. Bennett speaks to this issue:

> For most of us, this point is within a day-by-day relationship in which we function. In these daily relationships with superiors, colleagues, and subordinates, a leader is likely to know more accurately what can be expected of other persons and what is expected of him. This is also the network of relationships in which he has the most self-control. He can do more about his own attitudes and actions to be of help to the person who will be directly affected by the change. A supervisor may expect to have little

> success in changing the behavior of the president of the company, but he can expect to have considerable influence in bringing about change among subordinates.[5]

The leader dare not innovate unless he has clear-cut goals relative to the direction that innovation will take and the ultimate results of the change. Since one resistance to change is due to fear of the unknown, the wise leader will provide as much information as possible about where the group is going in the new context.

CHANGE IS SMOOTHER WHEN PEOPLE PARTICIPATE IN ITS PLANNING

If the leader develops and hands down a report of what he wants to see changed, the change will be much more difficult to implement than if the people themselves or at least their representatives have a voice in planning the change. Involvement in the planning process tends to generate the necessary force for the change itself. Facts personally researched are better understood, more emotionally acceptable, and more likely to be utilized than those given by someone else. Participation in analysis and planning helps bypass resistance which arises from proceeding too rapidly or too slowly.

THE PROCESS OF CHANGE INCLUDES THE OVERCOMING OF RESISTANCES

People resist change primarily out of fear. While fear of the unknown is probably the most drastic factor in resistance, fear of disorganization or confusion is also a factor. People tend to get comfortable in the status quo. And the leader who suggests change is, in effect, suggesting that the organization is not functioning satisfactorily. Indeed, this is why many people in the church are suspicious of research or evaluation.

Information from such an evaluation process about the functioning of a system may introduce a need for change, especially when the new data is seen as objective and at variance with common perceptions and expectations of what the organization is supposed to be doing. The leader's responsibility is to help persons to manage and reduce the anxiety and fear involved.

Vested interest and/or conflict of interest are both detriments in the process of change. People are threatened by the thought of innovation in something of which they have long been a part. An obvious example in the church's educational program is the agony that confronts almost all church leaders in moving adults from one class to another in an age-group Sunday school organization. Cliques have entangled themselves around the roots of the class, and people want to stay with "their group" and "their teacher," fighting the change of atmosphere which will be part of any reorganization. In the responding to resistance to change, Bennett claims that there are six attitudes which the local leader must not develop: defense, advice giving, premature persuasion, censoring, controlling, or punishing.[6]

THE SUCCESS OF CHANGE IS DIRECTLY RELATED TO THE GROUP'S MATURITY

Mature groups tend to change more quickly and more thoroughly than immature groups. Maturity, of course, is not directly related to age or chronology of existence of the group but is defined more properly in an analysis of the facets of group dynamics which characterize the group.

Since change is inevitable in progress, church leaders must learn how to bring it about with the least amount of difficulty. Democratic leadership which depends upon the development of spiritual motivation is the best route toward achieving satisfactory change. This will involve meeting and overcoming opposition, and providing accurate and adequate information to all persons involved. Bennett suggests that a leader ask himself certain evaluatory questions regarding his desire for change and how he proposes to go about it:

1. What is the difficulty that requires change in the situation? How did this difficulty begin? What is maintaining it?
2. What are my motives for attempting this change? What are the bases of my desire to promote this particular change?
3. What seems to be the present, or potential, motivation of others to make or resist the change?
4. What are my resources as a leader for giving the kind of help that seems to be needed now, or may develop as the change effort continues?
5. Once the change has begun, what do I need to do to stabilize and maintain it?[7]

SOURCES OF CONFLICT IN CHANGE

As with any disease, human relations problems in an organization are best handled by dealing with causes rather than symptoms. The symptoms are quite obvious: dissatisfaction, frequent resignations, friction between subordinates and supervisors, and a general atmosphere of gloom. Achievement in such surroundings is propelled only by a neurotic compulsion to duty rather than the joy of service. Many of the conflicts isolated in the research of secular organizations are also common to Christian organizations.

One of the major causes of conflict is the absence of the positive factors identified in the chapters of this book. When supervisors are not properly relating to subordinates, when outmoded forms of motivation are employed, when power is abused, friction develops and imbalance occurs in institution-individual relationships. But to be more specific, let me delineate some of the sources of difficulty which stem from external factors (environment away from the job) and internal factors (inadequate work situation or poor administrative behavior).

ORGANIZATIONAL EXPECTATIONS VERSUS INDIVIDUAL NEEDS

Strain and conflict arise between the individual and the demands of the institution when expectations and needs are not properly harmonized. The worker begins to feel like a hired hand rather than a member of the team. We do well to remember our Lord's words to his disciples just before the crucifixion: "No longer do I call you slaves; for the slave does not know what his master is doing; but I have called you friends, for all things that I have heard from my Father I have made known to you" (John 15:15). There is no question that the Christian must have unyielding commitment in his service. But that commitment is to the Person of Jesus Christ and the universal church, not necessarily to a given local representation of that church.

SELF-ACTUALIZATION VERSUS ASSIGNED ROLES

This is uniquely true in situations in which there are discrepancies between the expectations which an organization holds for a man and the kind of personality development he sees for himself. That is why some pastors are frequently unhappy in new churches. It is also true of some Sunday school teachers who plod on in misery, Sunday after Sunday. And do not forget the Christian college teacher who feels that his talents and training are being "used" by his institution, without proper concern for his own individual development and self-realization.

Many individuals choose to act entirely in accordance with the expectations of their organizations, but such a decision frequently brings unhappiness, and perhaps even incompetence. On the other hand, a choice to follow the nature of one's own personality may well result in job loss.

DIVERSE ROLE EXPECTATIONS

There may be honest differences of opinion among the members of any group as to what an individual is supposed to do. One Christian worker often caught in this dilemma is the director of Christian education. Perhaps he has been called to a church which has never before employed a person of his skill and training. Fifteen different church leaders are expecting him to orient himself to fifteen different aspects of the task. To some he is really a youth director. To others, an administrator of the Sunday school. To still others, a visitation pastor. This multiplicity of role expectation surely contributes to the short terms of service of directors of Christian education during the last twenty-five years.

MOBICENTRISM

The mobility of the American family is a continuing problem in the matter of developing solid administrative and leadership styles. The concept of mobicentrism goes a step beyond mere mobility. It suggests, "Movement is not so much a way to get some place or a means to an end as it is an end in itself."[8] Eugene Jennings claims that a person who is mobicentric values action in itself, and is content with extended mobility because it always guarantees change.

Here again Toffler's *Future Shock* offers insight because it indicates that, for some people, the necessity of change is real, and the absence of change would in itself be a cultural shock! If in Christian service there is a premium on longterm commitment to a ministry, and I believe there is, then mobicentrism is a deterrent to competent Christian service and adequate leadership.

LACK OF SUPPORT AT HOME

Has anyone kept statistics on the number of men who have had to leave the ministry because of deficiency in their family relations? The supporting and encouraging wife is a crucial factor in the hiring and training of executives, as well. One business management magazine reported a survey of wifely drawbacks. This survey was put together by personnel executives, consulting psychologists, and executive recruiters, who cited these negative characteristics:

Prone to drink too much
Domineering
Poorly informed

Mentally underdeveloped compared to her husband
Resentful toward the company for taking away her husband or forgetting her
Excessively interested in her own career or activities, either social or business, to the detriment of her husband's[9]

With the exception of the first (hopefully), any of these items could be a problem for the Christian leader. Most seminaries have fellowship programs for students' wives, but it is surely safe to say that even the best of such programs falls considerably short of adequately preparing women to hold up their half of the executive syndrome in modern organizations, including the church.

STRESS ON AND OFF THE JOB

There is a reciprocal relationship, positive or negative, between the kind of environment a man experiences at home and the kind of situation in which he works during the day. Research has indicated, for example, that when a worker is surrounded by various different people who depend heavily on him, have power over him, and exert high pressure on him, he typically responds with apathy and withdrawal. He experiences a sense of futility. In such circumstances, his feeling of role conflict is very high, and his job satisfaction is low.[10]

There is probably no way we can alleviate the stress in the modern organization. So it becomes necessary to change the individual in some way, to prepare him to face the pressures and frustrations of executive leadership in today's world. In Christian ministry, this is primarily the responsibility of the Christian college and seminary.

ORGANIZATION OR INDIVIDUAL: WHO NEEDS TO CHANGE?

In an attempt to refocus the management camera on the worker instead of on the organization, the human relations advocates were led to the assumption that the most satisfying or rewarding organization would be the most efficient. According to some modern writers such as Etzioni, however, both of these approaches have one common deficiency: "Neither saw any basic contradiction or insoluble dilemma in the relationship between the organization's thrust for rationality and the human search for happiness."[11]

While the old scientific management school narrowed its scope on the formal organization, the human relations movement emphasized the informal organization. What is essential is to recognize the balance between the two. The more recent structuralists attempt to formulate a synthesis theory, relating informal and formal organizations without dwelling on a concern for either the institution or the individual. This broadened outlook takes into consideration:

1. The articulation of both formal and informal elements of the organization
2. The scope of informal groups, and the relations between such groups inside and outside the organization
3. Both lower and higher ranks
4. Both social and material rewards, and the effects on each other
5. The interaction between the organization and its environment
6. Both work and nonwork organizations

Etzioni recognizes the problem, but he does not actually make much of a step toward solving it when he reminds us:

> The ultimate source of the organizational dilemmas reviewed up to this point is the incomplete matching of the personalities of the participants with their organizational roles. If personalities could be shaped to fit specific organizational roles, or organizational roles to fit specific personalities, many of the pressures to displace goals, much of the need to control performance, and a good part of the alienation would disappear.[12]

Meanwhile, Zaleznik is concerned with changing the individual rather than the organization. He rejects the conclusions of the structuralists, whom he does not consider to have really come to grips with the problem any more effectively than have the exponents of the purely human-relations approach. According to Zaleznik, "The unsolved problem in understanding man in organization centers around the inability of existing theory to grasp the essential dynamics of the individual, and from this understanding to formulate a truly psychosocial theory of organization and leadership."[13]

While agreeing with much of what Zaleznik says, I find myself halting short of reverting to what almost seems to be a revival of the "great man" theory of leadership. Furthermore, I am not nearly so concerned about developing a "psycho-social theory of organization and leadership" as I am about developing a biblical model. It is interesting, of course, that many of the biblical components described in chapter 21 are also the elements of leadership style which have been discussed most positively in much of the psycho-social literature coming out of the management professions.

Is it possible, then, to be both spiritual and competent? Can the Christian leader be biblical as well as in line with the contemporary thinking of administrative science? It is my contention that he *can* and that administrative science has, in fact, spent millions of dollars to discover that *the biblical pattern of balance between a concern for the individual and the necessity of promoting the goals and productivity of the organization is essentially the best approach to leadership.*

Although in management science there is still a great deal of research with respect to changing either the man or the organization, many of the experts have decided upon the transactional approach between the nomothetic and the idiographic dimensions. In reality, these dimensions exist in constant relationship to and interaction with one another rather than in separate spheres. The individual's values will ultimately determine his behavior, unless he compromises his values for some item of secondary importance, such as salary or position. Therefore the organizational values must somehow be integrated with those of the individual.

The model below was developed by Getzels and Guba and clarifies the kind of difficulties which arise in the institution-individual balance game.[14] The top line indicates institutional plans and roles. The bottom line focuses on the idividual. The vertical arrows show the necessity of bringing the conflicts into creative tension to achieve harmony in the organization.

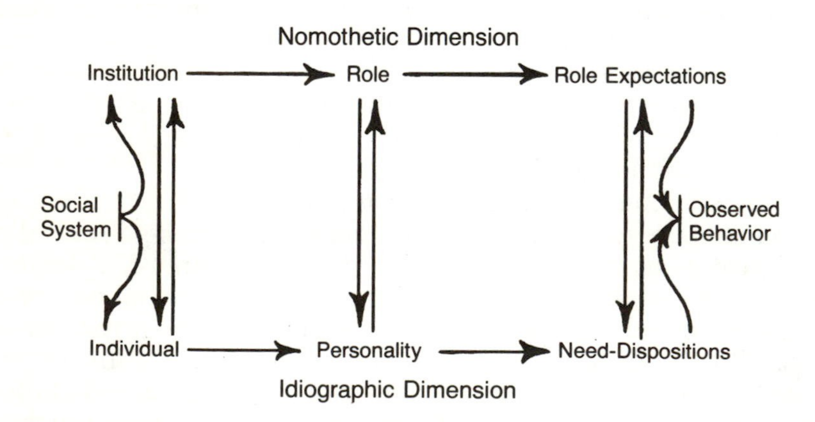

A Christian position argues that *both* the organization *and* the individual can change but an emphasis on changing either one to the sacrifice of the other will lead to confusion and turmoil.

Shaping the Idiographic Church

It is surely with design that the Scripture speaks frequently of the church as a building and of its members as various blocks of stone in the framework of that building. And just as the architects of a physical building take into account the qualities of the material with which they are working, so must the organizational architects of the church (or other Christian organizations) consider the characteristics of the personnel who make up the structure of their institutions.

The tasks of the human architect are considerably more complex. Qualities of human materials are only partially known, and furthermore, they are notoriously changeable. Some people reject the organization because they feel they have given but have not received. Others pose the opposite problem of taking but wanting to give nothing in return. The result is a sterile organization which, if Christian, becomes a liability rather than an asset to the ongoing ministry of God's work in the world.

Another problem is mobilizing the great amount of human resources the church has and is not using. Industrial science recognizes that the organization can become a deepfreeze in which human resources are stored, rather than an educational experience where the immature become mature; the undeveloped, developed; and the small, increasingly large in outlook and perspective. Douglas McGregor says,

> We have not learned enough about the utilization of talent, about the creation of an organizational climate conducive to human growth. The blunt fact is that we are a long way from realizing the potential represented by the human resources we now recruit into industry. We have much to accomplish with respect to utilization before further improvements and selection will become important.[15]

It is surely possible to substitute the word *church* for *industry* in the above quotation, and to nod to the truth of McGregor's words. The organization is not an end in itself, but rather a means to accomplish the tasks of the worldwide program of Christ.

Church administrators must become aware of the possibility that physical properties can demand such an inappropriate amount of time, talent, and funding that they are no longer an instrument to be used for God's glory, but an object to be hurdled before that glory can be communicated.

A focus on *program* instead of *people* is another albatross in the eighties. In our success-oriented society, we tend to see a large church with a large program as the model, with small churches running along as fast as their tiny, organizational legs can carry them, trying to match the big one. The result if frequently fatigue, disinterest, and rank disillusionment.

It has been said that churches provide a marvelous illustration of the futile attempt to apply raw principles of management to their operations. In the old days, before the pyramid began to crumble, organizational problems were successfully solved by generous applications of things called "techniques of management." But the current stress calls for flexibility rather than rigidity in coping with institutional tensions. Spontaneity and openness are the raw materials out of which creative energy can come to recharge the batteries of Christian organizations in these days of opportunity.

All of the information we can gather about restructuring, administrative forms, leadership styles, and human relations ought to be gathered. Then it should be carefully compared with, and run through, the grid of special revelation. Perhaps what we have left then will be a desirable integration of God's truth revealed in natural forms of order and design, and God's truth in special revelation.

It is *not* a question of baptizing secular research and stuffing it, still damp, into the organizational potholes on the road the church must travel. It is, rather, the application of biblical principles of administration, better understood because we have taken the time to grapple with the secular research.

We are institutions made up of individuals. Our needs are both similar to and diverse from those of secular organizations. But one thing is clear: unless we learn how to be laborers together with each other and with God, our personnel problems will trip us up, just when the world is beginning to see the supernatural dynamic of the body of Christ in the darkness of our contemporary, pagan culture.

FOR FURTHER READING

Barnard, Chester I. *The Functions of the Executive*. Cambridge, Mass.: Harvard U., 1938.

Bennett, Thomas R. *The Leader and the Process of Change*. New York: Association, 1962.
Bennis, Warren, et. al. *The Planning of Change*. New York: Holt, Rinehart & Winston, 1961.
Bower, Robert K. *Administering Christian Education*. Grand Rapids: Eerdmans, 1964.
Buchanan, Paul C. *The Leader and Individual Motivation*. New York: Association, 1964.
Dubin, Robert. *Human Relations in Administration*. New York: Prentice-Hall, 1968.
Gangel, Kenneth O. *So You Want To Be a Leader!* Harrisburg, Pa.: Christian Publications, 1973.
Lippitt, Ronald; Watson, Jeanne; and Westley, Bruce. *The Dynamics of Planned Change*. New York: Harcourt, Brace & World, 1958.
May, Rollo. *The Courage To Create*. New York: Norton, 1975.
Schaller, Lyle E. *The Change Agent*. Nashville: Abingdon, 1972.
Weschler, Irving R. *The Leader and Creativity*. New York: Association, 1962.
Zaleznik, Abraham. *Human Dilemmas of Leadership*. New York: Harper & Row, 1966.

NOTES

1. Thomas R. Bennett, *The Leader and the Process of Change* (New York: Association, 1962), p. 23.
2. Ibid., p. 25.
3. Ibid., p. 27.
4. Abraham Zaleznik, *Human Dilemmas of Leadership* (New York: Harper & Row, 1966).
5. Bennett, p. 27.
6. Ibid., pp. 37-39.
7. Ibid., pp. 57-59.
8. Eugene Jennings, "Mobicentric Man," *Psychology Today*, July 1970.
9. "Executive Wives: A Factor in Hiring," *Printers Ink*, August 3, 1962, pp. 19-25.
10. "Stress: From 9 to 5," *Psychology Today*, September 1969, pp. 34-38.
11. Amitai Etzioni, *Modern Organizations* (Englewood Cliffs, N.J.: Prentice-Hall, 1964), p. 75.
12. Ibid.
13. Abraham Zaleznik, *Human Dilemmas of Leadership (New York: Harper & Row).*
14. *J. W. Getzels and E. G. Guba, "Social Behavior and the Administrative Process," The School Review* 65 (Winter 1957): 423-41.
15. Douglas McGregor, *The Human Side of Enterprise* (New York: McGraw-Hill, 1960), p. vi.

PART VII

The Leader Training Other Leaders

32

Recruiting Workers in the Church

SOMEONE HAS SUGGESTED that we face three basic problems in utilizing people in the service of Christ through the church: misuse, disuse and abuse. The first is a reference to the employing of unqualified teachers and workers; the second, to the many uninvolved Christians who throng our church pews; and the last, to the problem of overburdened workers in the church.

WHY IS THERE A SHORTAGE OF WORKERS IN THE CHURCH TODAY?

Actually, most of the specific answers which can be given to the question of why there is a shortage of church workers categorize into problems which are either spiritual or organizational. The spiritual problems direct attention to the individual Christian and his relationship to Jesus Christ, whereas the organizational problem focuses on the program itself and on deficiencies which hinder rather than promote recruitment of workers.

MANY CHRISTIANS ARE INDIFFERENT TO THEIR RESPONSIBILITY OF SERVICE

Some choruses used in music ministry with children and youth give the impression that the purpose and end of salvation is service. This is not in accordance with Scripture, which indicates that the believer has been brought to God through Christ in order that his life might be a witness to Christ's glory and grace. Nevertheless, service is a very distinct part of Christian living. The dynamic passage in Matthew 9:35-38 indicates that the necessity of harvest laborers began in the days of Christ and continues on to the present. A Christian who is unwilling to share responsibilities for service is demonstrating thereby that his spiritual life is deficient. He has not come to grips with the demands upon his time, talent and entire being, which are stressed clearly in the New Testament.

SOME WORKERS LACK CONFIDENCE IN THEIR ABILITY TO TEACH OR LEAD

The problem of lack of confidence could be either organismic or organizational. If it results from an unwillingness to trust Christ and the Holy Spirit for effectiveness in teaching or witnessing, then the cause points once again to a spiritual inadequacy. If, on the other hand, lack of confidence has developed in the worker's mind because of confusion and chaos in the structure of the program or because the church has not adequately trained him, the problem is organizational.

SOME LACK CONSECRATION TO CHRIST AND ARE UNWILLING TO PUT HIS WORK FIRST

"I don't have time" is a common excuse offered when Sunday school superintendents and pastors begin contacting potential workers. Of course, everyone has the same amount of time—twenty-four hours in a day and seven days in a week. What is at stake is a decision on the priority use of that time!

Sometimes it is important for a Christian to bypass an offer to serve Christ in the church because he must work additional hours to support his family or must spend more time with his family in the role of a biblical father. Many times, however, the excuse is invalid because the time taken away from a ministry of service is invested in some materialistic enterprise. Income produced may be wanted but not needed. The attention and time of that individual have been directed to a life of self-centeredness and pleasure rather than Christ-centeredness and service.

MANY POTENTIAL WORKERS MISUNDERSTAND THE TASK THEY ARE ASKED TO PERFORM

To the question "Will you take the primary class?" a potential teacher ought to direct a number of counter questions. How long? How often? What do I have to do? What other duties or standards are expected of me?

The necessity of job analysis for all church tasks is obvious because no worker can satisfactorily function in a given role unless he understands exactly what that role entails. He should have this information before he is asked to decide whether he wishes to undertake the task. A concomitant problem is that some workers turn out to be misfits because they have not been placed in positions corresponding to their qualifications and interests.

Here again cognizance must be taken of leadership theory in the relationship between organizational and individual goals. The church must realize that workers have personal and spiritual needs of their own which must be met and, although they might not be able to specify them accurately, goals which must be satisfied. When the goals of the individual can correspond directly with the goals of the organization, a satisfied worker is employed; and generally, an efficient task is completed.

POOR ORGANIZATION OF THE CHURCH'S PROGRAM MAY HINDER TEACHER RECRUITMENT

Secular business organizations spend millions of dollars in recruiting new talent. They assume that the organization's progress and continued existence depend upon its ability to enlist, train, and retain people who can competently perform the tasks which are a part of the organizational goals. Many churches, on the other hand, just expect workers to walk through the door and ask to be used. If they do, very little concern is given to their capabilities since it would be foolish to turn down anyone who would be interested in working in the church (or so it seems).

If the church is to have adequate staff, it is essential that adequate methods be employed to secure that staff. This is not to undermine for one minute the essentiality of the call of God and the importance of prayer in bringing workers to the ministry. Indeed, sensitizing people to the call of God and praying clearly for them are a part of the biblical, spiritual methodology of worker recruitment.

SOME HAVE NEVER BEEN ASKED

Their number may be small, but some have never been asked to help. In some churches they may not even exist at all. Nevertheless, there are some people who are not serving Christ through the church today because no one has ever asked them to accept such responsibility.

I remember one time being called in by a local church to assist in worker recruitment. One of the tasks to be filled was the leadership (coordination) of a nursery program. The pastor indicated that the committee had looked carefully over the church lists and asked three or four people, all of whom had declined. There was simply no one left. In looking over the list one more time, a name was mentioned that had not been discussed previously by the committee. Upon asking about this particular worker, I was told that she surely would not be interested and so had not been considered. Talking to the woman herself, however, produced a completely different story. She was not only interested but delighted to be asked to serve in this way. With a brief period of orientation and training, she undertood the task and performed at a high level of efficiency.

Are There Certain Proper Techniques for Securing Workers?

Is there a single best way to secure workers? The answer is probably no. *Christian education is best learned in principles which are workable when adapted to a number of different situations.* These principles may culminate in specific techniques which can be applied to varying situations for the achieving of satisfactory results. The following seven-step pattern is no magical formula, but I have seen it increase the worker productivity in a number of churches where it has been put into operation in one form or another.

CONDUCT A COMPLETE NEED AND TASK SURVEY

The administration of this survey resides with the board of Christian education. If a director of Christian education is employed by the church, he will obviously implement the board's program. The object is to gather a storehouse of information on every church task.

The first time these data are procured they may take the form of a complete listing of every ministry in the church. However, it is actually a *continuing survey.* Departmental superintendents, sponsors, and leaders regularly report through their supervisors to the board of Christian education concerning projected needs, long-range goals, and patterns of growth in their particular ministries.

It is extremely important to keep a long-range projection on need analysis at all times. Now the church is looking forward to the kind of program it will carry on and the kind of workers it will need in two, five, and even in a general way, ten years. On occasion it may happen that a given job becomes vacant without the foreknowledge of the Christian education board. This should be the rare exception. If it happens with any amount of frequency, it denotes a deficiency in the recruitment policies and the long-range planning.

CONDUCT A TALENT AND ABILITY SURVEY

A survey of talent and ability can be held to establish a personal file on every church member. Information in the file could include service interests, experience, abilities, and other pertinent data which will be helpful in placing a given worker in a given position. Part of the ministry of the board of Christian education is to act as a personnel office in properly matching people and jobs.

The survey can be taken in a number of different forms. The most common is probably the use of a regular questionnaire sheet (see sample in Appendix B). Some churches call the sheet a "privilege and responsibility chart." The emphasis is that church membership is a distinct privilege, and the privilege is accompanied by a responsibility.

Such a file of information is not gathered in a short period of time. It may take several years to bring it to a place where it can be effectively used in worker recruitment. At that point, however, the time and effort spent in the securing of the data will begin to reap dividends in the form of more, better equipped, and properly placed workers for church ministries.

CONTINUALLY PROMOTE AND INSTRUCT PEOPLE IN THE CHURCH'S TOTAL EDUCATIONAL TASK

Promoting and instructing the congregation in the church's total educational task is not something that is done once in a particular step of the process. It is the continuing ministry of the pastor, director of Christian education, superintendents, board of Christian education, and other church leaders. The instructional program utilizes all of the media open to the educational leadership: sermons from the pulpit, bulletin boards, church bulletins, mailings, church newspaper, personal interviews, Sunday school classes, and even casual conversation. Public relations is in view here. The purpose of the instructional program is to tell people what Christian education really is and to show them the urgency of the teaching and nurturing ministry in home and church.

RELATE EVERY POSITION TO THE ULTIMATE GOAL OF THE CHURCH'S EDUCATIONAL PROGRAM

The content of chapter 1 is not just for pastors and directors of Christian education. It is essential that every Christian become familiar with the basic tenets of the doctrine of ecclesiology. He must understand his relationship to the collective body and to the ministries of that body in conformity to Ephesians 4. He must grow up unto Christ through engaging in the process of mutual edification with other saints.

There is no room in the educational program of the church for entrepreneurs because a Christian leader dares not view a particular ministry as his own piece of work. Stewardship is not ownership, and discipleship is not lordship. The students in that Sunday school class belong to Christ and not to the teacher.

By the same token, no teacher has the right to become discouraged or disheartened because his class is small. First Corinthians 12 teaches that the less comely parts of the body are just as important (and sometimes more important) for bodily functions as those parts which are more pleasant to look at. Just as the human body must have all of the parts working together to satisfactorily accomplish its functions, so it is with the spiritual body, which is the church. It can also be said that the educational program, like a body, must function smoothly in all its parts.

MAKE THE APPROACH PERSON-CENTERED

It is important to sell people on the need of ministering in the church, but to do so does not require describing the predicament. Indeed, the conveying of crisis is indicative that the organizational structure with its recruiting policies has not been functioning properly. Rather than a general call from the pulpit ("Anyone interested in being a youth sponsor please see the pastor after church."), the board of Christian education should send its representative to ask *specific people* for *specific jobs* for a *specific length of time.* When making the contact it is assumed that the board will consider the person's likes and interests.

One progressive St. Louis church has a member on the board of Christian education whose only responsibility is to seek out and contact potential church workers. He makes the initial contact which places the person on the list of potential workers to be trained and enlisted in the various church ministries. His approach is personal as he takes people out to lunch, visits in their homes, and talks with them about what it means to serve Jesus Christ in the church. The results of such a ministry are rewarding.

OFFER EACH POTENTIAL WORKER A CAREFULLY PREPARED JOB ANALYSIS

Job analysis (sometimes called "job description" or "role definition") outlines what the worker is being asked to do when he accepts a given position. If, for example, the church wishes the Sunday school teacher to attend prayer meeting, make a minimum number of calls each week, spend a certain amount of time in lesson preparation and arrive at church at a given time on Sunday morning, all of this should be specified in the job description.

Included in the job description should be some indication of what the worker may expect from the church, as well as what the church expects from the worker. Consider the following items copied from a local church vacation Bible school personnel letter:

What We Expect from You

1. Willingness to serve.
2. Spiritual readiness to serve.
3. Preparation for service.
4. Faithfulness in service.

What You May Expect from Us

1. Competent administration.
2. Training sessions.
3. Early and thorough planning.
4. Guidance at all points.

DO NOT HURRY THE WORKER'S DECISION

If, indeed, the church is presenting an opportunity, a responsiblity and a need rather than a predicament, there should be no necessity for hurrying the decision. The potential worker should be allowed to study carefully the job description, consider the matter in prayer before the Lord, and finally make his decision. If divine sovereignty is at work within the framework of the local church (and it is), then the worker's response to the request after prayerful and intelligent consideration must be viewed by the church leadership as within the will of God.

The above procedure is not particularly profound. On the contrary, it is simple enough to succeed in almost any size church, regardless of how limited the administrative situation. If properly followed, it can provide not only for more workers but for those who will approach their tasks with a greater sense of responsibility, a more positive attitude in service, and a willingness to accept and utilize training which the church should provide.

WHAT PLACE DO STANDARDS PLAY IN WORKER RECRUITMENT?

One of the most needed emphases in the church's program of

education is elevation and dignifying of the calling of its workers. The church which communicates the concept that "just anybody" can be a Sunday school teacher is asking for inferior workers as well as destroying the motivation which can result from properly recognizing the importance of the teaching ministry. Satisfactory recruitment standards actually provide workers these necessary elements:

1. Incentive. God's people should *want* to work for Him in the church. That desire, however, does not spring up automatically in the heart of the Christian—particularly the Christian whose level of maturity is somewhat retarded. It becomes the responsibility of the church's educational leaders to try to build incentive into the recruiting program. When the potential worker looks at the educational program, he tries to determine whether it is something with which he wants to be identified. If the standards are high and the requirements are significant but reasonable, he will seek that identification more quickly than if it appears that he may be joining a shoddy enterprise.

2. Improved efficiency. In any given church situation there are some current problems which are causing extreme difficulty to the church leadership. Nothing can be done about them now without really upsetting the whole program. What ought to be our concern, therefore, is to see that these problems do not breed more problems. Meodiocrity can only reproduce itself or its retarded offspring, inferiority. The efficiency of the church's education program ought to be always improving, but this is an impossibility if the standard of the workers recruited does not rise continuously.

3. Evaluation guides. If the educational program is going to be evaluated (and, indeed, it must), the teachers and workers will have to be compared with some acceptable norm or standard. To ask a teacher to assume the task and then evaluate that task on the basis of a norm that is developed a posteriori is unfair and yields a very distorted evaluation. The teacher must know what is required of him and expect that he will be judged on how he has measured up to that requirement. Evaluation always relates to objectives, and in this particular case the objectives ought to demonstrate some clear indication of standards.

At times it will seem that high standards impede the progress of worker recruitment, but in the final analysis they will lead to better teachers and a higher opinion of the teaching position among the congregation. A church ought to have clear-cut expectations of its workers and be able to provide them with the wherewithal to do the task.

A periodic check of the workers' accomplishments, needs, and problems will be beneficial to them and to the supervisory staff. Self-evaluation is important as well, and it is carried on through workers conferences, questionnaire sheets, and group discussions.

It is improper to say that worker recruitment exists as an end unto itself. Rather, it is a means to an end—the maturing of people through the church's educational ministry. The means, however, is important, and in the process one strategic key is to involve as many people as possible in the church's educational program.

How Important Is Recognition?

Part of the task of elevating and dignifying the position of working in the church is a genuine demonstration of appreciation by the church for those who have served. There are some very obvious benefits in a thorough appreciation program:

1. The workers who have served feel noticed. They can see that the church leadership is not taking them for granted but rather is interested in them and thankful for the work they have performed.

2. Potential workers can see that the church really does consider teaching an important ministry—important enough to recognize publicly the work which has been done.

3. The total congregation is made aware of the importance and centrality of the teaching ministry in the local church. Every member may not be invited to some special event which honors only the teachers and workers, but the announcing and carrying out of it will serve as a reminder that *that particular church is a teaching church by design and not by accident.*

A number of methods demonstrate appreciation for teachers and workers. The following is only a partial list:

1. an annual appreciation banquet
2. a dedication service at the beginning of each year
3. personal letters from the pastor and/or other church leaders
4. periodical notes of appreciation in the church bulletin or other literature produced by the church
5. special elections such as "teacher of the year" or "teacher of the month"

6. a public wall chart that shows who is carrying on what particular ministry in the church and perhaps even a listing of what training courses each individual has completed

7. free transportation and expenses to Sunday school conventions or professional training conferences

8. an annual appreciation picnic

9. giving of gifts (such as a book or a magazine subscription) at Christmastime

10. the regular and sincere personal "thank you" given by the pastor, director of Christian education, superintendents and other educational leaders.

The recruitment and enlistment of workers and teachers for the church's educational program depends upon the alleviation of spiritual and organizational problems. When the church's spiritual standards are raised and immaturity gives way to maturity in Christian living, the innate conviction of the dedicated life will solve any of the spiritual problems faced in recruitment.

It must be recognized, however, that personnel problems have a twofold origin. Organizational deficiences contribute as much to the delinquency of workers as do spiritual problems. Both causes must be attacked and removed before a church can expect to achieve its goals in recruiting satisfactory leadership for the church's educational program.

FOR FURTHER READING

Bower, Robert K. *Administering Christian Education.* Grand Rapids: Eerdmans, 1964.

Buchanan, Paul C. *The Leader and Individual Motivation.* New York: Association, 1964.

Byrne, Herbert W. *Christian Education for the Local Church.* Grand Rapids: Zondervan, 1963.

Crossland, Weldon. *Better Leaders for Your Church.* Nashville: Abingdon, 1955.

Dobbins, Gaines S. *Learning to Lead.* Nashville: Broadman, 1968.

Edwards, Mary Alice Douty. *Leadership Development and the Workers' Conference.* Nashville: Abingdon, 1967.

Gangel, Kenneth O. *Lessons in Leadership from the Bible.* Winona Lake, Ind.: BMH, 1980.

Johnson, James L. *The Nine-to-Five Complex, or the Christian Organization Man.* Grand Rapids: Zondervan, 1972.

33

Establishing a Climate for Leadership Training

WHEN WORKERS have been recruited for the church's educational program, the task of supplying personnel has just begun. Next it is essential that the church provide those workers a satisfactory training program to prepare them for their tasks. Obviously, the Christian workers' ultimate competence resides only in God's power (2 Cor. 3:1-6). But humanly speaking, the greatest need of the church has always been and is today the need of trained leadership. The churches that are making the greatest strides are those who are taking time to train leaders.

WHY TRAIN LEADERS?

If Christian service is instigated at the call of God and accomplished by the power of the Holy Spirit, why train on a human level? Isn't it enough to allow people to fulfill their tasks by simply using the Bible and functioning as best they can under the Spirit's direction? Such an attitude is born of ignorance and not of faithfulness to the Word of God. Just as Jesus trained His disciples; as Paul trained Silas, Barnabas and Timothy; and as Moses trained Joshua, so a distinctive part of today's Christian leadership is for the leader to reproduce other leaders.

DELEGATION OF AUTHORITY IS A BASIC PRINCIPLE OF GOOD LEADERSHIP

When authority is delegated it is necessary not only to expect from the delegatee a certain level of performance commensurate with the responsibility of the task, but also to provide that worker competent training which will enable him to produce effectively. In the volunteer work of Christian service, many subleaders are essential. Down through its history the church has carried out its ministry by means of a large army of lay workers led in their ministries by a much smaller contingent of captains and generals.

One problem brought about by a lack of training is an overloading of the willing and talented few. If many people are standing back and not working in the church because they don't know how to do the necessary jobs, it behooves the church to remove this barrier (and its accompanying excuse) by offering the training. Ultimately then, a training program will involve *more* people. It puts some "teeth" in the program and argues that the church is serious about its teaching ministry.

WHO SHOULD BE TRAINED IN THE CHURCH?

Every Christian has the responsibility for teaching and ministering and, therefore, a need for training. Unfortunately, not all people recognize this need, so part of the training task is to influence people sufficiently so they will *want* the kind of training that the church can provide in spiritual matters and Christian leadership.

The Evangelical Teacher Training Association has been involved for many years in the business of training teachers for the local church. It suggests that training be offered to prospective teachers, parents, present teachers, Sunday school leaders and officers, and even people of the community. The church which offers solid leadership education is not only serving itself but other evangelical churches in its area as well as furthering the cause of Christ in a much more thorough way.

INFLUENCES ON LEADERSHIP BEHAVIOR

Leadership training is more than the offering of a certain program, a study of certain books, or the viewing of a set of filmstrips. It is the production of future leaders by any process available, providing the process lines up with a biblical methodology.

Ability to lead depends largely upon previous experiences with leadership attempts, because the leader transfers learning from what he has done before to the new task. The principle of apperception, as developed and described by Herbart, plays a significant role in the process of leadership development. As we watch a developing leader move through various age levels, attempting different and increasingly more difficult and responsible tasks, it becomes apparent that all of life is preparation for leadership.

The transfer of learning which takes place can be either positive or negative:

1. *Positive transfer of learning facilitates the leadership performance.* The more a new leadership situation is like previous ones, the more the behavior patterns which may be transferred. The fact that a person knows how to play the trombone, for example, would not be of any appreciable effect in learning to play the organ. If, on the other hand, the same person had been playing the piano for several years, a transfer to organ might be made with minimum difficulty.

One evangelical church sees the role of Sunday school superintendent as a developmental task toward the chairmanship of the board of Christian education. A worker serves for three years as Sunday school superintendent and then automatically assumes chairmanship of the board for three more years. The transfer of learning from the largest and, in many ways, most significant agency of the church to the supervision of the entire educational program, is a natural one, and performance in the new role is facilitated. By the same token, many high school principals were formerly successful classroom teachers, and many college presidents have functioned as deans.

2. *Negative transfer of learning is detrimental to performance.* Negative learning transference can happen when a new situation is different but the leader still carries over old behavior patterns that fit his former role. Consider, for example, a rural pastor whose homespun, folksy style helped rural folk feel right at home. Moving into the city and assuming the pastorate of a larger and more sophisticated church, he applies the same jargon, goes visiting without a tie and suit coat, and acts as though he had not changed positions. The carry-over of behavior in this situation is negative and hinders effective leadership.

A similar situation occurs when a high school student comes to college. In high school there was a fixed schedule which indicated his presence was required in a given room at a given hour all through the day. Homework assignments were specified, and there was very little need for independent thinking and making one's own decisions. Now in college he not only chooses his courses but must do individual research and be responsible for his own learning. If he continues to expect the same kind of enforcement that characterizes high school days, he may soon be listed among the college dropouts.

If it is true to say that all of life is preparation for leadership, then there must be certain kinds of experiences and situations during the various age levels which help or hinder leadership development.

CHILDHOOD INFLUENCES IN LEADERSHIP TRAINING

The earlier the effectiveness as a leader, the greater the present success in leadership. Leadership training does not begin in the adult department or in the senior-high training-hour group; it begins during the preschool years. Children are being influenced at all times in many ways. Some of the influences are negative, others are positive, but influences they are. The church needs to be aware of the need for control and revitalization of the various opportunities for leadership influence during the childhood years. There are four central points at which this influence can take place:

1. *The home.* How a child is taught to act and react within the context of his own home is the most crucial factor in leadership development for the first five years, and maybe for the first fifteen. There must be a climate of acceptance, love and faith bounded by a clear-cut fence of obedience. Discipline is extremely crucial during these years and is not to be confused with punishment. It is the setting of boundaries—the narrowing of the line so that the child walks in the path which the parents have set up for him. Punishment becomes necessary only when discipline fails.

A child who is properly loved in his own home; who learns to live within the proper biblical bounds of obedience and discipline; who learns to accept himself, his parents, and his social status with ease and understanding; who learns consideration for others as well as proper care for his own things; and who develops a perception of God's will and Word in his own life, is on the road to satisfactory Christian leadership.

2. *The total church program.* The church which is really serious about training leadership will set up its entire educational program so that from the earliest years in the nursery department its children will learn how to grow to maturity in Christ and accept a proper responsibility for serving Him. The curriculum will be so constructed that the child early develops an appreciation for the Word of God and learns how to apply it in his everyday life.

Proper departmentalization and competent organization of educational experiences all through the childhood years contribute to the establishing of a leadership training climate. It is necessary for the child to establish and maintain a proper concept of the church so that, as soon as possible, he comprehends his role and responsibility in the body of Christ on a local level.

3. *The individual classroom.* It is obvious that the teacher of an adult Sunday school class is in the business of reproducing leaders. It is not quite so obvious in the nursery, kindergarten, and primary departments. Nevertheless, it is necessary there as well.

Teaching methodology and the atmosphere in which the child learns at church are significant factors in his growth into leadership. Simple participation, such as the recitation of Scripture verses, the giving of reports, the use of flannelgraph figures, and various kinds of group work, lays a foundation for accepting more significant responsibility in later years.

4. *The Christian school.* The development of civic leadership and social responsibility is one objective of the public school. Likewise, the development of Christian leadership is an objective of the Christian school. It should logically follow that church leadership is developed more thoroughly in a Christian school than in a public school. For this reason many churches are developing Christian elementary and secondary schools as a part of their educational programs, and Christian schools are now opening at the rate of three per day.

An increase in size and quality of church educational plants, a result of the Christian education movement of the last twenty or twenty-five years, now makes it possible for the church to provide satisfactory educational activities for the entire week instead of just on Sunday. In a parochial organization the church controls the educational program and the selection of teachers. It can therefore provide an instructional setting that will lend itself effectively to the preparation of leadership. Some students will become effective laymen. Others will go on to further Christian education to become professional workers in the church's program.

ADOLESCENT INFLUENCES IN LEADERSHIP TRAINING

As children mature into adolescence, the leadership pattern changes from coercive to persuasive, that is, from overt enforced discipline to less dependent, problem-solving procedures. As independence increases, leadership potential becomes more apparent and leadership opportunities more frequent.

In training adolescents in leadership, the greatest single factor, both negative and positive, is the "crowd." Teenagers are profoundly influenced by the thought and behavior patterns of whatever clique, group, or gang they have chosen to identify with during the teen years.

The "crowd" provides several essential ingredients of teen life:

1. Social relationships with members of his own sex and members of the opposite sex.
2. Competition within the crowd and between his crowd and other crowds.
3. The sharing of peer problems. These problems may never be solved, but the opportunity to share them without adult interference is one of the attractions of the group.
4. Opportunities to exercise leadership in various capacities. This can range from being the toughest kid on the block to being a duly elected student-body president in high school.
5. A source of strength against adult authority.

Any Christian leader seeking to train other leaders at the youth level must face and handle the matter of crowd pressure in the teen years. Many social proficiencies, which are essential to leadership, must be learned during this time of life:

1. Christian social ethics and relationships
2. Christian etiquette
3. proper grooming
4. group activity, both as a follower and as a leader
5. public oral communication.

Other skills, such as athletic development, may not be essential to present and future leadership but can be very beneficial. The pastor who has learned how to play basketball in high school can use that skill later in working with the teenagers in his church. This may be an avenue to leadership which might not be open to him if he possessed no athletic ability.

The influences of the crowd are not necessarily bad. The wise Christian leader will use them to positive advantage in training the teenager in the church for present and future leadership.

ADULT INFLUENCES IN LEADERSHIP TRAINING

Now we arrive at the point toward which we have been moving through the childhood and adolescent years, namely, a formal program of leadership training. The training influences during childhood were important but very informal. During the teen years they become more definite, and we even conduct what is called a "training hour." Nevertheless, final "polish" of leaders for Christian service in the church is generally reserved for the adult years.

In terms of leadership training, one might well ask the question, What is an adult? Peter Person suggests that "an adult is one who has reached maturity. Achieving this maturity is not a matter of the number of years we have lived, but rather the sum total of our experiences as well as certain inherited patterns."[1]

It is important to understand that this "maturity" is not a completion of the educational pattern. Adults are not people who have learned all there is to learn, but are in need of continuing learning experiences throughout all of life. Educationally speaking, adults are "growing up," not "grown up."

Adulthood is a stage of life when fellowship as well as education is necessary. This the church must supply if it is to do its job properly. Zeigler has drawn three general conclusions which are relative to training adults for church leadership:

1. Adulthood is the longest period of living, lasting at the present life-expectancy for fifty years or more.
2. All periods of adulthood are probably equally important.
3. The culture in which adulthood is maturing contains both assets and liabilities.[2]

One task that the church faces in adult leadership training is teaching its adults that they *can* learn. People must be convinced of learning *ability;* they must have *desire* for training generated in minds and hearts; and there must be adequate *situations* provided in which the training can take place.

The aging process in human beings is slow and continues until death. The learning process coordinates with this, and learning ability never really wears out. Part of inciting adults to want to learn is the presentation of their *need* to learn. They must be shown why they must continue learning and then be given activities in which they can put to use what they have learned.

One error that many churches make in providing training situations for adults is to conceive of this training only as technical specialization for a particular task, such as Sunday school teaching. Adult leadership training should be a much more comprehensive and embracive program. Certainly we want more effective teachers in our Sunday school classrooms, but we also want more effective parents in the homes of our congregation. Leadership is just as important at family devotions as it is in the worship session of the junior department.

Sometimes we frighten away many adults in need of training by tagging a given program "teacher training." They identify the class with people who have a given educational responsibility of a classroom nature in the church's program. In a real sense then, the church's total program of adult education is one of training. It is an effort to bring interests and needs of adults into proper relationship with one another.

The last two decades of the twentieth century will be a time of adult education. The church that wants to get serious about growth will evaluate and enrich its adult leadership-development ministry.

Developing a climate in which effective leadership training can take place is just as important as constructing specific training experiences. People of all ages must feel that the church exists to help them become better disciples and more effective workers for Christ. When they learn to expect this, it is much easier to draw them into responsibilities for the Lord and to train them for those responsibilities.

FOR FURTHER READING

Bell, A. Donald. *How to Get Along with People in the Church.* Grand Rapids: Zondervan, 1960.

Bergevin, Paul; Morris, Dwight; and Smith, Robert M. *Adult Education Procedures.* New York: Seabury, 1963.

Bower, Robert K. *Administering Christian Education.* Grand Rapids: Eerdmans, 1964.

Byrne, Herbert W. *Christian Education for the Local Church.* Grand Rapids: Zondervan, 1963.

Crossland, Weldon. *Better Leaders for Your Church.* Nashville: Abingdon, 1955.

Deboy, James J., Jr. *Getting Started in Adult Religious Education.* New York: Paulist Press, 1979.

Edwards, Mary Alice Douty. *Leadership Development and the Workers' Conference.* Nashville: Abingdon, 1967.

Gangel, Kenneth O. *So You Want To Be a Leader!* Harrisburg, Pa: Christian Publications, 1973.

———. *Lessons in Leadership from the Bible.* Winona Lake, Ind.: BMH, 1980.

Wedel, Leonard E. *Building and Maintaining a Church Staff.* Nashville: Broadman, 1967.

Wilbert, Warren N. *Teaching Christian Adults.* Grand Rapids: Baker, 1980.

Zeigler, Earl F. *Christian Education of Adults.* Philadelphia: Westminster, 1958.

Zuck, Roy B. and Getz, Gene A., eds. *Adult Education in the Church.* Chicago: Moody, 1970.

NOTES

1. Peter Person, *Introduction to Christian Education* (Grand Rapids: Baker, 1958), p. 117.
2. Earl F. Zeigler, *Christian Education of Adults* (Philadelphia: Westminster, 1958), pp. 19-20.

34

Constructing the Program of Leadership Training

THE CHURCH'S STRATEGIC EDUCATIONAL TASK can only be accomplished through the use of an army of lay workers performing various duties under the direction of a few professional workers and educators. Adequate fulfillment of the task requires more than willingness; it requires training.

To become a teacher in even the youngest grades of the public school system, one must study content and methods for several years after high school. In contrast to this requirement, willing workers in our churches assume posts of responsibility without even knowing what is expected of them, much less having been trained for the job. Wyckoff says,

> Leadership is a function of the church. Leadership training is basically a matter of making the nature and mission of the church clear, establishing the functions of leadership in light of the nature and mission of the church, and selecting and educating persons to know those functions well and to perform them skillfully.[1]

The purpose of training workers is quite obvious, although many of the "fringe benefits" of a formal training program are often overlooked. The teacher should be given basic training in the content of Scripture and the methodology of education. In the thorough program, however, the trained worker will also learn to understand the entire church program and to see his place in it. There are many individual problems facing the leader which will be dealt with in the training sessions. Also, a certain fellowship is experienced as teachers and workers learn side by side in the training program.

DEVELOPMENT OF THE TRAINING MOVEMENT

Through the years the work of Christian education has been carried on by lay workers. Such names as Peter Waldo, Charles Finney, D. L. Moody, Robert Raikes, Marion Lawrence, William

Carey and a host of others demonstrate the impact of God's working through laymen. The ministry of great church leaders such as Luther and Wycliffe was often carried on largely by laymen who followed their cause.

Formal leadership training in the church probably resulted from the success of the normal schools in training public school teachers. The Chatauqua Movement, started by J. H. Vincent and Louis Miller, purposed at its inception to train Sunday school teachers. However, the temptation to broaden curricula and teach secular subjects was too great, and within a few years Chautauqua's spiritual fires were only dusty coals.

In the beginning of the twentieth century, the publishing of graded lesson manuals increased the need for teacher training. In 1910 the International Sunday School Association published the first standard course which included thirty Bible lessons: seven lessons on the pupils, seven on the teacher, seven on the school and nine related to any of the above. An Advanced Standard Course was also prepared. In 1917 the association withdrew the two former standards and set forth a longer course of one hundred and twenty units. A "unit" consisted of an hour of preparation and forty-five minutes of recitation. The great fault of the new course was an undue lessening of Bible content.

In 1926 the International Council of Religious Education (successor to the ISSA) revised the Standard Training Course and renamed it the Leadership Course. This is the basic pattern of many denominational training programs today.

In 1931 articles of organization were drawn up for the Evangelical Teacher Training Association, an organization which continues to serve churches and schools in the area of Christian education. ETTA licenses qualified teachers in churches and schools. These teachers are then permitted to teach the various courses for credit which the trainee obtains toward a diploma or certificate. Three complete courses are offered for recognition: the Standard Training Course of 432 hours of study, the Gold Seal Certificate Course of 144 hours, and the Preliminary Teacher Training Course of 96 hours. A Standard Teacher's Diploma and a new Christian Education Diploma are offered through Christian education departments of higher education.

The 1960s and 70s saw the development of training records, filmstrips, correspondence courses, and a host of books geared to provide formal training experiences for workers in church's educational program. It can no longer be said that the materials are not available. Many denominations have developed their own training program geared specifically to the distinctive needs of their churches. Southern Baptists have led the way in this area with their training-union program which serves all ages and seeks to develop specific leadership at the adult level.

DETERMINING CONTENT FOR LEADERSHIP TRAINING

What does a church worker really need to know? What is a proper balance between Bible content and methodology? How many different types of content training are essential?

The Evangelical Teacher Training Association generally has provided courses that equally divide the time and emphasis between content and methodology. The Preliminary Course contains three units on content (Old Testament Survey—Law and History; Old Testament Survey—Poetry and Prophecy; and New Testament Survey) and three units on educational proficiency (Understanding People, Teaching Techniques or Understanding Teaching, and Understanding Sunday School). The Advanced Course in ETTA carries the same balance with Bible Introduction, Bible Doctrine I and II, which complement courses in Evangelism, Missions, and Vacation Bible School. Several optional courses are available, including an excellent survey of church education called *Church Educational Ministries*. The church ought to provide training for any task for which it needs workers. Although no list of subject matter areas would be complete nor would any one list satisfy all church leaders, nevertheless, the following is an attempt to delineate at least ten or more specific lines of curricula which ought to be included in local church leadership training programs.

SCRIPTURE CONTENT

There must be adequate requirement of courses in the various books of the Bible to assure each worker a knowledge of the entire Scripture. These courses should not only teach the information in the books of the Bible but also develop Bible study techniques so that the lay leader can inductively approach the Bible on his own without always having to get his information secondhand from pastors or commentaries.

THEOLOGY

A course in theology should be offered which would include basic fundamentals of evangelical doctrine as well as denominational distinctives necessary to leadership in a given church situation.

CHURCH HISTORY, MISSIONS, AND CULTS

If history is for the race what memory is for the individual, it is important for the church leader to see what the decades of the past have experienced in leading us to the present state in church history. Missions philosophy and methodology is rapidly changing in this last third of the twentieth century, and local church leaders must keep abreast of these developments. An increase of cultic groups requires that a local church leader be sufficiently aware of heretical beliefs and practices to function defensively and offensively as a soldier of the cross.

HUMAN BEHAVIOR

Courses in psychology of all age groups should be offered so that teachers and leaders understand the students with whom they work.

PHILOSOPHY AND PRINCIPLES OF EDUCATION

Church leaders need to know what learning is, how it takes place, and how people are helped in learning experiences.

ORGANIZATION AND ADMINISTRATION

Superintendents, board members, and leaders at all levels in the educational program need to understand how to conduct themselves within the organization and how to administrate their particular area of responsibility effectively.

TEACHING METHODS AND MEDIA

Instruction in the use of lesson materials, utilization of audio-visual aids, and the construction of classroom learning experiences is essential.

VISITATION AND EVANGELISM

Too often the church encourages and perhaps even requires its teachers to "go calling" without giving them adequate instruction in visitation procedures and teaching them how to witness effectively for Christ outside of the church itself. Therefore, courses must be given in visitation and evangelism.

CHURCH MUSIC

Instruction of song leaders, pianists, and vocal instrumental musicians should be a formal part of training that the church provides for its leaders.

TRAINING FOR SPECIALIZED AGENCIES

Special leadership courses directed toward service in specialized agencies, such as vacation Bible school, weekend clubs (e.g., Christian Service Brigade, Pioneer Girls or AWANA) or camp counseling, have an important role to play in the overall program of leadership training.

Ross and Hendry quote McMurry's statement that certain numerous skills can be inculcated by formal instruction in leadership training. This is not quite the same as delineating areas of content, but it closely relates to what will be taught in the training curriculum:

1. The ability to see problems in broad perspective and to make decisions on the basis of long-run rather than short-run goals.
2. The capacity to delegate *authority* as well as responsibility.
3. An open-minded receptivity to suggestions and criticisms from peers and subordinates as well as superiors.
4. A willingness to risk the loss of the approbation and support of others, if necessary, by thinking independently and taking a firm stand (as, when necessary, saying "no" to administer discipline).
5. A knack for discovering and utilizing previously undetected relationships among the things and conditions of his environment.
6. Competence in carrying on, integrating, and coordinating a number of highly varied interests and activities simultaneously.[2]

Structuring a Training Program

Once again a good pattern for beginning a leadership training program is laid down in the helpful little book by Ross and Hendry. They suggest six steps for actually putting the program together:

1. An inventory of possible leaders based on intimate contact.
2. An audit of all tasks within the organization for which leadership is required.
3. Plan strategy for placing and developing leaders.

4. Develop a framework for appraising groups, tasks, and leaders.
5. The development of a program of supervision.
6. The development of leadership courses.[3]

What the authors are obviously saying is that the actual construction of courses cannot be effectively done until preparatory work has provided a satisfactory organizational climate for leadership training. It is for the same reason that this chapter on specific programming for leadership training is placed last in a series of three chapters on the subject. The organization and impetus of a leadership training program in the church must come down from above. That is, the initiation comes from the pastor, the director of Christian education, or other top administrative personnel.

The church which has had the foresight to employ a full-time minister of education will certainly benefit from his leadership in this area. A properly trained director of Christian education will supervise the training program as well as teach several of the courses himself. The board of Christian education must give wholehearted support to the training project. Enthusiasm and cooperation are incumbent upon every church leader, including deacons, elders, trustees, and members of any official board.

WHO WILL TEACH IN THE PROGRAM?

Many churches have college graduates in their membership who can be utilized as teachers in their specific fields. Elementary and secondary school teachers can be very effective because of their formal training and experience. If there is a Christian school in the area, the church might employ some of the faculty members in its training program. In situations where the church is too small to conduct a thorough program of its own, cooperation with other churches or the use of denominational specialists can greatly enhance the value of the program.

Some courses may be taught by the Sunday school superintendent or even effective teachers already serving in the educational program. Obviously the pastor and the director of Christian education will be strategically involved.

VARIOUS METHODS OF TEACHER TRAINING

There is probably no one *best* method of leadership training in the local church. The church which is really actively producing leaders is involved in various approaches to training methodology. Perhaps no church will utilize all of the following methods, but a flexible approach with several opportunities to prove one's leadership skills is preferred over a single course program.

1. *The coaching plan.* According to Wyckoff, "This very practical approach permits the previewer to help the leader in his preparation for using the curriculum materials for the next lesson, unit, or quarter."[4] This is a personal approach to leadership training, focusing on the pastor or Sunday school superintendent working with one teacher on a personal counseling approach.

2. *Utilization of a training consultant.* Sometimes it is helpful for the church to hire a specialist to direct a training program, which may include evaluation and recommendations for educational change in the church.

3. *Apprenticeship or cadet teaching.* In this system new teachers are trained by watching and helping experienced teachers. After serving in this capacity for three or perhaps even six months, a new teacher may be ready to assume the responsibility for her own class. A cadet teaching program should be accompanied by a more formal leadership training approach.

4. *Supply teachers.* Every department should have a corps of substitute teachers who teach periodically under the supervision of a trained teacher. This is different from the cadet teacher program in that a person may serve as a substitute for a number of years, teaching quite sporadically until he or she finally takes a class of his own.

5. *Visits to other churches or schools.* The worker learns by watching a better trained worker in action, therefore the teachers and leaders should be given some time off to involve themselves in such observation.

6. *Workshops.* Laboratories or clinics in Christian education are conducted at Bible conferences and Christian school campuses periodically, and church leaders should be involved in such programs.

7. *Conventions.* Regional, state and national conventions of NSSA or denominations provide much help for the local church worker.

8. *Leadership conferences.* Syrstad offers the following suggestion to Sunday school superintendents:

> At least annually, you should plan to get your entire staff together for a full day or a weekend. You may want to travel to some conference center or meet at your church. The purpose of such a gathering would be to evaluate the work of your Sunday school, plan for activities in the coming months, and spend time together

> in earnest prayer. Such a conference can be a source of great spiritual encouragement and growth to your workers. It can do more to build a spirit of teamwork than many other staff activities.[5]

9. *Cooperative training schools.* Leadership training can be conducted on a one-night-a-week basis for a period of three months or so. If a single church is unable to provide this kind of training program, perhaps it can be made a cooperative venture with several churches participating.

10. *Regular evening Bible school.* One night of the week is set aside as leadership training night. Several courses are offered (ETTA, Moody Correspondence School, etc.), and the school operates regularly for at least nine months of the year.

11. *Regularly scheduled training classes.* Classes can be held year-round at the Sunday school hour, during the Sunday evening training hour, or on a week night.

12. *Regular workers conferences.* The workers conference must be viewed as a leadership training time. Gable is correct in assessing that the purpose of the workers conference is to bring "workers together for inspiration, for planning, and for sharing of ideas. This is not a business meeting."[6]

13. *Library.* The church library should make books available on all phases of the church educational program. Active circulation is necessary here. Having the books on the shelves is not sufficient.

14. *In-service training.* This is a general term involving many of the above methods. Its main distinguishing feature is that it emphasizes the training of teachers who are already involved in the program rather than working with potential teachers. Leaders should never be allowed to feel that they have "arrived" because they have earned a diploma or certificate. New methods, new ideas and solving of continuing problems are brought into focus in a proper in-service training program. Several curriculum publishers now conduct weekend seminars for teachers and administrators in local church education programs (e.g., Gospel Light's ICL and Scripture Press's TDS training programs).

15. *Correspondence courses.* The church has actually less control over this kind of program, and it is more difficult to build motivation. Nevertheless, satisfactory courses are available from Moody Bible Institute, Biola College, and Fort Wayne Bible College, among other sources.

Enlisting Trainees

The church has a task even more difficult than that of providing a training program, and that is getting the constituency to make use of it. Several things are to be considered in recruiting leaders for the training program. If the need and task surveys are in order and the board of Christian education has access to this information, it will be possible to approach *specific people for specific jobs for a specific length of time*. If this is done, the same approach can be made in the leadership training program with respect to the projected needs which are obvious.

The other part of a leadership training program, however, is a general approach in seeking to train *all* the adults of the church so that they will be made more ready for leadership opportunities as they become available. Perhaps the following seven steps to securing cooperation may be helpful:

1. *Use personal appeal.* It's fine to advertise a leadership training class and attempt to inform everybody through various media that it will be offered. In the final analysis, however, it is quite important to speak to specific individuals about becoming involved in the program. Just as some volunteer for service and others need to be asked, so some will volunteer for training but others will need to be asked.

2. *Use all available public promotion and publicity.* This will include the church bulletin, any mailings that are sent out periodically, posters, bulletin boards, and verbal announcements. No one in the church should be able to say that he did not know the leadership training program was being conducted.

3. *Impress present leaders with their responsibility for producing leadership.* They should see themelves not only as holding office in a given agency or organization but also as sharing in the developing process of other leaders for that agency. Every leader is a potential recruiter of other leaders.

4. *Make much of the recognition for leadership achievement.* One church has an entire section of the vestibule devoted to the names and pictures of teachers and leaders, specifying what tasks they are performing in the church. Under each name and picture is a long ribbon, and placed upon the ribbon are the diplomas or achievement awards which have been earned through leadership training programs. This is not unlike a medical doctor displaying his credentials on his office wall. Such a high respect for leadership training tends to dignify the position of a trained church leader and draw others to that position.

5. *Have high standards for all tasks.* Elevate the total educational program. The use of certificates or diplomas is helpful in this regard, as is a genuine appreciation of the teacher's desire to better himself. A dedication service at the beginning of the educational year and an appreciation banquet at the end help build incentive for training service.

6. *Put people to work.* Like college students, adults want to see the practical value of what they are learning. To be always sitting in adult education classes or training programs and never utilizing the information is a stagnating experience. This is the reason why in-service programs more highly motivate trainees than programs which deal with potential workers.

7. *Require reports of all workers.* The reports should have a place for recording what professional growth has taken place during the year and how the teacher or worker has sought to improve himself in his leadership role.

The standard objections will continue to be "no time," "not interested," and "we've never had a training program here before." The leaders must not be discouraged when these problems arise, but work even harder to pinpoint the fallacy of such reasoning and the absolute necessity of training leadership in the local church.

What the church is attempting to do in the securing and training of its leadership is not dissimilar to what industry does in obtaining employee commitment. Milton Valentine and Robert Graham, writing in the *Northwest Business Management* magazine, apply the so-called "stages of identity development" to this whole problem. They demonstrate the process of bringing a worker from mistrust to trust, from self-doubt to initiative, from inferiority to industry, and from despair to integrity. The conclusion of the article bears reproduction here:

> What all of this seems to suggest is that the pattern of identity development also fits the pattern of work development, and that Erickson's pattern can be used to suggest some new lines of development or analysis. Clearly, the pattern fits the companies, groups, and individuals with whom the authors have worked. Equally the application of the pattern must be an individual one.
>
> Specifically, what is suggested is a planned induction of each employee through each level and stage of development. Begin by providing a firm, clear structure; modify this to allow the employee greater individual involvement and commitment as time goes on; and be consistent with general recognition. Begin, too, by developing trust. Look for signs of trouble and provide possible

> answers: poor quality performance, for example, perhaps suggests feelings of inferiority and non-involvement. . . . Management is, after all, an individual and clinical business, an art based on several sciences, but it is always and necessarily a spontaneous and ever-changing art. It involves the activity of maintaining and advancing the human condition by human beings and through perception.[7]

The same basic principles are operative in a church. True, the commitment is not to the organization but rather to its Head, Jesus Christ. Nevertheless, the New Testament demonstrates that a greater commitment to Christ will bring a greater commitment to the work of His church. The kind of training program suggested in this chapter is a vast undertaking for any local congregation. Yet it is necessary, and the benefits are sufficient to outweigh the trouble and expense involved. Too long has the church floated down the educational stream using broken oars to propel a leaky boat. The time has come to patch up the holes, mount the motor, and head for specific ports.

FOR FURTHER READING

Bergevin, Paul; Morris, Dwight; and Smith, Robert M. *Adult Education Procedures.* New York: Seabury, 1963.

Bower, Robert K. *Administering Christian Education.* Grand Rapids: Eerdmans, 1964.

Byrne, Herbert W. *Christian Education for the Local Church.* Grand Rapids: Zondervan, 1963.

Crossland, Weldon. *Better Leaders for your Church.* Nashville: Abingdon, 1955.

Edwards, Mary Alice Douty. *Leadership Development and the Worker's Conference.* Nashville: Abingdon, 1967.

Gable, Lee J., ed. *Encyclopedia for Church Group Leaders.* New York: Association, 1959.

Gwynn, Price H., Jr. *Leadership Education in the Local Church.* Philadelphia: Westminster, 1952.

Knowles, Malcolm, and Knowles, Hulda. *How to Develop Better Leaders.* New York: Association, 1955.

Kraft, Vernon R. *The Director of Christian Education in the Local Church.* Chicago: Moody, 1967.

Murch, James DeForest. *Christian Education and the Local Church.* Cincinnati: Standard, 1958.

NOTES

1. D. Campbell Wyckoff, *The Gospel and Christian Education* (Philadelphia: Westminster, 1959), p. 165.

2. Murray G. Ross and Charles E. Hendry, *New Understandings of Leadership* (New York: Association, 1957), p. 147.
3. Ibid., p. 138-45.
4. Wyckoff, p. 161.
5. Ray Syrstad, *The Superintendent and Teacher Training* (Wheaton, Ill.: Scripture Press).
6. Lee J. Gable, ed., *Encyclopedia for Church Group Leaders* (New York: Association, 1959), p. 68.
7. Milton Valentine and Robert Graham, "A Method for Obtaining Employee Commitment," *Northwest Business Management* magazine, Spring 1967.

35

Church Education at the End of the Twentieth Century

Andrew Jackson supposedly once remarked that the quality of American life would be flatly ruined if the printing of paper money ever drove the price of bacon to four cents a pound. Jackson's insightful sensitivity to the dangers of inflation is commendable, but his capability as a prognosticator is highly questionable. Prediction is risky business, which is why futurists develop multiple scenarios and tend to be quite general in their analyses of what the future holds. The statistics are also very confusing. For example, while we enjoy much greater longevity because of miracle drugs and general improvement of health conditions, 3.2 million Americans still undergo needless surgery each year, and sixteen thousand die annually as a result.

Unfortunately, there is really no other option but to study the future. Christian educators must take the long-range view, or the planning of future ministries is totally negated. A consistent analysis of demographic trends, an awareness of change and what it will bring with it, a sensitivity to the "global village" philosophy popularized in the 1960s by Marshall McLuhan and now coming into stark reality, and a filtering of these through a biblical value system will all force the Christian educator to think more than a week or two in advance concerning his ministry.

Change and Diversity

Part of our problem with forecasting is the rapidity of change described so thoroughly and with such frightening examples by Alvin Toffler, first in *Future Shock* and more recently in *The Third Wave.* Perhaps the blatant paganism of the last half of the twentieth century has finally caught our attention. Christian education in various forms is the last alternative to supply the moral and spiritual fiber which has been excluded from our nation by a complete embracing, particularly since World War II, of secular humanism.

Against such a backdrop a genuinely evangelical education in home, church, and school emphasizes the lordship of Christ, the centrality of the Scriptures, the necessity of Spirit-filled teaching, the importance of adequate communication techniques, and an increasing commitment to flexibility in patterns and forms. Thereby the task of confronting the culture with Christian truth can go forward on several fronts.

In a barbarian, materialistic society, whose punk rock heroes make more money than its college professors, Christian education has a seemingly insurmountable task. Yet the very enormity of the task provides opportunity and responsibility that is unprecedented in the history of the church. If there is one word that characterizes the evangelical church in the last two decades of this century it is *diversity*.

Within a city one can find a church bursting its facilities, ministering to thousands of people in two or even three morning services, filling the building again on Sunday evening, and carrying out a sophisticated program of ministry to varying age groups and social untis from all over its community.

Meanwhile, just a few miles away in the same city is a struggling congregation of fewer than one hundred Christians. More empty places than filled ones greet the pastor each Sunday; the youth ministry has died out; the choir has dwindled to eight faithful ladies scattered across alto and soprano parts, with two men grinding out the bass while the director sings along in an attempt to assist the one remaining tenor. The church is desperately clinging to its Sunday evening service and prayer meeting, but attendance at both of those gatherings hardly justifies paying the utility costs involved. The budget is a struggle not only on an annual basis, but month by month, and gifts to missionaries are often late.

What is the difference between these two churches? Generally, one would expect to find much more dynamic preaching in the active church, but the faithful pastor of the struggling congregation may be no less true to the Word of God and may very well be exercising the gift he has in the very best way he knows how. Is it the program? Again one has to ask if the size of the church permits the expanded and diverse program or if the attempt at such a program builds the size of the church. There simply are no easy answers to this kind of obvious dichotomy. The problem, of course, is that people tend to want to leave a struggling church where they are desperately needed, to go over to an exciting, more glamorous congregation where they may never be noticed, much less needed.

FORMER PREDICTIONS

More than a decade ago the last chapter of *Leadership for Church Education* suggested that "we can look for developments of some kind in the following twenty areas during the 1970's."[1] It is always interesting (and sometimes embarassing) to go back and re-examine one's prognostications. Here then are those twenty items, listed just by title:

1. Family Orientation in Church Education
2. Increased Emphasis on Adult Education
3. Increased Use of Media and Mass Media
4. Innovative Approaches to Communication
5. Improved Training for Witness
6. Establishment of Parochial Christian Schools
7. Increasing Use of Professional Personnel
8. Flexibility in Programming
9. Popularity of Club Programs
10. Decentralization in Camping
11. Christian Education Emphasis on the Mission Field
12. Short-term Service Programs for Youth
13. Better Organization at the Local Level
14. Cooperative Curriculum Projects
15. Programmed Bible Instruction
16. Disappearance of Small Rural Congregations
17. Increase of Apostasy, Worldliness, and Materialism
18. Continued Suburban Captivity
19. Bigger and Better Buildings
20. Necessity for Legal Counsel[2]

Most of the twenty items look reasonably accurate in retrospect, though I have serious misgivings about the implementation of numbers 8, 10, 14, and 19. Some have been lost because of the enormous inflationary pressures of the last decade, whereas others have suffered simply because of lethargy and lack of commitment on the part of local congregations. Others were certainly not stressed strongly enough. For example, "Increased Emphasis on Adult Education" is only now coming into its own and will surely be the banner of church education for the 1980s. And who could have known in 1969 that the late 1970s would see the establishment of Christian day schools at the rate of three per day? In most places Christians have lost the battle to retain consistent Christian principles in the public schools but have now resumed the war against secular humanism by developing their own school system.

Facing the Future

As we look ahead to the years remaining in this century, it seems imperative that the people of God give attention to the role the church will play in society during those critical times. Such an analysis of role will surely bring forth several observations that can be "plugged in" to evangelical congregations as both preparation for change and serious commitment to improvement. What must we do?

We Must Reaffirm Our Goals

Part of the significance of absolute truth is the necessity to retain goals and roles that are distinctly linked to biblical revelation. Of course needs change, and with changing needs come revised goals. Even while certain things ought to be changing, other things ought never to change, such as our commitment to distinctive but hard to maintain Christian values. Perhaps the crisis of the hour points up again the desperate need for congregational nurture, which is simply another word for what we call *church education*. The emphasis on evangelism, worship, fellowship, and teaching is hardly a new one, but it certainly bears reaffirmation as we attempt to keep the ministry of the evangelical community in balance during the coming decades. I am reminded again that Ephesus and Colossae, Philippi and Thessalonica were neither large nor small, glamorous nor plain, aggressive nor passive. By that I mean we know nothing about these qualities in the churches of the New Testament. What we *do* know is that they carried out a balanced emphasis of preaching and teaching, sharing and worshiping, all geared to lead God's people into maturity and to equip them to do the work of ministering in the congregation and the community. That emphasis dare not change. No matter how greatly the environment around the congregation may change, it is a biblical absolute, it is an eternal goal, which continues as mandate until the Lord comes again.

We Must Reawaken the Church to the Issues

Sometimes we become so preoccupied with past and future that we forget we must serve the present society where it is. Thousands of Christians, very intelligent and skilled in their areas of business expertise and even many aspects of congregational ministry, are not able to articulate Christian responses to the current problems that plague Western society. Are Christian education programs really preparing people of all age levels to speak a Christian response to such pressing issues as abortion, pornography, terrorism, capital punishment, crime, child abuse, and drug abuse? Indeed, can we even say we are effectively dealing with issues within the church such as inerrancy, the use of various Scripture versions, the role of women in leadership, and a distinctly biblical plan of financial stewardship? These are the issues, and Christian education programs which focus only on the historical significance of the Pentateuch or minor prophets, without genuinely relating the relevance of biblical mandate to the problems of today, are not carrying out their tasks and can be considered neither competent nor biblical in terms of current ministry.

WE MUST REASSESS THE CHOICE OF INVESTMENT

It surely is apparent by now that financial resources are not limitless even though the 1970s saw the expenditure of enormous amounts of money on elaborate church buildings, Christian television programming, and the development of several new massive college complexes. Millions more were spent on political involvement. Meanwhile, people starve in Cambodia and central Africa, and missionaries are unable to return to the field because inflation both at home and abroad has cut their support to a level below minimum standards. Furthermore, most of the churches of America can not identify with million-dollar buildings and media programs. According to Schaller, "Approximately 60 percent of all Protestant churches in the United States and Canada contain fewer than 200 members each, and two-thirds of them average less than 120 at worship. In other words, at least one-half of all Protestant congregations on the North American continent can be classified as small."[3]

I have used this quotation earlier in the book (chapter 19, page 220) but repeat it here for emphasis. So many Christian workers spend their ministry in such a setting.

WE MUST RETHINK THE ROLE OF THE SUNDAY SCHOOL

Here is an item that could not have been foreseen in 1969 when Sunday school was just coming off a decade of enormous popularity. But the bottom dropped out during the 1970s, and we look now at a very different picture. But the very fact that we have seen significant change in Sunday school during the '70s indicates something of its elasticity and resilience. It *has* changed, it *is* changing, and *will* continue to change. In some churches that change will affect name, in others, emphasis. Relationships with the Christian school movement must be carefully considered, and the format of the Sunday morning learning-worship program could be changed any number of ways.

We also need to work at better integration between Sunday school and church. This is a false bifurcation that has plagued us throughout the entire history of the Sunday school, perhaps stemming from the way Sunday school began as a parachurch social organization. I am not at all sure it is legitimate to make a distinction between the goals of the Sunday school and the goals of the church any more than we should sever the mid-week prayer service from the rest of the congregational ministry.

Veteran Christian educator D. Campbell Wyckoff emphasizes the necessity of local congregations' calling upon all the help they can find to analyze the future and construct a ministry that will effectively reach and teach people as they are and as they will be, rather than as they once were. In speaking about the cooperative work of a "concerned core of Christian educators in the local church," Wyckoff writes,

> It hardly matters what the group is called or how it is constituted and organized, so long as the future of Christian education in the congregation is its mandate, and so long as this is the heart of the concern for each of its members. The role of the minister or director is to get such a group together, help them to set their tasks and to get into it, and to maintain fruitful liaison between this core group and the officers of the church, on the one hand, and the Sunday school and other aspects of the Christian education program on the other.
>
> The issues and possibilities that are important for Christian education in the 80's will come to the local concerned core group from a number of sources, chiefly from the world outside the church, from the church itself, and from those who are giving a major portion of their time to the consideration of what Christian education is to become.[4]

These are great days to carry the banner of Jesus Christ. The light shines brightest where the darkness is deepest, and the salt is most pungent where the danger of rottenness is greatest. We have the promise that the gates of hell shall not prevail against the cause which we seek to forward. Perhaps the words of Charles

Wesley's hymn were never more relevant for the church than they are in the 1980s:

A charge to keep I have,
A God to glorify;
A never-dying soul to save
And fit it for the sky.

To serve the present age,
My calling to fulfill;
O may it all my powers engage
To do my Master's will!

Arm me with jealous care,
As in Thy sight to live;
And O Thy servant, Lord, prepare
A strict account to give!

FOR FURTHER READING

Collins, Gary R. *Our Society in Turmoil.* Wheaton, Ill.: Creation House, 1970.

Kahn, Herman; Brown, William; and Martel, Leon. *The Next 200 Years.* New York: Morrow, 1976.

Schaeffer Francis A. *How Should We Then Live?* Old Tappan, N. J.: Revell, 1976.

Toffler, Alvin. *The Third Wave.* New York: Morrow, 1980.

NOTES

1. Kenneth O. Gangel, *Leadership for Church Education* (Chicago: Moody, 1970), p. 357.
2. Ibid., see pp. 357-63.
3. Lyle Schaller, ed., *Preaching and Worship in the Small Church* (Nashville: Abingdon, 1979), p. 7.
4. D. Campbell Wyckoff, "Looking Ahead At the '80's," *In Focus*, vol. 2, no. 2, p. 2.

APPENDIX A

Glossary of Leadership Terms

ANTHROPOLOGY—The scientific study of the nature of man.
AUTOCRATIC LEADERSHIP—Leadership that focuses on the importance and control of the "top man."
AXIOLOGY—The scientific study of values.
BUREAUCRACY—A term describing the size and administrative detail characteristic of large organizations.
CENTRALIZATION—A philosophy of organization that vests authority or programming in a few persons, places, or ideas.
CENTRICITY—Attitudes and activities of group members that cause them to reflect inwardly on themselves rather than the group.
COMMUNICATION—The transmission of ideas from one person to another in a language that is common to both.
COMPENSATION—A mechanism that enhances self-esteem by overcoming a failure or deficiency in one area through achieving recognition in another area.
CONTROL—The extent of regulation upon group members by the leader or the group itself.
COUNSELING—The process of helping other people to understand, face and solve their own problems.
CYBERNETICS—An attempt to bring together and reexamine lines of research; study of behavior on the basis of a theory of machines, particularly computers.
DECENTRALIZATION—A philosophy of organization that vests authority or programming in as many persons, places, or ideas as possible.
DELEGATION—The consigning of certain tasks and authority to other persons in the organization.
DEMOCRATIC LEADERSHIP—Leadership that focuses on the group and its goals, ideas, and decisions.
DIFFERENTIATION—The process of correctly discerning or identifying the perspective between two items that appear to be similar.

EMERGENT LEADERSHIP—Leadership that is neither elected nor appointed but develops from among the group itself, probably as a result of the situation.

EMPATHY—Identifying oneself with the members of the group.

EPISTEMOLOGY—The scientific study of the nature and limits of knowledge.

EQUALITARIANISM—The leader treating group members as equals.

FRUSTRATION—A state of being unable to discharge a painful or uncomfortable excitation.

GROUP ATTRACTIVENESS—The degree to which a group promises rewards to its members.

GROUP EFFECTIVENESS—The degree to which a group rewards its members and achieves the goals which it sets out to perform.

HABITUATION—The process of forming patterns of behavior which become almost automatic through repetition.

HAWTHORNE EFFECT—The behavior that results in individuals as a result of noncontrolled variables in an experimental situation.

HEDONIC TONE—Satisfactory group relationships. The atmosphere that makes a member "like" his group.

HETEROGENEITY—The degree to which outsiders are able to get into a group. Also, the diverse makeup of the group itself.

HOMOGENEITY—The degree to which members of the group are similar with respect to socially relevant characteristics.

HOSTILITY—A feeling of enmity or antagonism between people or perhaps on the part of one person toward others.

IDEATION—The process of thinking which produces ideas.

IDIOGRAPHIC ORGANIZATION—Organization that places heavy emphasis on the needs and personal goals of individuals, possibly to the point of insufficient concern for the achievement of the institution.

INITIATIVE—The leader or a member of the group originating ideas, developing new procedures, and starting the group out on progress.

INSIGHT—One's ability to perceive the underlying or genuine nature of things.

INTERACTION—Confrontation of group members with one another (usually verbal).

INTIMACY—The degree to which members of the group are mutually acquainted with one another and familiar with personal details of one another's lives.

JOB DESCRIPTION—A specification of the duties and responsibilities that accompany a given task. Sometimes called "role definition" or "job analysis."

LAISSEZ-FAIRE LEADERSHIP—Leadership that withdraws authority and control in favor of extreme permissiveness.

LINE-STAFF RELATIONSHIPS—Line relationships refer to vertical positions of authority or subordinancy as shown on the organizational chart. Staff relationship is shown horizontally and generally depicts equal authority. Any leader is in line and/or staff relationship to someone else in the organization.

MEDIA—Plural of medium: the channel used to communicate the message, such as a recorder, film, etc.

METAPHYSICS—The scientific study of the nature of reality.

MOTIVE—A conscious or subconscious factor that serves as an impetus in determining behavior.

NOMOTHETIC ORGANIZATION—Organization that places heavy emphasis on the goals and achievements of the institution without proper consideration to the individuals who work in it.

PERCEPTION—Any differentiations the individual is capable of making in his perceptual field whether an objectively observable stimulus is present or not.

POLARIZATION—The centering of interest, discussion, or thought on one person or idea.

PROJECTION—The process of shifting the responsibility for an act or thought from oneself to an outside agency or to another person; taking an attitude of oneself and attributing it to someone else.

RADICITY—Attitudes and activities of group members that cause them to reflect on the group and its projects rather than themselves.

RAPPORT—The relationship between people marked by attitudes of friendliness, harmony, and cooperation.

RATIONALIZATION—A device whereby the individual provides plausible reasons for his behavior rather than the actual reasons which are too painful to acknowledge; the substitution of a socially approved motive for a socially disapproved one.

REGRESSION—The process of relieving anxiety or threat by falling back upon the thoughts, feelings, or behavior which worked successfully during an earlier period of life.

REINFORCEMENT—Rewards and recognition that will serve as an impetus for group members to continue to perform in a constructive capacity.

REPRESSION—An unconscious process wherein shameful thoughts, guilt-producing memories, painful experiences, or distasteful tasks are removed from awareness or forced below the level of consciousness.

ROLE—A description of how a person is supposed or expected to behave in a given situation.

ROLE SET—A structure of defined relationships involving two or more people in given positions.

SELF-ACTUALIZATION (Self-realization)—The process of "becoming" a complete person realizing one's own abilities and goals and accepting one's self realistically.

SELF-CONCEPT—One's image or evaluation of himself. It has been determined by his environment in the past as well as internal spiritual factors. Now it governs the way he behaves in various situations.

SPAN OF CONTROL—The number of officers in an organization over which a given leader has authority and for whose work he bears responsibility.

STABILITY—The extent to which a group persists over a period of time with essentially the same characteristics.

STRATIFICATION—Process of a group's placing its members in status hierarchies.

SUBSTITUTION—A device that makes it possible to discharge tensions by diverting one's energies from a desired goal to an alternative goal.

SUPERVISION—The directing of the activities of other people toward the accomplishing of organizational goals.

SUPPRESSION—The deliberate, conscious control of one's hazardous and undesirous thoughts or impulses.

SURGENCY—Generally defined in terms of personality, talkativeness, outreach, and gregariousness.

SYNTALITY—The prediction of group performance or effectiveness.

TRANSACTIONALISM—An attempt to reconcile structurally and otherwise the goals and needs of the organization with those of the individuals who work in the organization.

TRANSFERENCE—Reaction toward people in present situations motivated and controlled by one's attitudes toward important people earlier in life.

VALUE SYSTEMS—The importance and truth that a person places upon concepts or people which in turn determines the way he treats them.

VISCIDITY—The group's acting as a unit, working together toward group goals.

APPENDIX B

Sample Form for Worker Recruitment

P & R Sheet
(Privilege and responsibility)
for Christian Service

P The privilege of being a Christian is difficult to describe, for mere words are insufficient vehicles to express the wonders of salvation, redemption, peace, and spiritual joy. This privilege is best experienced by an active faith, constantly nourished by daily communion with the Lord through His Word and prayer, and is best expressed by sacrificial service through the agency of the local church.

Therefore, as you read the list below, do so with a sense of gratitude to God and a willingness to demonstrate your faith by service in the areas indicated.

R Check your desired area of service:

Sunday School

1. Teacher ______________________
2. Helper ______________________
3. Secretarial work ______________________
4. Transportation ______________________

Please note age group preferred and approximate years of experience ______________________

Other Agencies of Youth or Children's Work

1. Jet Cadets Sponsor ______________________
2. Home open for youth parties ______________________
3. Transportation to youth events ______________________
4. Vacation Bible School teaching ______________________
5. Helping in VBS ______________________
6. Pioneer Girls ______________________
7. Christian Service Brigade ______________________
8. Children's Church ______________________
9. Graded prayer groups ______________________

Music

1. Pianist ____________
2. Choir ___________ (part you sing) _______________________
3. Vocal soloist ___________
4. Instrumental soloist ___________ (type of instrument) _____
5. Songleading __________

Committee Work

1. Pioneer Girls ___________
2. Brigade ___________
3. Christian Education ___________
4. Building ___________
5. Hospitality ___________
6. Missions ___________
7. VBS ___________

Miscellaneous

1. Ushering ___________
2. Nursery worker ____________
3. Visitation ___________
4. Manual service ___________ (list what type) _____________

Name ___________________________ Address ____________________

Telephone ____

This sheet is your invitation to Christian service through your local church. We are interested in helping you to train for a position and then faithfully and joyfully serve the Lord in that position. This P & R sheet will greatly facilitate the total service program of our church. Thank you.

Board of Christian Education.